CHURCHILL'S
AMERICAN
ARSENAL

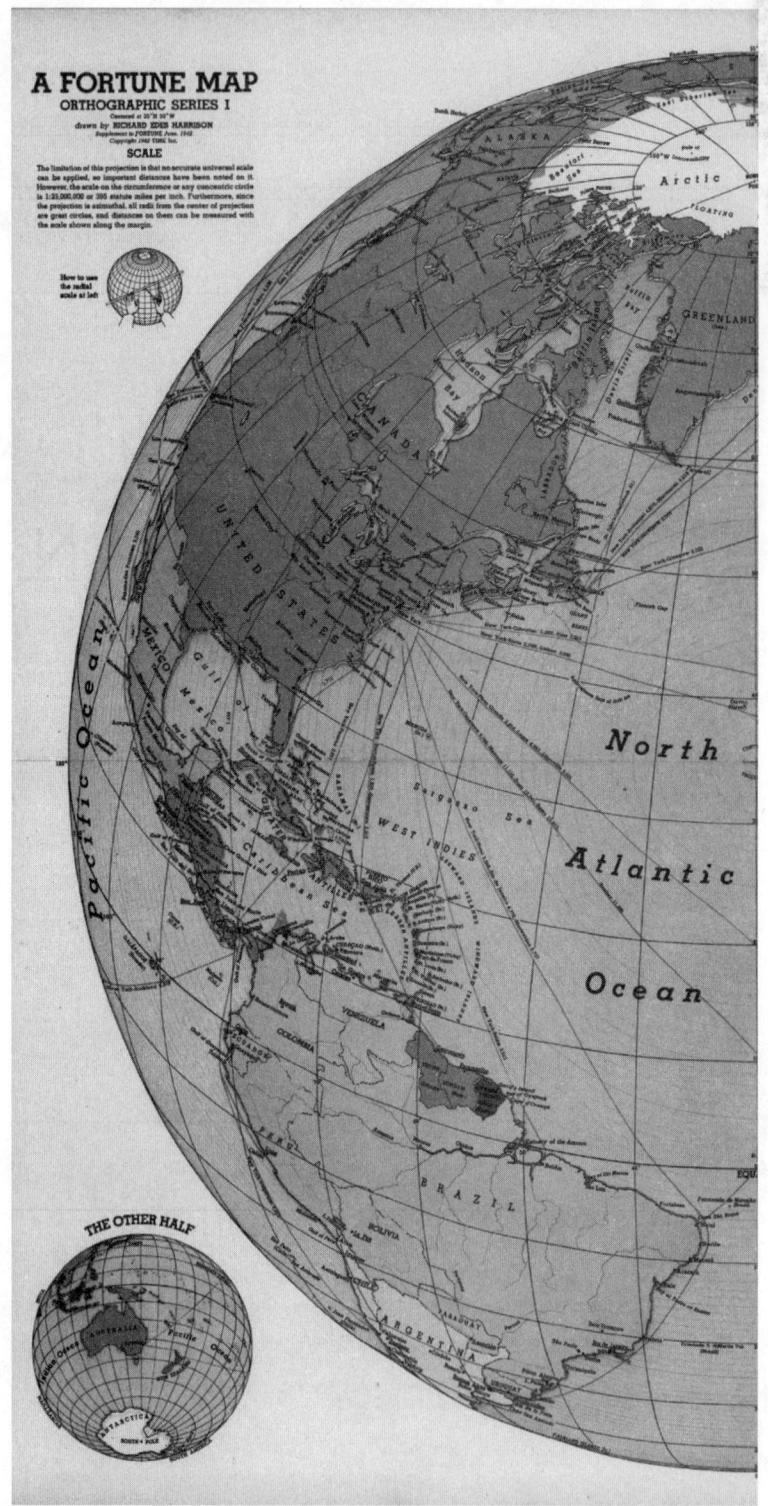

Atlantic Arena, by Richard Edes Harrison, 1942 (Curtis Wright Maps)

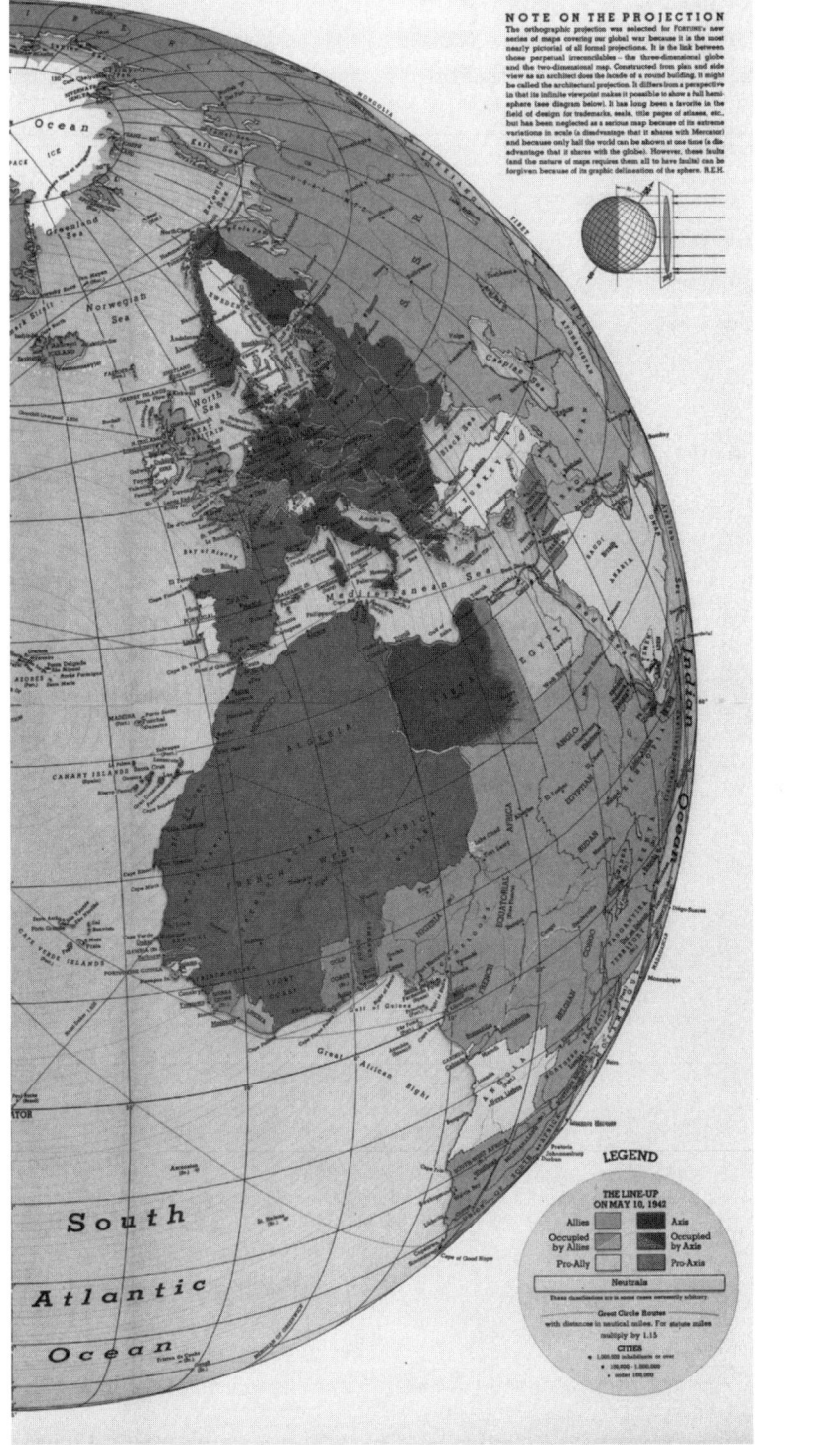

NOTE ON THE PROJECTION

The orthographic projection was selected for FORTUNE's new series of maps covering our global war because it is the most nearly pictorial of all formal projections. It is the link between those perpetual irreconcilables – the three-dimensional globe and the two-dimensional map. Constructed from plan and side view as an architect does the inside of a round building, it might be called the architectural projection. It differs from a perspective in that its infinite viewpoint makes it possible to show a full hemisphere (see diagram below). It has long been a favorite in the field of design for trademarks, seals, title pages of atlases, etc., but has been neglected as a serious map because of its extreme variations in scale (a disadvantage that it shares with Mercator) and because only half the world can be shown at one time (a disadvantage that it shares with the globe). However, these faults (and the nature of maps require them all to have faults) can be forgiven because of its graphic delineation of the sphere. R.E.H.

LEGEND

THE LINE-UP
ON MAY 10, 1942

Allies

Occupied
by Allies

Pro-Ally

Axis

Occupied
by Axis

Pro-Axis

Neutrals

These classifications are in some cases necessarily arbitrary.

Great Circle Routes
with distances in nautical miles. For statute miles
multiply by 1.15

CITIES
● 1,000,000 inhabitants or over
✦ 100,000 - 1,000,000
○ under 100,000

CHURCHILL'S AMERICAN ARSENAL

THE PARTNERSHIP BEHIND
THE INNOVATIONS THAT WON
WORLD WAR TWO

LARRIE D. FERREIRO

OXFORD
UNIVERSITY PRESS

OXFORD
UNIVERSITY PRESS

Published in the United States of America by Oxford University Press
198 Madison Avenue, New York, NY 10016, United States of America.

CIP data is on file at the Library of Congress
ISBN 978–0–19–755401–2

DOI: 10.1093/oso/9780197554012.001.0001

1 3 5 7 9 8 6 4 2

Printed by Lakeside Book Company, United States of America

As always, to my family, Mirna, Marcel, and Gabriel

CONTENTS

PREFACE

Due in large part to the fact that they had been engaged in a life-or-death struggle with an enemy of high technical competence for more than two years before the United States entered the war, the preponderance of basic ideas came from the British. Great Britain's scientific mobilization for war was extremely impressive, but her engineering resources were not of comparable strength. America's engineering capabilities proved fully adequate to support the fine contributions made by her scientists. We were, therefore, able to adopt and benefit greatly from British ideas.[1]

—Bennett Archambault, head of the Office for Scientific
Development and Research, London Mission (1946)

The partnership during World War Two between the United States and Great Britain, two sovereign nations that were twice adversaries in war, was unprecedented at almost every level. Coalition warfare had traditionally been conducted between senior military commanders of allied armies and navies, with little interaction at the lower officer and enlisted levels. In World War One, for example, American forces operated independently from British and French units, and almost all coordination was carried out only between high-level staffs. In World War Two, the relationship was very different. British and American staffs jointly planned operations on land, at sea, and in the air. Allied troops fought literally shoulder to shoulder; convoys consisted of an assortment of Allied warships and merchant ships; British fighters routinely escorted American bombers, and vice versa.[2]

This cooperation was nowhere more evident than in the development of the weapons and technologies that they used on the battlefront. The transfer of military technology between nations had been commonplace for some time. British officers in the Crimean War were armed with American Colt pistols. The American Civil War was fought with British Lee-Enfield rifled muskets, French Minié balls, and the French 12-pounder Napoleon model. The American Steel Navy of the 1880s was based on British cruiser designs. But these transfers occurred largely in peacetime, usually as direct commercial purchases from foreign companies. In World War Two, the British and American governments, working together, developed entirely new weapons, and those weapons would decide the course of the war.

At the forefront of weapons research and development (R&D) was the American agency that carried those words in its name—the Office of Scientific Research and Development, or OSRD, which was led by Vannevar Bush. In World War One, Bush had seen firsthand the results of a disjointed, ad hoc approach to weapons development, and he was therefore determined to bring the full might of American and British science and engineering to bear on fighting the Nazis. At the vanguard was the OSRD London Mission (as it was called), led by Bennett Archambault, with a cadre of 600 American scientists and engineers who worked closely with their British counterparts to create the most advanced weapons the world had yet seen: airborne radar, radio navigation, proximity fuzes, and the atomic bomb, to name a few. Each was begun on British soil and brought to fruition with American assistance, in universities, laboratories, and factories on both sides of the Atlantic.

Before America entered the war in December 1941, the British government had quite a different cooperative arrangement in mind: in August 1941, four months before Pearl Harbor, the Foreign Office asked its US ambassador, Edward Wood, Earl of Halifax, to request a limited number of American personnel for work in British facilities. The Ministry of Supply wanted electrical and general engineers, chemists, and physicists; the Ministry of Aircraft Production specified a few dozen engineers for wind tunnels and flight test; and the Admiralty wanted a handful of radio and electronics engineers. But with Britain's scientific infrastructure dispersed or damaged by regular attacks from the Luftwaffe, this arrangement would have deprived Allied technical cooperation of its most valuable resource: American research, development, and production facilities, far removed from the threat of war, with ample space, energy, and above all people to carry out the work of two nations. In the event, over the course of the war, Americans and British continuously crossed the Atlantic to work in each other's facilities, while the OSRD London Mission established two American radar laboratories in the rolling hills of western England, side by side with their British counterparts.[3]

MANY HISTORIES OF WORLD War Two are told from the top down, focusing on leaders like Winston Churchill, Franklin Roosevelt, and Dwight Eisenhower. Others are bottom-up, telling the stories of the British soldiers at Sword Beach, or the Tuskegee Airmen who escorted bombers to Berlin. In both approaches, weapons and equipment often appear suddenly, unheralded, on the battlefront. This book heralds them, and their creators. It falls squarely in what historian Paul Kennedy calls "history from the middle"— portraying those who worked in the space between the leaders and the front lines, producing the weapons and innovations that converted strategy into operational solutions for the foot soldier, airman, and deckplate sailor.[4]

Some of these weapons and innovations were credited with winning World War Two. The claim of Lee Dubridge, the head of the MIT Radiation Laboratory, is often cited: "The atom bomb only ended the war. Radar won it." Other candidates for winning the war have included the P-51 Mustang fighter, the Liberty ship, the proximity fuze, and the Landing Ship, Tank (LST). While any one of these may have helped turn the tide, all were products of the close partnership between British and American scientists, engineers, and workers.[5]

This book not only describes the technologies and how they were used in battle, but also portrays those who developed them. It is not often realized that for every front-line American fighter, there were five people behind him, carrying out the critical jobs of designing, building, and equipping him with what he needed for the fight. Roosevelt himself recognized that the home front was every bit as important as the battlefront; as he stated for his budget to Congress in January 1942, just after America entered the war, "Powerful enemies must be outfought and outproduced."[6]

My book *Brothers at Arms: American Independence and the Men of France and Spain Who Saved It* describes the collaboration between the three nations in the title, and how they defeated their common British adversary and cemented the creation of the American nation. Soon after its publication, my agent, Michelle Tessler, asked the question that every agent poses to an author: "What is your next book about?" I knew I wanted to pursue the theme of collaboration, and after several false starts, I hit upon that between the United States and Great Britain during World War Two. The subject has been tackled in parts—airborne radar in one book, the Rolls-Royce Merlin engine in another—but I found that no one had put together all the pieces to give a full picture of the vast extent of that effort. It was, as I discovered, industrial-scale cooperation for an industrial-scale war. World War Two was the largest conflict ever fought, which spanned every continent including Antarctica. It therefore would be impossible to discuss cooperation on every battlefront and with every Allied nation. This book focuses on the "life-or-death struggle"—Archambault's words—of the British-American alliance against Nazi Germany, "an enemy of high technical competence."[7]

I was fortunate enough to receive help from many people whose parents and grandparents were part of this effort, and who kindly opened the family histories to me, in several cases locating the classic forgotten-trunk-in-the-attic filled with letters and photos that had remained untouched by historians. The story of the British-American partnership is personal for them, as it is for me. I'm an American naval architect who was trained as a British naval constructor, and I learned warship design from the people who were taught at the knees of Rowland Baker and John Niedermair, the designers of the LST discussed in this book. This story became even more personal when I realized that the OSRD London Mission was at the heart of the narrative. I was for several years a liaison scientist at the Office of

Naval Research Global office in London, the direct successor to the OSRD London Mission and just a few minutes' walk from its wartime location. My work there in supporting transatlantic partnerships exactly paralleled that of the OSRD scientists—albeit without the worry of falling V-1 buzz bombs.

ACKNOWLEDGMENTS

FIRST AND FOREMOST, thanks to Tim Bent, my editor at Oxford University Press, and my agent, Michelle Tessler.

I owe thanks to many individuals and institutions for assistance in my research and for critiques of the first drafts of this work. I list the most significant ones by country and in alphabetical order. I make no distinction whether they are still with us or have already passed. Even with their assistance, all analyses as well as any errors are mine alone.

Great Britain: David Andrews, Charles Betts, David K. Brown, Stuart Burgess, Ian Buxton, Sebastian Cox, David Edgerton, Eric Grove, Nick Hewitt, Peter Hore, Andrew Hussey, Barbara Jones, Thomas Kelsey, Andrew Lambert, Bryan Lovell, Peter Mallet, Hugh Murphy, Allen Packwood, Séan Scullion.

Canada: David Zimmerman.

Sri Lanka: Arthur C. Clarke.

United States: David Allison, Walter L. Alvarez, Michele Archambault, Tyler Bamford, Colin F. Baxter, Stephen Budiansky, Spencer Churchill, Roger Connor, Erik M. Conway, Daniel Else, Norman Fine, Norman Friedman, Allen Galson, Ed Galson, Thad Garrett, Marion Greer-Knowles, Alan L. Gropman, Shaun Hardy, Jamie Holmes, Thomas Hone, Andrea Kalas, Alan G. Kirk, David Kohnen, Jean Langmuir, Edward Lengel, Barbara Long, Patricia Long, Brandon C. Montanye, Margaret Moodie, William M. Murray, Douglas E. Nash, George E. Niedermair, John C. Niedermair III, Philip E. Niedermair, William D. O'Neil, Randy Papadopoulos, Stephen Phillips, Norman Polmar, Jerry E. Strahan, Craig Symonds, Dana Wegner, Dan Wilt.

A NOTE ON CURRENCY

CONVERT THE CURRENCY exchange rates from 1938 to 2020 US dollars. I have used two broad comparators depending upon what is being measured. When discussing the price of individual goods, outlays, and salaries, I use the real price comparator that measures consumer goods and services and is based on the consumer price index (CPI). When discussing large national outlays like government budgets and military building projects, I use the economy cost comparator that is based upon the national gross domestic product (GDP) deflator. These give very different modern values, as GDP growth historically has been much faster than CPI growth. I have converted modern British pounds sterling (£) to US dollars ($) at $1.45/£, using the OECD (Organization for Economic Cooperation and Development) purchasing power parity 2020 rate, which is more reliable than the market exchange rate to compare the value of currencies.[8]

Based on CPI (salaries, etc.)		Based on GDP (government projects)	
Britain £1.00	US $1.00	Britain £1.00	US $1.00
$90	$20	$570	$250

Note that during World War Two, the market exchange rate between British and American currencies was pegged at Britain £1.00 = US $4.00.[9]

CHAPTER 1

DEFEND OUR ISLAND

THE IDEA OF a "special relationship" between Britain and the United States was most famously articulated by Winston Churchill in a speech just months after the end of World War Two. Churchill was no longer prime minister at this point, his Conservative Party having been decisively voted out of office soon after Germany's surrender in May 1945. That October, Churchill had just returned from a painting holiday in Lake Como, Italy (staying, ironically enough, in the former villa of one of Mussolini's fascist supporters), when he received an invitation from the president of the small (300-student) Westminster College in Fulton, Missouri, to deliver a lecture on "economic, social or political problems of international concern." President Harry Truman, himself a Missouri native, wrote an endorsement at the bottom of the letter—"Hope you can do it. If you come, I will introduce you"—at the behest of his military aide, who was a Westminster alumnus. Churchill accepted the invitation, replying directly to Truman, "I should feel it my duty—and it would be a great pleasure—to deliver an address... on the world situation, under your aegis." With the date of his speech set for the following March, he spent January and February of 1946 enjoying the tropical weather in Miami Beach and Havana, with brief visits along the East Coast, before boarding a train to Missouri in the company of Truman.[1]

Churchill's speech at Westminster College on March 5, 1946, delivered before 2,000 guests packed into the gymnasium, was titled "The Sinews of Peace"—an allusion to Cicero's utterance about "the sinews of war" being the steady stream of money to buy all the arms necessary to wage battle. Although his speech quickly became known for its observation (added at the last minute) that "an iron curtain has descended across the Continent"—referring to the Soviet Union's sphere of influence— it was, in fact, intended to lay out the mechanisms and identify the resources needed for achieving a "permanent prevention of war." Churchill reached back to the recent wartime alliance between the United States and Great Britain as the model for the kind of joint military and security force needed to maintain the peace: "This means a special relationship between the British Commonwealth and Empire and the United States of America."[2]

This was not the first time Churchill had used the phrase "special relationship" to describe a world in which the United States and Britain would be the joint guarantors of peace. In September 1943, during the middle of the war, he gave voice to this idea in a speech at Harvard, where, recognizing its many ties with British universities (Harvard had recently adopted Oxbridge-style residential programs for its students), he called upon the "united effort of the British and American peoples" to oversee global security after the war. In February 1944, he instructed his senior advisors to prepare for a postwar future in which "Britain and the United States are joined in a special relationship." And in November 1945 he trotted it out again in a speech before the House of Commons. Once Churchill had seized upon a catchy turn of phrase, he never hesitated to reuse it. In the afterglow of an Allied victory, the idea of a British-American "special relationship" had seemed almost inevitable, given the shared language and history of what Churchill called "the English-speaking peoples."[3]

Churchill's speech at Westminster College was greeted with "marked applause"—even Truman clapped at the appropriate moments. Afterward, both received honorary doctor of laws degrees. Churchill repeated his "sinews of peace" themes in several more speeches before returning home later that month to a nation that was about to lose an empire and would soon have to find a role in the world alongside the United States.

A Unique Relationship Is Born

Churchill was not wrong that the two nations had a relationship that was unique in the world, but for most of their shared history, "special" was a modifier too far. It began almost immediately after the War of American Independence, when Great Britain recognized the United States' sovereignty in the 1783 Treaty of Paris. Within just a few years, trade between the two nations had reached its prewar levels; by contrast, after the Dutch Republic became independent from the Spanish Empire in 1648, those two countries later came to blows over empire and trade, engaging each other in a series of conflicts in Europe and Asia. Economic ties between the United States and Britain continued to grow stronger through the early nineteenth century, eventually accounting for half of America's foreign trade; even when the United States went to war against Britain in 1812, the American war effort was largely financed by the London-based Barings Brothers bank (which also had acted as middleman in the American purchase of French Louisiana in 1802; technically, the United States bought the land from Barings and not from France). The ties between these former belligerents also were political. From 1818 to 1846, Oregon Country was jointly governed by both Britain and the United States (Britain had *never* shared territorial jurisdiction before). The 1823 Monroe Doctrine, which held that no European powers (namely, Spain and France) should interfere with emerging South American nations, was originally proposed as a joint action by Britain; it was instead unilaterally appropriated by the Americans, with the unspoken understanding that the powerful Royal Navy, not the tiny US Navy, would actually enforce the doctrine—while admittedly favoring British interests.[4]

The Monroe Doctrine fitted with America's growing belief that its national character was exceptional among countries, and that it was manifestly destined to carve out a much larger place for itself in the world. But American exceptionalism was aided and abetted by Britain (London, for instance, invested heavily in the westward expansion of American railroads) because the interests of the two nations, notably those of free trade and strengthening democratic institutions, were beginning to converge in unique ways. Even the friction created by the American Civil War, during which the British government largely supported (though never formally recognized) the Confederacy, did not wholly arrest the Anglo-American rapprochement. As a democratic America was becoming more like an empire, imperial Britain was becoming less like a monarchy, and both sides were beginning to recognize a shift in their global responsibilities. Rather than fall into the so-called Thucydides Trap, in which an existing hegemonic power goes to war with a rising power, Britain seemed at times almost to encourage the up-and-coming United States in ways that would have been unthinkable in an earlier era. For example, Britain actively supported the United States during the 1898 Spanish-American War, while in the past it would more likely have supported the weaker nation in order to maintain a balance of power in its own favor. Just a few years later, in 1902, Britain allowed the American financier J. P. Morgan to buy the White Star and Leyland lines, the very icons of Britain's self-image as a maritime power.[5]

The unique nature of the British-American relationship was perhaps most clearly on view with the advent of "titled Americans." It had long been commonplace for British aristocrats and royalty to marry other titled Europeans (Queen Victoria, of course, married the German-born Albert, Prince of Saxe-Coburg and Gotha). But starting in the 1870s, the landed British gentry began seeing a dramatic fall in the income from their estates due to competition from agricultural imports, including American wheat. At the same time, the post–Civil War industrial boom created a new class of wealthy Americans who coveted the social status that a title would bring.

One of the first marriages to trade American dollars for a British title was that of Jennie Jerome, daughter of a New York financier, to Lord Randolph

Churchill of the House of Marlborough, one of the newer peerages in the kingdom. Jennie's own ancestry was also notable—a claim of Iroquois blood from her mother's side of the family, and two paternal forebears who fought against the British in the American War of Independence. But Jennie Spencer-Churchill (she normally went by the full double-barreled name) banked on her British title to move in the highest social circles in London and abroad. After her firstborn son, Winston, arrived in 1874 (the same year as her marriage), Jennie, like most aristocrats, left him largely in the care of nannies and rarely saw him. When Winston was eight years old, she saw him just thirteen times, though she dined with one friend twenty-six times. Winston's first "special relationship" with an American, his mother, was thus complicated and often one-sided. He later said of her, "[She] shone for me like the Evening Star. I loved her dearly—but at a distance." This would prove a harbinger of the larger relationship that would ensue between the British and Americans.[6]

A Relationship Fractured by War

An observer in the 1920s and 1930s would have used the words "suspicious," "uncertain," and even "fraught"—any word *except* "special"—to describe the relationship between Washington and London. The Great War had ended the rapprochement and laid bare the rifts between the two polities. At the start of the twentieth century, after the American victory in the Spanish-American War and other diplomatic successes in South America, the Anglo-American alignment was stronger than ever. "The one indispensable feature of our foreign policy," said secretary of state John Hay in 1899, "should be a friendly understanding with England." Churchill's lecture tour of the United States in 1900 (his second visit in five years) cemented for him the idea that the two nations would form a fraternal association of "English-speaking peoples."[7]

That all changed in August 1914, when after a month of ultimatums telegraphed around Europe following the assassination of Archduke Franz Ferdinand, the Allied Powers of France, Britain, Russia, and Japan went to war with the Central Powers of Germany and Austria-Hungary. President Woodrow Wilson made clear that the United States would not be pulled into the same alliances that got Britain into trouble. The American people, many of whom claimed recent (and vocally anti-English) German and Irish ancestry, agreed. The only sector that stood by Britain was Wall Street, led by J. P. Morgan's financial empire, which became London's fundraiser and arms purchaser. By 1916, American financiers were raising $4 million (equivalent to $1.5 billion today) every day for the British war effort, and would soon cover one-third of Britain's war costs.[8]

The British government was hemorrhaging money because at that point the war was largely a stalemate, with enormous resources being expended for little gain. On mainland Europe, the initial Anglo-French maneuver warfare had ground to a halt by late 1914, with a line of trenches that stretched from Switzerland to the North Sea; attempts at breakthroughs at Verdun, the Somme, and Ypres were deadly (and costly) disasters. At sea, the 1916 Battle of Jutland saw the British Grand Fleet lose three major warships in as many hours, and while the German High Seas Fleet had been unable to break out into the Atlantic, the battle was widely viewed at the time as a failure for the Allied Powers.

Churchill himself was considered the father of one of the worst debacles of the war, the 1915 Dardanelles-Gallipoli campaign. As First Lord of the Admiralty (the political head of the Royal Navy; the First Sea Lord was the military head), Churchill believed that the Allies could put an early end to the conflict by bringing a combined French-British fleet through the Dardanelles Straits, which would cut off the Ottoman Empire from its German ally, while also aiding the Russians by opening their Black Sea ports. But in March 1915, Ottoman mines and artillery sank several battleships with great loss of life. The campaign now switched to an Allied amphibious assault on the Gallipoli Peninsula. This proved equally disastrous, and troops were withdrawn by the end of the year. Churchill was demoted from his position and resigned soon afterward, his reputation stained; "I was ruined for the time being in 1915 over the Dardanelles," he noted ruefully in his World War Two memoirs.[9]

Wilson had until then heeded his country's wishes to stay out of the war, but a combination of American shipping losses to German U-boats (including the sinking of *Lusitania* in 1915) and the infamous Zimmerman Telegram, which revealed Germany's attempt to bring Mexico into the war on its side on the promise that it would help Mexico recover American territories, changed the popular mood. Wilson persuaded Congress to declare war on Germany in April 1917. However, the United States was not joining as a member of the Allied Powers; it was very careful to call itself an "Associated Power," and the American Expeditionary Forces (AEF) remained an independent command that fought alongside, and not under, other members of the Alliance.

The US Navy was also wary of getting too close to the Royal Navy, which it saw as its main rival for command of the sea. The chief of naval operations (CNO), Admiral William Benson, told his liaison officer, Rear Admiral William Sims, then en route to London, "Don't let the British pull the wool over your eyes. It is none of our business pulling their chestnuts out of the fire. We would as soon fight the British as the Germans." Even so, the two navies managed to coordinate and even cooperate in their activities, although keeping each other at arm's length. By mid-1917, a combination of British and American destroyer squadrons was effectively hunting U-boats in the Western Approaches, and by December five American battleships were integrated into the Grand Fleet, though as an independent squadron. The same month saw British and American naval constructors exchange places in each other's design bureaus to cooperate on the design of battlecruisers (similar to battleships but faster and more lightly armored). In June 1918, assistant secretary of the navy Franklin D. Roosevelt sailed to Europe to coordinate with his French and British counterparts (he also briefly met Winston Churchill at a social function, but neither thought enough of the experience to mention it in their correspondence).[10]

Wilson kept the United States out of the Alliance because he saw American war aims as substantially different from Britain's. The Americans wanted a "new international order," as he phrased it, free of imperialism and military alliances. The Americans were represented on the Supreme

War Council—the body that coordinated the Alliance's strategy—though their command was independent from that of the British and French. This made combat logistics and operations difficult, even as the AEF poured troops into the Western Front at the rate of 10,000 per day. While Americans learned how to use the novel weapons of their associated powers, like aircraft (the First Army Air Service used a combination of French and British biplanes) and tanks (George Patton's Tank Corps employed British heavy and French light tanks), they never attempted to work with France and Britain on their development and production. In fact, there was almost no time to do so; the period between the first major American actions in May 1918 and the armistice on November 11 was not even six months.[11]

After the war, the United States was in a position of global authority, unprecedented in its history. Its dominance on the battlefield during the 1918 counteroffensives had been crucial to bringing the war to its final, sudden conclusion (the new German government initially asked Wilson, not the Allied Powers, for an armistice). Its industrial and financial power had surpassed even that of Britain, which saw its leadership role assumed by America. Wilson arrived in January 1919 at the Versailles Peace Conference on an equal footing with his counterparts, British prime minister David Lloyd George and French prime minister Georges Clemenceau. Wilson, who brought a far bigger delegation (1,300 staff versus 200 under Lloyd George), at first dictated the direction of the peace negotiations with his "new international order." His statement of principles, the Fourteen Points, largely reflected the Anglo-American convergence on broad principles like free trade and strengthening of democratic institutions.

But Wilson also wanted to establish a League of Nations, which would put paid to balance-of-power disputes, reserving the use of force to maintain justice and enforce laws. Lloyd George understandably saw many of the League's provisions as threatening to Britain's empire. As the negotiations wore on through the spring, Wilson's idealistic vision was gradually overtaken by realpolitik considerations, including German disarmament and punitive reparations to Allied nations. The treaty signed in June 1919 included the charter for the League of Nations but little else of Wilson's

Fourteen Points. In a final irony, Britain joined the League but the United States did not, prevented by Republican opposition in the Senate.[12]

A Relationship Sundered by Peace

As noted, the 1920s and 1930s were marked not by British-American rapprochement, but by the great-power competition that Wilson had specifically sought to avoid. Partners in the Great War, the two nations were now contenders on the world stage. The sentiment was felt keenly on both sides of the Atlantic. William Wiseman, a British intelligence officer based in New York City who frequently met with Woodrow Wilson, reported to London on "the growing consciousness that after the war there will be only two great powers left—Great Britain and the United States. Which is going to be the greater, politically and commercially?" Edward House, Wilson's advisor who helped him draft his Fourteen Points, told his boss soon after the Versailles Treaty was signed that he sensed an antagonism to the United States. "The English are quite as cordial and hospitable to individual Americans as ever, but they dislike us collectively. . . . The relations between the two countries are beginning to assume the same character as that between England and Germany before the war." The previously unique relationship had become soured primarily by two sources of friction: naval rivalry and finance.[13]

Naval rivalry between the United States and Great Britain predated the American entry into World War One. In 1916, spurred by Germany's sinking of *Lusitania* the year before, Wilson had proposed—and Congress had passed—the Naval Appropriation Act, promising to build a navy "second to none" (meaning "equal to the Royal Navy") that would ensure free trade on its own terms and not be subordinate to British interests, as had been the case for enforcement of the Monroe Doctrine. The following year, however, battleship construction was temporarily sidetracked to build destroyers capable of hunting submarines, and merchant vessels for carrying troops and war matériel across the Atlantic. When Congress passed Wilson's new postwar Naval Appropriation Act in 1919 promising even more battleships and battlecruisers, the race was restarted. The United States was now the stronger power, with the resources to outbuild Britain; moreover, the Royal Navy, which was perceived to have failed at Jutland and the Dardanelles (and had needed US destroyers to defeat the U-boats), was facing steep budget cuts. Britain was well aware of the threat of an expanded US Navy. Stanley V. Goodall, the British naval constructor working on exchange in the American warship design bureau, wrote his boss back in London, Eustace Tennyson d'Eyncourt, that the United States "means to have a big navy" that "gravely endanger[s] the future of the British Empire."[14]

In March 1921, Warren G. Harding assumed the presidency, having campaigned on a promise to reduce Wilson's profligate defense spending. By this time, the US Navy had determined that Japan, not Britain, would be the most likely enemy in a future war—they were routinely labeled, respectively, as "Orange" and "Red" opponents in Naval War College war games— and that America's military planning should focus on Japan and the Pacific (collectively known as "War Plan Orange"). Nevertheless, both policy and public perception still demanded a "navy second to none." It therefore made strategic as well as economic sense to call for a general halt in the arms race among all the major sea powers. Four months after he took office, Harding's administration invited eight other nations, including Britain, France, Japan, and Italy, to Washington to discuss naval arms limitations. From November 1921 to February 1922 the delegates deliberated over a complex agreement to limit the number and size of capital ships (battleships and battlecruisers), halt or scrap existing ships then under construction, place a ten-year moratorium on new capital shipbuilding, and stop the expansion of naval bases in the Pacific.

But the real cut-and-thrust of negotiations occurred behind the scenes of each delegation. Harding's desire for budget reductions prevailed over the strategic demands of secretary of the navy Josephus Daniels, who wanted more ships and referred to the proceedings as "my own funeral." Lloyd George overruled his own First Sea Lord, David Beatty, who rejected the idea of a shipbuilding "holiday." In its final version, the Washington Naval

Treaty was a political document, not a strategic one. It capped British and American capital ship tonnage at 525,000 tons each, while Japan was limited to 315,000 tons. This simultaneously established the United States on a par with Britain and superior to Japan, although solely in terms of big-gun capital ships.[15]

And yet this did not stop the continued frictions between the two navies. The Royal Navy bridled at the treaty limits, believing that Britain's much larger empire and commitment to protecting trade routes required more ships. It refused to accept the idea of parity with the United States. Although most believed that in the end continued naval cooperation between the two nations was preferable, Winston Churchill himself (then chancellor of the exchequer) stated in a July 1927 memo to the Cabinet, "Although it was quite right in the interests of peace to go on talking about war with the United States being unthinkable, everyone knows that this is not true." He added bluntly, "We do not wish to put ourselves in the power of the United States. We cannot tell what they might do if at some future date they were in a position to give us orders about our policy." By the same token, the United States Navy felt it had given too much away to the British; American naval historian Dudley Knox spoke for many of his fellow officers in his book *Eclipse of American Sea Power*, arguing that by signing the Washington Naval Treaty, "America resigned to Britain the predominance in Sea Power." The United States Navy made no bones about its aversion to the United Kingdom, pointedly naming its new aircraft carriers *Lexington*, *Saratoga*, and *Yorktown* for American victories over the British in the War of American Independence.[16]

Calvin Coolidge, who assumed the presidency when Harding died in 1923 and won it outright the following year, continued his predecessor's policy of limiting naval spending. With capital ships now strictly regulated, competition between America and Britain centered on cruisers, which were smaller and less heavily armed than battleships. The Royal Navy wanted great numbers of them to patrol imperial waters and protect trade; the United States simply saw them as smaller versions of capital ships and did not want to be outbuilt by the British. Coolidge, following in Harding's footsteps, called for another naval disarmament conference to be held in Geneva in 1927. This time there was no postwar political will to bridge the yawning strategic chasm between Britain and the United States. The Geneva talks, according to the Americans, were not "negotiations at all, but merely a form of hostilities." The failure to arrive at a treaty plunged Anglo-American relations to their lowest level in decades; in 1928 Congress, distrustful of British intentions, was contemplating a massive cruiser buildup to counter the Royal Navy, while Churchill referred to the "Yankee menace" as a reason for defending the Admiralty's large budget requests. But the threat of a new arms race was derailed the following year, when the London Stock Exchange crashed in September 1929, followed by the crash of the New York Stock Exchange in October.[17]

The subsequent descent of both nations into the Great Depression (the British referred to it as the "Great Slump") reinvigorated the political will to rein in naval spending by mutual agreement. The new leaders, Prime Minister Ramsay MacDonald and President Herbert Hoover, took swift action. The London Naval Conference on arms limitations opened in January 1930, just weeks after the stock market crashes. By April the delegates had established national limits for the number and total tonnage of cruisers, destroyers, and submarines, once again putting Britain and the United States at parity while placing Japan in a secondary position. The effect of the 1930 London Naval Treaty (and a second London treaty signed in 1936) was to remove one of the two main sources of friction between the United States and Britain, their naval rivalry; the United States was finally able to achieve its goal of having a navy "second to none," the Royal Navy could continue to protect its empire, and neither goal would break the bank since both nations tacitly agreed that they would never fight each other.[18]

While the naval rivalry was largely eradicated due to the Great Depression, the second source of Anglo-American friction, finance, was only exacerbated by it. Their financial rivalry, like their naval rivalry, predated the American entry into World War One. Before 1914, the City of London was the global destination for businesses and governments to raise capital, and the pound sterling was the reserve currency that underpinned those transactions. Wall Street aspired to such a status, but the history of American bank panics—which the newly created Federal Reserve was intended to rectify—deterred would-be international borrowers. In July 1914, the threat of war led European nations to start pulling their gold reserves from Wall Street, repatriating them in order to finance their arms buildup. At the time, the world operated on a gold standard pegged to the British pound (£4.247727 per troy ounce of gold). Hence, when, say, Barings Brothers bank sold its Wall Street shares in the Great Northern Railway Company, those shares would be converted to gold bullion, which was shipped across the Atlantic to London. The sudden flight of capital would have rapidly depleted America's gold reserves, which could have led to another panic.

However, in that crisis lay the seeds of an opportunity. A Boston banker, writing to President Woodrow Wilson just as Germany was executing the Schlieffen Plan against France and Belgium, unambiguously summarized that opportunity: "England has been the exchange place of the world. . . . Today we can take this place if we choose." Wilson forwarded this note to his secretary of the treasury, William G. McAdoo, who had already launched his own Schlieffen Plan against Britain's financial empire. McAdoo shut the New York Stock Exchange for four months—by far the longest hiatus on record—to stop Britain from selling American stocks and bonds, halting the outflow of gold. Other nations quickly exhausted their own reserves to pay for the war, so when Wall Street reopened in November, American banks were in a position to lend money to Britain and other warring nations. Within a few months of Wall Street's reopening, the dollar had effectively replaced the pound as the world's reserve currency, and America became its "chief money lender." This was why J. P. Morgan and other American banks were able to raise funds, primarily through the issuance of Liberty Bonds, for such a large percentage of Britain's war costs.[19]

By the end of the war, Britain had borrowed just over $4 billion from the Americans, and when accrued interest was added, the British government's debt amounted to $4.7 billion, the equivalent of over $1 trillion in today's currency. Almost immediately the two nations were at loggerheads over repayment. Britain was already in a precarious financial situation, having lost a considerable percentage of its export market. Overall unemployment jumped from 2 percent to over 10 percent in just a few years, and vital economic sectors like steel and shipbuilding saw 30 percent unemployment. As the British economy contracted, the American economy grew at close to 5 percent per year, with less than half the unemployment rate of the United Kingdom. The Roaring Twenties (the phrase started to appear toward the end of the decade) saw the United States supplant Britain as the world's largest exporter, with increased wages going toward new consumer goods, such as automobiles and electric refrigerators.

The fact that the Americans continued to demand payment from the increasingly impoverished British created barely disguised hostility. In early 1921, the incoming British ambassador, Auckland Geddes, linked the financial crisis with the upcoming Washington Naval Treaty talks when he told Whitehall, "The central ambition . . . is to win for America the position of leading nation in the world." To Geddes, the United States appeared to "look for the opportunity to treat us as a vassal state so long as the debt remains unpaid." Even Churchill, as chancellor of the exchequer, attacked the Americans for draining Europe of its capital. Although Britain (along with France and other European nations) tried several tactics to have the debt forgiven, such as the British argument that American loans were essentially political debts—a payment in kind for Britain's enormous death toll—a series of American administrations, from Coolidge through Roosevelt, refused to relent on the terms of the loans.[20]

The London and New York stock market crashes of September and October 1929 did not immediately trigger a global depression. Stock markets actually rebounded for a time. However, by 1932, a complex series of actions, including protectionist tariffs, panicked monetary policies, and a lack of leadership on the parts of both Britain and the United States, brought about a sickening slide in economies worldwide. Soon after Roosevelt came into office in 1933, the London Economic Conference failed to bring any agreement on measures to fight the Depression, in large part due to Roosevelt's decision not to support any stabilization of world currencies until the domestic crisis in America had been sorted. Roosevelt's refusal further heightened Britain's mistrust of America, which was felt especially by Neville Chamberlain, now in Churchill's old position as chancellor of the exchequer, who accused Roosevelt of having "completely smashed" the conference. Britain soon followed other European nations in defaulting on its war debt repayment. Meanwhile, relations between America and Britain were fraying under the economic strain.[21]

As the financial contagion spread from the United States to Europe and then to Asia, trade, industrial output, and employment dropped off a cliff. In the United States, industrial production dropped by half, while unemployment grew sixfold. The incoming Roosevelt administration threw together a series of policies, collectively labeled the "New Deal," that were intended to get Americans back to work. Many of these government-created jobs were devoted to building infrastructure, such as highways, bridges, buildings, shipyards, airports, and dams. While military spending was pared—in part due to the London Naval Treaty—some projects, like the construction of the aircraft carriers *Yorktown* and *Enterprise*, were paid for with public works funds. Even with massive government stimulus, many Americans struggled throughout the 1930s to get back to work. Britain's Great Slump was not nearly as severe. This was, in part, because its postwar economy was already in dire straits, so there was no comparable Roaring Twenties heights from which to fall. Britain also enacted a series of fiscal and monetary policies (including abandoning and then later reestablishing the gold standard) that helped the economy recover more quickly. Industrial production was dented but not damaged, unemployment was a fraction of that in the United States, and real wages actually rose.[22]

The Depression hit Germany far worse than either Britain or the United States. It was already struggling to pay war reparations, and the American loans that backed those repayments were called in after the 1929 crash. Without cash, and with less demand for German goods, banks and industries failed, unemployment skyrocketed, and the German people lost faith in the ability of their government to manage the crisis. This toxic mix allowed the fringe National Socialist German Workers (Nazi) Party to come to power in 1933, with Adolf Hitler as chancellor and soon dictator, promising to restore the German economy and its national pride. Hitler was actually late to the rise of postwar dictators, having been preceded by Benito Mussolini in 1925 and Joseph Stalin in 1927.

The rise of dictators worried many Americans, who sensed another European conflict looming on the horizon. At least some of the anti-British sentiment at the time reflected the idea—popularized by the Senate Special Committee of the Investigation of the Munitions Industry, and led by Senator Gerald P. Nye—that the United States had been suckered into World War One by pro-British interests. The corollary to this argument was that peace was best maintained not by treaties, but by removing the profit incentive through neutrality legislation. Congress subsequently passed a series of four Neutrality Acts from 1935 to 1939, placing an embargo on American exports of arms and "implements of war" (e.g., airplane engines and parts) to any nation that was openly at war. The 1936 act extended the provisions to prohibit loans to warring nations. While these acts were not purely isolationist in nature, they did put up high barriers to American in-volvement in the increasingly likely European wars.[23]

Britain saw the rise of dictators, and most notably Nazi Germany, in an entirely different light. As early as 1932, when Hitler was ascending in power but not yet chancellor, members of Parliament were already begin-ning to sow doubt on the wisdom of disarmament as a cost-saving measure, in the face of the growing threat. At a late-night debate in the House of Commons on November 10, Stanley Baldwin, then part of Prime Minister Ramsay MacDonald's coalition government, stated that "disarmament in my view will not stop war." He went on to point out that any future war would hinge on an aerial campaign, given the rapid progress of the airplane since the Great War: "I think it is well also for the man in the street to realise that there is no power on earth that can protect him from being bombed. Whatever people may tell him, the bomber will always get through . . . the only defence is in offence."[24]

Within months of Baldwin's statement, Hitler had taken over the German government, rejected the Versailles limitations, withdrawn from the League of Nations and the Geneva Disarmament Conference, and begun a massive program of rearmament. By 1934 the threat was so evident that the British government decided to establish parity in the air with Germany. Building upon his statement of two years earlier, Baldwin again warned: "The truth is that a bomber will always get through. . . . Since the days of the air, the old frontiers are gone. When you think of the defence of England you no longer think of the chalk cliffs of Dover; you think of the Rhine. That is where our frontier lies." Britain's former barrier to enemy attack, the celebrated "wooden walls" of its navy, was rapidly being overtaken by the airplane.[25]

When Baldwin became prime minister in 1935, he continued the policy of rearmament. Even Neville Chamberlain, the tight-fisted chancellor of the exchequer, believed that the best way forward was to pursue diplomacy with Germany (later referred to as appeasement) while simultaneously rearming Britain. The increased spending particularly favored the Royal Air Force (RAF), whose budget doubled every year from 1935 through 1939, eventually surpassing that of the Royal Navy.[26] Both Britain's rearmament and Roosevelt's New Deal provided the stimulus to help get their respective economies back on track. But while Britain, faced with the existential threat from Germany, was putting money and people to work in its military factories, the United States benefited from its neutrality to build roads, dams, electrical grids, and bridges. By 1938, Britain was spending seven times as much as the United States (as a percentage of GDP) on the military and employing three times more British workers (as a percentage of the workforce) in defense industries. In real terms, they were producing 70 percent more munitions than the much larger United States.[27]

This difference in priorities was nowhere more evident than the comparison of two major construction projects from 1938 (Figure 1). At first glance, the two sets of latticework towers appear similar. All along the British coastline, Chain Home radar towers were being built as part of a series of integrated air defenses against the German Luftwaffe. Meanwhile, in Flushing Meadows, New York, the Trylon was erected as the centerpiece of the upcoming World's Fair, itself the symbol of America's industrial might. There, the World of Tomorrow brimmed with electric household gadgets and studiously avoided any mention of war-related applications. In Britain, the most talked-about home appliance was the new Anderson air raid shelter being distributed to households across the island.

The World's Fair opened in April 1939. Two months later, amid rising tensions in Europe—Germany had just finished its conquest of Czechoslovakia, after reoccupying the Rhineland and subsuming Austria—King George VI and Queen Elizabeth visited the World's Fair British Pavilion, where one of four original copies of the Magna Carta was displayed (it would remain in the United States for the duration of the war). They then called on Roosevelt at his home in Hyde Park on the Hudson. It was a flying visit, less than twenty-four hours, but it allowed Roosevelt to develop a personal relationship with the British monarch. George VI came back with notes to his government that hinted at, though did not promise, American support in the event of war: "If London was bombed," he wrote hopefully, "USA would come in." More importantly, the informality of their visit made the royal couple, and by extension Britain itself, more sympathetic in the eyes of the American public. It was among the first of several tentative steps toward thawing out the US-British relationship in the face of the growing German threat.[28]

A Special Relationship Emerges

The United States and Britain had already been talking about possible military cooperation for over a year before George VI's visit. The first cracks in the wall of separation appeared not in response to Hitler's actions in Europe, but rather to a series of unprovoked Japanese attacks on the gunboats USS *Panay* and HMS *Ladybird*, as well as several American and British oil tankers, near Nanjing, China, in December 1937. Japan then was in the first stages of its war with China. Neither the British nor the American government was prepared to enter the conflict, nor was either navy individually able to respond to further Japanese "outrages." Roosevelt dispatched a naval officer to London in January 1938 to explore options for cooperation with the Cabinet of the recently elected prime minister, Neville Chamberlain.

The resulting Record of Conversation only outlined the most tentative of plans for Pacific fleet cooperation in the event of a joint blockade of Japan. Nonetheless, they represented the first forays into coalition planning since World War One.

The next foray took place in Washington, DC, June 12–14, 1939, starting the day after George VI's visit with Roosevelt. A British naval officer secretly met with CNO Admiral William Leahy at his residence. The main subject was cooperation in the Atlantic theater of operations, given the increasingly likely event of a European war. Once again, the discussions only resulted in a vague outline of how the two navies would work together should America join the hostilities—Britain would take the lead in the Atlantic, the United States in the Pacific, and the two would share naval intelligence. While no major action resulted from these talks, planners from both sides of the Atlantic gained insight into each other's priorities, and discovered that they were not very far apart.[29]

There were no further discussions of military cooperation beyond these initial forays, and even the fact of war did little at first to bring the two nations closer. Germany invaded Poland in the early hours of September 1, 1939. Forty-eight hours later, Neville Chamberlain declared war on Germany, and formed his war cabinet. He appointed Winston Churchill— who had long been a vocal critic of Hitler—as First Lord of the Admiralty, the same position he had held in World War One. It was at this point that Roosevelt and Churchill developed the close partnership that would endure for the entire war. It was clear from the start that this "special relationship," like the unique relationship that had begun two centuries earlier, hinged on the shared interests of the two nations, and was further bolstered by the strong bond between Roosevelt and Churchill. That bond certainly did not exist between Roosevelt and Chamberlain, whose distrust of Roosevelt's interests stemmed from the president's failure to support the stabilization of world currencies at the 1933 London Economic Conference. Roosevelt equally distrusted the British prime minister for rebuffing his offers, made the previous year when European tensions were mounting, to convene a peace conference and to participate in a naval quarantine of Germany.

On September 11, Roosevelt penned two letters, each very different in tone. To Chamberlain he perfunctorily said that the prime minister had "been in my thoughts," although he revealed his belief that "we shall repeal the embargo [i.e., Neutrality Acts provisions] within the next month." His letter to Churchill was of a different tenor, revealing both their shared naval background as well as their common interest in history (even if he could not properly spell Churchill's family title):[30]

> It is because you and I occupied similar positions in the World War that I want you to know how glad I am that you are back again in the Admiralty. Your problems are, I realize, complicated by new factors but the essential is not very different. What I want you and the Prime Minister to know is that I shall at all times welcome it if you will keep me in touch personally with anything you want me to know about. You can always send sealed letters through your pouch or my pouch.
>
> I am glad you did the Marlboro volumes before this thing started—and I have much enjoyed reading them.

Churchill replied just days after receiving the letter, puckishly opening it with "Naval Person to President Roosevelt" in tribute to Roosevelt's observation of their shared backgrounds. Churchill continued to use that nom de guerre in their correspondence (Roosevelt called him by it as well) until he became prime minister in May 1940, after which he was "Former Naval Person."

Given Roosevelt's strong naval roots (he typically referred to the navy as "we" but the army as "they"), it was unsurprising that his first action after the outbreak of hostilities was to initiate the Neutrality Patrol of western Atlantic and Caribbean waters, consisting of cruisers, destroyers, and seaplanes, designed to keep any foreign warship at least 300 miles from American shores. In November 1939 he kept his word to Chamberlain, finally convincing Congress to overturn the arms embargo sections of the Neutrality Acts, allowing arms trade with Britain and other nations on a "cash-and-carry" basis (of which more in Chapter 2). Meanwhile, the fairly small naval attaché office in London—consisting of just three officers and led by Captain Alan Goodrich Kirk, who arrived in June 1939—found itself short-staffed in the face of the sudden demand for intelligence sharing. Within twelve months the number of officers increased tenfold, in addition to many other temporary personnel, and this was still insufficient. Despite previous promises to Admiral Leahy, the British were understandably reluctant to give too much away to the still-neutral Americans. Kirk was nonetheless able to obtain important information on naval developments, including the new German magnetic sea mine. He also became an expert on one of the Royal Navy's specialties, the use of landing craft in amphibious operations—expertise that would later serve him well during the Allied landings in Sicily and Normandy.[31]

If the United States remained decidedly neutral, the British government was happy to keep it so. In January 1940, Chamberlain wrote his sister, "Heaven knows, I don't want the Americans to fight for us—we should have to pay too dearly for that." Chamberlain's minister for rearmament, Ernle Chatfield, echoed an undoubtedly widespread sentiment when he told Philip Kerr, Marquess of Lothian—the newly installed British ambassador in Washington, DC—that the Americans "will indeed fight the battle for freedom to the last Briton." This assumption about America's lack of resolve was only reinforced by the mission to Europe of undersecretary of state Benjamin Sumner Welles in February 1940. Welles had long been one of Roosevelt's confidants, and as the so-called Phoney War dragged on (the eight-month period when Germany marshaled its resources after the invasion of Poland, while France and Britain were unfairly accused of inactivity), the president asked Welles to go on a fact-finding mission about "present conditions in Europe." Welles spent a month on his tour, mostly speaking with German and Italian leaders, to explore the admittedly remote possibilities of disarmament and a peaceful resolution to the looming conflict. Although Welles spent only a few days in London, American ambassador Joseph Kennedy was highly suspicious of what he saw as a personal envoy performing the duties of an accredited diplomat. Chamberlain and his government were equally suspicious of Welles's (and by extension Roosevelt's) motivations, fearing that the American president once again was going to scuttle their own efforts, as they believed he had back in 1933 at the London Economic Conference.[32]

The Welles mission buttressed the American suspicion that Britain and Europe were too weak to forestall an expanded war, which was confirmed just a month later when Germany began its invasions of Denmark and Norway. Partly because of Welles's attempts at diplomacy with the enemy, the British government became doubly cautious about revealing too much to the Americans, especially about its own dire financial conditions. The Foreign Office instructed Lothian "not to create the impression that we are in acute difficulties . . . and that we cannot win the war without borrowing from the United States," lest Roosevelt use that as an excuse to sue for peace instead of supplying the British with "aeroplanes and other essential war means." While Lothian remained circumspect about British finances— he never uttered the phrase misattributed to him, "Well, boys, Britain's broke"—he could not obscure the truth when, on returning to the United States in November 1940, he told the press waiting at LaGuardia Airport, "England will be grateful for . . . planes, munitions, ships and perhaps a little financial help."[33]

Britain's continued mistrust of American intentions, and the exchequer's own rapidly depleting reserves, meant that the British government intended to limit purchases from the United States, even for airplanes and other "essential" matériel. The chancellor of the exchequer directed the "restriction of payments by the Defence Services, especially in North America, to the absolute minimum of essential and speedily available services." There were also technical reasons that Britain minimized its purchase of American war matériel. As early as 1938, the RAF was placing small orders at Lockheed Aircraft Corporation and North American Aviation for non-military aircraft for reconnaissance and training. When British envoys visited the plants, they found that the design and production capability for these planes considerably lagged those of its own civilian aircraft, and were far behind the British fighters and bombers now entering service. The same was true for other weapons, with the exception of American machine tools, which Britain needed for its rapidly expanding factory capacity.[34]

CHAMBERLAIN'S GOVERNMENT WAS CONFIDENT that it could stand against Germany without relying on American assistance, and even defeat it, for two reasons. First, its munitions production capacity was poised to overtake Germany's; second, it had a strong alliance with the equally powerful France, while Germany stood alone. The first advantage, that of munitions production, was largely due to Chamberlain's policy of rearmament as a necessary precondition for appeasement. The British economy was already capable of matching Germany in building weapons; with an overall productivity about 20 percent higher and more access to coal and iron ore, it had significantly greater potential to ramp up manufacture. The Kriegsmarine (German navy) was just a fraction of the size of the Royal Navy—two battleships and three heavy cruisers for Germany, versus twelve battleships, three battlecruisers, and seven aircraft carriers for Britain. Chamberlain's budget, as we have seen, was already favoring the RAF over the Royal Navy, and by the start of the war that choice was paying off. In the summer of 1939, the Industrial Intelligence Centre (a small, secretive organization within the Board of Trade, located well away from Whitehall) reported that British and German aircraft production would be running "neck and neck" by the fall. By the spring of 1940, the air minister announced that "allied output of aircraft now exceeded that of Germany." British tank production during the first eight months of the war was actually higher than that of Germany (600 versus 530, respectively). British tanks were on par with German ones, and the British Army, though smaller, was actually more tank-intensive than Germany's. Although British industry had serious shortfalls in small arms and ammunition, those could be overcome by the powerful Canadian industry.[35]

The second advantage Britain had over Germany was that it entered the war alongside its longtime ally France, with whom it had defeated Germany just twenty years earlier. Germany, as noted, entered the war alone (Italy would not join the fight until June 1940). France's military was equal in capability to that of Britain, and in some cases superior. The French Char B1 series tank was recognized as having the best armor and heaviest weaponry of any tank in Western Europe, and France was building hundreds more tanks per month than Germany. The Anglo-French alliance had grown stronger in the days after Germany's dismemberment of Czechoslovakia, with staff talks to coordinate military strategy (for example, the French navy would patrol the Mediterranean, while the Royal Navy would control the Atlantic) and economic activity (such as purchases of raw materials from neutral states). So effective was the coordination that within twenty-four hours of Chamberlain's declaring war on Germany, he was able to dispatch the 400,000-man-strong British Expeditionary Force (BEF) from British ports across the English Channel to take their assigned positions between the equivalent-sized French First and Seventh Armies along the French-Belgian border. Merely days later, the first meeting of the Supreme War Council took place in Abbeville, France.[36]

A whole slew of other joint activities began to take shape, albeit haltingly; the possibility of joint tank and anti-aircraft gun production; the formation of an Anglo-French Purchasing Board to go to the United States for aircraft and machine tools; and a combined Allied landing in Norway. In December 1939, three months after the war's outbreak, Ernle Chatfield was able to tell the public with confidence that "we have the closest cooperation with our great ally. . . . Anglo-French staffs in all sections are completely organised and sit together daily to study the problems of war. Never have allies started fighting with such a complete mechanism, such complete plans and such identity of spirit."[37]

While Britain stood protected from German invasion by the English Channel, which no nation had crossed in anger for 250 years, the Phoney War was waged from September 1939 to May 1940. It was not, in fact, a phony war, but one combining economic offense and military defense. Economic war was waged by preventing German trade and shipping, block-ading its ports, and cutting off its exports. Meanwhile, British and French troops waited anxiously along the Belgian border for an attack they increasingly doubted would ever come.[38]

The combined German forces of the Wehrmacht and Luftwaffe struck suddenly and savagely across the Netherlands, Luxembourg, and Belgium on May 10, 1940. Two days later, they breached the supposedly impenetrable Ardennes Forest, where Allied resistance was lightest. Any parity that existed on paper between French, British, and German tanks disappeared in actual combat, as the Germans deployed Stuka dive-bombers and heavy anti-tank guns in tightly organized thrusts to race through Allied defenses. The British and French forces were surrounded and overwhelmed, and within two weeks had been pushed to the coast around Dunkirk. If the BEF were destroyed or captured, it would cripple any possibility of a future British counteroffensive. So, in a feat of both derring-do and making do, a fleet of small craft, ferries and naval ships evacuated the great majority of the BEF (as well as some French and other Allied troops) across the English Channel. By June 4, the human evacuation was complete. The toll in matériel, on the other hand, was immense—tens of thousands of tanks, artillery pieces, anti-aircraft guns, and motor vehicles were abandoned in place, along with tons of munitions (Figure 2). Britain would need months or even years to rebuild, and its factories and industries were already stretched to the limit.

The German invasion of the Low Countries coincided with the failure of the Allies to stop the German occupation of neutral Norway. The two events led Chamberlain, who had overseen the failed stranglehold strategy for nine months and the failed appeasement strategy before that, to deliver his resignation to King George VI and recommend Winston Churchill as his replacement. The evening of that same day, May 10, the king summoned Churchill to Buckingham Palace to form a government.

Churchill's first month as prime minister was marked by defeat after defeat, as the BEF was rolled back to the sea. Only the Dunkirk evacuation stood as anything close to a success, though, as Churchill noted in his "War Situation" speech to the House of Commons on June 4, as the last of the British troops were being landed in Britain, "wars are not won by evacuations. But there was a victory inside this deliverance." After explaining to the assembled ministers how Britain had arrived at this situation and admitting that "our losses in material are enormous," he then described how he saw the nation's future: "We shall prove ourselves once again able to defend our Island home, to ride out the storm of war, and to outlive the menace of tyranny, if necessary for years, if necessary alone."[39]

He conceded that France was no longer an equal ally, and that Britain would eventually have to come to its rescue. In the speech's famous peroration, Churchill vowed:

> We shall go on to the end, we shall fight in France, we shall fight on the seas and oceans, we shall fight with growing confidence and growing strength in the air, we shall defend our Island, whatever the cost may be, we shall fight on the beaches, we shall fight on the landing grounds, we shall fight in the fields and in the streets, we shall fight in the hills; we shall never surrender.

Despite his insistence that Britain would fight, "if necessary, alone," Churchill understood that the island was never really alone; the (now) Former Naval Person evoked the nation's maritime heritage and the promise of its empire with a half-billion residents. Even should Britain be "subjugated and starving," its fleet and empire would continue the fight, until "in God's good time, the New World, with all its power and might, steps forth to the rescue and the liberation of the old."

Churchill all but acknowledged that, with the sudden downfall of France and the enormous losses at Dunkirk, his nation would have to depend upon assistance from America, first to defend itself and then to defeat Germany. To encourage the "New World" to step forth in that role, Britain would need to develop an entirely new relationship with the United States, one unlike any in their long and shared history.

CHAPTER 2

FIGHT WITH GROWING CONFIDENCE

WHEN CHURCHILL GAVE his "War Situation" speech on June 4, 1940, he was well aware that the two pillars of Britain's prewar strategy to defeat the Nazis—outbuild them and, with France at its side, outfight them—now lay as broken and derelict as the tanks and artillery left on the beaches and around the countryside of Dunkirk. Neither he nor Chamberlain before him had believed that France would fall so swiftly; they had expected a protracted battle for Europe, one that would allow British and French industries to replenish battle losses. Now Britain would have to bear the brunt of the fighting without outside help, and its industries would have to somehow keep pace, at least in the short term. Still, Churchill's claim that they would "fight with growing confidence" was not without foundation. Almost a decade of preparation for war had resulted in scientific and engineering breakthroughs that promised, if not speedy victory, then a bulwark against defeat.

Churchill had long been fascinated by inventions, and even proposed his fair share of them. As a young officer serving overseas, he became an avid reader of H. G. Wells's futuristic novels, which envisioned long-range bombers, "land ironclads" (which helped inspire Churchill's push to develop the tank), heat rays, and even the atomic bomb, a term Wells coined. The two began a correspondence in 1901, met in person the following year, and kept up their friendship until Wells's death in 1946. Churchill's interest in technology was constrained by his education at Harrow School and the Royal Military College at Sandhurst, which focused on the classics, mathematics, military studies, and horsemanship, and not physics, chemistry, or engineering, which might have given him a firmer basis for understanding these advancements.[1]

Fortunately, thanks to his wife, Clementine (whom he married in 1908), Churchill befriended the physicist Frederick Lindemann, who could summarize abstruse scientific concepts and "explain to me in lucid, homely terms what the issues were," as Churchill later recalled. Lindemann's father was German, and, like Churchill, his mother was American. Lindemann spoke German fluently—he studied physics at the University of Berlin— and spoke English with a German inflection. During World War One, he developed theories of aeronautics and learned to fly airplanes to test them. In 1919, Lindemann was appointed professor of experimental philosophy (physics) at Oxford, largely on the recommendation of another Oxford professor, the chemist Henry Tizard, whom he had befriended while both were at the University of Berlin. In 1921, Clementine Churchill and Lindemann, both avid tennis players, were paired at a charity exhibition tennis tournament, after which Winston and Frederick became lifelong friends (and Clementine and Frederick lifelong tennis partners). In 1924, Churchill leaned heavily on Lindemann's scientific acumen to write an article entitled "Shall We All Commit Suicide?," a reflection on the increasing lethality of modern weapons in which he anticipated (like Wells) a future with "electrical rays" able to destroy airplanes or people, and a "bomb no bigger than an orange," based on recent atomic research.[2]

When Churchill was appointed First Lord of the Admiralty in September 1939, right at the start of World War Two, he carried with him a demand for brevity, alacrity, and attention to detail among his subordinates. This was a trait that had marked his earlier tenure during the Great War, when he required that information be delivered to him on a "single sheet of paper." Now he instated a three-tier response system to his minutes and memoranda: "Action this day," "Report within three days," "Report as soon as possible." The second and third tiers rarely were used, and soon disappeared entirely; instead, he circulated the red-labeled "Action this day" documents throughout the Admiralty, a practice he would take with him to the premiership.[3]

A frequent recipient of these missives was Lindemann, whom Churchill had brought on as an unpaid "Personal Advisor to the First Lord on Scientific Development," a remit that soon expanded to economics and war production. Long known as "Prof" in honor of his position as an Oxford don, Lindemann's actual job was head of the Statistical Branch, in which his uncanny ability to synthesize vast amounts of information and present it to his boss made Churchill one of the best-informed members of the war cabinet. As he would throughout his career, Churchill depended heavily on the Prof's scientific and technical advice, and their discussions on these subjects often lasted well into the early hours. For all that, Winston sometimes had an odd way of expressing his sentiments toward one of his "oldest and greatest friends." After a member of Parliament once dared to question Lindemann's loyalties—that German accent and heritage—Churchill was livid, and in an aside to his parliamentary secretary that was both devoted and dehumanizing, said, "Love me, love my dog, and if you don't love my dog you damn well can't love me."[4]

When Churchill became prime minister in May 1940, he brought Lindemann with him as his personal science advisor, appointing him head of the renamed Prime Minister's Statistical Department (Lindemann would become an official Cabinet member in 1942 as paymaster general). In addition to his premiership, Churchill appointed himself minister of defense, a previously unknown title that put him above the chiefs of staff of the Royal Air Force and British Army and above the First Sea Lord of the Royal Navy. He also established a civilian war cabinet, consisting of five (later eight) ministers. Now he could give free rein to his passion for promoting technology to advance the state of warfare. One of his early actions was to reorganize a military intelligence unit into a new department called Ministry of Defence 1 (the first and only department in the Ministry of Defence, better known as MD1), which was a specialized research and development center for unusual weaponry such as limpet mines (so called because they magnetically stuck to ship hulls) and antitank mortars. Churchill and Lindemann were frequent visitors to the department—which was nicknamed "Churchill's Toyshop" and housed just a few miles from the prime minister's country house, Chequers—witnessing trials of prototype weapons and proposing new ones.[5]

Churchill's penchant for proposing inventions was well known but sometimes derided; while he was the one who pushed the development of the tank to become an effective weapon, he also dreamed up a giant trench-cutting machine that proved useless in the face of German maneuver warfare. General Alan Brooke, Viscount Alanbrooke, the chairman of the Chiefs of Staff and Britain's highest-ranking military officer, privately complained that "[Churchill's] military plans and ideas varied from the most brilliant conceptions at one end, to the wildest and most dangerous ideas at the other." This was somewhat unfair; Churchill's failures in World War One, notably the Dardanelles campaign, had taught him to recognize his own limitations. MD1's administrator and chief inventor, Stuart Macrae, said of him: "When faced with any problem, the first thing Churchill would do would be to summon a selection of people best able to give him information on the subject and another selection best able to advise him as to the decision to be taken. Very seldom would he go against their advice."[6]

A War of Boffins

The development of British radar—certainly one of the most important reasons for Churchill's "growing confidence" after Dunkirk—began with an Air Ministry request for a death ray. The belief that such a weapon was feasible had grown every decade since Wells's 1898 *War of the Worlds* introduced the Martian "heat-ray" to the public. In science fiction, in "the next war" novels, and with inventors like electricity pioneer Nikola Tesla, the death ray captured the popular imagination. Even Churchill, following a claim by a British inventor, asked his friend Lindemann to make inquiries into "a ray which will kill at a certain distance," which subsequently became fodder for "Shall We All Commit Suicide?" Ever since then, a regular stream of proposals had been arriving at the Air Ministry (the civilian authority for the Royal Air Force), which offered a prize of £1,000 for any device that could verifiably kill a sheep at a range of 100 yards.[7]

The Air Ministry was concerned mainly with defending against enemy aircraft. By 1934, that enemy had been positively identified as Germany, with Hitler's new, openly belligerent government and its withdrawal from the League of Nations and the Geneva Disarmament Conference. Coupled with Baldwin's warning that "the bomber will always get through," the annual Air Exercises now took on increased urgency. The 1934 exercises, which over three days and nights in July simulated a series of German bomber attacks against London (defended by fighters, anti-aircraft guns, and searchlights), showed that the lack of a viable early warning system meant that fighters and gunners had very little chance of intercepting the bombers before they got through. Even the development of acoustic mirrors, which in theory could hear aircraft at a range of 10 miles—twice as far as the visual range of about 5 miles—was in fact severely limited by wind noise and could be spoofed by the sound of horse-drawn carts. Moreover, aircraft engineering was advancing at such a rate that bombers would soon be able to cover that theoretical distance in less than three minutes, not enough time to scramble defensive fighters. Longer-range detection would be imperative for the coming war.[8]

Before these results were even known, the Directorate of Scientific Research in the Air Ministry, led by the engineer and former Royal Navy pilot Harry Wimperis, was considering how to improve Britain's air defense in general, and long-range detection in particular. Wimperis's assistant, Albert Percival Rowe, searched the Air Ministry archives and found nothing had been done to address the early-warning problem, aside from the aforementioned acoustic mirrors, which fell under the War Office, a separate branch of government. By October 1934, Wimperis had decided that further scientific work was needed. Being careful not to tread upon the War Office's territory, he proposed establishing a new Committee for the Scientific Survey of Air Defence with a broad remit to investigate scientific advances, and which would belong to neither the Air Ministry nor the War Office. Wimperis instead proposed to the government an ad hoc advisory committee with himself and Rowe as members, along with Patrick Blackett (an experimental physicist and a naval gunner in World War One), Archibald "A.V." Hill (Nobel laureate physiologist and former army gunner), and chair Henry Tizard, president of Imperial College London. This combination of scientific acumen and military experience would make the Air Defence Committee (known also as the Tizard Committee) a highly influential body.[9]

Well before the committee's first meeting, Wimperis had approached Hill to "have a good talk with him on radiant energy as a means of AA [anti-aircraft] defence." Wimperis then met with his friend Robert Watson-Watt of the National Physical Laboratory (Britain's premier government laboratory) to inquire about the "prospects for some form of damaging radiation in defence against enemy air attack." Watson-Watt had spent much of his early career at the Meteorological Office, investigating the use of radio waves as a means of predicting thunderstorms. He subsequently began using radio to probe the ionosphere, recently discovered by the American physicist Merle Tuve. Watson-Watt had enough experience to know that Wimperis's innocuous phrase "damaging radiation" meant "death ray," so he and his assistant developed some quick calculations that showed that radio waves could never damage a pilot or the aircraft. But a series of pulsed radio waves could reflect back to the source and thus determine an enemy's position, long before it could be spotted visually or heard acoustically.[10]

Watson-Watt conveyed these findings to the Air Defence Committee before its first meeting in January 1935. The discussion that day ranged from death rays to gunnery. Watson-Watt's "radio-detection" of aircraft, however, received the greatest interest. Watson-Watt subsequently submitted a final memorandum on February 27, 1935, "Detection and Location of Aircraft by Radio Methods," which explained how pulsed radio waves could detect, locate, and track an aircraft at a range of over 200 miles, far greater than any visual, acoustic, or infrared methods. It also explained that a method would be needed to identify friend from foe, that a "line of [radio] senders" would be needed across a wide front to provide continuous coverage, and finally that a command and communication system would need to be developed in order to vector defensive fighters to enemy targets. In short, Watson-Watt's final memorandum, which he later called the "birth certificate of radar," laid out a complete description of what would become Britain's Chain Home system against the Luftwaffe.[11]

The Air Defence Committee, convinced of the significance of this radio detection system, petitioned Air Marshal Hugh Dowding for development funding. Dowding had risen through the ranks of the RAF and now was head of Supply and Research, overseeing the development of the new front-line aircraft, specifically the Hurricane and Spitfire fighters, both of which were ordered in the autumn of 1934. Wimperis brought Watson-Watt with him to make the case. Despite Dowding's nickname, "Stuffy"—which Watson-Watt attributed to the "high respect and partial frustration" that Dowding's all-business attitude elicited from his men—the Air Marshal was quick to understand the potential benefit of this new idea. However, he demanded a demonstration before authorizing monies. On February 26, 1935, Watson-Watt and Rowe set up a pair of receiving antennae in a farmer's field near Daventry in middle England, close to a BBC shortwave transmitter. Using a converted ambulance as their control room, they were able to see on a cathode-ray tube display the trace of a biplane bomber as it flew through the BBC radio beams and bounced the signals to the antennae. When Dowding was informed of the results, he sanctioned £10,000 (a considerable sum at the time, about $6 million today) for Watson-Watt to develop a working system at large scale.[12]

Watson-Watt and his team established a laboratory on a remote spit of land at Orfordness in Suffolk to begin working on a series of experiments and demonstrations, cobbling together antennae, transmitters, and receivers (some built with American vacuum tubes) to detect and track aircraft at longer and longer ranges; in June it was 17 miles, by July 40 miles, and in August 60 miles. Meanwhile, the RAF was casting about for a code name "which did not immediately indicate its method of operation." They hit upon the meaningless initials RDF, a mash-up of RD, for "radio detection," and DF, for "direction-finding." (RDF was used in Britain until 1943, when it was replaced by the American Navy's acronym for "radio detection and ranging," or "radar.")

Although the Air Defence Committee regularly visited Watson-Watt's team and received briefings on RDF, it was also considering other anti-aircraft systems. This was often at the instigation of Lindemann, who had joined the committee in July at Churchill's behest. Lindemann supported the development of RDF, but like many on the committee, he was disappointed by what he saw as slow progress. Moreover, he believed that the committee was singularly focused on RDF as a solution to the problem of daylight interception by fighters, whereas he believed that the greater threat lay in nighttime and overcast bombing, which had been the case during the previous war. Because fighters operating in the dark or in overcast skies would be unable to visually locate bombers even after being given RDF bearings, Lindemann—backed by Churchill—advocated for more work on aerial minefields (rocket-launched bombs that descended on long wires via parachute), better searchlights, radar-directed anti-aircraft guns, and even a proximity fuze for bombs that could be automatically detonated when it was near the target. Tizard himself was concerned that even building a system for the "simpler" problem of daytime interception still would be enormously complex, and therefore should be the focus of their efforts. As these two longtime colleagues continued to talk past each other, the resulting friction led to the breakup of both their friendship and the Air Defence Committee.[13]

BY MAY 1936 THE experimental work had outgrown the wooden huts at Orfordness and was moved down the Suffolk coast to a Victorian country house at Bawdsey Manor, and it formally became the Air Ministry Research Establishment (later known as the Telecommunications Research Establishment or TRE). It was led by Watson-Watt until 1938, when his assistant Rowe took over. While the team at Bawdsey was building and testing the RDF antennae equipment for detecting Luftwaffe bombers, the Air Defence Committee began work on developing the rest of the system. As Watson-Watt had indicated in his original memorandum on RDF, a reliable command and communication system had to be developed that could take radio detection information and turn it into orders for vectoring defensive fighters to intercept the bombers.

In July 1936, working closely with Dowding—now promoted to commander, Fighter Command—Tizard set up a series of trials at Biggin Hill airfield near London, to establish how the communication flow would take place—what information needed to be transmitted and how pilots would respond. What started as a two-month experiment eventually stretched to two difficult years, as more RDF stations were erected and the kinks were worked out. The 1936 Air Exercises were particularly disastrous: RDF information never reached Biggin Hill before Dowding heard the attacking aircraft pass overhead. The final system, collectively known as Chain Home but often referred to as the Dowding System, included RDF stations (Chain Home and Chain Home Low towers, which supported seaward-facing antennae to detect and track incoming aircraft at high and low altitudes); Royal Observer Corps for visual identification and tracking after the enemy aircraft crossed inland; high-frequency direction-finding and Identification Friend or Foe to "tag" friendly aircraft on RDF cathode-ray tube displays; filter rooms, where plotters would synthesize all the information and indicate positions of incoming bombers and available fighters; and the fighter squadrons themselves. All of these had to be brought together into an integrated whole.[14]

The Chain Home system marked the full integration of scientists and engineers into the British military hierarchy, which in the past had often held them at arm's length. Now RAF officers affectionately referred to them as "boffins," a new term with no discernable etymology but which was widely embraced by the scientists themselves. Churchill preferred "wizard" (he called the radar battle against Germany "The Wizard War"), perhaps due to its popular use meaning "clever," or to his own affection for the film *The Wizard of Oz*. Few scientists adopted it.[15]

Even as the boffins were working closely with RAF officers at Biggin Hill, they were fighting among themselves in London. In July 1936, Lindemann's excoriation of the Air Defence Committee for its prioritization of RDF and its lack of support for aerial mining had reached the resulted in the resignations of Patrick Blackett and A. V. Hill, crippling the committee's work just as the Biggin Hill experiments were beginning. Despite Churchill's fervent defense of Lindemann, the Air Ministry decided that RDF work was too important and reconstituted the committee with Tizard, Blackett, and Hill, and without Lindemann. Instead, one of Britain's premier radio physicists, Edward Appleton, was invited to join, solidifying the ministry's support of RDF. In an ironic twist, with Lindemann now gone, the committee spent even more time on nighttime and overcast air defense, including better designs for aerial mines and experimenting with acoustic and photoelectric devices for proximity fuzes. Tizard kept a close eye on promising work being done by one of Watson-Watt's assistants, Edward G. Bowen, to develop an air-intercept RDF unit that was small enough to fit on aircraft, allowing night fighters to find and target German bombers.[16]

Ground-based early-warning RDF—radar—was still the Air Ministry's top priority. Teams under Stuffy Dowdy and Robert Watson-Watt continued to build, test, and expand the Chain Home system. When Britain declared war in September 1939, the Air Defence Committee was folded into the larger Committee for the Scientific Survey of Air Warfare (over which Tizard still presided), whose remit extended to offensive weapons. The committee even brought aboard the nuclear physicist John Cockcroft— the first scientist to split the atom—to examine the possibility of "producing atomic bombs during this war," as nuclear fission had recently been discovered. Meanwhile, Chain Home became a fully operational arm of the RAF, covering the entire eastern coast of Great Britain. Watson-Watt was justifiably proud of this accomplishment, entitling his autobiography *Three Steps to Victory* for his list of achievements, beginning with radar (the other two steps, operations research and high-frequency direction-finding, are discussed later in this book). Although happy to be known as the father of radar, he personally disliked the acronym: "a synthetic palindrome invented by our friends the Americans," he derisively called it.[17]

Watson-Watt was also quite aware that like most successes, radar had a hundred fathers, of which he was just one. In fact, at the same time Watson-Watt was working on his earliest experiments, radar in one form or another was being independently developed in at least seven other nations, including Germany and the United States. German radar systems were primarily developed by two companies, GEMA and Telefunken, each for different purposes. GEMA built early-warning radars, first for the Kriegsmarine (named Seetakt) and then for the Luftwaffe (Freya), the latter of which began land-based testing in 1937. Telefunken built Würzburg intercept radars, used for guiding anti-aircraft guns, after 1940. While the two radars eventually became integrated into a defensive system similar to Chain Home, rivalry between the two companies over licensing and patent rights, combined with the Nazi government's scorn for physicists and basic scientific research (which previously had pride of place in German engineering), meant that German radar was never developed into the offensive weapon that it became in Britain and the United States.[18]

Radar development in the United States was also subject to rivalries, not just between companies like RCA and Westinghouse, but also between the navy and army. The antecedents to American radar dated back to 1922, when navy engineers discovered that radio waves beamed between two stations on the Anacostia River (near Washington) were blocked by passing ships. Eight years later, other engineers at the Naval Research Laboratory (NRL) in Washington found that radio waves reflected off aircraft. NRL physicist Robert Morris Page began experimenting with radar in December 1934, just a few weeks prior to Watson-Watt's efforts (though neither knew of the other's work at the time). By 1936, NRL was building prototype radars for surface warships, culminating in the production in 1940 by RCA of the CXAM early-warning radar, which saw extensive use in the Pacific theater of the war. The Army Signal Corps Laboratory (SCL) in Monmouth County, New Jersey, which served both the Army Ground Forces and Army Air Forces, was well aware of NRL's work, and built upon it to develop its own radars—first the SCR-268 gun-laying radar in 1937, then by 1940 the Westinghouse-built SCR-270 and SCR-271 early-warning models (it was the SCR-270 that detected the Japanese aircraft en route to bomb

Pearl Harbor, but this information was misinterpreted and never acted on). Neither the NRL nor SCL scientists were ever called "boffins," but they were recognized early on as being crucial to the war effort. Just three months before Pearl Harbor, the nuclear physicist Arthur Compton—brother of Massachusetts Institute of Technology (MIT) president Karl Compton— remarked in the journal *Nature*, "If the War of 1914–18 was a chemists' war, the present affliction . . . is a physicists' war." The trope that World War Two was a "physicists' war" would be reprised throughout the conflict.[19]

Whether it was called a boffins' war, Wizard War, or physicists' war, the first major engagement to put science directly on the front lines occurred right after Dunkirk evacuation, when the Chain Home system was put to the test. Beginning in June 1940, the Luftwaffe began the Battle of Britain, followed in September by the Blitz, which lasted until May 1941. During those eleven months, thousands of bombing raids were launched against cities, military bases, airfields, port facilities, and factories across the whole nation, with London bearing the brunt of the attacks. The two campaigns were really an overlapping series of aerial assaults by the Luftwaffe, following different strategies and tactics that ultimately failed to open Britain to invasion or to bring it to its knees. Hitler's aim was to knock Britain out of the war—first by blockade, then by a combined amphibious and airborne assault—before his planned invasion of the Soviet Union. For Germany's effort against Britain to succeed, the Luftwaffe needed to gain air superiority in the English skies. During the Battle of Britain, air attacks on coastal cities and shipping in the English Channel soon gave way to daytime bombing of RAF airfields and aircraft factories, with the goal of exhausting British fighter defenses.[20]

By September 1940, when it became apparent that Germany could not attain sufficient air superiority to allow an invasion or coerce Britain into a peace, the Luftwaffe's tactics changed to the Blitz, marked by day and (mostly) night bombing of London and industrial cities like Coventry, Manchester, and Liverpool to destroy its war-making capability and cow its citizens into submission. The Nazi air assault eventually petered out after May 1941, when bombers were withdrawn east for Operation Barbarossa, Hitler's ill-fated invasion of the Soviet Union.

The Chain Home system had been confronting problems ever since the first towers were erected in 1936, and was barely operational when the first major air attacks began in July 1940. Under Dowding's command, the system and its operations rapidly evolved and adapted as the Battle of Britain and Blitz continued. Chain Home radars were often given most of the credit for directing the fighter defenses, but this was not the case. Since they faced the ocean, the radars would lose track of aircraft once they crossed the Channel. As Churchill pointed out, "The observers, with field-glasses and portable telephones, were our main source of information about raiders flying overland." Nor were Chain Home radars of much help during the nighttime raids. Lindemann had been correct that day fighters could not hope to intercept bombers in the dark, although his preferred method of defeating German aircraft—the use of aerial mines—proved ineffective. Emerging technologies such as jamming the German navigational beams, radar-guided anti-aircraft guns, and radar-equipped night fighters blunted the Luftwaffe's effectiveness, but they came too late to significantly diminish the size and number of raids.[21]

A War of Factories

In the end, cities like London and Liverpool mostly had to endure the incessant bombings, while major industrial plants continued to set up "shadow factories" around the country to keep vital war production going. The scheme of creating government-owned, industry-operated factories had been established in 1935 under Stanley Baldwin's government, as part of its rearmament response to Hitler, alongside diplomacy. The term "shadow factories" was taken from "shadow cabinets," a long-standing tradition by which parliamentary opposition parties developed alternate policies to the sitting cabinet. Baldwin's rearmament strategy had focused on building up the RAF aircraft fleet. Since Britain's mass-production capability lay in primarily in its automobile industry, motorcar companies such as Rover, Austin, Daimler, Morris, and Ford (as well as some aircraft engine companies like Rolls-Royce) were paid to build, equip, and operate shadow factories for aircraft and engines, alongside existing plants. In this way, skilled workers could be placed on the production lines to oversee the influx of new laborers. Much of the automobile industry was based in the Midlands, especially in and around Coventry, which is why that city suffered so much bombing. Even before the Coventry Blitz, the government was dispersing manufacturing to sites in the countryside, which were harder for the Luftwaffe to target but also decreased productivity. Most of the government capital ($3 billion modern equivalent per factory) went to such machine tools as metal planers, drill presses, milling machines, lathes, and press brakes, all of which were in increasingly short supply as the war dragged on. Yet these tools were so sturdy that they generally survived even the worst bombings, so full production was often reestablished within days or weeks of an attack.[22]

Even the increased production from shadow factories would not be enough for the sustained aerial campaign that faced Britain after the fall of France. Churchill prioritized this issue two days after he took office, when he appointed his longtime friend Max Aitken, Baron Beaverbrook, minister of aircraft production, removing that portfolio from the overburdened Air Ministry. Beaverbrook—who derived the title from his childhood home in Canada—was a press baron and a former minister of information, recognized for his skill at organizing large enterprises. He immediately consolidated the manufacturing lines for the most critical bombers and fighters, began rationalizing the logistics train, and started his practice of setting intentionally unrealistic production goals to push industries to stretch their capabilities. Arming the nation would be made even more challenging by the devastating losses at Dunkirk, along with further losses during the later British evacuations at Le Havre, Brest, Cherbourg, and other French ports.[23]

Before Dunkirk, when Britain had been certain of having France by its side, with the British Expeditionary Force firmly anchored on European soil and German air and sea bases far from England. That was why British leaders were convinced that it could win the war without American assistance. After Dunkirk and the fall of France, they understood that they could not possibly do without it. The speed of the human evacuation from the beaches and quays—338,000 men in nine days—had meant that almost every piece of equipment, large and small, was left behind and would have to be replaced. Over 700 tanks had been lost, for example. Moreover, Britain required countless more armaments just to defend the island from Nazi assault, which could now be launched by sea and air from an occupied France just a few miles away. On top of all that, its entire military—army, navy, and air force—would have to be completely rebuilt, first to weaken Germany through bombardment, then to land on the Continent and reconquer Europe. None of this had been counted in the war plans formulated only two months earlier.

By June 1940, the British Army had barely enough heavy tanks and artillery to equip two armored divisions, compared with Germany's ten divisions. Those 700 destroyed tanks would take seven months to replace at the then-current rate of production, and this did not account for the huge backlog of new orders. Tens of thousands of machine guns, trucks, motorcycles, and even personal arms had been discarded in France; a third of a million Lee-Enfield rifles, the mainstay of British infantry, were left strewn among the dunes. Ships and landing craft were destroyed and had to be replaced, with many more needed for a future amphibious invasion. The RAF also suffered enormous losses: 458 aircraft were downed, two months' production even with shadow factories. Though bombers were needed in the long term to take the offensive to Germany, for now defensive fighters were the key. As Churchill explained to the House of Commons in his "finest hour" speech, given weeks after the evacuation, "The Battle of France is over. . . . I expect that the Battle of Britain is about to begin." For Britain to survive, fighter production would have to be the first priority. Beaverbrook succeeded in his initial task, ensuring that fighter numbers increased dramatically; monthly production rose from 256 in April to 467 in September, surpassing Germany and more than covering the losses in battle. By October 1940, when the Battle of Britain ended, the RAF had more fighters than when it began.[24]

Even with the increase in fighter production, it was obvious that Britain would require many more months to build up its bomber fleet, and years to rebuild its other forces to retake Europe. "We have no continental army which can defeat the German military power," Churchill admitted to

Beaverbrook in July 1940. With these limitations in mind, the Chiefs of Staff Committee outlined its post-Dunkirk plan to take the fight to the Germans in a paper presented on September 4, 1940. Although the document, called "Appreciation of Future Strategy," was never formalized as official policy and was revised over the following months, it established the framework that Britain—and later the Allies—would follow in the European campaign, and is worth summarizing here. The British military, it argued, must avoid direct confrontation with the German armed forces in the short term, instead undermining the enemy by naval blockade, sabotage, and subversion largely carried out by the recently formed Special Operations Executive and Combined Operations Command, and by laying the groundwork for a major assault. That operation would follow four main steps. First, the RAF would carry out a strategic air campaign, a "devastating, exterminating attack by very heavy bombers from this country upon the Nazi homeland." Second, Britain would build up "very powerful naval forces and maintain our merchant shipping tonnage" to keep open the transatlantic supply lines from North America and its empire. Third, it would "exploit . . . our amphibious power to the full" by conducting offensive operations on the peripheries of Europe and in occupied territories, then attack Italy as the weaker of the two Axis powers. In the final step, the army would "provide a striking force on the Continent when the morale of the enemy forces has been considerably weakened," inflicting the final blow against Germany itself.[25]

The day before his Chiefs of Staff finalized the details of this strategy, Churchill spelled out his own thinking in a minute to his war cabinet: "The Navy can lose us the war, but only the Air Force can win it," he argued. "Therefore, our supreme effort must be to gain overwhelming mastery in the air. The Fighters are our salvation, but the Bombers alone provide the means of victory." Defeating Germany would involve gaining the explosive power "to pulverise the entire industry and scientific structure on which the war effort and economic life of the enemy depend, while holding him at arm's length from our island." This was the only way to win the war.[26]

Despite Beaverbrook's early success with exhorting British industry to quickly churn out Hurricanes and Spitfires, he knew that shortages of machine tools, manufactured parts, and skilled labor hobbled its ability to produce heavy bombers in the enormous quantities needed. The problem of skilled labor—which had been identified long before the war broke out—was especially felt in the aircraft industry, where companies resorted to poaching each other's workers as the supply of new male recruits dried up due to war conscription. Bringing in women was one obvious answer to this problem. In fact, they had already been finding work in munitions plants. After 1941, however, they were required under the National Service Act to report for duty in either the armed forces, civil defense, agriculture, nursing, or an "essential industry." Recruiting posters pleading, "Women of Britain, come into the factories" went up around the country. By 1942, women made up as much as two-thirds of employment in the various war industries, often at the same skill levels as the men.[27]

Meanwhile, the factories themselves were expanded to take on the additional workers and production lines, now running twenty hours a day and on weekends. The industrial bottlenecks only grew worse as the Blitz dragged on, for the German bombing raids disrupted the supply of raw materials and manufactured parts. Although Britain's industries were still supplying over 90 percent of its military requirements, the nation was already looking to the United States to provide the rest; even before Dunkirk, munitions and supplies from the United States were double those of Canada and the rest of the empire combined. With France out of the picture, much of Britain's weaponry lying in smoldering ruins, and its needs outstripping its capacity almost by the hour, Churchill and his Cabinet understood that above anything else, Britain now required America's manufacturing might.[28]

Roosevelt would have been happy to oblige at an earlier point, but his hopes of providing arms and munitions to Britain and its allies had long been hamstrung by American public sentiment for staying out of war, which Congress embodied in the aforementioned Neutrality Acts, forbidding trade in arms with friends and potential enemies alike. In November 1939, just weeks after the German invasion of Poland, Roosevelt, sensing a shift in public mood, convinced Congress to enact the "Cash-and-Carry" provision (the phrase was popular before then, even extending to the title of a Three Stooges film) that ended the embargo on arms export, as long as a belligerent nation paid for them on a cash basis, and as long as the arms were not shipped by American vessels. When the American pipeline began opening, Britain and France established a complex arrangement of joint committees and boards to avoid competition over raw materials, munitions, and shipping. In November 1939, the Supreme War Council had established the Anglo-French Coordinating Committee in London, with the French businessman and diplomat Jean Monnet at its helm to coordinate production and imports. Operating underneath the committee was the Anglo-French Purchasing Board, led by British-born Canadian industrialist Arthur Purvis, intended to coordinate North American arms purchases (although many transactions continued to be made on an ad hoc basis). The board quickly grew, involving over a thousand personnel in its office at 15 Broad Street in Manhattan, directly opposite the New York Stock Exchange. There would be no J. P. Morgan as middleman, as in World War One; the British and French governments had direct access to the American financial system.[29]

The Purchasing Board wasted no time, immediately placing millions of dollars of orders for machine tools, rifles, and above all, aircraft—nearly 10,000 trainers, seaplanes, dive-bombers, and fighter planes were ordered in the first few months, and orders for another 16,000 soon followed. The "cash" part of the deal ($1.6 billion, worth more than $400 billion today) was accomplished through using Britain's reserves of gold bullion, which were being secretly transported to Canada aboard battleships, cruisers, and passenger liners, to keep the nation's wealth from falling into Nazi hands in the case of an invasion. The "carry" part was more onerous at first. For example, Congress prohibited aircraft from being flown into Canada (a belligerent nation, having declared war on Germany just days after Britain did). This meant that aircraft had to fly to American airfields at the Canadian border, where they were hitched to a team of horses and towed across the border (one farmer in Manitoba charged $5 per tow) to be flown off by a Canadian pilot. A tweak to the law in July 1940 allowed the planes to be flown to Canadian ports, where they could be loaded on cargo ships.[30]

THE SUDDEN INFLUX OF these Anglo-French purchases had the effect of jump-starting both Canada's and America's military-industrial complex, which had almost ceased to exist after World War One. These purchases would account for nearly all of Canada's aircraft orders and 40 percent of American aircraft orders prior to Pearl Harbor. Not just aircraft and arms builders benefited; their suppliers did as well. Steel mills that had been dormant for years came back to life: in late 1939 in Pittsburgh, one woman called the fire department to report smoke coming from across the hill. "That's no fire, lady," came the reply, "them's the mills." This flood of cash, coming on the heels of the 1937–1938 downturn during the Great Depression, allowed many manufacturers to retain their cadre of skilled production workers, many of whom were on the brink of dismissal due to lack of business, and retool their assembly lines for mass production. By 1941, two years after arms sales began, American manufacturers saw employment double and their backlogs triple in value.[31]

While other nations also queued to buy American equipment during this period (which coincided with the Phoney War), their orders were minuscule by comparison with those of Britain and France, and were usually sent to the back of the line. British and French delegations traveled around the United States, often seeking idle factories to fulfill their orders. One such plant was the underused American Locomotive Company facility in Schenectady, New York, slated to produce what would become the M3 tank (of which more later). Other delegations were focused on combat aircraft, having cast aside previous concerns that American companies were simply not up to snuff. They tended to focus on airplanes already in production, such as Curtiss-Wright's P-40 fighter and Consolidated PBY seaplanes. In some cases, however, they put money toward developing models not yet in American service. One such example was at the Lockheed Aircraft Corporation, which was known for building Amelia Earhart's Electra airliner, but whose production lines were underutilized. There the British delegation found Clarence "Kelly" Johnson designing a prototype Army Air Corps twin-engine fighter, designated the YP-38. They gave Lockheed a set of battle-tested requirements to modify the design, $100 million ($2.5 billion today) to set up a new production line, and a name for the aircraft—Lightning. The resulting P-38 model would become one of the most successful fighters of the war.[32]

Machine tools were the second-largest category of purchases after aircraft. British and French artillery and gun manufacturers were clamoring for lathes and presses, while Rover alone required over 400 machine tools for its aircraft shadow factory. The shadow scheme itself was always present in the mind of the commissioners as a model for American purchases. To set up new manufacturing facilities for smokeless gunpowder, for example, they established and fully financed the Tennessee Powder Company, which then contracted with E. I. du Pont de Nemours (DuPont) to build and operate a shadow facility in Memphis. Another American chemical company, Hercules, built and operated a shadow gunpowder plant financed by the British-owned New Jersey Powder Company.[33]

In most cases, however, American industry—especially aircraft manufacturers—dismissed the idea of shadow factories, preferring to use British and French money to expand their own facilities and build their own products instead. Even so, the shadow scheme would soon prove its merit when the Packard Motor Car Company began building Rolls-Royce Merlin aircraft engines in June 1940, as Chapter 3 describes.

June 1940 also saw the fall of France, after which the Anglo-French Purchasing Board became the British Purchasing Commission (BPC). Britain immediately took over France's purchases, which caused logistical problems great and small; Westinghouse, for example, had to completely redesign 500 milling machines, originally destined for France, from metric to English units. As the likelihood of America's entry into the war increased, the BPC found itself in competition with the US Army and Navy for orders. In September it moved 150 senior staff from New York to the Willard Hotel in Washington, taking over the entire ninth floor. Two blocks from the White House and historically favored by presidents and politicians, the hotel would enhance the BPC's lobbying efforts. The British had used the term "lobbying"—and were highly skilled at it—long before it was purportedly coined in the lobby of the Willard. Churchill's secretary of war,

Anthony Eden, had already made it clear to the prime minister that "the United States Administration is pursuing an almost entirely American policy, rather than one of all possible aid to Britain." The BPC's move was part of an all-out campaign to counteract that. It was placed under the umbrella of the British Supply Council in North America, which soon outgrew its digs at the Willard and took over the entire former Hotel Grafton, near Dupont Circle, from where it conducted lobbying efforts on behalf of the Air Commission, Tank Mission, Merchant Shipbuilding Mission, and Ordnance Commission.[34]

Churchill also focused on swaying American public opinion from its overwhelming opposition to entering the war. The British Ministry of Information cultivated American broadcasters like Edward R. Murrow to present favorable coverage of the war, while the Secret Intelligence Service (today more commonly known as MI6) dispatched, at Churchill's orders, the Canadian-born William Stephenson to run an operation in New York City, aimed at countering anti-war efforts by Charles Lindbergh and others.[35]

By this point—well into the Blitz—Churchill made personal entreaties for assistance to Roosevelt, now signing them "Former Naval Person." His first telegram, dated in May 1940, had asked for "forty or fifty of your older destroyers," a request Roosevelt declined. Instead, in June, the president declared that hundreds of thousands of rifles, machine guns, artillery pieces, and tons of ammunition—similar to what was left at Dunkirk— were surplus to US Army needs and could be released (in a complicated maneuver, they were transferred to US Steel Corporation, which then sold them to Britain on the same day). By August, Roosevelt had worked out a deal to declare fifty World War One–era destroyers (many in poor condition) as surplus, and exchange them to Britain for ninety-nine-year leases on bases around the Caribbean. Roosevelt laid the groundwork for further American involvement by dispatching Rear (soon Vice) Admiral Robert L. Ghormley to London, alongside two other general officers, to observe British technical developments and determine where the two nations could cooperate in wartime.[36]

After he won the November 1940 election for a historic third term in office, Roosevelt was able to expand American assistance to the British, as he noted in a press conference on December 17: "The best defense of Great Britain is the best defense of the United States, and therefore that these materials would be more useful to the defense of the United States if they were used in Great Britain, than if they were kept in storage here," he explained, using the analogy of lending a neighbor one's garden hose to fight a fire, rather than selling it to him. Roosevelt's argument was given concrete form by Jean Monnet, who began living in exile in the United States after the fall of France. Working in the British Supply Council and also as part of Roosevelt's informal circle of advisors, Monnet argued that because Britain was reaching the end of its credit, the limitations of Cash-and-Carry had to be cast aside. After Roosevelt's reelection, Monnet insisted that the imminent buildup of American arms manufacture, which was being set in motion with the $10 billion ($2.5 trillion today) military budget the administration was proposing, be used not just for American forces, but also to arm the Allied nations fighting Germany. Just days after Roosevelt's garden-hose speech, Monnet remarked to a gathering of his fellow advisers, "The United States must become a great arsenal, the arsenal of democracy." Supreme Court justice Felix Frankfurter, an influential advisor to the president who was at the event, told Monnet to hold off using that phrase again, so that Roosevelt could take it over. The president employed Monnet's turn of phrase in his fireside chat on December 29, which appealed to American industry to "produce arms and ships with every energy and re-source we can command . . . We must be the great arsenal of democracy." Five weeks later, on February 9, 1941, Churchill echoed this message in a BBC broadcast he knew would be heard across the Atlantic: "We shall not fail or falter; we shall not weaken or tire. . . . Give us the tools, and we will finish the job." The combined efforts of British propaganda and the speeches of Churchill and Roosevelt helped turn American opinion; polls conducted by George Gallup showed that while in October 1940 only 16 percent were in favor of helping Britain by entering the war, the number had grown to 22 percent in April 1941 and to 64 percent in July (and would reach 85 percent just before Pearl Harbor).[37]

AS POPULAR SENTIMENT SHIFTED, Roosevelt initiated two actions that solidified American support to Britain, one highly secret, the other overt. In January 1941, picking up from where Ghormley and the other American observers left off, undisclosed meetings began in Washington, with five British military staff and nine Americans to "determine the best methods by which the US and British Commonwealth could defeat Germany should the United States be compelled to resort to war." The ensuing reports, ABC-1 on joint strategy and ABC-2 on aircraft production allocation—the initials coming from "American-British Conversations"—were issued and approved in late March. The ABC-1 joint strategy largely followed the outline arrived at by the British Chiefs of Staff Appreciation of Future Strategy in late 1940: undermine the Germans by naval blockade, sabotage, and subversion; conduct air offensives while maintaining the transatlantic supply line; conduct initial offensive operations on the periphery and eliminate Italy early in the game; and build up forces for an eventual assault on the Continent. Although by early 1941, Japan was identified as another probable foe, it was given secondary priority to reconquering Europe. ABC-2 confirmed Britain's order of 26,000 aircraft, and established its primacy for an additional 24,000 planes.

The Lend-Lease Act of March 11, 1941, confirmed the Roosevelt administration's commitment to helping Britain. It was an overt declaration of American support to Britain and reflected the tacit acknowledgment that the two nations' war economies were to be merged against the Axis, with matériel allocated according to joint strategic needs. Officially titled "An Act to Promote the Defense of the United States," it pointedly carried a patriotic number, House Resolution 1776. The act—following Roosevelt's garden-hose analogy—removed the restrictions of Cash-and-Carry, allowing the United States to provide almost unlimited food, oil, and equipment to Allied nations (at this point the British Empire and Greece, with dozens more subsequently added), with the stipulation that the equipment would be returned after the war—a provision that would be largely ignored. Britain was by far the main beneficiary, but more importantly the act had the effect of opening the monetary spigot that brought American production to a war footing. To properly coordinate this sudden rush of orders between nations, various intergovernmental mechanisms—most notably the Joint Aircraft Committee—were established to take over the BPC contracts and strategically allocate them between Britain, the US Army, and the US Navy. Jean Monnet considered Lend-Lease, not Pearl Harbor, the turning point of the war; he later related how an American soldier, after the 1944 Normandy landings, met a French farmer whose wall calendar said March 11, 1941. When asked why, the farmer replied, "We stopped the calendar on the day we heard on the radio that the United States had voted for Lend-Lease. That day, we knew that Germany had lost the war."[38]

It is no exaggeration to state that the aircraft and munitions purchases from Britain and France, prior to Lend-Lease, had given American industry considerable lead time—many months if not a full year—to prepare for the moment when the country entered the war. Those purchases helped keep the American military aircraft industry afloat, accounting for 10,000 orders in early 1940, when the US Army and Navy together had ordered barely 5,000 planes. Not only did British and French money pay to develop new facilities and keep old factories from being boarded up, it also prevented the loss of skilled workers from going on the dole and losing those critical skills. Although aircraft production was the main beneficiary, other war industries profited as well. When Henry L. Stimson took the position of secretary of war in July 1940, he noted, "We did not have enough powder in the whole United States . . . for anything like a day's fighting; and what is worse we did not have the powder plants or facilities to make it." Britain and France had financed the construction of sixty-one new munitions plants throughout the country, including those shadow powder factories run by DuPont and Hercules, which had kick-started the multibillion-dollar ammunition industry. Meanwhile, British dollars financed the construction of dozens of new shipyards, many of which rose on greenfield sites, laying the keels of ships even as the molding lofts and assembly buildings were erected around them.[39]

With American manufacturing on the rebound, the government moved quickly to strengthen its control of war production. In May 1940, Roosevelt established the Advisory Commission on National Defense (soon to be the Office of Production Management), led by automobile executive William S. Knudsen, to establish precisely what those war needs were and to coordinate the activities of American industries, so as to avoid both wasteful duplication and critical omissions of production. In August, Congress chartered the Defense Plant Corporation, a federal agency that took over British-financed factories and plants and directed tens of billions of dollars to expand industries to meet British and American war needs. This industrial expansion was almost entirely government funded. Many critical industries (aircraft, ships, munitions) were 90–100 percent owned by Uncle Sam. Even Henry Ford's Willow Run B-24 bomber production plant, a shadow factory in all but name, received every penny of its $95 million capital investment ($2.4 billion today) from the federal government—though Henry Ford himself was opposed to any government intervention. Unlike women in Britain, American women never were required to report for war work, but nevertheless arrived at factories in increasing numbers. They found jobs not only in traditional airplane factories and shipyards, but also in smaller commercial firms that were hastily converted for military applications—lock and safe companies that built anti-aircraft guns, and air-conditioning manufacturers repurposed to fabricate anti-submarine mortars. The Steinway & Sons piano factory in Queens, New York, constructed wooden gliders.[40]

Mobilizing American Science

Knudsen and the Defense Plant Corporation could only ask American industry to produce what was already on the drawing boards. To fight Germany, the United States would also need to create entirely new weaponry. For almost half a century, Germany had shown the way in combining academics, scientific research, and industrial production into formidable research universities. German engineers received the same kind of polytechnic education as had Albert Einstein, which they applied to world-leading advances in aerodynamics, chemistry, metallurgy, and electronics. While the new Nazi government belittled some of these advances, many had already been woven into the basic fabric of German military production. Robert P. Patterson, who was undersecretary of war during the conflict, stated in a postwar speech that one reason for the Allied strategy of attacking Germany first and Japan second "was the danger of the German scientists, the risk that they would come up with new weapons of devastating destructiveness. There was no time to lose in eliminating German science from the war. There was no comparable peril from Japanese science."[41]

The United States government was no stranger to recruiting scientists to meet military needs, but historically had done so in a largely piecemeal fashion. Abraham Lincoln created the National Academy of Sciences during the Civil War, an independent body whose first works were devoted to minor improvements in telegraphy and magnetic compass corrections for the new ironclad warships, which did not materially affect the war's outcome. As World War One raged in Europe, the US government established several new science agencies: the National Advisory Committee for Aeronautics (NACA), an independent agency for aircraft research (and the precursor to NASA); the Naval Consulting Board, presided over by Thomas Edison; and the National Research Council, part of the Academy of Sciences, which was designated by the Council of National Defense (Woodrow Wilson's temporary executive office to coordinate resources and industry) to organize the "scientific forces of the country." All these bodies helped direct scientific research into areas of specific needs, such as aircraft engines, submarine detection, and high explosives, but their efforts went largely ignored by the time the war ended.[42]

Between the wars, the United States continued to take an ad hoc approach to military research. In fact, almost all federal research money went for agriculture, primarily through land-grant colleges. Apart from armor plate and naval artillery, most science-based weapons development was in the hands of private industry, such as Carl L. Norden, Inc. for bombsights, Colt and Winchester for small arms and machine guns, and Sperry Corporation for fire control systems.

Vannevar Bush, who would lead the mobilization of American science in World War Two, knew from personal experience that the earlier ad hoc approach could never bring America's full scientific might to bear on Nazi Germany. During World War One, Bush had been working with a small radio company when he approached the National Research Council to endorse his concept of a magnetic detection system for submarines, which could be fitted to surface ships carrying depth charges. Bush (Figure 3) was then a newly minted PhD in electrical engineering, and his expertise was buttressed by considerable practical experience in industry. In his basement shop he made everything from his omnipresent hand-carved tobacco pipes to fishing rods to a surveyor's mapping device that he patented. The navy allowed him to test his magnetic detection system on a ship, and while it appeared to work successfully, a few glitches caused the navy to remain skeptical and refuse to finance further development. Bush later learned that several other groups were working on similar detection systems and also were experiencing glitches, but because there was no coordination between them on the part of the navy, those problems were never ironed out. This highlighted for him what happened when there was a "complete lack of proper liaison between the military and the civilian in the development of weapons in time of war."[43]

After the war, Bush became a professor, later vice president, of his alma mater, MIT (Massachusetts Institute of Technology), while co-founding the Raytheon Company, which focused on making radio vacuum tubes. He turned his apparently boundless energies to creating a mechanical computer and an electronic codebreaking machine, and he worked on special projects on education with the National Research Council. He even was chair of NACA. With such widely varied interests, and given his previous experience with the military, Bush was convinced that the United States was technologically unprepared for Germany's advanced weaponry. Left to their own devices, he believed, the army and navy would simply revert to type and build more of the same. Bush told his friend and fellow engineer, the former president Herbert Hoover, "When military men are queried they usually reply that the answer to a plane is another plane." An entirely new approach would be needed to meet the growing threat.[44]

By September 1939, Bush was already working with a small group of like-minded men, whose unhappy experience with scientific mobilization in World War One made them determined to create a better way of meeting the threat head-on. Bush had left MIT in 1938 to become president of the Carnegie Institution of Washington, one of almost two dozen organizations established by the industrialist Andrew Carnegie (almost all, confusingly, with "Carnegie" in the title) that funded advances in education, diplomacy, and the sciences (the long-necked dinosaur *Diplodocus carnegii* was named in honor of his support for natural history). The Carnegie Institution of Washington, then as now, was a monumental, neoclassical building on 16th Street NW, with a columned portico, a two-story rotunda, and a vast Beaux Arts auditorium. Its scientific departments—geophysics, astronomy, terrestrial magnetism, and so on—attracted top-flight scientists, several of whom had fled the Nazi regime. Bush lived out of a suitcase (he and his wife were at the Wardman Park Hotel until they could buy a house), continuing his service with NACA and with the National Research Council. This put him in regular contact with his old boss, MIT president Karl Compton; James Conant, president of Harvard University; Frank Jewett, head of Bell Laboratories; and several other scientists who had dealt with military bureaucracies during World War One.

On May 24, 1940, as German forces were sweeping through Belgium, this small group met at a luncheon at the Century Association, a private club in New York City, and agreed to a proposal for a strong, centralized government body, similar to NACA and firmly independent of military branches, that could marshal funds and direct scientific research to war needs. Bush, well connected in Washington circles, emerged as the obvious leader of the group. He approached Frederic Delano, a trustee of the Carnegie Institution and Roosevelt's maternal uncle, to get him an audience with Harry Hopkins, the president's close friend and advisor, who had just moved from working on the New Deal to prepare for a war everyone knew was coming. Hopkins persuaded Roosevelt to meet with Bush, which they did on the afternoon of June 12, 1940. After ten minutes Roosevelt scribbled on Bush's one-page planning memo, "OK—FDR."[45]

THE NATIONAL DEFENSE RESEARCH Committee (NDRC) was formed two weeks later under the hastily-resurrected Council of National Defense, with Bush as its chair and Conant, Compton, and Jewett forming part of the eight-man committee, which included Rear Admiral Harold Bowen and Major General George Strong, representing military interests. Bush asked Carroll Wilson, who was on Compton's staff at MIT and a research manager, to "spend a few days" in Washington helping him with the NDRC, a task that evolved into a position as Bush's executive assistant that would last six years. With government office space rapidly dwindling in Washington (the Pentagon was not yet conceived, let alone constructed), Bush offered his own Carnegie Institution as headquarters. Setting up makeshift offices in the vast rotunda, the NDRC established five divisions to handle different research areas—ordnance, chemistry, radio, and so forth—and began appointing scientists and engineers to lead various projects. Like NACA, the NDRC would not carry out any research, instead acting as a coordinator, clearinghouse, and funding authority. Projects were culled from inputs by the military committee members, and then contracted out to be performed by universities and industry (unsolicited inventions, such as Austrian-born Hollywood actress Hedy Lamarr's now-famous torpedo guidance system, were handled separately by the Department of Commerce). Even with the NDRC closely tied to the military, Bush considered its creation an "end run, a grab by which a small company of scientists and engineers, acting outside established channels, got hold of the authority and money for the program of developing new weapons."[46]

By the beginning of 1941, the NDRC had placed almost 200 contracts for projects ranging from oxygen systems to proximity fuzes to uranium research. Although scientists made good progress in understanding the fundamental of these new technologies—the "research" part—it was rapidly becoming clear that this needed to be followed by "development" in order to create weapons that would eventually get into the hands of the soldiers and sailors. Additionally, Roosevelt wanted to see medical research and development included in the remit. On June 28, 1941, a year after the first "OK—FDR," Roosevelt signed an executive order creating the Office of Scientific Research and Development (OSRD). The OSRD superseded and subsumed the NDRC. Headed, again, by Bush, it was structured to be far more powerful and with greater funding, allowing for development and production of weapons and innovations (medical research was also folded in) after the initial discoveries. Led by Conant, the NDRC became an advisory body inside the organization to recommend projects.

The executive order located the OSRD within the newly created Office for Emergency Management, an omnium gatherum of agencies directed toward mobilizing the economy for war. The OEM was placed under Roosevelt's direct control so that he could rapidly make changes without congressional approval. Bush himself was elevated to a virtual cabinet-level position, becoming Roosevelt's de facto science advisor—similar to Lindemann's role with Churchill, except that unlike his British counterpart, Bush also directed much of the national science infrastructure. With these new powers came greater complexity: by December 1942, there were nineteen divisions plus special sections and committees on medical research, uranium development, and proximity fuzes. Funding and personnel grew so dramatically that in March 1943, the Carnegie Institution's huge auditorium was decked in to provide additional office space. Even this was not enough; several OSRD divisions were forced into remote locations; for example, Division 15, Radio Countermeasures, moved into the largely unoccupied Empire State Building in New York. Meanwhile, "Van" (which most people called Bush, not being able to properly say "Vuh-NEE-ver") entrusted the day-to-day running of the OSRD to his subordinates. "As long as I could keep abreast of things well enough to keep the organization on good terms with the Congress, the President, and the military services," he later said, "I thought I was doing my job."[47]

The complexity of the OSRD reflected the enormousness of the task ahead. One of the most significant offices to emerge within this growing scientific bureaucracy was Division D-1 (Detection) of the NDRC, which became Division 14 (Radar). Instead of improving existing early-warning radar for defense like the SCR-270—large systems that operated at relatively long wavelengths of around 3 meters—both offices were focused on a promising new technology, microwave radar, whose short wavelength, less than 1 meter, meant that the devices could potentially be made small enough to fit inside an aircraft (a radar's physical size is proportional to wavelength). This would allow for offensive operations like air intercept and bombing through overcast skies.

Compton's choice of Alfred Lee Loomis to head the so-called Microwave Committee was highly unusual yet completely logical. It was unusual because Loomis was not a scientist in the traditional sense. Loomis was close to his first cousin Henry Stimson, and followed in his footsteps at Yale University and Harvard Law School, then became a Wall Street financier. He saw the 1929 crash coming and got out of the market early by investing in gold. He used those investments to buy depressed stocks cheaply, earning him even more money, then used those earnings to leave the finance world and follow his passion for science, devoting his full attention to his private laboratory at his Tudor mansion in a tony upstate New York community called Tuxedo Park (from which the men's formal wear was named). Even without formal training, Loomis became a conscientious scientist. Moreover, he had access to researchers and funding needed to turn scientific theories into reality; for example, he was a frequent visitor to Ernest Lawrence's laboratory at the University of California, Berkeley, and was key to funding the cyclotron (atom-smasher) that earned Lawrence a Nobel Prize and revolutionized nuclear physics.[48]

Loomis was the logical choice, because by 1940 he was one of the nation's foremost experts in microwaves. He and Compton had been close friends since 1927, when Loomis hosted a physics conference at Tuxedo Park. Three years later, Loomis was instrumental in getting Compton the MIT presidency. In 1939 Compton had suggested that Loomis join the promising microwave research being done by Edward Bowles, MIT's foremost radio expert. The klystron, a vacuum tube capable of generating microwaves, had just been invented, and MIT was teaming with Sperry Corporation to develop a microwave-directed blind-landing system that could guide commercial airplanes to runways even at night or when fogged in. Loomis immediately saw the military advantages of such a system, and hosted Bowles's MIT team at Tuxedo Park. When the NDRC was created the following year, the Microwave Committee examined the existing research to develop it for military applications like long-range detection and targeting of aircraft. But existing klystrons were too weak at the desired wavelengths (around 10 centimeters) to generate sufficient power to bounce a signal from an approaching aircraft, and no laboratory was contemplating tackling the subject. "At the end of the summer [of 1940]," Bowles recalled, "we [the Microwave Committee] decided to write a report," which was "a sign that we didn't know what to do next."[49]

The Boffins Visit Washington

Bowles and Loomis did not know that even as they were typing up their report, "what to do next" was being packed into a heavy black lacquered tin box, normally used by British solicitors to carry deeds, and placed under close guard at government offices in the Savoy Hill House on the Strand in London. Inside that deed box was a cavity magnetron that had been invented just a few months earlier by John Randall and Harry Boot at the University of Birmingham. While the Chain Home radar system was being developed under Robert Watson-Watt, one of his assistants, Edward Bowen, was working separately on the problem of installing air-intercept radar on aircraft. This required a small transmitter that could generate microwaves on the order of 10 centimeters wavelength (like the American blind-landing system) and with enough power to "see" over long distances. Bowen's work led the Air Ministry to contract with the physics laboratory at the University of Birmingham and the General Electric Company (GEC, no connection to the American company General Electric) to design and develop such a device.

At first, British scientists experimented with variations of the klystron, but as the Americans had discovered with their blind-landing system (of which more later), it was too weak—about half a kilowatt—to bounce a beam off a distant aircraft. In February 1940, working under the direction of

Boot's PhD advisor, Mark Oliphant, Randall and Boot began experimenting with a novel idea—using a solid copper cylinder with holes (cavities) drilled around the perimeter like the cylinder of a revolver pistol, then encased in a powerful electromagnet. A heated filament generated electrons that were circulated around the holes by the electromagnet, and as they passed over the cavities they resonated, creating electromagnetic (radio) waves at very short wavelengths. By June 1940, their first cavity magnetron was generating a full kilowatt (kW); by July, 10 kW; by September, 100 kW, or 200 times that of the klystron, while remaining compact and rugged (no breakable glass vacuum tubes). This was the microwave breakthrough that Bowen and the Air Ministry had been looking for. Britain was then in the early days of the Blitz, and the biggest problem would be manufacture—by the autumn of 1940, only twelve cavity magnetrons had been built by GEC. The Air Ministry knew that America had the capability of manufacturing cavity magnetrons on an industrial scale, but government officials were unsure that sharing any information about such innovations with the Americans was a good idea.[50]

The uncertainty was hardly one-sided; American officials had similar views about sharing vital information with the British. Even in summer 1940, after a full year of war, mutual mistrust remained. At the political level, suspicions about American intentions lingered from Chamberlain's administration, while Sumner Welles's fact-finding (and peace-exploring) mission had only reinforced American views of Britain's weakness in the face of Germany. At the technical level, British officials believed that since American engineering lagged far behind the British, any exchange would be one-sided. Americans worried that any technologies they gave to the British would likely be captured by Germany in the first weeks of the war.

The greatest source of transatlantic contention had been the Norden bombsight. Invented by the Dutch-born American engineer Carl L. Norden and first produced in 1931, it was gyroscopically stabilized and promised far greater accuracy for putting bombs on target than any existing device. Tests from 12,000 to 15,000 feet altitude (one witnessed by the RAF air attaché) demonstrated that bombs could hit within 160 feet of the target, leading to the oft-quoted claim that Norden-equipped bombers could hit a pickle barrel. The fact that these tests were run under clear skies with no anti-aircraft fire—completely different from European skies filled with clouds and flak—did not dissuade the British from requesting it. Even with personal appeals to Roosevelt by Chamberlin and Churchill—the latter offering a quid pro quo exchange of Norden information for British ASDIC, an early form of sonar—the Americans balked at sharing what it considered its crown jewel. After repeated US stonewalling, the British war cabinet decided not to pursue the matter further, claiming in December 1939— without any justification—that the Americans had "no weapons of special value for the purpose."[51]

Henry Tizard saw the matter differently; he wanted facts, not uninformed rationalizations. Shortly after war was declared, he was placed at the head of the Committee for the Scientific Survey of Air Warfare, which gave him substantial influence at the Air Ministry. Like several other scientists, Tizard had long advocated for technical exchange with the Americans, and used his new position to stump for a proposal to review the state of American research by sending a scientific attaché to Washington. The Air Ministry viewed this proposal as another means to eventually get the Norden bombsight, and approved it.[52]

Tizard arranged to send his colleague A. V. Hill to visit and speak with dozens of scientists in government, academia, and industry, and report back to the Air Ministry on the usefulness of American technology and industry to the British war effort. Hill sailed first for Canada in early March 1940, to take the pulse of research there. He arrived in Washington on March 22. For the next two months he toured America's scientific establishments, a trip that included a visit with Alfred Loomis to discuss microwave research. Hill's messages convinced both Tizard and British ambassador Philip Kerr, Lord Lothian, of the importance of a technology exchange with the Americans, despite the fact that officials back in London believed they lagged far behind. "All offers to exchange information with them would, I am sure, be welcomed," Hill said. He later recalled thinking that the Americans "would have much to gain from our operational experience," and the British would "gain by being given an entry to the great scientific resources of America." In parallel efforts, Tizard told RAF officials that cooperation with the Americans "meant a great deal considering their facilities for applied research and production," while Lothian sent a telegram to the Foreign Office that argued such technical exchanges would bring "the services of the two countries into closer liaison and sympathy [on] war preparation," and offered to approach Roosevelt personally on the matter.

When Churchill took office as prime minister in May 1940, he balked at the proposals for technical exchange, still smarting from his failure with Roosevelt the previous year on the Norden bombsight. Tizard had been the most vocal proponent of such an exchange, but with his adversary Lindemann now ascendant, his influence waned when the Air Warfare Committee was disbanded in June. He was literally packing up his office files on July 20 when he learned that he was to lead a technical mission to the United States. Three weeks earlier, following good progress on negotiating surplus American weapons and destroyers for British bases, Churchill had authorized Ambassador Lothian to propose an unrestricted (i.e., no quid pro quo) information exchange to Roosevelt, which the president quickly accepted. Several names were mooted to lead the team that would carry out the exchange, including Watson-Watt, who was seen as self-aggrandizing and rough around the edges, and the recently returned A. V. Hill, whose technical knowledge was seen as too narrow. Tizard, by contrast, was widely liked, carried a great breadth of knowledge, and despite Lindemann's black mark had earned Churchill's respect.

Tizard's official appointment letter of August 3—on behalf of the Ministry of Aircraft Production—outlined the subjects for exchange. Not surprisingly, at the top of the list were many of the technologies that Tizard's committees had been working on: RDF (radar), microwaves, proximity fuzes, and radar-directed anti-aircraft guns. High explosives (RDX), jet engines, and ASDIC were also included. The vaunted Norden bombsight was now almost at the bottom of the list, just above aircraft deicing. Nuclear fission was not explicitly mentioned, but the inclusion on the team of nuclear physicist John Cockcroft meant that it would be addressed. Along with Tizard and Edward Bowen (who covered radar research), there would be three senior military officers—one from each service—plus a civilian secretary and a recorder, for a total of eight members on what was officially called the British Technical and Scientific Mission to the United States but was widely known as the Tizard Mission.[53]

Tizard traveled ahead of the rest of the mission to lay its groundwork, departing by flying boat on August 14 during a lull in the incessant Luftwaffe raids. Like Hill before him, he first spent several days in Canada to shore up relations with the scientists there, since their close links with American scientists would be vital to the success of British-American collaboration. He arrived by overnight train in Washington on August 22 and was met by British Army attaché Charles Lindemann, the brother of Tizard's adversary Frederick. Charles was charismatic where his brother was brusque; he helped Tizard navigate the complexities of Washington, and the two became lifelong friends. After several days of meetings with Ambassador Lothian, various British purchasing missions, American military officials, and President Roosevelt—who apologized for not being able to share the Norden bombsight—Tizard met Vannevar Bush, at the time head of the NDRC, to discuss scientific exchanges.

On the evening of August 28, Bush invited Tizard to the Cosmos Club, whose members came from the Washington scientific and cultural elite, and which Bush had joined in 1938 when he came to the Carnegie Institution. The Cosmos Club was a far cry from the elegant Athenaeum Club on Pall Mall, where Tizard was a member. The building on Lafayette Square had once been Dolley Madison's sparely appointed townhouse, and the Grill Room in the basement was rustic; its brick fireplace must have been blazing even in mid-August to stave off the damp from the unusually cold, rainy weather that day. The two men found common ground in seeking a direct exchange between scientists. Bush cautioned Tizard to first establish good relations with the American military, while Bush worked behind the scenes to begin a direct technical interchange between the NDRC and the British.[54]

The very same hour that Tizard and Bush were meeting at the Cosmos Club, Edward Bowen was asleep at the Cumberland Hotel near Marble Arch. Under his bed was the deed box with the GEC Number 12 cavity magnetron, which Bowen had picked up earlier that evening from John Cockcroft's Ministry of Supply office at Savoy Hill House. Bowen had orders to keep it close to him, and the box would not fit in the hotel safe. Bowen and Cockcroft had spent the previous two weeks collecting manuals, circuit diagrams, blueprints, and films, and forwarding them in nine crates labeled "Tizard Mission" to the passenger ship *Duchess of Richmond*, which would take them to Canada (some of those crates would be inexplicably delayed for two months). The ship was scheduled to sail on August 29, so that early that morning Bowen, carrying his deed box, left London on a train to Liverpool, where he met with the other mission members and secured the box in the ship's bridge. As the ship pulled away from the quay at dusk, German aircraft began bombing the city. It would be no safer in the U-boat-infested North Atlantic; Cockcroft took the extra precaution of having holes drilled in the box so that it would sink with the cavity magnetron if the ship were torpedoed, or if it had to be jettisoned in case of capture.

Duchess of Richmond arrived in Halifax on September 6, having safely conveyed hundreds of school-age evacuees, a thousand British sailors to man the American destroyers that had just been exchanged to Britain, the Tizard Mission scientists, and the cavity magnetron, which OSRD historian James P. Baxter called "the most valuable cargo ever brought to our shores" (it was always accompanied by armed guards). The mission members, along with a contingent of Canadian scientists, arrived by train in Washington on September 8. The following day the entire Tizard Mission (Figure 4) set up shop at the Shoreham Hotel to begin its technical work. Bush was able to secure agreements from the War and Navy Departments for direct interchange between the mission and the NDRC. On September 19, the Mission's members met with NDRC Division D-1 in Alfred Loomis's room at the Wardman Park Hotel, across the street from the Shoreham. Loomis related to them the successes of his Microwave Committee, but also the dead end they had encountered as to "what to do next." Then Bowen disclosed the cavity magnetron to the group. The sight of it generated palpable excitement.[55]

The following week the two groups assembled in Loomis's laboratory at Tuxedo Park, where it became obvious that if the apparatus worked as advertised, it would give the Americans "the chance to start now two years ahead of where we were," as Loomis breathlessly informed his cousin (and secretary of war) Henry Stimson the next day. Bowen agreed to have the magnetron tested in early October at the Bell Laboratories in Whippany, New Jersey, where it produced 10-centimeter radar waves at 10 kW, five times greater power than Bell had yet produced (and unknown to either group, GEC in Britain was already testing a unit ten times more powerful than the one in Bowen's hands). This was even better news than expected; while Loomis had thought the cavity magnetron might save the Americans two years, Bush told Conant at a dinner at the Cosmos Club that he was convinced it bought them five years. Conant, in turn, believed that "a special lab exclusively for the NDRC should be set up to speed this research."[56]

With the test results confirming British claims, Loomis revealed that he had already placed Bell Laboratories under NDRC contract to copy and build thirty units of the cavity magnetron within a month, using the British blueprints and drawings as well as X-ray photographs of the unit that Bowen and Tizard allowed to be left in his care. Once these prototype units were tested, mass production would follow. Given that GEC had only managed to build a dozen magnetrons over the course of several months, this boost in manufacturing capacity was exactly what the Tizard Mission had been hoping for. It was agreed that Britain would receive Bell-produced magnetrons for use in air-intercept fighters and sub-hunting planes.

Meanwhile, the Microwave Committee began planning for a new research facility devoted exclusively to microwaves, as Conant had suggested. For several weeks in October, Loomis presided over a series of meetings in Washington and New York to determine its location and structure. Both Cockcroft and Bowen were integral to these discussions, as they brought firsthand knowledge on the operations of the British radar laboratory (soon to be renamed Telecommunications Research Establishment or TRE, a name chosen to obscure its true purpose). Where the laboratory should be located became a sticking point. Bush did not want it at his Carnegie Institution—too much red tape—and stumped for MIT. Loomis eventually agreed, but Frank Jewett wanted it for his own Bell Laboratories. Loomis had spent his Wall Street career brokering deals, and he knew how to back Jewett into a corner. After Jewett protested that such a laboratory needed industrial-style management that would be too complex for MIT, he remembered that Bush was an MIT graduate and quickly softened his appeal by praising the school's facilities. Loomis immediately saw the opening and jumped in. "I am so glad," he said, "that you approve the idea of having the laboratory at MIT."[57]

The matter settled, the Microwave Committee convinced Karl Compton to free up 10,000 square feet of space for the new facility. They also decided it should be called the Radiation Laboratory, a name deliberately chosen, like TRE, to obscure its purpose—the same name was given to the cyclotron laboratory of Ernest Lawrence. Lawrence was also on the Microwave Committee, and he was instrumental getting one of his proteges, Lee DuBridge from the University of Rochester, made director. DuBridge was widely considered a capable and energetic administrator, and readily agreed both to the directorship and to allowing Edward Bowen to remain behind at MIT, to assist in setting up the new Rad Lab, as it was straightaway christened. Rad Lab established three projects for its initial focus—airborne microwave radar, radar-directed anti-aircraft gunnery, and long-range navigation—though within two years its portfolio expanded to include over fifty projects.[58]

While establishing joint research and development of microwave radar had been the Tizard Mission's core objective, its members revealed other British innovations, kicking off a transatlantic scientific exchange. The NDRC Uranium Committee was told of recent British advances in the separation of uranium. Both sides had been working on proximity fuzes, which showed great promise in improving the ability to bring down enemy aircraft, as well as Identification Friend or Foe to stop radar-directed weaponry from shooting down friendly aircraft. The Kerrison Predictor, which automatically directed anti-aircraft guns, was also of interest to the Americans; the British wanted it mass-produced in the United States. Americans got their first glimpse of the new British jet engine, learned of a precision radio navigation system called Gee, and discussed high explosives like RDX. Although some of these discussions did not occur until late November 1940, when those crates of British equipment finally arrived, the American

War and Navy Departments had cleared the way for an "intimate collaboration" with Britain and Canada, "freely disclosing information" to one another.[59]

The only exclusion would be the Norden bombsight. By this point, as we've noted, the British had lost almost all interest in the Norden, in part because Patrick Blackett was developing what became the British Mk XIV stabilized bombsight, comparable in accuracy to the Norden—and which, ironically enough, would later be manufactured by Sperry for use in American and British bombers. Of greater importance than the Norden was the fact that by the time the Tizard Mission wrapped up in late November, it had established the framework for a two-way channel of proposals, information, and research, combining the brainpower and manpower of Britain, the United States, and Canada to produce a series of innovations and weapons that could win the war.[60]

American Science Sets Up Shop in London

The Tizard Mission was one among many British delegations from the War Office, the Admiralty, the Air Ministry, and the Ministry of Supply, delegations that were arriving almost daily to establish collaborative links with their American counterparts, as the war economies of the two nations grew more interconnected. Ultimately, the two nations created five combined boards to coordinate and allocate munitions, food, raw materials, shipping, and production between them. They worked with varying degrees of efficiency during the course of the war.[61]

The exchange of scientific information required some means of directing traffic as well. Following on the heels of the Tizard mission, Britain and the United States agreed to establish scientific liaison offices in each other's capitals, while maintaining Canada—the British dominion with the closest ties to American manufacturing and academia—as a critical link. The British embassy had named A. V. Hill, during his pre-Tizard visit, as scientific attaché, but both his visit and the title were short-lived. John Cockcroft, at the behest of Vannevar Bush, sent Tizard a proposal in November 1940 for a permanent office in Washington, one that would act as a clearinghouse for scientific communications with Britain and Canada. The war cabinet agreed to the proposal and in February 1941 established the British Central Scientific Office (BCSO), which was housed in a mansion on Massachusetts Avenue. Charles Galton Darwin, grandson of the great naturalist and a celebrated physicist in his own right, was appointed head of the organization. The BCSO got into difficulties right from the start. Although BCSO helped with information flow concerning proximity fuzes, microwave radar, and atomic research, it was perennially understaffed (never more than seventeen scientists) and overwhelmed. Darwin himself was unfamiliar with many British and Canadian scientific needs, and his appointment, which lasted only six months, did not let him develop a good working relationship with his American contacts. None of his successors stayed long enough to develop those contacts or fix the personnel problems.[62]

Vannevar Bush had written to Tizard back in December 1940, proposing that the NDRC establish a liaison office at the American embassy in London, something equivalent to the BCSO, and that he would dispatch a delegation early the following year to establish with the British the terms of the information exchange. He didn't get a positive reply from the British government until February 3, after which planning went quickly. James Conant would head the diplomatic mission, accompanied by Bush's right-hand man, Carroll Wilson, and by the chemist Fred Hovde, who was selected to lead the liaison office. They departed Jersey City on February 15 aboard SS *Excalibur*, on the first of what would be thousands of exchange visits from American scientists to help with the war effort in Britain. U-boats were patrolling the North Atlantic almost at will, in what the Kriegsmarine called the "Happy Time," so the ship took a southerly route to neutral Lisbon, which was the main port of entry to and from Europe ("A mad place," Wilson called it, "no one has anything to do but try to get out of here"). There Conant boarded a charter flight to Britain along with the incoming US ambassador, John Winant, who was replacing Joseph Kennedy. They were greeted by an honor guard, and later met with Churchill and King George VI, whom he found "up to date" on secret programs like radar. Wilson and Hovde, meanwhile, waited a week before finally getting seats on a Dutch KLM flight, one of the few commercial services between Portugal and Britain.[63]

By March 4, 1941, the Conant Mission was at full strength with five academic scientists, and spent the next several weeks establishing relations with the British civil, scientific, and defense establishments and setting up operations for the new liaison office. All information at any classification level was to be exchanged freely, and the BCSO was to receive copies of all correspondence. The NDRC liaison office would start small and grow as necessary. The visiting Americans would have open access to all British military and scientific facilities. Both sides would fully collaborate on new technologies and divvy up responsibilities for research, production, and field tests.

The Conant Mission had arrived simultaneously with Roosevelt's special envoy to handle the Lend-Lease deal, Averell Harriman, who worked closely with the mission members and became an ardent supporter of the British-American technical exchanges. Despite the incessant fall of bombs and midnight bursts of anti-aircraft gunfire—they were in the throes of the Blitz—the sudden presence of so many high-level American officials gave both the British and the expatriate Americans hope for the future: Alexander Woollcott, a noted American commentator there, remarked, "With Winant, Conant [and] Harriman in England, I think we are more credibly represented than we have been since Dr. [Benjamin] Franklin was our spokesman in London." On April 11, 1941, with the diplomatic portion of the mission accomplished, Conant and Carroll Wilson flew to Lisbon and boarded *Dixie Clipper*, one of the first Pan American flying boats on the company's newly inaugurated transatlantic route, taking seventy hours to reach New York via Dakar in West Africa, Belém in Brazil, and Bermuda. Pan Am would soon become the official ferry system for the United States to deliver passengers and equipment to Allied nations, including many NDRC (soon OSRD) scientists and engineers.[64]

The man chosen to stay behind and temporarily run the NDRC London office, Fred Hovde, had been a Rhodes scholar at Oxford and even played on its varsity rugby team. Hovde barely recognized the lively city he knew from just a decade earlier; London during the Blitz was blacked out at night and heavily damaged. A family man with small children, Hovde had made it clear that this would be a six-month stint, until a permanent head of mission could be found. He and four other NDRC scientists (along with three secretaries) set up their office on the third floor in the already crowded American Embassy in Grosvenor Square, while sharing a pair of flats two blocks away at 40 Berkeley Square near Marble Arch. He soon learned that only "foolhardy Americans" would live on the top floor of a seven-story building in a city under siege. Just months later, two bombs destroyed the adjacent building. Meanwhile, Hovde's workload took a sharp turn upward over the summer of 1941, after Roosevelt created the OSRD, which included "development" in its portfolio. In theory, Hovde's tasks at the now-retitled OSRD London Mission should have been split with his Washington counterpart, Charles Darwin, at the BCSO, but in practice Hovde handled the bulk of duties coordinating research, setting up mail courier services via the State Department and military transport, handling visit requests, and forwarding critical information, as well as making frequent visits to British military and scientific facilities.[65]

In August, while Hovde was back home on a visit to his family, Roosevelt and Churchill met secretly aboard British and American warships in Placentia Bay, Newfoundland. Churchill arrived hoping that Roosevelt would soon promise to declare war, but the president was still hoping that Lend-Lease alone would be enough for Britain to stave off Germany— Harry Hopkins told the British delegation that Roosevelt was "a believer in bombing as the only means of gaining a victory." The two leaders hammered out what became known as the Atlantic Charter, a series of goals and plans on how the upcoming war should be carried out, and what a postwar world would look like (one clause, the right to self-determination, would prove especially bothersome, for Roosevelt saw it as the end of colonialism, while Churchill did not think it applied to the existing British Empire). When Hovde returned to London in November—after a ten-day marathon of flights and delays—his desk was piled high with paper. The Atlantic Charter had not led to an increase in his staff, only additional work. He found

London even darker, drearier, and more downtrodden than when he had left.[66]

On the evening of December 7, 1941, Hovde was "freezing to death in the Hotel Grosvenor on the south coast of England at Swanage, Dorset," after attending a regular Sunday meeting of British radar scientists at the nearby Telecommunications Research Establishment. On the BBC nine o'clock news he learned of the Japanese attacks on Pearl Harbor, and understood that the United States was now in the fight. Churchill learned the news from the same broadcast, and phoned Roosevelt, who told him, "We are all in the same boat now." Although the official declarations of war with Germany and Italy were still days away, Churchill knew that with America fighting by its side, they would win the war and "Britain would live." Overcome with emotion, he "went to bed and slept the sleep of the saved and thankful." Charles de Gaulle, then in London as the leader of the Free French government in exile, heard the news, too, and had a similar reaction: "Well, the war is finished. Of course, there will still be maneuvers, battles and combat, but the war is over because the outcome is now known. In this industrial war, nothing can stand up to the power of American industry." Hovde, meanwhile, was worried that he would have to stay in London, away from his young family, for the duration.[67]

Hovde's concern was soon allayed when he learned that his replacement had already been selected and was receiving a "cram course" in Washington, DC. Bennett Archambault was hardworking and ambitious, a 1932 graduate of MIT with a degree in business and engineering administration. Despite entering the workforce during the depths of the Great Depression, he had little trouble landing a series of management positions at New York financial firms, allowing him to put his sister through college. His career was occasionally helped along by his MIT connections, Conant and especially Carroll Wilson, who began recruiting him in August 1941 to head the OSRD London Mission. Unmarried, thirty-two years old, and a Wall Street businessman who was not a recognized scientist, Archambault was hardly the obvious choice. As Vannevar Bush later admitted, "The British were, I think, jarred by this appointment. But they later agreed that we had the right idea in choosing a younger man."[68]

After months waiting for security clearances, Archambault finally reached London on April 4, 1942, occupying Hovde's old flats (which they soon had to vacate in favor of the Office of Strategic Services, instead moving to nearby hotels). Although a civilian, he arrived with an assimilated rank of colonel and usually came to work in uniform (though without rank insignia, Figure 5), which helped with military liaison. He had no need of the uniform to establish hierarchy. "Arch," as he was usually referred to, left "no shadow of doubt who he thinks is boss," according to David Langmuir, his technical aide, friend, and flatmate, but "always with humor that makes it quite bearable... especially as he accomplishes a lot." Archambault would head the OSRD London Mission throughout the war, and his long tenure ensured solid connections across many British circles—his personal address book included direct telephone numbers for scientists like Blackett and Watson-Watt, military officers like Air Chief Marshal Philip Joubert and naval attaché Rear Admiral Alan Kirk, ambassadors, and presidents of major munitions and electronics manufacturers.[69]

The embassy offices of the OSRD London Mission, as it was officially known, were taken over by Harriman's Lend-Lease office in October 1942, so Archambault had to find new offices nearby. Long before it became known as "Eisenhower Platz" during the buildup to D-Day, the buildings around Grosvenor Square were already almost entirely occupied by Americans, as were the rooms at Claridge's Hotel. At the nearby Grosvenor House Hotel, the Great Room was converted to a 1,200-seat American officers' mess, nicknamed "Willow Run" (Figure 6) because it could mass-produce meals as fast as Henry Ford's famous bomber production plant could build B-24s. One longtime London resident remarked that "American accents, from the New York twang to the drawl of the Southern States, replaced the warm, slow talk of the London streets."[70]

Archambault was able to secure three adjacent flats in Hereford House at 117 Park Street, at the corner of Oxford Street, to house the OSRD London Mission, though with barely enough room to accommodate the rapidly growing staff. Ultimately about fifty people at a time worked cheek by jowl, often sitting on top of one another's desks (Figure 7). Vannevar Bush, during one of his visits, remarked that "it was a beehive with people coming and going and in little groups talking excitedly. I'm pretty sure they were under Archambault's control. He controlled them all right, there wasn't any question about that." Most of the staff were British, many of them women, who undoubtedly looked upon their American employers (if modern experience is a guide) as somewhat gormless and in need of a firm hand. They may have even believed of the Americans, as did one anonymous British secretary during the war, that they were "capable of a greatness that has evaded them. I knew then, and used to tell them, that they needed to know more about the world before they could lead it."[71]

The OSRD London Mission administered the thousands of reports that kept the Allies up to date, often sent across the Atlantic in diplomatic pouches to avoid censorship and delays. It also mobilized over 600 American scientists and engineers who came to Britain between 1942 and 1945 as part of the war effort. The list of names who worked at or passed through the OSRD London Mission is a veritable who's who of prominent figures in postwar science: Luis Alvarez, recipient of a Nobel Prize in physics and creator of the asteroid extinction hypothesis; Isidor Rabi, Nobel Prize–winner in physics; William Shockley, inventor of the transistor and Nobel laureate in physics; Thomas Kuhn, renowned historian of science; Fred Terman, father of Silicon Valley; Guy Stever, architect of US science and space policy during the Cold War; Gerard Kuiper, comet astronomer; and many others. These Americans would work side by side with their British counterparts to develop, produce, and put into operation the weapons that went to the battlefront.

To win the war, the Americans needed the British as much as the British needed the Americans. Their first priority was to gain ascendency in the air war, for without that, there could be no hope for victory. And that required bombers equipped with radar to accurately locate targets; a means for the bombers to defeat German air defenses; and long-range fighters to escort them to their targets and back home again.

CHAPTER 3

FIGHT IN THE AIR

I N SEPTEMBER 1940, at the height of the Battle of Britain, over a year before the United States entered the war, Churchill had summarized his
plans for a strategic air campaign in a minute to his Cabinet: "Bombers
alone provide the means of victory . . . we must develop the power to carry
an ever-increasing volume of explosives to Germany." He knew that the current state of heavy bombers was inadequate to the task. The first few daylight
raids against Germany, conducted by unescorted bombers in December
1939, had resulted in the loss of almost half the aircraft and crews, first to
anti-aircraft guns and then to fighters. RAF Bomber Command subsequently operated its squadrons—composed mostly of Halifax, Stirling, and
Lancaster bombers—at night. However, without precise navigational aids
they could barely find, let alone hit, their targets. When the pilots and crews
of the American 8th Bomber Command came into the war in early 1942,
they discovered that operating in overcast conditions—typical of Britain
and northern Europe—also required precise navigational aids.[1]

The combined strategic air campaign would depend on building three capabilities: locating targets at night or in overcast conditions; running the gauntlet of German radar-enabled anti-aircraft guns; and (though this would be slower in coming) arriving over the targets escorted by long-range fighters. All of these required novel technical solutions, as the prime minister explained in another Cabinet minute in October 1940. This war would not be about "masses of men hurling masses of shells at each other." It would be won by "devising new weapons, and above all by scientific leadership." Churchill announced that "very highest priority in personnel and material should be assigned to what may be called the Radio sphere." This meant finding "scientists, wireless experts, and many classes of highly skilled labour and high-grade material. Not only research and experiments, but production, must be pushed hopefully forward."[2]

The scientific leadership for developing the "Radio sphere"—read "radar"—was located in the aforementioned Telecommunications Research Establishment, or TRE, a part of the Ministry of Supply. As noted, its name had changed several times since it was first established in 1936 at Bawdsey Manor by Robert Watson-Watt. One staff member suggested that TRE stood for Touring 'Round England, since the organization had moved from Bawdsey to Scotland in 1939 in order to avoid potential German attack, then back south to Worth Matravers, Dorset, in 1940. For two years, TRE had been under the direction of Albert Percival Rowe, who was usually known by his initials, A.P. (only his closest friends and colleagues called him "Jimmy," a nickname that still eludes explanation). As a teenager, he apprenticed as an electrical fitter in the Portsmouth Royal Naval dockyard, then studied physics at the University of London before working at the Air Ministry and joining Henry Tizard's Committee for the Scientific Survey of Air Defence in 1935.

Rowe ran TRE much like a university department—a natural arrangement, since much of its staff were former academics—and with the same levels of improvisation and openness. Unusually for a defense establishment, a small but significant number of women worked in the technical arena—Renie Warburton (later Adams) was a radar instructor, Stella Budden carried out mathematical modeling, and Joan Curran was a physicist who developed radar countermeasures. Rowe also instituted an academic-like routine called the Sunday Soviets, which were informal meetings held at the Grosvenor Hotel in nearby Swanage, Dorset. These morning meetings, as Rowe described them, were "attended by Cabinet Ministers, Commanders-in-Chief, Air Marshals, Admirals and Generals, University professors, Service personnel straight from the heat of battle, those who controlled our destinies from Headquarters and, not least, scientists working in or alongside the laboratories," including American scientists (it was after one of these Sunday Soviets that Fred Hovde heard the news of Pearl Harbor). Government officials appreciated the opportunity for a seaside retreat away from the London bureaucracy, and TRE staff were given Saturdays off (instead of the traditional Sunday) so that they could attend.[3]

The purpose of the Sunday Soviets was to provide a frank exchange of views on what worked in the field and what hadn't, and how new applications of radar might help the progress of the war. Rank and position did not matter, and it was this lack of hierarchy that gave the sessions the nickname "Soviet." "You can say anything in Rowe's office on a Sunday" was the watchword, and it had the effect of quickly weeding out impractical ideas or ones that would not prove useful in combat. Lee DuBridge, Rowe's opposite number at the MIT Rad Lab, was astonished that almost all of TRE's developments were brought into operational use; by contrast, fewer than one-quarter of the Rad Lab's devices ever made it into service (DuBridge was undoubtedly also astonished that TRE was so productive with just one-tenth of the Rad Lab's 4,000 staff).

Blind Bombing

One of the most consequential Sunday Soviets, held on October 26, 1941, was called by Robert Watson-Watt, by then promoted to the Air Ministry's scientific advisor on radar, and accompanied by Churchill's scientific advisor Frederick Lindemann. They had both been supporters of strategic bombing, which to that point had only been carried out in the western parts of Germany, those closest to Britain. Raids on industrial targets like oil refineries, railroads, and factories in the Ruhr Valley, Hamburg, and Frankfurt seemed to have had little impact on German war production, so in August 1941 Lindemann had asked his assistant David Bensusan-Butt to study the bombers' effectiveness by analyzing night bombing photos taken at the moment the bombs were released. The resulting Butt Report was damning; the accuracy of strategic night bombing was so poor that fewer than one in three bombers got within five miles of their targets (over the Ruhr Valley it was one in ten), and the resulting damage to the enemy was minimal. Churchill began to question "whether bombing by itself would be a decisive factor" and demanded his Air Staff give the matter the most urgent attention.[4]

It was with this in mind that Watson-Watt and Lindemann met that Sunday with Rowe and his TRE staff, including Herbert Skinner and Philip Dee, heads of, respectively, Groups 8 and 12 (out of thirty groups total at TRE), which were at the moment testing the 10-centimeter microwave radar in aircraft. The subject of this Sunday Soviet, as Rowe recorded in his later memoir, was "how to locate targets" that were "unseen," but also to do so with greater accuracy and at far greater ranges than had been possible. The conversations that morning began with the two precision radio navigation systems, Gee and Oboe, which TRE was already developing to assist with "blind bombing" (the term originated after World War One to connote indiscriminate civilian casualties, and only later was used to differentiate from visual bombing). Gee used ground stations in Britain to send out timed radio pulses that formed an invisible grid of position lines over Western Europe ("Gee" stood for "grid"), which could be detected and plotted on a special navigational chart; any aircraft equipped with a Gee receiver could navigate up to 300 miles (about the distance to the Ruhr Valley) with a positional accuracy of about one mile.[5]

"Oboe" was the code name for a radio transponder system also using British-based ground stations, and therefore with the same range of about 300 miles. However, it was accurate to within a few yards. Oboe required the pilot to fly a specific course indicated by one ground station until he reached the drop point indicated by a signal from a second ground station.

As Lindemann and Watson-Watt foresaw, the problem was that the limited ranges of both systems prevented the deep-penetration raids that Churchill demanded—Berlin was twice as far from London as the Ruhr Valley. Moreover, they could be systematically jammed by German radio operators. Lindemann insisted that any bombing aid must be self-contained within the bomber itself, so that it could not be readily jammed and would not limit the precision bombing range of the aircraft.

Although Gee and Oboe would continue to be fitted to British bombers for precision navigation and bombing at shorter ranges, they were not deemed useful for long-range strikes. Other methods were raised and dismissed at the meeting, such as following electrical power lines, but the gathering was adjourned with no result. However, Philip Dee (and others at TRE) had already been thinking about blind bombing using radar, and by that Sunday evening he concluded that his group's 10-centimeter microwave radar, powered by the cavity magnetron, was the best option. Throughout 1941, Dee's group at TRE, as well as his counterparts at the MIT Rad Lab, had been experimenting with microwave radar fitted in aircraft (the Rad Lab's Project 1, its highest priority), though both groups had been focused on problems other than blind bombing—specifically, detecting U-boats at sea and shooting down German bombers with night fighters.

On Monday morning, the day after the Sunday Soviet, Dee instructed his staff to modify the radar in their test aircraft, a Blenheim fighter-bomber, so that it could be used over land. The following Saturday, November 1, 1941, with the modifications complete, the crew flew east along the coast and then north toward the Salisbury Plain, armed with a camera to take pictures of the cathode-ray tube display. They were gratified to see that the cities of Southampton, Warminster, and Salisbury were clearly distinguishable on the display from other radar scatter coming from the ground, even though the skies were overcast. This was proof to them that microwave radar could indeed locate "unseen" strategic targets, both through clouds and at night, which would allow Churchill's bombing campaign to proceed.[6]

The next morning, before the usual Sunday Soviet, Dee developed the photographs of the radar displays and rushed them, still wet from the fixing bath, to Rowe's office and laid them on his desk. To anyone else, these photographs simply showed blurry white blobs on black circles. For Rowe, however, they were an epiphany. "This is the turning point of the war," he told his colleagues. Rowe sent Lindemann the news, and after some high-level meetings, the Air Ministry ordered TRE to proceed with development of the microwave blind-bombing system.[7]

The November 1 experiments may have been a turning point of the war, but as Churchill himself would say just one year later (about the North Africa campaign), it was not the end, it was not even the beginning of the end, but it was, perhaps, the end of the beginning. Only a handful of cavity magnetrons had yet been built in Britain, not nearly enough to outfit even a few bombers, much less carry out an entire strategic air campaign. The GEC factory at Wembley, which had promised 500 sets, was slowly hand-crafting each unit "using the chamber of a Colt revolver—which just happened to be the right size—as a drilling jig." This was one reason the Tizard Mission had, the previous year, brought the cavity magnetron to the United States (as related earlier): to take advantage of the nation's manufacturing prowess. But the situation there was scarcely better. Despite the early enthusiasm shown by the Americans, at this point in 1941 neither the MIT Rad Lab nor Bell Labs were having much success in building magnetrons, or even figuring out how they worked.[8]

Lee DuBridge had built the MIT Rad Lab on the promise of the cavity magnetron (Figure 8), which showed potential for air intercept for fighters, anti-aircraft gun-laying, and submarine-hunting. He took over the first two floors of MIT's Building 4, overlooking the main courtyard, filling them with equipment and painting the windows black. He then took advantage of an MIT conference on applied nuclear physics to begin finding suitable candidates; like TRE, he intended to hire university scientists to carry out the work. Also like TRE, several of the scientists recruited were women, including Pauline Morrow, a recent MIT graduate, and Monica Healea, a physics professor at Vassar. Indeed, women made up the majority of the teams of human computers that carried out complex calculations.

Another recruit was Isidor Isaac Rabi, then a professor of nuclear physics at Columbia University. Rabi, born into a Jewish Polish family who emigrated to New York soon after his birth in 1898, was, like many Americans, ambivalent about the war before its outbreak. On the one hand, he was convinced that Germany "was motivated by anti-Semitism" and was intent on "destroying Western civilization." On the other hand, he thought that stopping Hitler was France's and Britain's job. Still, when offered a position at the Rad Lab, he later recalled saying to himself, "I want to be in on it." In the middle of the semester, he left his classes, his students, and his family and went to Cambridge to be part of the war. Rabi was not the only scientist to drop everything to come to the Rad Lab. George E. Valley Jr. and Edward M. Purcell, both physicists at Harvard University, were "drafted" for the effort, and within weeks answered the call. Ernest Pollard's departure from Yale was even hastier. After receiving the telegram from DuBridge, he put it in the pocket of his lab coat, hung the coat on a hook in his laboratory, and then walked out. When he returned to Yale five years later, he found his lab coat hanging on the same hook, DuBridge's telegram still in the pocket.[9]

On November 11, 1940, as the Battle of Britain gave way to the Blitz, the Rad Lab held its first meeting. It was soon organized into twelve divisions, with Rabi taking over Division 4 (research), which focused on developing the cavity magnetron and microwave radar. Drawn primarily from universities around the country, the staff quickly grew from a few dozen to a few hundred and then to several thousand. Scientists were often assigned to multiple divisions and worked on several projects at once, depending on their expertise. The Rad Lab's collegial structure took its cue from TRE, largely due to the influence of Edward Bowen, who had been closely involved in the NDRC Microwave Committee's planning for the laboratory and agreed to stay behind in the United States after Tizard's departure. Thanks in part to bonding during Friday night drinking sessions—during one of which he demonstrated how to leave footprints on the ceiling—Bowen was now an integral part of the Rad Lab staff. He received his nickname, "Taffy," because his Welsh accent called to mind the old British nursery rhyme "Taffy was a Welshman." He not only was knowledgeable about the practical aspects of building a radar system, but also could share TRE's experience of fighting a war with radar.[10]

Even so, the Rad Lab needed additional help, and by mid-1941 placed a request to TRE for a scientist to come on temporary assignment. One of Philip Dee's colleagues, Denis Robinson, was an MIT graduate, and his wife and family had already moved to Cambridge, Massachusetts, for safety. Within a few weeks he was on a flight to the United States, accompanied by a US Army major named Curtis LeMay, who would become one of the key players in the American strategic bombing campaign that would depend mightily upon microwave radar.

DESPITE THE INFORMALITY THAT reigned at the Rad Lab, Rabi, having shed his previous ambivalence, knew the importance of the work and took it quite personally: "When someone approached me with an idea," he later explained, "I'd look at him coldly and say, How many Germans will it kill? Our objective was to win the war." The initial task of Rabi's division was to create a working prototype of a 10-centimeter microwave radar. Even with Taffy Bowen's assistance, the microwave team—which included Pollard, Purcell, and Healea, among many others—was unsure how the cavity magnetron worked. For the most part, their academic studies and careers had been about nuclear physics and recently discovered subatomic structures, but they had little experience with electronics, magnets and radio waves. They knew that when electrons, guided by magnets to travel around a circular path, passed over open metal cavities, their oscillation produced microwaves. However, it was not clear to them how that happened—when Rabi explained to another physicist, "It's just a kind of whistle," he was stumped when asked, "Okay, Rabi, how does a whistle work?"[11]

They had to move quickly, not just to understand the physics but also to build a working microwave radar, as they were worried that the funding provided by Loomis's Microwave Committee might not last. The committee, meanwhile, gave several companies a thirty-day timetable to produce components for a radar prototype. Bell Laboratories, which had been given the original GEC cavity magnetron brought by the Tizard Mission, was assigned to copy it from plans and X-rays of the device. By mid-November Rabi and his team had put the magnetron together with a Westinghouse pulse generator, a Sperry-built transmitter, a Bell Laboratories receiver, and a General Electric cathode-ray tube display (the radar scope), and made a crude microwave radar.[12]

On a freezing January morning in 1941, they sent out their first microwave radar beam from the rooftop experimental station on MIT's Building 6. The magnetron bounced radio pulses off the buildings in Boston across the Charles River and showed up on the radar scope. A month later, they were able to track aircraft taking off from nearby East Boston Airport (today's Logan Airport). They then fitted a microwave radar set inside a B-18 Bolo bomber, which on March 10 flew sorties off the coast of New England and was able to detect ships from 9 miles away—a sure indication that the system would be useful for aircraft hunting U-boats in the Atlantic. That very same day, unknown to the Americans or even to Bowen, Philip Dee's group at TRE had also been conducting its first experiments with airborne microwave radar, fitted to their test Blenheim fighter-bomber flying out of the nearby aerodrome at Christchurch. These British tests were aimed at a different goal than the Americans' were: that of using night fighters to hunt down German bombers. Their experience showed that the radar could detect other aircraft at a range of several miles.[13]

In the course of the following months in 1941, both the British Blenheim and American B-18 tests showed that radar could locate aircraft at night and submarines at sea. While on an inspection tour of American military installations in April 1941, Hugh Dowding (now an envoy of the Ministry of Aircraft Production after leaving Fighter Command) witnessed some of the American tests. Impressed with the speed of American manufacture, he ordered 200 sets of the Rad Lab 10-centimeter radar for the RAF. Microwave radar had shown its potential on both sides of the Atlantic. The challenge was getting it mass-produced.

Bell Laboratories in New York City had been able to make a few prototype models of the cavity magnetron, but for full-scale production they had to rely on their manufacturing subsidiary, the Western Electric Company, whose massive Hawthorne Works outside Chicago produced almost all the telephone equipment for "Ma Bell," the Bell Telephone monopoly.

The 45,000 workers there—many of them women, even before World War Two—were well acquainted with precision work, and had even provided Watson-Watts's group in Britain with vacuum tubes for its early radars. Nevertheless, the levels of precision needed to build the cavity magnetron (Figure 9) stretched the limits of Hawthorne Works' manufacturing, causing countless problems that had to be solved one by one. The Monday after Pearl Harbor, Bell scientists were despondently staring at some nonworking magnetrons; that particular batch had leaky vacuum seals. Other flaws soon cropped up—such as problems with brazing the waveguides, and with machining the cavities to exacting tolerances. Not only did these have to be solved, but the equipment had to be made rugged enough to stand up to wartime use and reliable enough to trust airmen's lives with it, all while trying to increase its power output (higher power meant longer range) and improve its performance.[14]

The entry of America into the war transformed polite cooperation with Britain into a strong sense of solidarity—Denis Robinson later recalled that when he went into the Rad Lab on the day after Pearl Harbor, they all shook his hand and said, "We're allies now," before redoubling their efforts. Orders were starting to flood in for magnetrons designed for a variety of functions—locating submarines, air intercept and air-to-air combat, gunlaying, navigation, and a host of other roles. And these orders came not just from the US Army and Navy, but also from the British—in addition to Dowding's initial order. Like thousands of other companies around the United States, Western Electric suddenly had to hire and train tens of thousands of new workers and set up dozens of satellite plants, some of them in former laundromats and shoe factories. Antennae were subcontracted to a slot-machine manufacturer, and frames to a bicycle-maker. Rad Lab personnel were frequent visitors to Bell Labs and Western Electric (as well as its Canadian subsidiary, Northern Electric), continually tweaking the design and production of what would turn out to be fifteen separate variants of the magnetron.[15]

Two magnetrons were destined for installation on a pair of B-24 Liberator bombers that were ordered by Britain under the Lend-Lease program. Denis Robinson took charge of converting the aircraft for anti-submarine operations, which involved installing the microwave radars in a bulbous dome underneath the nose. The resulting configuration made the already unwieldy aircraft look like a flying elephant, so naturally they were christened "Dumbos." The first test flight took place on December 11, 1941, the day Germany declared war on the United States, and subsequent experiments demonstrated that the radar could detect submarines on the surface.[16]

After several months of testing both the sub-hunting and air-intercept capabilities of microwave radar, American and British officers became convinced of its worth. At that point in early 1942, it made sense to concentrate on these defensive capabilities of airborne radar—even after the Blitz, Germany was still sending bombers over Britain, and the Battle of the Atlantic was raging. But the Rad Lab knew that sooner rather than later their new radar would be called upon for offensive operations, meaning bombing Germany. In March 1942, Robinson extensively tested the 10-centimeter set over land, flying over Connecticut, New York, and even as far as Pittsburgh, personally tweaking the controls to get the performance he was looking for. The results were disappointing—Bowen later reported that "townships . . . were quite invisible on a [10-centimeter set]. . . . [T]he biggest failures were Pittsburgh and, to a lesser extent, the Schenectady-Albany metal and electronic production centres. Neither could be seen on a 10 cms radar."[17]

This was a completely different result from TRE's "turning point of the war" experiments just four months earlier. Robinson wrote his colleague Philip Dee that radar for targeting cities and industries "did not work in America" and thus was useless for blind bombing. This discrepancy between the British and American results was not resolved until almost a year later, in early 1943, when George Valley at the Rad Lab, while fixing a malfunction in one of the radars, discovered that the American radar set had been equipped with a limiting device that improved its performance over water but reduced its sensitivity over land. Once that device was switched off, cities and factories showed up perfectly on the radar scope. Unfortunately,

Valley's discovery came too late to repair the rift over blind bombing that had opened up between the Rad Lab and TRE.

Back in Britain, the "turning point" news of November 1, 1941, had led the Air Ministry to direct TRE to proceed with blind-bombing experiments using the 10-centimeter radar on a heavy Halifax bomber, which the newly appointed commander in chief of the RAF Bomber Command, Arthur Harris (the press, not his men, nicknamed him "Bomber" Harris) planned to use for attacking the Nazi homeland as early as the autumn of 1942. Lindemann dubbed the radar "Home Sweet Home," because it allowed a bomber to home straight in on the target, and suggested "H2S" as its nickname, which stuck. Rowe selected Bernard Lovell, a young science officer who had been working on cosmic rays before the war, as the director of the program. By April, the first trials on a heavy Halifax bomber seemed so faultless that Churchill himself demanded a "really large order for H2S" to be produced.

Within weeks, unexpected problems delayed progress. In late May 1942, TRE was moved yet again from the Dorset coast to a spa town far inland named Great Malvern. The move came in response to the threat of German bombardment or paratroop invasion, as reprisal for a recent raid on a Nazi radar site in France (of which more later). Over the course of just forty-eight hours, all the laboratory equipment was dismantled, packed into trucks, driven 150 miles to the new site, and reinstalled in a hastily requisitioned boarding school. Then just two weeks after the move on June 7, the test Halifax suffered an engine fire and crashed, killing the crew and seven radar engineers who were vital to the H2S program, as well as smashing the radar itself. Lovell was tasked with recovering the still-secret cavity magnetron amid the wreckage and bodies, "a searing experience as a young man," as he recalled.[18]

The very day of the crash, though before he knew of it, Churchill sent a missive to the Air Ministry. "I am deeply disturbed at the very slow rate of progress promised for its production," he wrote. "Three sets in August and twelve in November is not even beginning to touch the problem. We must insist on getting, at any rate, a sufficient number to light up the target by the autumn." Neither the disruption of TRE's move to Great Malvern nor the news of the Halifax crash deterred Churchill's demands. He had already seen multiple defeats in North Africa and Singapore, and needed to carry the fight to the enemy. On July 3, 1942, Churchill called a meeting with Lindemann, Harris, and executives from Electrical and Musical Industries (EMI) Ltd., which was now manufacturing 10-centimeter radars in disappointingly limited quantities. Churchill announced to the group that he needed 200 sets of H2S radars by mid-October, as long-range bombers were "our only means of inflicting damage on the enemy." The need for blind-bombing radar was so great that Churchill personally ordered his point man, Robert Renwick, to remain at TRE to ask every day if there was "any news, any problems" and if so, to immediately contact the prime minister to resolve them.[19]

Even with Churchill's personal oversight of the microwave radar program, Britain was quickly losing control of it to the Americans. When the Tizard Mission showed the cavity magnetron to the Americans back in September 1940, it had been clear that the British were in the ascendancy. Since then, the Rad Lab and TRE had been developing airborne radar in parallel, with considerable exchange of information and personnel between them, and not a small amount of competition. The Americans were certain that they could beat TRE at developing a working model, because they had Taffy Bowen's assurances that it could be done "and weren't to be outdone by any Britisher," said Ernie Pollard. When Bowen made a visit to TRE in July 1941 to demonstrate a Rad Lab 10-centimeter set installed in a modified Boeing 247D airliner (he thought the Rad Lab set was "clearly ahead of its equivalent in Britain"), his British colleagues' reaction was "lukewarm." But as Denis Robinson noted, the day after Pearl Harbor the Americans "worked twice as hard as ever before," and given their massive advantage in resources and their sheer number of scientists and engineers, it seemed inevitable that they would outstrip the British in terms of research, engineering, and production. This shift in the power dynamic was noted by Taffy Bowen, who in an unsigned letter back to Britain in February 1942 noted, "We no longer have the Americans in our pocket. There are two reasons for this: they now have enough experience to stand on their own feet, and they have their own problems which are sometimes different from those in England."[20]

—————————

TIZARD'S RETURN FROM HIS mission to the United States in the fall of 1940 had reversed his waning influence. He was appointed as a specialist to a scientific advisory panel for Churchill's war cabinet, which gave him wider access to policy decisions than had his narrower portfolio with air warfare. The same month (February 1942) that Bowen recognized the power shift in radar development, Tizard circulated a long memorandum to the war cabinet that echoed those same points: now that the United States had joined the war, it had both the incentive and the capacity to assume the bulk of the radar effort, and therefore the United States, not Britain, should become the primary location for radar research. The reaction to Tizard's memo was swift and encouraging; with the approval of the British government, Averell Harriman sent a cable to Vannevar Bush recommending that the two nations standardize equipment (presumably to American standards), establish joint research teams in the United States, and allocate projects to each nation. At the level of the working scientists and engineers, however, the reaction was quite different; TRE was not about to let the Rad Lab run the show. Friction between the two laboratories came to a head with a visit by Isidor Rabi and Edward Purcell of the Rad Lab microwave team to TRE in July 1942, a visit that threatened to derail one of the most critical strategic bombing initiatives of the war to date.[21]

During the month of July, Rabi and Purcell made their home base in the crowded offices of the OSRD London Mission, from which they fanned out across Britain to coordinate American and British radar activities. The first few days were devoted to bringing high-level British officials, including Rowe and Watson-Watt, up to speed on American developments. Rabi reported that the British thought the Americans "were streets ahead of them," to the point where Watson-Watt suggested that "certain developments could be thrown entirely to the United States." Rabi and Purcell were then invited to the TRE Sunday Soviet on July 5 at the new Malvern site. As there was no nearby hotel available, these Soviets were now held in

Rowe's office, and therefore more restricted affairs. Blind bombing was at the top of the priority list, and TRE wanted to know whether they could "procure American equipment and fit it to British aircraft." Rabi demurred, concerned about the "difficulties of fitting American equipment to British aircraft," an understandable reaction at a time when British nuts could not screw onto American bolts, and vice versa. A separate closed-door meeting in Herbert Skinner's office that afternoon "came to no conclusion" on the matter, but all sides agreed that "a great deal would be gained" by improving US-British cooperation.[22]

When Bernard Lovell, in charge of the H2S blind-bombing radar, was subsequently told of these meetings, he mistook Rabi and Purcell's reluctance for outright opposition to his radar-guided blind-bombing project, much later claiming—incorrectly—that the Americans said the system was "unscientific and unworkable" and that if an H2S-equipped aircraft was downed, "the Germans would obtain the secret of the magnetron" (it was a nearly solid block of copper and almost indestructible). Like Rabi, Lovell took his work personally. Not only was this Lovell's first major project, but he had just lost eleven men in its development; he now had Churchill's personal envoy literally looking over his shoulder on a daily basis and reporting back to the prime minister; and, like the rest of TRE, he was unhappy that the Americans had largely taken over the development of a system that the British had created. In his accounts, written a half century after the facts, Lovell mistakenly claimed that American opposition to radar-guided blind bombing had colored the views of British officials, which resulted in a significant delay in the deployment of H2S against Germany. Although Lovell's interpretation was wrong, Rabi's own concerns about the compatibility of British and American equipment would also turn out to be overblown. These miscommunications and missteps on both sides threatened to disrupt the close relations between TRE and the Rad Lab.

Despite Lovell's concerns, Rabi and Purcell's visit would actually lead to an agreement between American and British officials, one that acknowledged that the Rad Lab and TRE needed better coordination, preferably on a day-to-day basis. At this point in midsummer 1942, almost all of the coordination was being handled by the relatively small OSRD London Mission, which was becoming overwhelmed with the job of passing information between the two nations and fielding inquiries from both. It was also handling a growing stream of American scientists and engineers, some of whom stayed for weeks and months in the European theater to see operational problems with radar and electronic systems at first hand. Meanwhile, the British Central Scientific Office in Washington had never been staffed sufficiently to share the workload with Bennett Archambault's team, and was largely on the sidelines.

SOME MONTHS LATER, FROM April to June 1943, Karl Compton from OSRD and Lee DuBridge from the Rad Lab came to the OSRD London offices to conduct a wide-ranging visit of British radar research, production, and operations facilities, aided by two scientists stationed at OSRD London, Horton Guyford (Guy) Stever and David Langmuir. The United States Special Mission on Radar—usually referred to as the Compton Mission—was authorized by the Joint Chiefs of Staff (the four senior officers of the armed services) in recognition of the difficulties experienced by the American 8th Bomber Command after it had started bombing missions over Europe in mid-1942. For ten months, B-17 Flying Fortresses had been striking targets in France, Belgium, and the Netherlands, their range limited by that of the British fighter squadrons that protected them. Unlike the RAF's night bombings, the American strategy called for daylight raids, on the assumption that it allowed for precise targeting of military and industrial facilities. The dilemma was that European skies were often cloudy, obscuring the targets and rendering the Norden bombsight largely ineffective. Bombing through overcast was proving to be as difficult as bombing at night, as both required a means of locating targets without visual reference. DuBridge wrote in his post-mission report in June, "The most urgent radar problem in the war . . . is that of blind bombing."[23]

Although B-17s were being fitted with British-built Gee radio navigation systems, most crews relied on traditional methods of dead reckoning and celestial navigation (of which more in Chapter 4). Stever and

Langmuir, recognizing that the crews needed better navigational aids, had prepared for Compton a secret summary of all British radar and radio devices to date. They almost caused a major security breach when they lost it in a London cab, and had to scramble to recover it. They showed that while Gee and Oboe had good results so far, Lovell's H2S system was still in its infancy and proved somewhat disappointing. The British, for their part, acknowledged American dominance over the radar effort, asking them to take primary responsibility for eight projects while retaining only two for themselves. DuBridge's aforementioned report underscored the fact that TRE, with its "appalling scarcity of ordinary laboratory test equipment," needed American help with its radar efforts. The scientists at the Rad Lab, he noted, were already developing a new radar that operated on a shorter (3-centimeter) wavelength, which promised to give better results than the 10-centimeter H2S. Compton, meanwhile, reported to the Joint Chiefs of Staff that instead of sending a steady stream of visitors to Britain, as they had been doing, the Americans should establish permanent teams collocated with TRE to jointly work on radar and other developments.

As a result of the Compton Mission, in September 1943 the Americans established a British-based satellite office of the Rad Lab, initially carved out of several rooms and huts vacated by TRE in Great Malvern. Called the British Branch of the Radiation Laboratory (BBRL), it was placed under the OSRD London Mission for administration and support, but otherwise operated independently. Although its primary purpose was to support the US Armed Forces in Europe with the "development and effective employment of radar equipment required for their operations," it was also tasked with cooperating with and assisting British scientists. BBRL started with sixteen American scientists, who shipped over crates of MIT Rad Lab equipment to supplement TRE's, and showed their British counterparts how to use it. The team was led by Lauriston C. Marshall of MIT, a specialist in microwaves, who also had to establish personnel, staffing, housing, and financial arrangements for the new laboratory. Expenses were drawn on a special account set up through Midland Bank, the British agent of the First National Bank of Boston.[24]

By March 1944, the rapid Allied buildup for the upcoming D-Day invasion led to Marshall being replaced by John G. Trump, a physicist who originally was developing hospital X-ray machines before coming to OSRD as Compton's aide (where one of his side duties was to investigate Nikola Tesla's claims for a death ray, after Tesla died in January 1943). Trump's managerial experience at OSRD was seen as crucial to the rapid expansion of BBRL, which at its height employed almost 200 American scientists and engineers, working in hastily built tin-roofed huts whose discomforts were made up for by superb views of the cricket grounds and rolling countryside around Great Malvern.

The second result of the 1943 Compton Mission was that both TRE and the Rad Lab abandoned further development of the 10-centimeter radar despite its initial successes (though it remained in limited production) and began work on 3-centimeter systems. In January and February 1943, the first 10-centimeter H2S systems were installed and in use in two dozen Stirling and Halifax bombers (though the Nazi air defenses shot down one of the bombers over Rotterdam and captured an H2S set, it took the Germans until the end of the war to duplicate it). In March, the commander of the 8th Bomber Command, Brigadier General Ira C. Eaker, sent a formal request for H2S to his opposite number in the RAF Bomber Command, asking for "sufficient quantities of this equipment" so that they could continue bombing through overcast when the skies clouded over in late summer and early fall.[25]

This request came as an "unwelcome" surprise to Lovell, who was busy installing H2S in British landing ships and anti-submarine aircraft, and in any event was convinced that the Americans had rejected his H2S system the previous year. Nevertheless, Lovell's multinational team—and in particular a Canadian flight officer named Joseph Richards—marshaled a group of American airmen and mechanics to handle the installation and testing of the radars. By August 1943, Lovell and his team installed four (later increased to eighteen) British H2S radar sets in American B-17 and B-24 bombers, putting paid to Rabi's concerns over equipment compatibility between the two countries. These aircraft led daylight raids on the

German port of Emden in September 1943, bombing through overcast to destroy U-boat shipyards and cargo facilities.[26]

As operational experience with H2S in both British and American bombers grew during the fall of 1943, it became increasingly obvious that the 10-centimeter sets lacked sufficient resolution; cities and industrial facilities simply looked like white blobs on the radar screen, without enough detail to target even large-scale strategic assets. Scientists on both sides of the Atlantic had foreseen this and were already working on 3-centimeter sets, whose shorter wavelength could resolve major areas of cities and built-up portions of industrial facilities. Back in January 1943, George Valley at the Rad Lab had led the development of the 3-centimeter cavity magnetron model 725A. By October, Western Electric, Northern Electric, and Raytheon were turning them out by the thousands—eventually 300,000 would be built during the entirety of the war. These American and Canadian magnetrons became the heart of both the British version, called H2S Mk III ("Mark" or "Mk" indicated the version number), and the American version, H2X (because the 3-centimeter wavelength is called X-band).[27]

The overall H2X system, nicknamed "Mickey" because its original radar dome evoked the cartoon mouse (Figure 10 shows a later version), was manufactured by the Philco Corporation, a Philadelphia-based electronics company that had already built thousands of Identification Friend or Foe sets for the Americans and British (discussed in Chapter 4). As the H2X and H2S Mk III were deployed in front-line bombers, American scientists at BBRL worked side by side with their British TRE counterparts to improve both systems. By late 1943, the combined Allied bombing raids were beginning to push deep into Germany, using a combination of radar and optical bombsights; radar would guide navigators to their targets by comparing their radar scope images with their charts and maps, while the bombsights (with radar data fed to them by the bombardiers) could be used if the skies cleared over the targets.

However, in order for these raids to even reach their targets, British and American bombers had to overcome a Nazi anti-aircraft defense system that had no equal in the world.

Foiling German Radar

Shortly after midnight on the morning of February 28, 1942, the first sticks of the 2nd Paratroop Battalion, C Company—120 men total—dropped through a small opening in the floor of the fuselage of their modified bombers, floating down and landing in a foot of fresh snow on level farmland, about 600 yards from their intended target. A perfect drop, despite heavy anti-aircraft fire. The waxing moon, almost full, reflected off the snow and allowed the paratroopers to carry out their complex assignment. Their target was a German Würzburg air-intercept radar, located just a few yards from the cliff edge near the town of Bruneval on the Normandy coast.

Led by Major John Frost, who would later distinguish himself in the unsuccessful attempt to take the bridge at Arnhem during Operation Market Garden, the first group of fifty men quickly surrounded the radar dish and the nearby chateau, which had belonged to a prominent French surgeon and was abandoned. Other paratroopers protected the operation from nearby German troops. Engineers and technicians dismantled the 10-foot-diameter radar while others captured one of the Würzburg operating technicians. So far, the raid—code-named Operation Biting—seemed to be proceeding just as planned. But only half the forty paratroopers assigned to clear the evacuation beach had hit their landing zone; the others had to sprint two miles through the darkness to reach the shore. Fierce firefights broke out as Frost and his men, hauling the radar in pieces and manhandling the German technician, withdrew down a ravine to the beach. It was now past 2:00 a.m. and there was no sign of the Royal Navy's evacuation force. Frost sent up red signal flares, which also gave away their position to the Germans. Thankfully, the six landing craft drew up to the beach before the counterattack could begin. The evacuation was messy, but within a few minutes the paratroopers and their prize were heading across the English Channel back to Portsmouth. Though it had resulted in the loss of two men and another six captured, the raid was counted as an overwhelming success—for the first time, British scientists would have a good look at German radar and begin to devise the means to defeat it.[28]

While Robert Watson-Watt was inventing the British version of radar in the 1930s, the German companies GEMA and Telefunken were developing their own versions for the Luftwaffe (called, as noted earlier, Freya and Würzburg, respectively). Baldwin's belief that "the bomber will always get through" was dismissed by the Luftwaffe's leader, Hermann Goering, who claimed in August 1939 that the Ruhr Valley would never be bombed. "If an enemy bomb reaches the Ruhr, my name is not Hermann Goering; you can call me Meier," he said, using a Jewish surname to underline the depths of his certainty. The Freya radar performed successfully against British bomber raids against Wilhelmshaven in December 1939, after which Goering ordered the deployment of an integrated air-defense system, comparable to Chain Home, later dubbed by Churchill the Kammhuber Line for its commander. Each air-defense zone had a Freya early-warning radar to detect the incoming bombers and then alert two Würzburg intercept radars, which located the bombers and guided German fighters to them; they also cued dozens of anti-aircraft guns with searchlights. Occupied France also had an extensive network of early-warning radars constructed by Germany to alert the homeland long before an attack. The German radar system was so effective against the bombers that the RAF looked to the boffins for solutions.[29]

The boffins had been on the case even before the war began. In 1937, Lindemann had suggested to Churchill, then a backbencher in Parliament, several potential ways to spoof enemy radars. It was already obvious to the scientists that a new battlefront had opened, and it involved radio waves. The first evidence of this novel type of warfare was revealed on June 5, 1940, the day the Dunkirk evacuation ended, when cryptographers at Bletchley Park (of which more later) decoded German transmissions that indicated a new radio navigation system for blind bombing of British cities. Reginald V. Jones, a young physicist who had briefly worked at Bletchley before being assigned to the Air Ministry Intelligence Directorate, figured out how this system—named Knickebein (Crooked Leg), according to the coded messages—employed radio beams during the Battle of Britain and the Blitz, to guide German bombers through the night skies to drop bombs with deadly accuracy. When Jones and his team developed a countermeasure for those signals, the German engineers switched tactics to a system called X-Gerät (X-Apparatus), and when the British jammed those signals, they deployed Y-Gerät, which Jones again defeated for a while, this time by means of an unused BBC television transmitter. While this Battle of the Beams, as it was later dubbed, was successfully diverting many German bombs from falling on cities, a very different technology to defeat German radar was in the works.[30]

Jones became one of the most noted forces behind Operation Biting. British signals intelligence had been identifying the radio signatures of Freya, Würzburg, and other radars since mid-1940, but not until December 1941, a year and a half later, did Jones receive RAF reconnaissance photographs of the Würzburg radar at Bruneval, which helped set into motion the daring raid that captured it. Within a week the radar was brought to TRE at Worth Matravers and dissected by Groups 5 and 6 (Countermeasures), headed by Robert Cockburn, a former science teacher turned physicist. Once the Würzburg's inner workings were uncovered—aided by intelligence from the captured German radar technician—the groups began designing an airborne jamming system, code-named Carpet. The early sets were too weak to be effective, however, and their work was interrupted in late May, when, as mentioned, TRE was moved from the British coast to Great Malvern, for fear of reprisals for the Operation Biting raid.[31]

Cockburn's groups also began experimenting with a way of literally foiling German radar that had first been proposed by Lindemann—scattering from aircraft clouds of aluminum foil that reflected back to the radar, which would pick up the large return and thus be blinded to the actual location of the bombers. In December 1941, Cockburn made Joan Curran, a twenty-five-year-old junior scientific officer, the lead in developing foil reflectors. For months she experimented with dozens of different shapes and sizes of foil, from tinsel strips to notebook-paper-sized sheets that could serve double duty as propaganda leaflets. Curran settled on foil strips about a foot long and a half-inch wide. Albert Rowe, his tongue firmly in his cheek, code-named this method of making the skies opaque to radar Window.[32]

After the United States joined the war, it also joined in the quest to thwart German radar. The MIT Radiation Laboratory had of course been originally established to develop microwave radar, but, like TRE, it was soon pursuing many other avenues of research, including how to defeat enemy radars. In January 1942 the Rad Lab officially established a radar countermeasures team headed by Fred Terman, who had been one of Vannevar Bush's most accomplished students at MIT and was now working at Stanford. It quickly became obvious to them that the same laboratory developing radar should not also develop the means to defeat it; internal politics could prove too great a barrier for innovation. In July, Terman and his team—many were his former Stanford students—decamped to an underused biology laboratory at Harvard, just down the road, where they established the Radio Research Laboratory (RRL), whose name, like the Rad Lab, hid its true purpose.[33]

Shortly after Terman had established the RRL at Harvard, he and several other radar experts went to Britain to spend two months at the OSRD London Mission, from which they made numerous site visits to British radar and research establishments. Terman felt that his most valuable meetings were with Robert Cockburn and his countermeasures teams, who shared the information on the Würzburg radar gleaned from Operation Biting, and TRE's work on Carpet and Window. Cockburn also explained to Terman that the Germans had just successfully jammed British radar with their own countermeasures, allowing the battleships *Scharnhorst* and *Gneisenau* and the heavy cruiser *Prinz Eugen* to dash through the English Channel from Brest to Germany, right under the noses of the Royal Navy and the RAF. Radar could be defeated, as Terman learned, and this could make a difference in the outcome of a battle.

"When I arrived back from England," Terman later recalled in an interview, "I had a much clearer idea of what we should be doing at RRL." Each radar operated on a very specific wavelength—early-warning systems had longer wavelengths for range, intercept radars had shorter wavelengths for accuracy. Terman assigned teams to work on different jammers against each of the several German radars that TRE had identified—Carpet against the Würzburg, Mandrel against Freya, and so forth. He also assigned a former Hollywood soundman, Winfred Salisbury, and a pair of young planetary astronomers, Fred Whipple and Gerard Kuiper, to further investigate Window. They realized that the best way to decoy radar was not simply to reflect it back with aluminum strips, but rather to create thin dipole antennae—not unlike television "rabbit ears"—that resonated when hit by radar and retransmitted the waves back to the source, spoofing the radar with much stronger and brighter images on the operator's screen. This could be best accomplished with slivers of aluminum foil, each the thickness of a penny, with a length half that of the wavelength of the specific radar. For the Würzburg, which was operating at a 53-centimeter wavelength, this meant slivers 10 inches long.[34]

Now the problem was how to manufacture such thin slivers, at the right length, in the enormous quantities (about a billion per day) needed to defeat the German radar. Terman assigned this task to his friend Harold Elliott, the engineer who had invented the push-button radio for automobiles. Though the foil slivers were incredibly thin—they acquired the name "chaff" after fine wheat husks—they had to be folded into a V-shape so they would not curl up in the air, then packaged into bundles that could be dispensed out of chutes in the aircraft fuselage. Elliott and his machine shop crew tried various types of paper cutters, finally developing in the summer of 1943 a workable prototype with high-speed whirling blades. RRL did not have the capabilities to manufacture such large quantities of chaff, so they approached the director of OSRD Division 15, Radio Countermeasures, in search of funding for industrial production. The director, Chauncy Guy Suits (a research executive at General Electric, who always went by his middle name), noted that "getting financial support was never a problem . . . we would describe what we were doing, what additional resources we felt were necessary and what it would cost. Almost without exception, they accepted the figures we gave them."[35]

With almost unlimited funding from OSRD, the Harvard-based RRL contracted out to a dozen commercial firms, including Reynolds Metals Company in Richmond, Virginia, International Paper Box Machine Company in Nashua, New Hampshire, and Standard Rolling Mills in Brooklyn, New York. By war's end, 20 million pounds of chaff had been produced, accounting for three-quarters of all the aluminum foil produced in the Unites States. The British were unable to manufacture chaff (still known there as Window) at the same speed as the Americans, so in September

1943 RRL sent Elliott and seventy-five of his machines to Britain to fill the demand. David Langmuir, who took on the job of radar countermeasures liaison in addition to his myriad other duties for the OSRD London Mission, wrote to Guy Suits in September 1943 about the British use of American chaff, "I have never seen any American development assimilated over here with anything like the speed which has been shown in this case." In November, a British RAF general admitted to his American counterpart that "much of the RAF's [countermeasures] program depends absolutely on American production," in part because Britain's precious aluminum supply was largely assigned to aircraft manufacture. Within months, British and American bombers were deploying thousands of pounds of chaff daily to blind German radars. During the Christmas season, chaff did double duty as tinsel foil to decorate the RAF Christmas trees.[36]

ELLIOTT'S ARRIVAL IN BRITAIN in September 1943 coincided with the establishment of a new radar countermeasures research facility at Great Malvern. Called the American-British Laboratory of Division 15 (ABL-15), it was a branch of the Harvard-based RRL but administered under the OSRD London Mission. For about a year, a series of directors rotated through the division, brought over from American industries such as Columbia Broadcasting System (CBS) and General Electric. Much of ABL-15's staff of 105 scientists and technicians also came from those companies, and as the war progressed, staff members were increasingly deployed to the front lines in support of the US Army Air Forces and the RAF, to install, test, and evaluate an increasingly wide variety of radar countermeasures systems and chaff dispensers. For example, Thomas Kuhn, a twenty-two-year-old physics graduate from Harvard, was sent from Great Malvern to Cherbourg, France, in August 1944, soon after D-Day, to assess the effectiveness of Carpet and Window on bomber operations.[37]

With ABL-15 personnel coming on top of the almost 200 scientists at BBRL, the influx of Americans at Great Malvern in the fall of 1943 put an enormous strain on the little town's ability to provide food and housing. Great Malvern was no stranger to visitors. Since the Middle Ages, its spring-fed waters had been touted as a cure-all for a variety of maladies, from stress to tuberculosis, making it a popular spa retreat. In the Victorian Age, the most famous of the spas was Dr. James Wilson's Establishment, the favored destination for Charles Darwin, Alfred Lord Tennyson, Florence Nightingale, and other luminaries who sought the "water cure" for their ailments. By World War Two, Great Malvern was home to boarding schools and retirement homes, with Wilson's Establishment now the County Hotel for retirees. When TRE arrived in the town in May 1942, it took over several boarding schools, while its staff was crowded into billets at the County Hotel and other hotels and flats, much to the dismay of their displaced elderly residents. Meanwhile, a food queue was established at the Winter Gardens complex in the town center, manned by the Women's Voluntary Services, to feed the 1,500 new residents.[38]

Like BBRL, ABL-15 was administratively placed under the OSRD London Mission, but both operated largely independently. The Americans there worked to the TRE schedule, taking Saturdays off so that they could participate in Rowe's Sunday Soviets. Despite the crushing workload and relative isolation of Great Malvern, some of the scientists found solace in the natural beauty that had drawn visitors there for centuries. Langmuir, a temporary director at ABL-15 in its earliest days, described one memorable excursion in a letter to his wife. As they climbed down the hill behind the town one Saturday afternoon, "we had one of the typical English rainstorms which would be called freak in the US. The effect was stunning, particularly by the clearing up which brought a rainbow which went all the way round the semicircle."[39]

The British side saw the influx of Americans as a boon. Robert Cockburn spoke for many of his TRE colleagues when said that they had been "up to our ears in work" and "doing everything on a shoestring," when "suddenly this enormous fresh unit came in." It wasn't long before ABL-15 matched TRE in number, "with everybody beaming and shining with enthusiasm." Cockburn noted that "there was great fraternity between ABL-15 and my department; we borrowed equipment from each other and that sort of thing. But from the start it was clear that it was a separate effort and they were working on different things for their armed forces."[40]

Despite TRE's enthusiasm for American help, ABL-15 suffered from leadership problems. The CBS and General Electric executives who initially were brought over in the fall of 1943 to direct ABL-15 ran the field office as if it were a business and not a branch of the American military, promising equipment to front-line units and contracting with British electronics manufacturers like Plessey Company Ltd., for which they had no authority and no means of paying. These actions so threatened the delicate balance between American and British forces that in October, both Fred Terman and Vannevar Bush seriously considered recalling the executives from Great Malvern and "folding up the entire show." At the OSRD London Mission, Archambault, already overwhelmed with his day-to-day duties, found himself having to remotely manage his field offices while smoothing over relations with the British. Moreover, the planned invasion of France (cover name Operation Overlord) would demand far greater involvement of scientific personnel in radar and radar countermeasures, which would only add to the strain. After reviewing the situation in Britain, officials of the Army Air Forces in Washington recommended "strengthening this group [scientists] by additional personnel to produce the maximum influence" and "improving the relations between BBRL, London OSRD Office, and ABL-15." In February 1944, three months before D-Day, Bush directed a change in leadership of the field offices, dispatching John Trump to head BBRL and John N. Dyer from CBS to lead ABL-15 ("I have enormous confidence" in them, Bush told Archambault). Both men stayed on through the remainder of the war.[41]

Even with these frictions, American scientists at BBRL and ABL-15, working together with their British counterparts at TRE, developed a series of airborne radars and radar countermeasures that by late 1943 were transforming the RAF into an effective night bombing force, capable of hitting both cities and factories. American aircraft were also being fitted with the same systems as the RAF, but Army Air Forces doctrine still saw daylight bombing by mass formations of bombers as the best means of conducting precision attacks against specific German military targets, notably factories, oil refineries, and railroads. However, without adequate long-range fighter protection, unescorted American bombers, even in massive formations with mutually supporting gunfire, were being chewed up by the Luftwaffe before they could even reach their targets.[42]

British-Bred, American-Born Fighter

The P-51 Mustang was the iconic all-American escort fighter of World War Two—except it was developed with British money, built to British specifications, and designed by a German American engineer with assistance from a British aerodynamicist. Initially it was brought into service with the RAF, having been rejected by the US Army Air Forces. And in its most-recognized version, the P-51 was fitted with a British Rolls-Royce engine. Thomas Hitchcock, the American assistant air attaché in London, described the Mustang as "sired by the British out of an American mother." The P-51 (P for "pursuit") started as part of the buying spree that the Anglo-French Purchasing Board (soon to be renamed, as we've seen, the British Purchasing Commission or BPC) went on in April 1940, then flush with the several hundred millions of dollars in gold bullion that had been rushed overseas in secret and safely stored in the vaults of the Bank of Canada in Ottawa and the Federal Reserve Bank in New York City. First through the Cash-and-Carry program, and then through the Lend-Lease program, the British eventually placed today's equivalent of almost a half-trillion dollars of airplane orders, a lifeline to American aircraft manufacturers.[43]

At the time, North American Aviation (NAA) of Inglewood, California, was one of those manufacturers, building mostly small two-man trainers, and trailing the aviation giants such as Douglas Aircraft (which built the DC-3 airliner) and Boeing (the manufacturer of the Pan American Clipper flying boats). Even before the British began placing orders, the US Army had approached the firm as a second source for building P-40 fighters, which were being made by its rival Curtiss-Wright. Army officials suggested the BPC also contract with NAA as a second source. NAA's chief designer, Edgar Schmued, was the heart of the company. Schmued had been transfixed by aviation ever since he saw his first plane as an eight-year-old boy near his home in Hornbach in the German Rhineland, and after World War One had gained many years' experience in the German aircraft industry before moving to the United States in 1931. He told his boss, James "Dutch" Kindelberger, that instead of copying the Curtiss-Wright fighter, he was certain he could "design a better one and build a better one." Kindelberger took Schmued's designs to Britain in March 1940. He promised delivery of the initial prototype in 100 days, and full production within one year. On May 23, NAA received an order for 400 fighters, based on Schmued's drawings but meeting British specifications as to armament (the RAF demanded a mixed suite including heavy 20 mm cannon in the wings), armor, and speed. NAA dubbed the model NA-73X ("X" meant prototype) and proposed calling it Apache. In December the Royal Air Force, following its rule that "the names of RAF fighters should convey speed, activity or aggressiveness," instead named it "Mustang" for the American feral horse (though one story suggests it was named for the popular 1936 dance tune "Saddle Your Blues to a Wild Mustang").[44]

Schmued's colleagues rushed to develop the Mustang design. The wings were based on new research that showed how to get smooth laminar airflow over their surface, giving greater speed than older designs that created turbulent, higher-drag airflow. The underbelly air scoop was designed to increase thrust instead of robbing the plane of airspeed. As the design progressed, the British Air Commission (a sister organization to the BPC) arranged for Beverley Shenstone, the Canadian-born British aerodynamicist who had helped develop the Supermarine Spitfire, to come to NAA in February 1941 to assist with the aerodynamics of the plane, most notably improving the performance of the underbelly air scoop. The prototype (delivered on October 26, 1940, well past the promised 100-day mark) and initial production models were fitted with the same General Motors Allison V-1710 aircraft engines used on the P-40. NAA continued to test and modify the Mustang through mid-1941, after which several models were sent to the US Army Air Forces for acceptance. The Americans were unenthusiastic about the plane, now designated P-51; in a memo dated March 4, 1942, the Materiel Division stated that "production of the P-51 airplane at Inglewood should not be continued" after the British contracts were fulfilled.[45]

Meanwhile, the first production P-51s had been crated and shipped to England, arriving in Liverpool in October 1941, and flown for the first time in November. The RAF pilots at the Air Fighting Development Unit wrote in a report that month that they considered it "definitely the best American fighter that has reached England." It was designated the Mustang Mark I (shown on the front cover) and placed into British service in January 1942, even though the RAF requirements had changed since the first aircraft orders had been placed in April 1940, prior to the Battle of Britain. That campaign showed that fighters needed to climb to high altitudes—above 15,000 feet—to intercept German bombers, and the Allison engine performance was decidedly anemic at that height.[46]

In April 1942, while the US Army Air Forces were mulling over how to end the Mustang production line, a British test pilot named Ronald Harker made the suggestion—momentous, in hindsight—of how to fulfill the RAF requirement with the same airplane. After flying one of the Mustangs at the Duxford Aerodrome, he called it "formidable," with excellent maneuvering and speed. "The point which strikes me," he wrote in his test memorandum, "is that with a powerful and good engine like the Merlin 61, its performance should be outstanding, as it is 35 m.p.h. faster than a Spitfire V at roughly the same power." The Merlin 61 was the newest fighter engine produced by Rolls-Royce and was already installed in combat fighters; it generated 1,500 horsepower compared with 1,120 horsepower for the Allison. Further calculations by Rolls-Royce showed that a Merlin-powered P-51 would outperform Spitfires at every altitude, and could reach a speed of 432 mph. More importantly, it was the same length as the Allison engine, so installing it in the P-51 airframe "would be a relatively quick job."[47]

Harker's memorandum sparked discussion between the Air Ministry and Rolls-Royce on creating a Merlin/Mustang hybrid. Averell Harriman, Roosevelt's point man in London for the Lend-Lease program, suggested to both the British and Americans that P-51s be built in Britain and fitted with Merlin engines. However, given that it would divert British factories away from other critical projects, the idea was dropped. In June 1942, Rolls-Royce agreed to take an existing Mustang airframe and test-fit a Merlin engine from its Derby factory in the East Midlands. The modified plane made its first test flight in October. Its performance was as impressive as advertised, 433 mph at 20,000 feet, compared with just 380 mph for the Allison version. As every pilot knows, "speed is life" in aerial combat, and the re-engined Mustangs would now be fast enough at high altitude to go up against the top German fighters, the Messerschmitt Bf 109s and 110s and the Focke-Wulf Fw 190s.

The problem was that the Air Ministry could not afford to have Rolls-Royce re-engine all of the Mustangs that were arriving from the United States, as it needed the Merlin engines for the newest fighters and bombers. Ultimately only five Mustangs were converted as test platforms using original Rolls-Royce Merlins, though none saw combat. Instead, another source of production for Merlin engines had already been established some 3,600 miles away from Derby, at the Packard Motor Car Company in Detroit, Michigan.

Rolls-Royce Comes to Detroit

The manufacture of Rolls-Royce Merlin engines by Packard was not originally intended for the P-51. That arrangement took place two years prior to Harker's suggestion of fitting the engines into the Mustang's airframe, and by coincidence occurred within days of the BPC's initial order for the fighter aircraft. The British government and Rolls-Royce had been planning shadow factories since 1936, and by 1940 it had established several sites around England and Scotland. Even so, the wartime demands for new and repaired Merlins, which powered fighters and bombers like the Spitfire, Hurricane, and Lancaster, were far outstripping the industry's capability. Faced with this dilemma, Rolls-Royce approached Lord Beaverbrook—as mentioned, newly appointed as the head of the Ministry of Aircraft Production in early May 1940—to advocate for having engine parts manufactured in the United States. The company only envisaged using the Americans as subcontractors for lesser-skilled tasks, and not for constructing the entire engine.

Beaverbrook, however, had far bigger plans for what effectively was to be an American shadow factory for the Merlin engine. These plans required immediate action, and he used his near-dictatorial powers to carry them out. On May 28, while British forces at Dunkirk were being evacuated, he phoned Arthur Sidgreaves, the head of Rolls-Royce, with instructions to pack up a complete set of blueprints and specifications for the Merlin 61 engine and await a special train, whose crew would pick them up. Beaverbrook would not give further details, saying only that the blueprints were going to the United States. He had decided that the entire engine, not just its parts, was going to be built there, without even a production license from Rolls-Royce. Other company executives were justifiably concerned at the one-sidedness of the deal with the Americans, but Sidgreaves brushed them off: "If their having the drawings would enable us to win the war, we would willingly give them without any claim," he wrote. "If we lose the war it certainly won't matter about the drawings."[48]

The next day, the 2,000 drawings—as well as a disassembled engine—were collected, crated, and transferred to a special train that immediately went to Greenock, a small Scottish port town just downriver from Glasgow. The train stopped at the wharves, where the crates were loaded onto motor launches that made straight for the battleship HMS *Revenge*, lying at the Home Fleet anchorage at the mouth of the Clyde River. This was what Beaverbrook could not tell Rolls-Royce, for *Revenge* was also carrying a large part of the nation's gold bullion to Canada for safekeeping. As soon as Churchill took office on May 10, 1940, he had begun transferring the nation's gold reserves, mostly at the Bank of England in London, to Martins Bank in Liverpool, where it was safer from German attack.

On May 20, *Revenge*, returning from escorting a convoy from Canada, docked at Liverpool. There, its crew spent almost a week loading £40 million in gold bullion, which arrived at the pier in a convoy from Martins Bank just a few blocks away. The gold shipment weighed 340 tons, not much for a battleship but a lot for sailors who had to hump up ramps and down narrow ladders carrying 5,000 wooden boxes, each with 120 pounds of ingots packed in sawdust to prevent loss by abrasion, and then find all the ship's nooks and crannies—in mess rooms, storerooms, ammunition lockers, and gun turrets—to store the precious cargo. The reason for Beaverbrook's haste in phoning Rolls-Royce on May 28 was that *Revenge* was due to sail for Greenock the following day, where it was to rendezvous with its escorts and immediately depart for Canada.

On May 30 at midnight, laden with boxes of bullion mixed in with crates of Merlin parts and blueprints, *Revenge* and its escorting destroyers left their anchorage and made for the Firth of Clyde, picking up two passenger ships filled with more gold and thousands of British evacuees, mostly children sent by their parents for safeguarding in the United States and Canada. The convoy then headed into the North Atlantic, at a time when U-boat activity was becoming increasingly perilous, for the dash to Halifax. Some of the gold aboard HMS *Revenge* would pay for turning the blueprints it carried into actual engines.[49]

To everyone's relief, it turned out to be an uneventful trip. *Revenge* and its convoy arrived at Halifax on June 7, and immediately upon docking, its gold was offloaded and transported by rail to the Bank of Canada in Ottawa. The bank's president, Morris W. Wilson, was at pierside, not to oversee the bullion transfer but rather to handle a far more valuable shipment— the blueprints and disassembled engine. Wilson, who was also the North American representative for the Ministry of Aircraft Production, had received a message from Beaverbrook, instructing him to pick up the Merlin blueprints and deliver them "forthwith" to Washington, telling the president that he was handing them over on Beaverbrook's authority for immediate use in aircraft engine production. "The rights of Rolls-Royce," Beaverbrook added, "can be left for subsequent determination and adjustment between the two countries." Upon boarding *Revenge* toting a single empty brief-case to carry the drawings, Wilson was "consternated" to find they were in two tons of large crates mixed in among the smaller bullion boxes. After recovering from his initial surprise, he delivered the plans to the offices of US treasury secretary Henry Morgenthau on June 13, while sending the disassembled engine to the Army Air Corps Materiel Division at Wright Field in Dayton, Ohio, which was responsible for aircraft procurement, testing and maintenance. Now came the question of who would build the American version of the Merlin engine.[50]

ARTHUR PURVIS, HEAD OF the British Purchasing Commission, went to Morgenthau's office on Tuesday, June 18 to explain Lord Beaverbrook's proposal to manufacture Merlins in Detroit. Morgenthau and William Knudsen, who had just taken his position as the head of the Advisory Commission on National Defense, agreed with the idea and considered Ford Motor Company best suited to undertake this; Ford was already building Merlin engines at its Trafford Park shadow factory in Manchester, and prior to the fall of France it had separately committed to build Merlins at its subsidiary Fordair factory in the Parisian suburb of Poissy. On that Friday, Knudsen, who had worked for Henry Ford in his younger days, approached his son, Edsel Ford, the company president, with the proposal. Edsel and his right-hand man, Charles Sorensen, flew to Washington, examined the plans, and agreed to the contract for 9,000 engines, which would power British, Canadian, and American bombers and fighters. Ford and Sorenson returned to Detroit, apparently with the deal set. Morgenthau arranged for the Secret Service to transport the Merlin plans under guard to Ford, while the Army Air Corps delivered the disassembled engine to the company.[51]

The following Monday, June 24, as Knudsen later recalled, Edsel Ford called him with bad news:[52]

"Bill, we can't make those motors for the British."

"Why?"

"Father won't do it."

"But you are president of the company."

"I know, but father won't do it, and you know how he is."

Henry Ford had originally endorsed the plan, but when he realized that the production would go directly to British instead of American service, he backed away from the agreement. Knudsen flew to Detroit that same day to personally entreat Henry, now seventy-seven years old and fiercely opposed to most anything Roosevelt did, especially helping the British war effort. Knudsen arrived at Edsel's office in the Ford Rouge factory, only to be told by Henry that, indeed, he wouldn't make motors for the British government. He would do it for the American government, or no one. "Let the American government take over the contract," said Ford, "and I will make all of them." Knudsen explained that this was not possible, but Ford was still having none of it. "You're mixed up with some bad people in Washington," Ford told his former employee, "and you're heading for trouble." "They want war," he kept repeating after Knudsen had left, according to those who were there.[53]

Crestfallen, Knudsen drove to his summer home in Grosse Isle for a few hours before returning to Washington. There he telephoned Alvin Macauley, chairman of the Packard Motor Car Company, and explained his dilemma. Packard, nominally a high-end luxury car manufacturer, had built aircraft engines during the previous war and was currently producing them for use in high-speed patrol boats, so it seemed to be a logical second choice. Within a few hours, the Packard president, Max Gilman, and chief engineer, Jesse Vincent, were at Knudsen's home listening to his story. Gilman's decision was immediate: "The Packard Motor Car Company would be glad to consider any proposal which [Knudsen] cared to place before us." With that answer, Knudsen left for the airport, and two days later Gilman and Vincent were in Washington to finalize the deal and begin planning for production of the 9,000 engines. On June 28, they were at the Ford plant to arrange for transfer of the Merlin drawings and engine to their Packard plant twelve miles away. Meanwhile, Packard began rearranging its drafting rooms and shop floor facilities for what they assumed would be a straightforward job of simply copying the British drawings and building the engines, to become Rolls-Royce's most distant shadow factory.[54]

The statement "Britain and America are two nations divided by a common language," which George Bernard Shaw never said (but should have), applied equally to the language of engineering. British draftsmen used first-angle projection for their engineering drawings, which showed parts and components in exactly the opposite configuration from the third-angle projection used by American draftsmen. In practice, for American shop-floor technicians to use British drawings would be like reading Leonardo da Vinci's backward handwriting to build his inventions. British draughtsmen also left out hundreds of details that their own shop foremen would know by heart. And the foremen themselves sometimes made "shop modifications" for ease of production that were not always included in the blueprints—a one-piece cylinder block on the blueprints, for example, turned out to be made of two halves when the engine was opened up. American shop floor practice, by contrast, demanded that every bolt hole, screw, and finish be precisely defined on the drawings, and that no change could be made without modifying the drawings.

Once they set about disassembling the Merlin engine to measure it, Packard engineers were mortified to discover that their British counterparts paid little heed to standardization. One part of the engine would have left-hand British Standard Fine screws, another would have right-hand British Standard Pipe screws. They also learned that British and American standards were simply incompatible, a problem that would continue to plague the combined forces through the rest of the war; one Army Air Forces mechanic stationed in Britain complained, "We can't borrow parts from the British. We can't even steal them. They don't fit."[55]

Packard discovered that fewer than 10 percent of its tools could be used to manufacture the Merlin; the company would have to take apart the engine, remeasure it, and completely redesign it for the American and British variants. For the British Merlins they kept the various British screw standards for interchangeability with Rolls-Royce models overseas, while for the Army Air Forces they changed to a uniform set of American War Standard screws. Packard then had to retool the plant so that its factory workers, many of whom had just recently been farm hands or housewives, could mass-produce the engines. Seventy-five engineers labored four months, from mid-July to November 1940, to take the 2,000 original drawings and create 2,500 new drawings, 60,000 new gauges, tools, and jigs, and hundreds of thousands of prints.[56]

Packard also cabled Rolls-Royce for further technical assistance. Sidgreaves, for his part, understood that Rolls-Royce's reputation was now inextricably linked to Packard. "Although this is a direct contract from the

Figure 1 *Left:* Chain Home radar towers, undated (Imperial War Museums).
Right: Trylon and Perisphere at New York Worlds Fair, 1938 (New York Public Library).

Figure 2 The beach at Dunkirk with abandoned British vehicles and arms, June 1944
(National Education Network)

Figure 3 Vannevar Bush at his desk, c. 1940–1944 (Library of Congress)

Figure 4 Some members of the Tizard Mission, c. October 1940. *Front row (left to right):* Frederick Campbell Wallace, Vera King, Ralph Fowler, unidentified. *Back row (left to right):* Arthur Edgar Woodward-Nutt, Henry Tizard, Hugh Webb Faulkner. John Cockcroft is likely holding the camera. (Imperial War Museums, with thanks to David Zimmerman for locating it)

Figure 5 Bennett Archambault in uniform at his desk at OSRD London Mission, undated (Michele Archambault)

Figure 6 "Willow Run," the US officers' mess at Grosvenor House Hotel, London, undated (Michele Archambault)

Figure 7 The OSRD London Mission office, undated (Michele Archambault)

Figure 8 Henry Tizard visiting the MIT Rad Lab, probably c. 1943. *Left to right:* Unidentified, Henry Tizard and Lee DuBridge. Tizard is touching a prototype cavity magnetron, DuBridge is holding a production model of the magnetron (MIT).

Figure 9 Cavity magnetron production model built by Western Electric (Creative Commons license)

Figure 10 B-17 Flying Fortress with H2X radar dome under belly, c. 1945 (National Museum of the U.S. Air Force)

Figure 11 RAF P-51 Merlin Mustang Mark III fighters over Sussex, April 1944 (Creative Commons license)

Figure 12 Lancaster bomber dropping chaff over Duisburg, October 1944 (Creative Commons license)

Figure 13 AN/PPN-1 Rebecca/Eureka beacon system for paratroop operations, 1943 (Naval History and Heritage Command)

Figure 14 Liberty ship SS *William Blount* leaves the Delta Shipbuilding Co. Yard, New Orleans, Louisiana, September 1942 (Naval History and Heritage Command)

Figure 15 African American welders Alivia Scott, Hattie Carpenter, and Flossie Burtos welding steel onto the Liberty ship SS *George Washington Carver*, Kaiser Shipyards, Richmond, California, 1943 (National Archives and Records Administration)

Figure 16 US Navy bombe operated by a WAVE, undated (Creative Common license)

Figure 17 Hedgehog Antisubmarine Projector, 1956 (Naval History and Heritage Command)

British government to the Packard Company and therefore Rolls-Royce carry no responsibility," he told Beaverbrook, "it is inevitable that the success of the undertaking will depend on Rolls-Royce and it is certain we shall be blamed for any failure or difficulties which may arise." In August 1940, despite the fact that his company could ill afford the loss of such talent, Sidgreaves sent to Detroit three of his top engineers: chief designer Thomas Barrington, development engineer James Ellor, and production engineer John Reid.

It took a full year for the first prototypes to be delivered for testing. On August 2, 1941, Packard held a transatlantic ceremony to deliver its first two test engines, one that had been built for the British, the other for the Americans. An RAF navigator, broadcasting from an underground studio in London, relayed the signal to Detroit to start both engines. British ambassador Edward Wood, Earl of Halifax, speaking over the deep roar on another radio circuit from Washington, DC, said, "That may seem to most who hear it not much more than a loud noise. But I can tell you it is sweet music in the ears of any man who has heard, as I have, the whistle and crump of German bombs." Initial testing continued through the end of 1941 and the American entry into the war. The first nine production engines, now designated the V-1650, came off the assembly lines in January 1942. The three Rolls-Royce men—Barrington, Ellor, and Reid—stayed on with Packard well after that, although Barrington died in the factory from a heart attack, in June 1943.[57]

Creating the Merlin Mustang

In April 1942, while Packard was tooling for the Merlin, the Army Air Forces reversed its decision of a month earlier regarding production of the P-51 at Inglewood, and placed an order for 500 Mustangs with Allison engines, to be used as dive-bombers and not as fighters. Apparently, the Americans still did not fully understand the Mustang's potential as a long-range interceptor and escort. It took the intervention of Thomas Hitchcock Jr., the American assistant air attaché in London who had described the aircraft as having a

British father and an American mother, to revive interest in the Merlin/ Mustang combination as such a fighter. Despite working a desk job at the embassy, Tommy Hitchcock was "a chase pilot—first, last, and always." After flying as an American volunteer in the French Air Force in World War One, he led the US polo team to numerous international victories. He also moved in the highest business and social circles (he was a family friend of the Roosevelts). His charm was legendary—his friend F. Scott Fitzgerald modeled one of his characters in *The Great Gatsby* after him. The self-confident Hitchcock had no trouble gaining the assistance of Gil Winant, the American ambassador in London, in promoting the Merlin/Mustang combination.[58]

When the Chief of the US Army Air Forces, General Henry "Hap" Arnold, came to London in June 1942, Hitchcock explained to him the advantages of a Merlin-equipped Mustang, based on Ronald Harker's assessment that such a combination would give "outstanding" performance. Meanwhile, Winant wrote to Roosevelt and Harry Hopkins, applying pressure on the Army Air Forces from above. Arnold needed no further convincing; he immediately ordered the Wright Field engineers to test "a prototype P-51 equipped with [a] Merlin 61." In November 1942, just six weeks after Rolls-Royce flew its first prototype, the first Packard-engined Mustang flew. After resolving some technical problems with the cooling system, the American version proved even more impressive than the original British model, topping out at 441 mph at 30,000 feet. Even with Hap Arnold's influence, however, the Materiel Division at Wright Field was not enthusiastic about what they saw as a "British project" that had not proceeded through the regular development steps of establishing an official requirement, bidding for contracts, and so forth. No specific requirement for long-range interceptors had yet come through official channels; the Merlin Mustang was an answer to a problem that the Army Air Forces had not yet acknowledged existed.

Hitchcock provided the final push to get the Merlin Mustang into production. Once again leveraging his social network and his charm, during a trip to the United States in November 1942 he described to President Roosevelt the British experience with the Merlin-equipped Mustang.

Roosevelt sent a note to Hap Arnold: "I am told by an American friend returning from England that the British are very keen about the P-51 and feel they could use Rolls-Royce engines in them. Do you know something about it? They tell me it is essentially similar in design to the Focke-Wulf Fw 190. Can you give me a tip?" Arnold passed the president's question to the head of the Materiel Division, telling him he needed production numbers right away. Roosevelt's simple question, the Wright Field engineers immediately and fully understood, was in fact an order. Within hours, Arnold received the production numbers he requested. He then replied to Roosevelt that the RAF was "very keen" on the P-51, and installed Rolls-Royce engines in two of them—one in Britain and one in the United States. "Tests indicate that they will be highly satisfactory pursuit planes for 1943," he noted, adding that they had already ordered about 2,200 of them. "They are similar in design to the Focke-Wulf 190 but we believe them to be a very much better airplane on account of their ruggedness, superior armament, and equal, if not better performance."[59]

This short exchange of notes ensured that all future combat models of the P-51, whether flown by the RAF or the American Army Air Forces, would be powered by Packard V-1650 Merlin engines. The American P-51s were crated at Inglewood beginning in August 1943 and arrived at Army Air Forces air bases in Britain a month later, while the RAF models (designated Mustang Mark III, Figure 11) began arriving in December. Meanwhile, Packard ramped up its production of the Merlin engine, hiring thousands of new workers from across the country. Many of them were African Americans who had left low-wage sharecropping in the South to get higher-paying jobs in the war factories up North. Many white workers resented the Black migrants taking "their" jobs, and in June 1943, 25,000 Packard workers went on strike for several days to protest the promotion of three Black workers. This was a prelude to the larger race riots that engulfed Detroit later that summer, though Packard avoided the worst of them. Despite this, Packard would emerge as the largest builder of Merlin engines on either side of the Atlantic. Over 55,000 Merlin engines were built there for American, Canadian, and British aircraft, and of these, 14,000 went to the P-51 Mustangs.[60]

Bombers Reach Berlin

By mid-1943, the elements for an all-out air campaign against Germany were in place. The Casablanca Conference, which had taken place in January between Churchill and Roosevelt and included Charles de Gaulle as the leader of the Free French forces, identified the war aim as "unconditional surrender" by the Axis. It also established the strategy for the European land campaign—first attack the "soft underbelly of Europe," Churchill's preferred phrase for Sicily and Italy, and then plan for a cross-Channel invasion of Europe through France. Continuing with Churchill's original strategy of "absolutely devastating, exterminating attack upon the Nazi homeland," the Combined Chiefs of Staff of Britain and the United States met during the conference to provide direction for the next phase of strategic bombing. Issued in February 1943, the Casablanca Directive called for a combined bomber offensive that would result in "the progressive destruction and dislocation of the German military, industrial and economic systems and the undermining of the morale of the German people to a point where their capacity for armed resistance is fatally weakened."[61]

Beginning with the industrial Ruhr Valley and moving east, Germany's military infrastructure, in particular its arms producers, was to be systematically destroyed by round-the-clock bombing. British aircraft would attack at night with area bombing (which they continued to call "blind bombing"), killing civilian factory workers and destroying their houses, thereby crippling their ability to man the factories and arsenals. Americans would come during daylight for precision attacks against the factories and arsenals themselves (they preferred the term "bombing through overcast" to avoid any negative connotations associated with "blind bombing"). Without any letup, the bombing, the theory went, would prevent the Germans from recovering and rebuilding their production capabilities.

Window and chaff became the first elements to tilt the advantage in the air toward the Allies. Both the British and Americans had been reluctant to use it for fear that once the Germans found the bits of foil, they would know how it worked and develop their own countermeasures (actually, German scientists had already developed their own chaff system, called

Düppel), but the combined offensive meant that aircrews were given the go-ahead. Britain first used it in raids over Hamburg and Essen in July and August 1943, and with great success; the loss rate for their bombers was cut by three-quarters. The German ground controllers monitoring their radars to direct the fighters were swamped; the echoes from the bombers were indistinguishable from the chaff, and the chaff blooms kept growing as the bomber crews dispensed more and more bundles down the chutes, where the wind broke the bundles apart and dispersed the foil strips into the surrounding air (Figure 12). British radio intercept operators heard the German controllers tell their fighter pilots to break off because the bombers were "multiplying themselves." The British government learned that the Germans knew about Window and chaff when they began receiving complaints through diplomatic channels that some German cows had died after eating the aluminum strips.[62]

The German military adjusted its tactics in response—for example, by deploying longer-wavelength radar that was unaffected by Window. This in turn led the Allies to develop new types of Window and chaff, as well as new jammers, in what became an unending struggle of measure/countermeasure between the two sides. British and American scientists at TRE and ABL-15 were continually gathering operational information from the returning pilots, coming up with new devices (like improved deployment chutes for chaff) and installing them on the aircraft, and helping devise new tactics. For example, the lead bombers turned out to be vulnerable to radar tracking—chaff blooms, when released, only protected the trailing aircraft—so bomber squadrons were preceded by a "chaff screening force" of fighters (typically Lockheed P-38 Lightnings and de Havilland Mosquitos) that would release chaff to protect the lead bombers as well.[63]

Meanwhile, Archambault and his team at the OSRD London Mission had their hands full bringing scientists from stateside to work on specific technical problems, acquiring a B-17 and a Cessna for full-time use by ABL-15 to test countermeasures equipment, and smoothing over the friction points that inevitably arose between the military and civilians as the call for new types of chaff and jammers grew. Window's "initial spectacular success," David Langmuir explained to Guy Suits in September 1943, just weeks after the Hamburg and Essen raids, "has been lessened considerably by the adjustment of the enemy tactically to the new situation, but the result has been only to increase the demand, not to cause abandonment of the weapon."[64]

Chaff and Window helped the bombers get through German air defenses, but it was airborne radar that got them to their targets. By late 1943, both British and Americans were employing 3-centimeter radars, respectively the H2S Mk III and H2X, and over 90 percent of the bombing raids were guided by those systems. Both air forces used similar tactics, employing pathfinder aircraft and markers. For the British night-bombing raids, pathfinder bombers equipped with H2S Mk III and precision navigation equipment like Gee and Oboe would lead the main bombing force. Once over the target, they would drop target indicator sky markers (parachute flares) and ground markers (dropped flares or incendiary bombs) giving off different colors to provide the other non-radar-equipped bombers their aim point. At ground level, the inhabitants knew that the dazzling fireworks displays dropping through the night sky (which they called, with some irony, "Christmas trees") were one of the last signals to get to their bunkers. They received no such final warning for the daylight raids carried out by the American bombers. B-17 and B-24 pathfinders, also equipped with Gee and Oboe in addition to H2X, marked their targets with indicator bombs that left smoke trails above the clouds as the visual cue for other bombers to drop.[65]

The American daylight raid on the Schweinfurt ball-bearing factories in October 1943, the second strike on that target in three months, was relatively accurate in terms of percentage of bombs hitting the targets; over half fell within 1,000 feet. Soon after arriving in Britain in January 1944 to take over the U.S. Strategic Air Forces in Europe (which absorbed the 8th Bomber Command and other European bomber commands), Lieutenant General Carl Spaatz wrote to Hap Arnold, expressing confidence in H2X and asking for more radar-equipped pathfinder bombers: "A few H2X airplanes now will profit our cause more than several hundred in six months."[66]

The division commander, Brigadier General Curtis LeMay, declared that such precision bombing ensured "complete destruction of each target on the first attempt, making it unnecessary to return later." At the same time, the Schweinfurt raid was among the costliest of the war. The bombers had flown well past the range of their P-47 Thunderbolt escort fighters and were "mauled," according to the official Eighth Army Air Force history, by German fighters as they approached the city. Out of almost 300 B-17s, 60 were downed with their crews, and another 138 were damaged. Moreover, the raid (like the previous one) had little long-term impact on production; the factories restarted in just weeks. This kind of campaign could not be sustained; as the same official history stated, "The cost of such deep penetrations by daylight without fighter escort was too high to be consistently borne." No more daylight penetrations deep into German airspace were possible until late 1943 and early 1944, when shiploads of the long-range P-51 Mustangs began arriving by the hundreds each week (tragically, Tommy Hitchcock died in April 1944, while test-piloting one of the new P-51B production models).[67]

The arrival of the Mustangs in both RAF and American squadrons coincided with a renewed effort by the new Eighth Army Air Force commander, Major General James H. Doolittle, to pursue the campaign of "progressive destruction and dislocation" called for at the Casablanca Conference. Operation Pointblank, as it was called, depended upon the Merlin Mustang fighters, which were escorting the bomber squadrons, to pursue and destroy German fighters and their increasingly exhausted and inexperienced pilots. In January 1944, on one of the first deep raids escorted by Mustangs, a group of B-17s were left without protection when the escorting fighter squadrons went after a group of German fighters. One of the P-51 pilots, James H. Howard (a veteran of the Flying Tigers, a group of American volunteer pilots formed to oppose the Japanese invasion of China), returned to guard the B-17s, and found himself fighting alone against thirty Bf 109s, Bf 110s, and FW 190s. For thirty minutes, he and his Merlin Mustang outflew his opponents, downing or crippling six German fighters while spoiling repeated attacks on the bombers. He only broke off when three of his four guns jammed. When he returned to base, his squadron counted 15 kills and no losses. Howard was hailed in the press as the "One Man Air Force" and was awarded the Medal of Honor.[68]

A month after Howard's exploits, in late February 1944, the Army Air Forces and RAF launched Operation Argument, better known as "Big Week," which saw continuous day-and-night attacks far into Germany. As with the Schweinfurt raids, the actual bomb damage to German industries during Big Week was only modest, in part for one of the same reasons the Blitz failed to cripple British manufacturing—machine tools are notoriously hard to destroy. The real intent of the Big Week campaign was to begin, in anticipation of D-Day, the steep attrition of the Luftwaffe's pipeline of trained airmen, as Mustang pilots systematically downed Germany's aces.[69]

The Merlin Mustang—especially when fitted with drop fuel tanks that greatly extended its combat range and more accurate Sperry K-14 gyroscopic gunsights copied from the British Ferranti Mark II—went on to play a critical role as escort in other bombing raids. The most famous missions were made by the all-Black 332nd Fighter Group, the Red Tails of the Tuskegee Airmen, where in raids throughout Germany and into Austria, Poland, Romania, and Yugoslavia, their P-51s escorted bombers that knocked out oil refineries that supplied the Luftwaffe, and destroyed railroad marshaling yards that disrupted the Nazi supply lines. Tuskegee Airmen joined other pilots in the belief that the P-51 was the finest long-range fighter of the war, a belief that went all the way to the top of the chain of command. In congressional testimony after the war, Hap Arnold admitted that they could have used the P-51 in Europe earlier, and that this "was the Air Force's own fault." Nonetheless, continued Arnold, "one of the great 'miracles' of the war was the fact that the full long-range fighter escort did appear over Germany at just the saving moment, in the very nick of time to keep our bomber offensive going without a break."[70]

Berlin was the target for the raids in early March 1944. They were as bloody for the Allies as the Schweinfurt raid, with 70 bombers lost in one day. The Mustangs were even deadlier, however. The newest Bf 109s and Fw 190s were technically on par with the P-51s, but the aggressive approach taken by American and British pilots gave the Mustang the edge.

The Germans lost 160 aircraft and crew that same day. Meanwhile, more American planes kept arriving even as German aircraft factories were razed to the ground and much of the population was made homeless. The Berlin campaign did not end the war, which continued for another year despite the continued bombing, and had little impact on its outcome. British and American post hoc histories of Allied strategic bombing noted the failure of area bombing campaigns, like those on Berlin, to materially affect civilian morale. They also noted the inability of raids like those at Schweinfurt to halt war production. Yet those same histories also credited precision bombing with the destruction of key German industries, notably oil and munitions, which contributed to the wholesale collapse of the Nazi regime in 1945.[71]

In interviews by the Allies after their surrender, the German high command also viewed the combination of British/American radar-led bombers and long-range Mustang fighters as an Allied success. Albert Speer, Hitler's minister of armaments and the man who mobilized the Nazi war economy, told his British and American captors that the war "was decided through attacks from the air," and that the "system of assault[s] on industrial targets were by far the most dangerous." The bombing attacks "caused the breakdown of the German armaments industry." His testimony was corroborated by Hermann Goering—who never did call himself "Meier" after the Ruhr was bombed to rubble—during his interrogation by Carl Spaatz.[72]

SPAATZ: "Which had the more effect in the defeat of Germany, the area bombing or the precision bombing?"

GOERING: "The precision bombing, because it was decisive. Destroyed cities could be evacuated, but destroyed industry was difficult to replace.

SPAATZ: "When did you know that the Luftwaffe was losing control of the air?"

GOERING: "When the American long-range fighters were able to escort the bombers as far as Hanover, and it was not long until they got to Berlin."

SPAATZ: "Could Germany have been defeated by airpower alone, using England as a base, without invasion?"

GOERING: "No, because German industry was going underground, and our countermeasures could have kept pace with your bombing. The land invasion meant that so many workers had to be withdrawn from factories' production and even from the Luftwaffe."

Goering's testimony was a vindication of Churchill's overall strategy against the Nazis, which began by sending bombers to Germany "to pulverise the entire industry," though, as Churchill foresaw, this alone would never lead Germany to surrender. But even before the next phases of Churchill's plan could come into effect, those bombers would still have to return through British air defenses and arrive safely on their landing grounds.

CHAPTER 4

FIGHT ON THE
LANDING GROUNDS

GETTING BOMBERS AND their escorting fighters to their targets over Europe was only half the battle; those aircraft still had to return, more or less intact, to their home bases in Britain. First, they had to pass through the British Chain Home defense system, designed to keep out enemy aircraft. They then had to locate their airfields (tarmac) and landing grounds (usually grass) and touch down, sometimes even in darkness and poor flying conditions.

The first problem was that of being mistaken for the enemy and attacked by your own forces, a problem as old as warfare itself. In 1758 during the Seven Years' War, George Washington, then a young British colonial officer, was leading a Virginia regiment when he mistook another Virginia regiment for their French adversaries; the resulting melee killed or wounded forty men before both sides realized their mistake. The nineteenth-century Prussian strategist Carl von Clausewitz (best known for stating "War is the continuation of politics by other means") used the term "fog," later translated as "fog of war," to describe the problem of losing one's bearings in battle. This sometimes resulted in accidentally shooting at your own troops. By World War One, the term "friendly fire" was used to describe this problem, which now extended beyond ground troops and into the air. In March 1918, Robert Gregory of the Royal Flying Corps was mistakenly shot down by an Allied Italian pilot. His family friend William Butler Yeats immortalized the tragedy in his poem "An Irish Airman Foresees His Death," giving Gregory voice: "I know that I shall meet my fate / Somewhere among the clouds above / Those that I fight I do not hate / Those that I guard I do not love."[1]

In the British Isles, the term "fog of war" was not merely metaphorical. British skies were (and are) notorious for being darkened for days on end by clouds, mist, and rain. Bombers and fighters could take off in such weather; landing was a different matter. RAF Bomber Command, which operated primarily at night, did not fly missions if their meteorologists forecast that the ceiling over British bases would be less than 1,000 feet during the return flight. The US 8th Bomber Command, which flew daylight raids, did not sortie if the return ceiling was forecast to be less than 500 feet. For these reasons, half of all bomber missions that were cancelled were scrubbed due to overcast skies over Britain, not the skies over the target. With cloud decks so low, the anti-aircraft gunners surrounding the bases might have just moments to determine the identity of the approaching aircraft, and a split-second mistake could cost dozens of lives.[2]

Identifying Friend from Foe

Robert Watson-Watt's 1935 memorandum to the Tizard Committee, a memorandum that he later called the "birth certificate of radar," had laid out a complete description of what would become Britain's Chain Home system. Toward the end of the memo, he recognized the need to discriminate between British fighters from German bombers, giving it the initials IFF, Identification Friend or Foe. In the 1937 Air Exercises, a primitive form of IFF was tested in conjunction with Chain Home. Called Pip-Squeak after a popular cartoon strip, it employed the fighter's voice radio setup to send out a periodic tone that would be triangulated by ground-based receivers to determine the fighter's position, which would be then relayed to the filter rooms, where plotters would mark their locations. Though simple in design, in battle exercises Pip-Squeak proved too cumbersome for the plotters, and also interrupted the aircraft's voice radio, the vital link between pilots and the ground.[3]

Even before Pip-Squeak was introduced, Watson-Watt's team had been working on a more reliable, less cumbersome alternative, which he described as "a small device, later to be called by the horrific U.S. coined name of transponder [a portmanteau of 'transmitter' and 'responder'], which would receive the questioning pulses of the radar system." When illuminated by a Chain Home radar, the friendly aircraft transponder would send out return signals every few seconds, so that the radar operator's scope would identify "friend" as having an amplified, pulsating return, while a "foe" would have a smaller but constant return. The first transponder system, labeled IFF Mark I, was successfully tested in August 1939, just before Germany invaded Poland. Within hours of the British declaration of war on September 3, the first friendly fire incidents occurred. In one, a French airplane flying over the Channel was taken to be hostile, causing Londoners to scramble to their bomb shelters. In another, a flight of Blenheim bombers returning from a raid on Hamburg was targeted by British anti-aircraft guns, which fortunately missed. In a third, sardonically labeled "The Battle of Barking Creek," squadrons of Hurricanes and Spitfires mistook each other for Luftwaffe fighters, resulting in two downed aircraft and one pilot killed. These incidents underlined the importance of IFF, and an order for 1,000 Mark I sets was immediately placed with the Ferranti Limited electronic company in Manchester.[4]

These first IFF Mark I sets were tuned to the Chain Home radar wavelengths, but British aircraft would also need to run the gauntlet of Royal Navy and British Army radars, which were used for targeting anti-aircraft guns and set to different wavelengths. Even before the Mark I sets were produced, a new IFF transponder—the Mark II—was in production by Ferranti, using a complex system of motors, cams, and gears to automatically tune the system through the different wavelength settings. By the time the Battle of Britain commenced in July 1940, Mark I and Mark II transponders were available, but both were still problem-ridden and often did not respond to a friendly radar signal. By this time, IFF development had fallen under the Telecommunications Research Establishment (TRE) Group 14, a small team of ten scientists and engineers, led first by Freddie Williams and then by Vivian Bowden. Bowden, like many of his radar colleagues on both sides of the Atlantic, had been a nuclear physicist prior to the war, but academic research had not prepared him for the battle that lay ahead. He later told the story of how Hugh Dowding, commander of Fighter Command, had called him to his office in the summer of 1941, about an apparent failure of an IFF system:[5]

"You are in charge of this new identification system, aren't you?"

"Yes, Sir, I have been for three weeks," I replied.

"Well, last Saturday night, a Stirling Bomber came back from a raid on the Ruhr. It got lost, and it was assumed to be hostile. Two Beaufighters went to intercept it. One of them shot it down, and then it was itself shot down by the other Beaufighter. Two aircraft and a dozen lives lost! What are you going to do about it?"

And I think it was at that moment that for the first time in my life, I realised the fundamental difference between science and engineering, and between war and both of them.

Bowden responded promptly to Dowding's demand. The Group 14 team was much smaller than the other TRE groups devoted to radar, so they "worked night and day," as Bowden put it, to produce a simpler, more reliable IFF system. Williams and Bowden had already recognized the impossibility of trying to identify the increasing number of new radars, which had a bewildering variety of wavelengths. Instead, the new IFF Mark III would operate on a single, separate wavelength; every radar in ground stations, anti-aircraft guns, and ships would be fitted with a new IFF transmitter (an "interrogator"), while each aircraft would have a dedicated transponder that would respond only to that wavelength. Once again, they worked with

Ferranti to build working models, and after testing in August 1941 they were ready to begin production. But the requirements were daunting: for "every unit and every craft or vehicle to identify itself to every other, even so far as tank to tank," required "a hundred thousand aircraft sets, a thousand large ground installations, ten thousand smaller ground installations." Even then, it was evident to Bowden that "so many IFF sets were needed" that it would be necessary to mass-produce them in the United States.[6]

Of course, getting access to mass production in the United States was one of the stated goals of the Tizard Mission, which reached Washington in September 1940, just as the Battle of Britain was giving way to the Blitz. Tizard's colleagues Edward Bowen and John Cockcroft had included one of the IFF Mark II models in the crates of equipment they shipped across the Atlantic in August (Mark III was not yet off the drawing boards), but its arrival was delayed until late November 1940, just when Tizard himself was on the verge of returning to Britain. Bowen agreed to remain in the United States at MIT's newly formed Rad Lab, and he was placed in charge of demonstrating the Mark II's capabilities. The Americans were skeptical, not because they doubted what British scientists told them, but because they had a better IFF system already in the works. Early in the development of the CXAM early-warning radar by the Naval Research Laboratory (NRL) in Washington, American engineers had built an accompanying IFF system, Model XAE, whose interrogation and retransmission signals operated on a unique wavelength from the radar—essentially the same concept that the British were using for their Mark III system, still on the drawing boards. XAE had been first tested in 1937, with prototypes installed aboard ships in 1938 and tested in fleet exercises in 1939. By mid-1940, NRL joined the Army Signal Corps Aircraft Radio Laboratory to develop a model suitable for both services, designated Mark IV, which would be built by General Electric Company. The American scientists were confident that their IFF model would be superior to the Mark II system that the Tizard scientists had demonstrated.[7]

The military, however, demanded a working system as soon as possible, rather than a potentially better system a year or more in the future (the Mark IV unit for the early-warning radar at Pearl Harbor, which might have alerted the operators that the Japanese planes were not friendly, was still on back order when the attack happened). Since the British Mark II was already in full-scale production, NRL agreed to have the unit tested aboard a US Navy fighter. Bowen oversaw the modification and installation of the IFF Mark II by navy technicians, then witnessed as it was test-flown in November 1940 against NRL's CXAM radar, at a distance of 90 miles. NRL's chief radar scientist Hoyt Taylor told Bowen that "he understood the vital importance of a common method of radar identification between British and US Forces, [and] was satisfied that this was the equipment to use."[8]

While the scientists and engineers at NRL and the Army Signal Corps agreed on the "vital importance" of a single IFF system, not all were not convinced that it should be the Mark II. To resolve this impasse, a Conference on Coordination of American and British IFF was held at the British Central Scientific Office in Washington on July 1, 1941. There, the Americans complained of the same reliability problems that had so angered Dowding during the Battle of Britain. The British representatives, which included Watson-Watt, countered that they were aware of the problems and were addressing them with the new Mark III; furthermore, they argued, the American system operated at a wavelength close to the German Würzburg radar and would therefore be easy to fool. The discussions dragged on through the rest of the year, almost reaching an unhappy compromise in December, by which American aircraft in the Atlantic would have carried both US and British IFF sets, while Pacific aircraft would only have had American sets. That compromise was chucked out the window right after Pearl Harbor, when the Americans found themselves without an operational system. They immediately made the unilateral decision to simply adopt and mass-produce the British Mark II for the near term, while working jointly with Britain to co-develop the improved IFF Mark III for the long term.[9]

IF THE AMERICANS HAD dragged their feet before Pearl Harbor, they lost no time afterward. On December 11, just four days after the attack, the Army Signal Corps Aircraft Radio Laboratory summoned the vice president of engineering of Philco Corporation, along with three other engineers, to

Wright Field in Dayton, Ohio, for a secret meeting. The army officers asked them if they could redesign and begin mass production of the British IFF Mark II in just four weeks. Philco, best known for the elegant "cathedral radios" around which many Americans gathered nightly to hear Roosevelt's fireside chats, hardly seemed the obvious choice. However, another electronics company had told the army that coming up with a new design would take eight months, and by that point American military leaders were already planning for a rapid buildup in Europe and naval campaigns in the Pacific. Unusually for most mass-production electronics companies at the time, Philco had extensive research and development facilities, which enabled them to rapidly design, prototype, and test new systems. Their engineers promised to deliver two working IFF sets to Wright Field within thirty days. The Signal Corps quickly modified the British sets they had to American radar wavelengths, and Philco engineers rushed the sets back to the headquarters in Philadelphia. The company's postwar booklet picks up the story from there:[10]

Engineers called conferences, scoured the country for special parts, designed others in locked laboratories. Soon a picked production crew from the Philco automobile radio plant in Sandusky, Ohio was working night and day under armed guard in one of the company's Philadelphia plants. On December 27, 1941, just 14 days after the job was begun, the first two radar models had been completed and were being tested by Philco engineers. Four days later, 24 additional IFF equipments were about 90% completed.

That was on New Year's Eve. To rush these secret aircraft radar sets to Wright Field, Philco asked the Pennsylvania Railroad to couple a special baggage car on the *Spirit of St. Louis*. Feverishly, engineers and production men loaded IFF radar sets and test apparatus aboard this baggage car while the *Spirit* paused impatiently at North Philadelphia station. As the *Spirit* sped across sleeping Pennsylvania and Ohio, Philco engineers and production men, protected by armed guards, celebrated the New Year by setting up laboratory equipment in the baggage car, and by completing production and testing on the unfinished IFF radar sets.

On the morning of January 1, with the Baggage Car Laboratory safe on a siding at Dayton, Philco engineers marched into the office of an Army officer at Wright

Field and presented him with two completed IFF sets. His amazement was un-printable, especially when he was told about the Baggage Car Laboratory . . . ready to work on flight tests and modifications . . . and the other 24 radar sets. . . . A total of 26 complete sets, instead of the two promised, in three weeks, instead of a month.

While the Signal Corps was testing the redesigned IFF system—now designated SCR-535, able to sweep through multiple wavelengths of British and American radars, both army and navy—Philco received purchase orders totaling 20,000 sets, worth over a billion dollars in today's currency. The company made an "all-out effort," as its vice president proudly told the army, and by the end of January 1942 it had converted its Sandusky car radio plant to full-scale manufacture of IFF (sales of commercial automobiles had been halted on January 1 by order of the Office of Production Management, so Philco's entire Ohio facility was available for military work). The first B-17 bombers arriving in Europe in 1942 were all equipped with the SCR-535 transponders. Meanwhile, the IFF Mark IV sets were held in reserve in case any of the Philco sets were captured and exploited by the enemy, but never were used in service.[11]

Most of the IFF sets had been intended for bombers and fighters headed to a rapid buildup of American forces in Britain, but by February, the Japanese assaults in the Philippines, Singapore, and the East Indies forced the United States to divert manpower and equipment to the Pacific. Getting the new IFF equipment to the Pacific-based aircraft carriers was daunting, since the ships had been at sea almost continually since the start of the war. For the carriers *Lexington* and *Yorktown*, which had not been at Pearl Harbor and had escaped destruction, only six of their 130 aircraft had SCR-535 sets by May 1942, when they were directed to interdict a Japanese invasion of New Guinea and the Solomon Islands. The ensuing Battle of the Coral Sea, the first major engagement between opposing fleet aircraft carriers, stopped the Japanese invasion but resulted in heavy damage to the American fleet. The lack of IFF played a central role in this; *Lexington* was first struck by torpedoes dropped from Nakajima B5N2 "Kate" torpedo bombers that had approached to within 400 yards. The Japanese bombers were not initially identified as hostile because the carrier had just launched several aircraft that resembled them. More torpedoes and bombs hit *Lexington*, which eventually sank, and throughout the rest of the battle, American gunners continually opened fire on returning planes, resulting in more friendly aircraft than Japanese being shot down.[12]

The value of IFF was shown just one month later, at the Battle of Midway. The Japanese Navy set its sights on using Midway Island as a jumping-off point for further attacks on Hawaii and the American Pacific fleet. The US Navy decrypted Japanese messages, deciphered their plans for invasion, and laid a trap with its remaining Pacific fleet carriers. *Yorktown*, which had been heavily damaged at Coral Sea but hastily patched up, steamed in company with *Hornet* and *Enterprise* to ambush the four attacking Japanese carriers. By now, all of *Enterprise*'s fighters and over half of *Hornet*'s were fitted with the SCR-535 IFF sets. Since *Yorktown* had far fewer IFF-equipped aircraft, the air officer arranged the squadrons so that each fighter section would have one IFF-equipped aircraft. On June 4, 1942, during the first Japanese counterattack after the destruction of three of its carriers, dive-bombers from the remaining carrier, *Hiryu*, were identified as hostile by *Yorktown*'s CXAM radar, which could distinguish them from friendly aircraft carrying the IFF transponder that were then returning along the same bearing at about the same time. This meant that *Yorktown* was able to launch aircraft to break up the attack and better prepare the ship for action; although hit and damaged, it was not crippled by a surprise attack, as had happened to *Lexington*, and was able to fight through the rest of the battle. (It was, however, sunk two days later by a Japanese submarine.)[13]

Despite the success of the IFF Mark II, both Britain and the United States understood by mid-1942 that it was only a stopgap measure until the improved Mark III, which used a separate wavelength for identification, was available. In theory, it was a straightforward task to remove the motorized tuning system from the old Mark II aircraft transponder and substitute one tuned to a single wavelength. The challenge lay in developing the corresponding system in ground or shipboard radar stations, which required a radar interrogator that would "ping" the aircraft transponder, and a responder that received the signal and displayed it on the radar scope. Ferranti continued that work in Britain, but many more IFF Mark III sets were needed from the United States. Radio set manufacturers had become the obvious choice for IFF mass production. Just before the war's outbreak, America accounted for half of the world's 90 million radio sets, and these manufacturers would have plenty of reserve capacity when commercial production plummeted after war broke out. In October 1941, the army and navy selected the Hazeltine Corporation in Little Neck, Long Island, to be the prime contractor for IFF sets. Like Philco, Hazeltine manufactured radios but also had a substantial research and development arm, which garnered it an early contract for mine detection. Hazeltine's contract was to re-design the Mark III sets for production to operate with US Army and Navy radars. The latest British sets from Ferranti were delivered to Hazeltine in October under armed guard, and the entire project was classified as secret.[14]

After Pearl Harbor, Hazeltine went on a six-day-per-week schedule, with over a hundred engineers doing the redesign, prototyping, and testing of the transponder and interrogator-responder sets, while two Chicago subcontractors, Belmont Radio and Wells-Gardner, would mass-produce them (Philco soon became a third subcontractor). Vivian Bowden and five TRE engineers arrived from Britain to assist Hazeltine with the circuit designs, while the first tests of the system were performed in June 1942 at an army base in Sandy Hook, New Jersey. Two models of the American variant of the Mark III, the Navy SCR-595 and the Army SCR-695, went into full production in October, with an initial order of 18,000 Navy and 62,000 Army sets. They entered service the following year, 1943. While Ferranti was able to build 85,000 Mark III sets for use in British and Canadian forces, US manufacturers (Hazeltine, Belmont Radio, Philco, Motorola, and others) produced 150,000 Army and Navy IFF sets—the single largest electronics order in the nation, worth several times the value of all the radar systems then under construction in the United States.[15]

THE MARK III BECAME the universal Allied IFF of World War Two, eventually installed on practically every ship and aircraft in British, Canadian, and American service—and even a few in Soviet aircraft. It also had significant shortcomings, which were recognized very early in its development. At the top of the list was the fact that it could be fooled by an enemy radar that happened to transmit at the correct wavelength and therefore registered on the scope as a "friend" (as noted, the British had rejected the original American IFF system because it operated too close to the frequency of the German Würzburg radar, conveniently overlooking the fact that their own system was close to the Freya radar). Mark III also had problems handling large numbers of aircraft, and could not pinpoint where the IFF signal was coming from, so radar operators had trouble figuring out which parts of the sky defending aircraft should avoid to reduce the chance of friendly fire. In a meeting with Vannevar Bush in March 1942, Watson-Watt was the first to propose creating a new IFF system to tackle these problems, as part of an Allied effort under a joint British-Canadian-American working committee.

Until this point, IFF had been deployed without much involvement of the Office of Scientific Research and Development (OSRD). However, the development of the new Allied system—designated IFF Mark V, since the Mark IV was never fielded—now was led by an OSRD office under Alfred Loomis's Microwave Committee. Loomis, in turn, established the IFF Group in MIT Rad Lab's Division 7, headed by Luis Alvarez. When Rad Lab's Isidor Rabi and Edward Purcell visited Britain in July 1942 to discuss the H2S microwave radar, they also came to an agreement with the British to consolidate the joint research program on the IFF Mark V in the United States. Within weeks, NRL was chosen as the site for the new IFF laboratory, a 60,000-square-foot facility hurriedly built to house the Combined Research Group of American, Canadian, and British scientists. The project was deemed so important that Vivian Bowden and four of his TRE colleagues were permanently assigned to NRL, while Bowden's second-in-command, Rennie Whitehead, took over IFF development at TRE. Because the new system would incorporate secret codes in the signal to prevent enemy spoofing, the IFF Mark V was considered "particularly sacred from the standpoint of military security," as the official MIT history reported. Alvarez's group at Rad Lab had been working on the system for about six months when they offered to travel en masse to NRL in the fall of 1942 to speed development. Their offer was rejected, because the Navy had decided that the project was so secret that only a handful of engineers from outside the laboratory would be granted access.[16]

It was inevitable that friction would develop between the two IFF factions, those in favor of all-out mass production of the current Mark III and those supporting development of the more secure Mark V. There was scant mention of this dilemma in April 1943 during Karl Compton's mission, which established the British Branch of the Radiation Laboratory (BBRL), but it took center stage at the follow-up British Radar Mission to the United States in late November and early December. Watson-Watt and Bowden spoke for both NRL and the British contingent in arguing for continued development of the Mark V to replace what they saw as an outdated system. Watson-Watt, never shy of hyperbole in the name of his cause, claimed that "our friendlies are killing one another in the air faster than our enemies. Thus, identification of friendlies is a prime necessity." While the recent invasion of Sicily involved several incidents where non-IFF-equipped gliders were shot down by friendly fire, it had never reached the epidemic proportions depicted by Watson-Watt. Lee DuBridge spoke for Rad Lab and many in the American military who questioned the need for an entirely new system, when troops were only just now receiving the Mark III and learning how to use it properly.[17]

A compromise was reached where both sides agreed to increase research for the Mark V while improving the Mark III. While the Combined Research Group continued its work (Bowden would be replaced in summer 1944 by the just-married Rennie Whitehead, who spent his honeymoon in Washington, DC, where he was very impressed by American air-conditioning), demands for more IFF Mark III units during the invasion of Europe, coupled with delays in research, meant that the Mark V system did not start limited production at Hazeltine until after the end of the war.[18]

Although the Mark III IFF was hardly a panacea—it was susceptible to being fooled by an enemy transmitter, or it could be inadvertently switched off or fail at a crucial moment—its almost universal use by Allied forces had a marked effect on operations around the world. Vivian Bowden, who was as much the "father" of IFF as Watson-Watt was of radar, related that Admiral Chester Nimitz, commander in chief of the US Pacific Fleet, "sent a signal to the engineers who were responsible for Mark III IFF to inform them that the Americans could not have captured Guadalcanal without it."

A modern study of friendly fire found that Allied aircraft that were fitted with IFF transponders suffered comparatively few friendly fire casualties—just fifteen incidents recorded (including the aforementioned gliders in Sicily), compared with over a hundred friendly fire incidents from ground troops, who often did not have IFF fitted. The British-American IFF system was even more effective than Germany's version, which was fitted to their Freya and Würzburg radars. In the last four months of 1943, the Allies shot down 967 Luftwaffe pilots over Germany, but 1,052 were shot down by the Germans themselves.[19]

Blind Navigation

IFF saved many Allied pilots from being downed by friendly fire, but these pilots faced another challenge when returning to their bases in friendly territory—the weather. Bad weather at home, as noted, cut down on the number of missions flown; it also meant that returning aircrews, often exhausted and traumatized, would sometimes get lost in conditions of fog, poor visibility, or overcast skies, resulting in forced or crash landings, and might even disappear completely. Overall, one aircraft in every 140 landings would crash or experience an accident on approach, and while this was much lower than the average 3 percent combat loss rate, it nevertheless added to the mental and physical toll on pilots and aircrew. David Langmuir at the OSRD London Mission, although primarily focused on countermeasures to make sure bombers were not shot down in the air over Germany, was equally aware of the dangers he saw at the other end of their mission. As he told Lee DuBridge at MIT Rad Lab in January 1943, "The need for improved ability to fly in bad weather in England" had become "most urgent."[20]

Bad weather affected American and British aircrews alike. An American brigadier general, writing after the war, complained about the thick fog and heavy overcast: "It is quite possible that the entire Eighth Air Force could be lost on a single afternoon by returning to England and finding all bases socked in." A recent history of 1 Group, the oldest of six RAF Bomber

Command groups, offers blow-by-blow accounts of crashes while landing. To take one particularly harrowing day as an example, on December 17, 1943, a group of bombers was returning to base from Berlin when bad weather unexpectedly closed in, bringing the cloud base almost down to the ground. Unable to see each other, two Lancasters collided while circling the airfield in opposite directions. Sixteen bombers were diverted from their primary airfields in Yorkshire and Nottinghamshire, of which five crashed, two made emergency landings, and one, whose crew could not find the landing ground and abandoned by parachute, was left to crash-land. That night, 1 Group lost a total of thirteen aircraft, killing fifty-nine men, including one Lancaster that circled in the gloom for forty-five minutes before running out of fuel and crashing into trees. The same story played out with 5 Group, based further south in Cambridgeshire, which lost seven aircraft in crashes due to the "vile and unexpected" weather conditions.[21]

Blind navigation systems had been developed in the interwar years, long before blind bombing became a subject of strategic importance, because aircraft were flying increasingly long distances to airfields around the world. During this period, blind navigation—flying without reference to visible landmarks—was accomplished by a combination of dead reckoning, celestial navigation, and radio direction-finding. Dead reckoning estimated the current location of the aircraft by accounting for the speed and direction after the last established position, so was notoriously unreliable, especially when winds were highly variable or the aircraft ran into unexpected conditions. Celestial navigation used the same basic instruments—the sextant and chronometer—that sailors had been using for 200 years to "shoot" the sun and stars, with almanacs providing the tabular data needed to do the calculations. As with ships at sea, unsteady motions and cloudy skies could make accurate sightings almost impossible. Radio direction-finding (DF) was relatively new, and therefore many pilots and navigators were unfamiliar with the systems. It used a loop antenna that swiveled to locate the bearing to known radio transmitters, which could be plotted to provide the aircraft's position. The early types of D/F used long-wavelength, low-frequency radio waves that could travel great distances but did not provide much accuracy. Amelia Earhart and Fred Noonan used such a system on their attempted round-the-world flight, and their disappearance has been ascribed in part to their unfamiliarity with the device.

Problems with blind navigation were evident even before the war's outbreak. During the two years prior to hostilities, according to RAF Bomber Command records, 478 aircraft on nighttime cross-country training flights in England—friendly and well-known territory—had become lost and were forced to land far from their bases. In wartime, over unfamiliar territory, the situation would become far worse. Bomber navigators, unlike their civilian counterparts, couldn't use celestial navigation because combat maneuvering (to avoid flak, for example) made sextant sightings almost impossible. Frequent course and speed changes also made dead reckoning highly problematic. Even in the best of circumstances, navigation was demanding both physically and mentally—a former pilot noted that doing it would "be difficult in the swivel-chair comfort of your office," let alone in an office reduced to "a five-foot cube size" that was engulfed in a constant roar of engines and operating at five miles off the ground. Yet, he added, "these are the conditions under which these men worked out the higher mathematical relationships . . . of altitude, wind drift, airspeed, groundspeed, position, and direction."[22]

The immediate solution to the blind navigation problem, which used simultaneous radio waves broadcast from transmitters located at great distances from each other, was arrived at by two engineers working simultaneously on opposite sides of the Atlantic. In 1938, William O'Brien, working for Douglas Aircraft Corporation in the United States, and Robert Dippy of TRE in Great Britain (neither knew the other) both hit upon the idea of fitting aircraft with receivers that could accurately measure the difference between two or more synchronized radio signals emitted from ground transmitters separated by dozens of miles. When plotted on a map, the differences between the radio signals formed a series of curved lines of position called hyperbolas, which is why the method is called hyperbolic radio navigation. The navigator would determine which hyperbolic lines his aircraft was on. Where the two lines intersected was his actual position. Although the principle was the same, O'Brien's system compared the phases of continuous radio waves, while Dippy's compared the timing of radio pulses.[23]

Neither system was adopted initially, but both were resurrected soon after the start of the war, when RAF Bomber Command was switching to nighttime operations after a disastrous series of daylight raids and needed a reliable blind-bombing system. O'Brien sent his proposal to friends at the Decca Gramophone Company in London, which forwarded it to Watson-Watt, who was Dippy's boss at TRE. Shortly thereafter, Dippy submitted his own proposal to Watson-Watt. Watson-Watt rejected O'Brien's Decca proposal as being prone to jamming, but he gave approval to Dippy's proposal for development. TRE called Dippy's system "Gee" for grid because (as noted in Chapter 3) the hyperbolic radio lines formed a grid pattern on a special navigational chart. TRE began testing it in late 1940, about the same time that the Tizard Mission brought news of the system to the Americans.[24]

The first Gee ground stations were established in July 1941, and a month later, TRE successfully installed and tested handmade Gee receivers on twelve Wellington bombers. After bringing Gee into full-scale production, it was first used in combat in March 1942, in raids against Essen, Lubeck, Rostock, and Cologne. Its limitations for long-range precision bombing were soon clear, however, in terms of both precision and range, which is why the more accurate Oboe system (also mentioned in Chapter 3) was introduced in late 1942, and the self-contained H2S microwave radar soon afterward. However, as Watson-Watt later explained, Gee was less useful as a precision bombing tool than as a precision navigation instrument, particularly for "marshalling in the assembly of a large night-bombing force," for maintaining a good track, and for "quick landings for damaged and lame-duck aircraft on their return."[25]

Demand for Gee sets jumped dramatically after the American 8th Bomber Command began bombing missions in mid-1942. Within months, a dozen B-17s and B-24s equipped with Gee were flying long-range missions. Their navigators found Gee easy to operate—an accurate fix could be made in under two minutes—and several considered it to be the best navigational aid at their disposal. By summer of 1943, Brigadier

General Ira C. Eaker formally asked that RAF Bomber Command deliver 2,000 Gee units at a rate of 300 per month (this was not long after Eaker had also requested British H2S radars for his American bombers). The British electrical and electronics industry, primarily AC Cossor, Dynatron Radio, and Metropolitan-Vickers, responded quickly, avoiding the delay that would have been involved in setting up a separate US production line. They also far exceeded initial production targets; as the British radio journal *Wireless World* crowed after the war, "The final achievement was a rate of production which enabled Britain to give 2,000 sets a month to her United States Allies," building a total of 60,000 Gee sets. Hugh Odishaw, an OSRD London Mission radar scientist attached to BBRL, reported that "by the end of the war, every operational heavy bomber in the Eighth Air Force, all 2,500 of them, had British Gee receivers on board as standard equipment." Postwar analysis showed that while 3.5 percent of bombers without Gee failed to find their home base, only 1 percent of Gee-equipped aircraft got lost. The history of the MIT Radiation Laboratory—which had no hand in its development—conceded that the successes of the Gee system, primarily radio navigational aid, were "far too numerous and too well known to need recounting."[26]

GEE NOT ONLY PROVED highly successful in the European campaign, but also provided the inspiration for the LORAN (long-range navigation) system that would see widespread use in the Battle of the Atlantic and in the Pacific campaign. The idea for LORAN came to Alfred Loomis on the evening of Sunday, October 13, 1940, at his Tuxedo Park mansion. That day, Cockcroft and Bowen of the Tizard Mission were briefing British radar developments to their American counterparts, including Loomis and Edward Bowles from MIT. Bowen outlined what little he knew of the Gee program, still under development back at TRE. The scientists then retired to their rooms to dress for dinner. When Loomis came back down he told Bowles that while in the shower he had had an "epiphany": he knew exactly how to build a hyperbolic navigation system, one capable of reaching across oceans and based on the same principles that he had just heard described for the much shorter-range Gee.[27]

The following day the group drove to Loomis's New York penthouse, where Loomis pulled Bowen aside and told him of his inspiration (Bowen marveled that Loomis "must have been working a 24-hour day"). Loomis suggested that by using much longer radio wavelengths that bounced off the ionosphere, with ground transmission stations many hundreds of miles apart but synchronized by highly accurate quartz clocks, they would be able to achieve ranges of over 1,000 miles with an error of less than 5 miles. Though the United States was not yet at war, it was obvious to all that the vast Pacific Ocean would become a major theater of battle. Within a few weeks, the system was being called LORAN at Loomis's insistence (the original acronym, LRN, was mistakenly thought to stand for Loomis Radio Navigation) and established as Project 3 at the newly formed Rad Lab under Division 11.[28]

Just weeks before the Tizard Mission had revealed the existence of Gee, the Army Signal Corps had established a set of requirements for a long-range navigational system: it had to have a minimum range of 500 miles and be accurate to within 1,000 feet. In November 1940, they accepted Loomis's proposed LORAN system, and work began on December 20, with a kickoff meeting at Rad Lab that included electronics engineers from RCA, Sperry, Bell Telephone, General Electric, and Westinghouse—all of whom, just months earlier, had been fierce competitors in the commercial radio market, but who were now joining forces. Edward Bowen—by now called "Taffy"—was an early participant but did not know enough about Gee to provide results from early testing. The team's prototypes in early 1941 showed that the LORAN system could achieve ranges of many hundreds of miles by using wavelengths of about 150–200 meters, which theoretically could enable the system to reach even greater distances by bouncing off the ionosphere (known at the time as "skywave"), making it useful for ships at sea.

In summer 1941, the team established the first LORAN transmitting stations at Montauk Point, Long Island, and Fenwick Island, Delaware. A hand-built LORAN receiver was installed in a station wagon, which in September was driven around the eastern half of the United States to establish range, picking up the signals as far as Springfield, Missouri, 1,300 miles away. By this time, the British were providing to Rad Lab more up-to-date information on Gee (recently tested in a dozen Wellington bombers), which helped the team settle on a final design for the receiver. In January 1942, just after the American entry into the war, two Rad Lab scientists brought a new LORAN receiver to Bermuda, where they were able to confirm the skywave propagation of the system that would allow LORAN to be used in the Battle of the Atlantic, which was already under way.

By the summer of 1942, LORAN had become a major Allied development program. In June, the US Navy conducted tests with one of its blimps, which led to high-level interest in the system. In July, the Royal Canadian Navy and the US Coast Guard joined the effort and established LORAN transmitters in mainland Canada, Newfoundland, Labrador, and Greenland, which provided coverage across the major North Atlantic convoy routes. As international participation grew, the Army Signal Corps was given the responsibility of procuring airborne receivers for all services to ensure complete interoperability. Later that summer, Dippy was temporarily transferred from TRE to lead Rad Lab efforts in standardizing LORAN receivers with Gee, so that the two systems could be readily swapped out in any aircraft, and assisted with the ground station design and development. By October, the North Atlantic Standard LORAN Chain was operational, with four ground stations and several receivers installed on warships. By the spring of 1943, the first of over 300 convoys, including their escorts and patrol aircraft, were being guided by LORAN through U-boat-infested waters. As convoy operations extended eastward to Murmansk, ground stations were added in Iceland, Scotland, and the Faeroes.

Many more LORAN stations were added to India and the Bay of Bengal, to aid pilots flying over the Himalayan "hump" to China. Constructing the Aleutian Island and Bering Sea chain to cover the northern Pacific Ocean proved particularly arduous. The islands had come under invasion and repeated attack by Japan, and even before the last Japanese forces were forced to depart in mid-1943, the US Coast Guard was shipping heavy construction equipment to build LORAN stations on several wilderness islands, which had to be continually resupplied since there were no natural provisions or even fresh water for their nineteen-man crews. The Coast Guard introduced small herds of reindeer to provide an emergency food source. By war's end, seventy-two LORAN stations were established from the North Atlantic to the Mediterranean to the Indian and Pacific Oceans, providing navigational fixes for both ocean and air transport.

Blind Landings

A good number of Allied bombers in the European theater during World War two carried both the British Type 62A Gee and the American AN/APN-4 LORAN sets for all-weather navigation. The first provided precise fixes at shorter ranges, while the second, though not as accurate, was good enough for deep penetration strikes at great distances ("AN" stands for "Army-Navy," denoting that the equipment was intended for multiple services). Neither LORAN nor Gee, however, could guide bombers to a safe landing at their airfields and landing grounds in darkness or poor visibility.

As noted earlier, the problem of providing safe all-weather landing had been recognized early and everywhere, by both governments and private concerns. In September 1929, the Guggenheim Fund, a private philanthropical organization that worked closely with the National Advisory Committee for Aeronautics (NACA), sponsored the first blind landing of an aircraft, flown by reserve pilot (and later Eighth Army Air Force commander) Jimmy Doolittle around Mitchell Field on Long Island, New York, using special radio equipment from the National Bureau of Standards (NBS). The NBS system used a pair of narrow, overlapping radio beams aligned to the runway, each of which transmitted a different Morse code. The pilot, listening intently on headphones, would hear "dash-dot" (letter N) if to the right of the beam, "dot-dash" (A) if to the left. Course-correcting into the overlap would provide a continuous tone, giving the pilot the right vector to the runway. A refinement the following year gave it three-dimensional capability, providing the crucial vertical glide path angle—too shallow and the plane could overshoot the runway, too steep and the plane could pancake into the ground. A further refinement placed the information on a cross-pointer in the cockpit instrument panel, so that the pilot operated on visual instead of audio cues.

By the early 1930s, several American airports adopted the NBS system, while its details spread quickly around the world. Many nations tried to copy it. The German electronics firm Carl Lorenz Aktiengesellschaft developed the most successful version, known as the Lorenz Beam, which was widely adopted at European airports during the 1930s and even reintroduced to America in a modified version by the Civil Aeronautics Authority (CAA) for commercial airports. The Knickebein, X-Gerät, and Y-Gerät systems deployed during the Battle of the Beams were, in fact, more powerful, longer-range variants of the Lorenz Beam, adapted for blind bombing instead of blind landing.[29]

The problem with the NBS system as well as the Lorenz Beam was that their long wavelengths rendered them inherently unstable due to local interference (buildings, rain, even distant mountains), which meant they were not safe enough for all-weather blind landings. From 1936 to 1938, Edward Bowles, working under a grant from the CAA, built a microwave blind-landing system at MIT that was inherently stable, but the transmitter was too weak to reach more than a mile, not enough to be an effective landing aid. As it happened, engineers at Stanford University had just invented the higher-powered vacuum-tube klystron, which when used in the Bowles blind-landing system could produce a beam detectable at 10 miles. In 1939, Bowles and his Stanford counterparts teamed with the Army Signal Corps Aircraft Laboratory, CAA, and Sperry Gyroscope to begin work on a klystron-based microwave blind-landing system that could allow even the largest bombers under development to land safely (this was the system that inspired Alfred Loomis to investigate the use of microwaves for radar). The Army Air Corps—which would have to use the same runways as commercial airlines—followed the CAA's lead in pursuing both the modified Lorenz system as well as the new Sperry microwave system. Both systems were based on the pilot control model, recognizing that the pilot had complete authority over the craft, following the same tradition as ships' captains and masters had for millennia. However, just before the United States entered the war, an upstart group at MIT Rad Lab upended this pilot-centric model, placing aircraft landing firmly in the hands of ground controllers.

―――――――

ALTHOUGH RAD LAB'S PROJECT 1 remained airborne microwave radar, close behind it was Project 2, radar-directed anti-aircraft gunnery, which also used the cavity magnetron to generate microwaves for the tracking radar. Research began in January 1941, carried out under two young physicists, Ivan Getting and Louis Ridenour, who were among the many university scientists recently recruited to fill Rad Lab's ranks. By April 1941 they had developed a working prototype of what would become the SCR-584 gun-laying radar and mounted it on the roof of MIT Building 6 (where, as noted in Chapter 3, Rad Lab was also running tests of its airborne radar). Over the next several months they conducted trials where they tracked a private plane flown by a friend of Ridenour for ten dollars an hour. In late summer, Luis Alvarez, joined Project 2. Alvarez observed that the radar, which was fitted with a 16 mm movie camera bore-sighted through a telephoto lens, could track the aircraft all the way to its landing at East Boston Airport. "What occurred to me," he later wrote, "was that if a radar could continuously and automatically track an enemy aircraft accurately enough to shoot it down, the same information should be adequate to guide a friendly pilot to a safe landing in bad weather."[30]

Alvarez was an amateur pilot himself—he had obtained his pilot's license in 1933 after only three hours of training—and was known for hands-on experimentation, which allowed him to look at a variety of problems in novel ways. Groomed to become a doctor, as were his father and grandfather, Alvarez was instead drawn to physics. Shortly after his marriage in 1936, he became one of Ernest Lawrence's cyclotroneers at Berkeley, where, despite having little training in electromagnetics, he spent hundreds of hours experimenting in the machine shop to develop an efficient 200-ton magnet, the heart of the new cyclotron that would pave the way for Nobel Prizes for discoveries in chemistry and physics. Alvarez barely missed out on the Nobel for the discovery of fission, which he was close to discovering at Lawrence's laboratory in 1939 when the news arrived that Otto Hahn's team in Germany had split the atom.

Alvarez impressed Loomis during the latter's frequent visits to Berkeley, and the two were close friends by the time Luie was at Rad Lab. Loomis, as part of his Microwave Committee work, selected Alvarez to lead a study on blind landing, just three days before Pearl Harbor. In February 1942, he submitted a report identifying the need to have a common blind-landing system between the services and with the British. Further, he recommended a radical departure from the system that Bowles had been working on at MIT for years. Instead of placing the landing in the hands of the pilot (Bowles's system), Luie contended that a ground-based controller should call the shots. Bowles, however, was leaving MIT and in no position to argue, having just accepted the post of scientific advisor to Secretary of War Henry Stimson.

Despite the tradition of pilot-controlled landings, for almost two decades the Navy had been using ground controllers—called Landing Signal Officers—to direct pilots landing their planes on aircraft carriers. The same concept, Alvarez believed, could be applied on land, which he called the "talk-down method." As his Rad Lab colleague Lawrence Johnston later explained, "Luie envisioned someone at the airfield seeing the airplane with radar and giving the [weary] pilot precise and simple steering commands to bring him down safely." At one stroke the combination of the microwave radar and a ground-based controller could solve some of the most pressing needs of both RAF Bomber Command and the US 8th Bomber Command, as the OSRD London Mission reported in January 1943:[31]

> The aircraft which are chiefly concerned are those which are most difficult to land—heavy bombers. The pilots are certain to be tired, and often will be wounded. In most British bombers there is only one pilot. Any system which depends upon cooperation from a second member of the crew is less reliable than a one-man system. Planes are likely to be damaged. Instruments may be in error, and certainly will be viewed with distrust by pilots after two trips across enemy territory. If there is a cross wind and the plane is crabbing, a visual touchdown will be essential for proper handling of the aircraft. With the expansion of the airforces the quality of flying personnel and of training is declining, and procedures must be simplified rather than complicated.

Alvarez, now at the head of Rad Lab Division 7, Beacons (which included both radio location transmitters as well as transponders), was given the go-ahead by Loomis's Microwave Committee to pursue the Ground Control Approach (GCA) system. The first tests in April and May 1942 using a truck-mounted version of the SCR-584 gun-laying radar were "disastrous," as Luie recounted, unable to lock on to the aircraft during approach. His team "returned to MIT thoroughly discouraged." Soon afterward, Luie had dinner with Alfred Loomis, where he explained the problems in detail. Loomis said to his friend that he was convinced GCA was the only way to blind-land planes, and told him, "I don't want you to go home tonight until we're both satisfied that you've come up with a design that will do the job." Working until almost midnight, they devised a new dual-antenna arrangement that promised to eliminate the ground reflections that plagued the gun-laying radar. Loomis funded Division 7 to build ten prototypes of the truck-mounted GCA, so that the US Army, the US Navy, and the RAF could all train with the prototypes while full-scale production got under way. Over that summer of 1942—"one of the happiest times in my life," Luie remembered—he and his team got to work.[32]

Alvarez's Division 7 was primarily staffed with scientists and graduate students, so Loomis arranged to bring in engineers from industry to help build the prototype. He had developed a good relationship with the Army Signal Corps from working on the LORAN project, and so turned to them for advice on whom to choose. The Signal Corps in turn suggested the Hollywood radio engineer Homer G. Tasker, who had worked with the Signal Corps on army training films when he was at Warner Pictures' United Research Corporation. Tasker had been a soundman on several films (he received two Oscar nominations for sound supervision) and was now at Paramount Pictures. He was no ordinary soundman, however; he had several patents to his name and was later described as "a brilliant engineer" by MIT Rad Lab, high praise from them for an outsider. In order to get Tasker, OSRD offered the GCA engineering contract to Paramount Pictures. Paramount wanted nothing to do with it. At the time, all Hollywood employees, not just film stars, were under contract—the studio system had not yet been broken up by the Supreme Court—so Tasker could not simply resign to work elsewhere. Instead, Paramount loaned him to a small Los Angeles electronics company, Gilfillan Brothers, Inc., which was awarded the GCA contract. Tasker brought three other engineers across the country to the Rad Lab in summer 1942, where they worked side by side with Alvarez's team to get the first prototypes into the field.[33]

December marked the first tests of GCA at the Naval Air Station in Quonset Point, Rhode Island, and somewhat to everyone's surprise, they proved successful. During a snowstorm on New Year's Day 1943, which closed the airfield and stopped all test flights, Alvarez's team received a phone call from the base commander, who reported that a flight of three PBYs (flying boats) had become lost and were low on fuel. "Can you guys find them and bring them down?" Alvarez of course agreed. The GCA radar detected the flight at 20 miles out. Alvarez called them and told them they had a system to bring them in. None of the pilots of the three aircraft even knew about the system, but Alvarez was able to accurately track their approach ("You lost fifty feet altitude in that turn," he told a pilot at one point) and, using just voice commands, guided them safely in, one by one. The PBY pilots were convinced that the system saved their lives, and soon the navy ordered twenty production models, designated AN/MPN-1, from Bendix Radio Corporation. In February, just before demonstrating it to Army Air Forces officials, several of the GCA's vacuum tubes burned out, which led Tasker to scramble for replacements. Despite this last-minute problem, the demonstration was successful, and the officials ordered fifty-seven sets from Gilfillan.[34]

The RAF was especially interested in GCA, as it required no new airborne equipment or special training, and asked for a model even before production started. Alvarez arranged for the prototype GCA, housed in a pair of army trucks, to be driven to the Norfolk Naval Shipyard and hoisted aboard HMS *Queen Elizabeth*, which had just completed a lengthy repair of damage caused by Italian naval commandos. The battleship, with the trucks lashed down as deck cargo, arrived in Britain in early June 1943, while Alvarez took a Pan Am Clipper from La Guardia Airport across the Atlantic. A week later, his four Rad Lab colleagues followed on the Clipper flight that carried the entertainer Bob Hope at the start of his two-month USO tour

of Britain and North Africa. Hope was not impressed with the scientists—
"four mysterious youngsters who could have been a backfield coming home
from a football game they'd lost," as he later wrote. "I never did find out who
they were," Hope said, but he was surprised at the "preferential treatment
they got" when they landed in Ireland. Hope's confusion was understandable; most of the scruffy (and airsick) Rad Lab bunch were freshly minted
college graduates in their early twenties, not distinguished-looking gray-
haired scientists, and even Alvarez's thirty-one-year-old second-in-command, George Comstock, had a round, boyish face that made him look a
decade younger.[35]

The Rad Lab team, whose "preferential treatment" was due to the RAF's
eagerness to begin work with the new landing system, caught up with the
two GCA trucks after arriving in London. Their drivers, a group of Women's
Auxiliary Air Force (WAAF) corporals, drove the trucks and the team to
RAF Elsham Wolds, a Lancaster bomber base in the north of England.
Alvarez, meanwhile, spent his first few weeks at the OSRD London Mission,
as the Rad Lab group would be under its administration during their stay in
Britain. He also spent time visiting military establishments, which left him
deeply impressed with how different the "attitude and atmosphere" were
from MIT. "The British," he noted, "were grimly aware of the seriousness of
war," because they "had personal experience with injury and death"—unlike their American counterparts, for whom "the war was far away."[36]

Alvarez joined his Rad Lab colleagues at Elsham Wolds in early July for
six weeks of testing. He talked down most of the aircraft himself, deriving
great satisfaction from the experience of landing "every type of plane the
RAF owned, every rank of pilot." Flying into a fog-bound airport after a
good night's sleep was one thing. It was "quite another to do so after eight
hours over hostile territory in a damaged aircraft with wounded aboard."
He was deeply moved by the experience: "We brought them in, those who
came back."[37]

Some of those who came back were twenty-one Lancasters returning
from a night raid on Hamburg in the early-morning darkness of August 24.
This was one of the first missions to successfully deploy Window, which
greatly reduced the causalities from flak; even so, three aircraft from Elsham

Wolds had been lost, and they could not afford more losses on landing. Alvarez's team talked down all aircraft in just over an hour and a half, with only four having to make a second landing attempt. This convinced the British Air Ministry of the worth of GCA; it asked for the production model, still on the drawing boards at Gilfillan, to be deployed to every airfield in Britain, and dropped all work on other blind-landing systems. With testing complete, it redeployed the GCA to RAF Davidstow Moor, to guide Coastal Command bombers returning from anti-submarine patrol through the notoriously foul Cornwall weather, and to train a new team of RAF officers to take over the system. At the end of August 1943, Alvarez passed the leadership of GCA to George Comstock and departed for MIT, to work on a special project he could not mention at the time, but which would transform the outcome of the entire war.[38]

The RAF officers arrived at Davidstow Moor on a typically foggy, rainy September day. Among the group was the recently promoted Pilot Officer Arthur Charles Clarke, who previously had been assigned to the Chain Home defense system. He and the others spent several months with Comstock and his team before the latter departed. During that time, they learned how to operate and maintain the GCA prototype with its 700 fragile vacuum tubes, in order to train other RAF officers for the new models due to arrive. Arthur C. Clarke was already writing both non-fiction and science fiction stories (he later would pen *2001: A Space Odyssey*), and his work with the Rad Lab team provided him ample material. When not learning how to operate and repair the GCA, Clarke, an active member of the British Interplanetary Society, wrote technical articles on space flight, including the now-legendary "Extra-terrestrial Relays," which predicted geostationary communications satellites (and appeared in the same October 1945 issue of *Wireless World* that lauded British wartime production of Gee). He also began writing the science fiction stories that would later make him famous, including his first published work, "Rescue Party." Clarke fictionalized his GCA experience in his 1963 novel *Glide Path*, barely disguising Luis Alvarez, who had left before Clarke arrived, as "Professor Schuster," and George Comstock, who turned out to be an avid sci-fi reader himself, as "Alexander Wendt." Clarke even described the Rad Lab team's encounter with Bob Hope (echoing Hope's description of them as "absurdly young") and claimed—perhaps with some basis—that the GCA trucks were shipped to Britain "stuffed with Scotch and nylons."[39]

Military pilots adopted GCA right away, as it needed no new equipment in already crowded cockpits, and only required following orders; as one RAF veteran recounted, "Any fool could use it." While the breakdown-prone Mark I was eventually cannibalized to resupply three other GCA prototypes deployed around Britain, Gilfillan and Bendix were racing to get the AN/MPN-1 production units into the field. The first of 256 GCA units began testing in January 1944, but they did not reach operational theaters until early 1945, with only a handful deployed by war's end. However, even with their small numbers they made a strategic impact on the war. Being portable—the MPN-1 was consolidated into a single truck pulling a trailer—they could rapidly be moved as the front advanced. In the European theater, they were located in southern France, Italy, and Sicily for the deep bombing campaigns in Germany and Axis countries. Other units were moved into northern France, Belgium, the Netherlands, and finally Germany as the British, American, and Canadian forces gained ground toward Berlin. And in the Pacific, GCA units followed the island-hopping campaign toward Japan—Iwo Jima, Leyte, Saipan, and, perhaps most significantly, the Tinian airfield from which two B-29 bombers, *Enola Gay* and *Bockscar*, would take off and land in August 1945 on the atomic bomb missions.[40]

Behind Enemy Lines

While IFF and blind-landing systems were developed by the British and Americans to solve well-known problems, the Rebecca/Eureka radio beacons were created before the problem they solved was even identified. The Battle of Britain was still being contested when the Chiefs of Staff outlined their future strategy against Germany in their paper of September 4, 1940. While building up their forces to take the fight directly to the enemy, the British Chiefs of Staff decided, the British military would also undermine them by sabotage and subterfuge. This plan was carried through in the joint strategy paper with the United States, ABC-1 of March 1941, which called for a "combination of blockade, bombing, and subversive activities." The logic was that these would so weaken the German defenses that "a direct attack would once more become possible." The British were first off the mark, creating the Special Operations Executive (SOE) in July 1940, just weeks after Dunkirk, "to coordinate all action, by way of subversion and sabotage, against the enemy." Churchill then told its director, "Go and set Europe ablaze!" In July 1942, the Americans created their own espionage and subterfuge organization, the Office of Strategic Services (OSS), led by William "Wild Bill" Donovan. From the start, the OSS and SOE shared intelligence, training, and matériel, including the radio beacons.[41]

"Invention is the mother of necessity," said historian of technology Melvin Kranzberg, turning Plato's dictum on its head, and this was the case for the development of the Rebecca/Eureka radio beacon system. The newly formed SOE did not know it needed a radio beacon to help insert special agents and supplies behind enemy lines until it learned that such a capability was even possible. The beacon was the brainchild of two (self-described) TRE boffins, physicist Robert Hanbury Brown and zoologist John Pringle, the latter of whom had actually studied biophysics before applying his skills to wartime radar research. In June 1941, both men were given the task of determining how to use TRE's microwave radar systems to help the British Army. After witnessing a training exercise at Old Sarum Airfield, just a few miles from Stonehenge, they hit upon the idea of assisting precision drops of supplies or troops by placing a small transponder beacon on the ground at the designated drop point that could guide an airplane fitted with a radar to find it. Their first trials a month later were successful, with a Blenheim bomber twice homing in on a well-hidden beacon starting 60 miles away.[42]

Nothing much came of these trials for several months, until in February 1942 Hanbury Brown received a call from the SOE, which had been tipped off to the beacon experiments, asking for his help. After arriving at its nondescript headquarters at 64 Baker Street, he learned that they intended "to drop agents and supplies from the air on to resistance groups in

Europe, who wanted equipment for sabotage, blowing things up, derailing trains and so on." Up until this point, the SOE had had mixed success in its agent drops, often losing soldiers and supplies as they attempted to reinforce the French and Polish Resistance. Drops zones were hard to identify; one valley or field looked remarkably like another in a distant country, and the danger of German troops seeing marker lights or flares was often too great. Hanbury Brown told the head of SOE, Colin Gubbins (he mistakenly assumed "Gubbins" was a cover name), that his radio beacon system could do what they needed, and arranged for a demonstration to take place.[43]

The SOE demonstration was also successful—the bomber dropped containers within 200 yards of the beacon after locating it 37 miles out—so TRE scrounged for spare electronic parts to build a dozen units that SOE could use behind enemy lines. The system consisted of two parts. Rebecca was the airborne part, essentially a low-power radar set that sent out a signal to be picked up by the ground transponder. SOE normally used medium or heavy bombers to make their drops, so Rebecca units were about the same size as other airborne radars. Eureka was the ground transponder unit, consisting of a battery, power supply, transponder, and tripod aerial, that would respond to the Rebecca radar signal and rebroadcast a new one, which the Rebecca operator would then home in on. The Eureka unit was heavy—about 100 pounds—and was smuggled into the country by advance SOE teams, usually concealed in a standard suitcase. Robert Watson-Watt gave the airborne set the name Rebecca, for "Recognition of Beacons," though the ground transponder name Eureka—Greek for "I found it"— seems to have arisen spontaneously. Both had explosive charges fitted to destroy it in case of enemy capture.[44]

The initial SOE operations using Rebecca/Eureka had mixed results. The first operations attempted to destroy the Vemork Norsk Hydro chemical plant in Telemark, Norway, which the British Tube Alloys program (of which more later) learned, through Norwegian intelligence, was producing heavy water for the Nazi atomic bomb efforts. In October 1942, the SOE inserted by parachute an advance team of Norwegian agents, who spent two weeks skiing to the Telemark site to establish a landing zone for a pair of British gliders carrying more troops. The agents set up the Eureka beacon near the landing zone and waited for the bombers towing the gliders to appear. Both bombers sent signals that Eureka picked up—the agents could hear the tone in their headsets—but the Rebecca units never registered the return signals, and the bombers went off course. The two gliders and one bomber crashed, killing most of their men and causing the operation to abort (the plant was later destroyed by Norwegian commandos and Allied bombers).

The experience in Norway led TRE to develop an improved and more versatile model, called the Rebecca/Eureka Mark II, built by Murphy Radio and Dynatron Radio. SOE had more success with these units in Poland and France, though the "reception committees"—local resistance fighters who guided and received SOE drops—were not happy with the Eureka transponders, because they were too large and bulky to manhandle across rough terrain, and the electronics could not be easily explained away to any German patrol that they crossed. Thus, the beacon system was used sparingly—in Poland only on nights with no moon to guide navigators, and in France to mark alternative drop zones in case pilots could not find the local reception committee.[45]

While Hanbury Brown was demonstrating the beacon system to SOE in 1942, the newly formed 38 Wing, the first of RAF's airborne forces for inserting paratroopers in enemy territory, approached TRE. The same demonstration that had intrigued SOE finally caught their attention, though their requirements were different from those of resistance agents. To prepare for the eventual invasion of Europe, 38 Wing was developing a new method of operation. Advance units of paratroopers—"pathfinders," the same term as used in bombing—would be flown to the designated landing zones 30 minutes to an hour before the main landings, in aircraft crewed by the most experienced pilots and navigators. The pathfinder paratroopers would jump while carrying Eureka transponders bundled in a canvas sack and strapped to their legs. Before the pathfinders landed, they would lower the Eurekas on a twenty-foot rope, so the transponder took the initial shock and helped cushion the paratrooper. The transponders therefore had to be lighter (60 instead of 100 pounds) but also more rugged than the older units. John Pringle at TRE was in charge of the design of the newer lightweight model, called Rebecca/Eureka Mark III, and gave the manufacturing job to AC Cossor.

Hanbury Brown was no longer part of the TRE team by December 1942; he was on his way to the United States to oversee the adoption and pro- duction of an American version of Rebecca/Eureka for the Troop Carrier Command of the Army Air Force. He boarded a Pan Am flight accompa- nied by a group of American entertainers just returning from tour. The performers, many apparently comedians, played all forms of pranks on him—in one instance, inviting unwanted attention from the press by telling the airport manager that he was a high-level British diplomat. But they made up for it: when he arrived at his New York City hotel, the troupe was waiting for him with champagne.[46]

Hanbury Brown spent the next few months demonstrating to American paratroop units the Rebecca/Eureka Mark II, which had been separately flown over on a C-47 Dakota transport (a modified DC-3 airliner). These demonstrations convinced the Army Air Force to adopt the British system, and Hanbury Brown's next job was to iron out the requirements and specifications for the American version. After spending several more weeks at the newly opened Pentagon and in Army and Navy laboratories, he "gave up" on the idea that the British and American teams could use interchange- able equipment. There were, he discovered, "far too many differences in standards, dimensions, voltages, plugs and ideas on how to do the job." The best he could hope for was to get equipment to "work together using the same frequencies and pulse codes." With that stipulation agreed to by all sides, the Army Signal Corps gave the contract for Eureka to Hazeltine and for Rebecca to Philco.

In March 1943 the Rebecca/Eureka Mark III units were flown to the United States so that the contractors could copy them. Philco seemed to have the Rebecca unit well in hand, so Hanbury Brown moved to New York (a "seedy hotel on 32nd Street," he complained), where he could be involved in Hazeltine's design of the Eureka unit. By now the Americans were used to having British engineers as advisors, with Bowden having served in that role the year before on IFF. Hanbury Brown worked closely with Hazeltine's engineers to design a lightweight and efficient version of Eureka, designated

AN/PPN-1 (Figure 13). It was just 25 pounds, small enough to fit in a back-pack, and with its spring-loaded aerial could be deployed in under two minutes—no more heavy and cumbersome drop bags to wrestle with. They began production in July. Meanwhile, Philco's version of Rebecca, AN/APN-2, was fitted just weeks later to new Dakota paratroop carriers coming off the assembly lines. The first beacon units were ready for American operations by the fall of 1943, in time for the initial assaults on the European continent.[47]

The Americans were, in fact, already operating with the Rebecca/Eureka system in assault operations. The OSS, having been briefed by their SOE counterparts, had used one of the British units in Operation Torch, the invasion of North Africa in November 1942. Though it was not successful, the OSS saw its potential and was clamoring for more. The first American beacons to come off the Hazeltine and Philco assembly lines were destined for the Operation Avalanche invasion of Salerno, Italy, in September 1943. There, they guided two waves of night drops by C-47 Dakotas, landing hundreds of paratroopers just yards from the designated landing point. Troop Carrier Command also saw the potential of the beacons, and kept increasing its demands—in February 1944 it asked for 650 sets; a month later, 750 sets. What no one could state, but everyone surely suspected, was that these units would be used in the upcoming large-scale invasion of Europe. But for this invasion to happen, the transatlantic supply lines that kept American troops and supplies pouring into Britain would have to be vastly expanded, and that meant they would need to be defended against the threat of U-boats.[48]

CHAPTER 5

FIGHT ON THE SEAS AND OCEANS

I N THE SECOND volume of *The Second World War*, his epic postwar memoir and history, Churchill writes, "The only thing that ever really frightened me during the war was the U-boat peril." Churchill's observation, like many of his postwar declarations, must be taken with a lot of salt. His fear of U-boats was mainly in hindsight. Churchill's strategy had always been to take the fight to the enemy in offensive operation; the fight against the U-boats (*Unterseebooten*) in the Atlantic was always going to be a largely defensive operation.[1]

Indeed, Churchill had never been interested in defensive anti-submarine measures like convoys, proposing during World War One to send an "Inshore Aggressive Fleet" to attack U-boats and other shipping in German waters. While First Lord of the Admiralty during the early phases of World War Two, he was reluctant to build up naval power at the expense of resources for the army and air force, and warships for escorting convoys across the Atlantic were often in short supply.

It was only in March 1941, after Churchill had been prime minister for ten months and it was clear that his strategic bombing campaign was faltering due to heavy losses in transatlantic shipping, did he fully turn his focus to the "U-boat peril." Even then, he attempted to reframe the fight in offensive terms, creating the Battle of the Atlantic Committee (the term was already in common use), which he chaired; its purpose was to direct efforts to improve shipping efficiency and provide protective convoys for the whole of the Atlantic crossing.

The Battle of the Atlantic was not a single battle, but the longest campaign of World War Two, beginning before Churchill "proclaimed" it in March 1941. It started the day Britain entered the war on September 3, 1939, and ended May 8, 1945, several hours after the German surrender. It was a massive campaign, eventually involving both offensive and defensive operations, and not just against U-boats. Unlike many other campaigns of the war, the primary Allied strategy was not to seek out and destroy enemy forces, but to avoid them whenever possible.[2]

U-boats were not originally seen as the primary threat in Atlantic waters. At war's outbreak, Britain was focused on Germany's capital ships (their battleships and heavy cruisers, the latter of which the British press labeled "pocket battleships") as the primary menace to shipping. In 1939, Germany had fewer than sixty U-boats, of which less than half could sortie into the Atlantic. Churchill's strategy of offense was to bottle them up in the North Sea with mine barrages and aggressive air and sea patrols. By contrast, long-range heavy cruisers like *Graf Spee* and *Prinz Eugen* and battleships like *Scharnhorst* and *Gneisenau* represented more immediate dangers to merchant shipping (*Graf Spee* was hunted down, damaged, and scuttled in December 1939). Britain's fear that after the fall of France the Nazis would commandeer French battleships for commerce raiding led to the attack by the Royal Navy on the French fleet at Mers-el-Kébir, Algeria, in July 1940. In August, Churchill told his chief of staff, General Hastings "Pug" Ismay, "The greatest prize open to Bomber Command is the disabling of *Bismarck* and *Tirpitz*," referring to Germany's newest super-battleships, not yet in operation (*Bismarck* would be at the bottom of the Atlantic nine months later, though not before sinking HMS *Hood*, the pride of the British fleet). When the Chiefs of Staff laid out their Appreciation of Future Strategy in September 1940, they tasked the Royal Navy to protect Britain's maritime communications, but they also placed the threats of Germany's U-boats and capital ships on an equal footing. Britain's naval strategy had shifted to a more defensive stance.[3]

Even after Churchill's proclamation of the Battle of the Atlantic, not everyone was convinced that U-boats were the main enemy. Churchill himself labeled the long-range Focke-Wulf Condor bomber, which was deployed from occupied France to attack convoys from the air, as a "scourge" equal to that of the U-boat. The Americans, who had been providing limited Neutrality Patrol convoy escort since mid-1941, saw other threats as equal to that posed by the U-boats. The first Allied planning conference, held in late December 1941 and January 1942 in Washington under the cover name Arcadia, confirmed the Allies' "Europe first" strategy. Admiral Ernest King, the commander in chief of the United States Fleet, argued that "the most mischievous naval operations which the Germans could make at this time would be a mass surface and submarine attack on convoy routes in the Atlantic." It was only later in 1942, after submarine attacks along the eastern seaboard of the United States made clear its vulnerability, that U-boats were universally recognized as the primary menace.[4]

By that point the United States had already become the "arsenal of democracy," and the food, supplies, and war matériel it produced had to come to Britain by sea, as did the vast number of American troops who shortly would be following in Operation Bolero, which was agreed to in the Arcadia Conference. The priority in the Battle of the Atlantic would be to keep open those vital lifelines to Britain. And for that, the Allies would need hundreds more convoys, thousands more merchant ships, and new ways of finding and defeating the U-boats.

Convoys Before World War Two

The use of armed warships to escort merchant ships for protection goes back to ancient times. The Greek, Carthaginian, and Roman navies routinely dispatched triremes (named for their three banks of oars) and other warships to sweep ahead of merchant fleets, to clear the ocean of pirates and enemies. Armed convoys took their modern form in the Age of Sail, with warships acting as bodyguards for the Spanish treasure fleets (1526–1778) that carried silver from Peru and Mexico back to Spain. One of the most famous naval battles of the American Revolution took place in September 1779, when John Paul Jones attacked a British convoy of timber-carrying ships and captured its escort, HMS *Serapis* (the convoy itself escaped unharmed). Less than a year later, in August 1780, when both France and Spain joined with the United States in the war against Great Britain, a combined Spanish-French squadron hunted down and captured a richly laden British convoy using a combination of naval intelligence (Spanish spies sent warning of the convoy's departure and route) and long-range acoustic detection (the squadron listened for British signal cannon booming at night to zero in on the convoy). During the Napoleonic Wars, the British navy built on their experience to conduct merchant ships through particularly dangerous chokepoints in the Baltic, Mediterranean, and Caribbean seas. Shipbuilding surged dramatically to constitute those convoys and make up for losses, often (as with the East India Company) using uniform, standardized designs to quickly build up the fleets.[5]

Convoys were deemed unnecessary in the Pax Britannica of the nineteenth century but were resurrected in World War One, as a result of commerce raiding by German U-boats. Beginning in 1916, Britain introduced armed convoys on selected routes, while relearning the harsh lessons of the Napoleonic Wars. In May 1917, three months after Germany had announced a policy of unrestricted submarine warfare (i.e., submarines would attack merchant ships without warning) and began sinking ships in large numbers, Britain finally began systematically employing warships to escort merchant convoys to and from France, Gibraltar, and Scandinavia. By then the United States was in the war, and the two nations operated a series of transatlantic convoys carrying troops and munitions from East Coast ports like Hampton Roads, New York, and Halifax to destinations in Britain and France.

The reason convoys were so effective is that it was almost as hard to locate a convoy in the vast ocean as it was to find a single unescorted merchant ship. However, while a submarine could easily sink a lone merchant ship, if it met with a convoy it would have to fight its way through escorts to get a shot. U-boat admiral Karl Doenitz had been a submarine captain in World War One, and remembered that after convoys began operating, "the oceans became bare and empty; for long periods at a time the U-boats, operating individually, would see nothing at all." On one occasion, he encountered "a huge concourse of ships" which was protected by escorts. He realized that "the lone U-boat might well sink one or two of the ships," but the rest of the convoy would escape. The logical conclusion to this was made clear in 1918 with a series of original studies by the British engineer Rollo Appleyard, who mathematically determined that larger convoys were more effective than smaller ones. Unfortunately, Appleyard's studies received little notice from the Royal Navy. Nevertheless, merchant ship losses dropped dramatically after the convoy system was instated in June 1917, and continued to decrease all the way to the end of the war.[6]

Britain Looks to America to Build Its Merchant Ships

The other lesson of Napoleonic-era convoys, one that had to be relearned, was that losses had to be replenished by robust shipbuilding, and that standardized designs were the best way to get ships in the water quickly. Even with its enormous shipbuilding infrastructure—before World War One, it was building more merchant ships than the rest of the world combined—Britain was forced in 1917 to look overseas for more ships, while limiting its own shipbuilders to producing just a dozen standard designs (lettered A through N), to speed up production. In April 1917, shortly after declaring war, the US government created the Emergency Fleet Corporation, which established a series of shipyards to be built on so-called greenfield sites, as well as a half-dozen standard ship designs to be built in them. The Hog Island Shipyard near Philadelphia was the largest (indeed, one of the largest shipyards in the world), and borrowed assembly-line and prefabrication techniques from both the automobile and bridge-building industries. Nonetheless, the first standard Hog Islander merchant ship was not delivered until three weeks after Armistice Day in 1918, far too late to see any action. Hog Island and other American shipyards continued in operation for several years, building these standard ships to supply the postwar trade boom, and, as will be seen, many continued in service during the next war.[7]

The lessons of using standardized designs were not completely lost during the interwar period. Despite the immediate postwar trade boom, however, the British share of shipbuilding diminished in the 1920s while American and European shipyards grew in size and capability. The Great Depression decreased world trade by 40 percent, but this resulted in a 90 percent drop in global shipbuilding. British shipyards were hit particularly hard; two-thirds of shipyard workers were unemployed in 1932, three times the national average, and many shipyards lay idle. Some yards kept their engineering staffs busy, however, designing newer fuel-efficient hull forms that were model-tested in the towing tank at the National Physical Laboratory in Teddington, outside London.

One of these shipyards was Joseph L. Thompson & Sons, in the Tyne and Wear region in northeast England. It had been in operation for almost a century and had built standard ships during World War One. Its managing director, Robert Cyril Thompson, led a team to produce inexpensive yet fuel-efficient cargo ship designs that proved especially attractive to shipowners. This coincided with the rearmament that began in 1935 under Prime Minister Stanley Baldwin in response to the Nazi threat, and breathed new life into British shipbuilding. Britain was soon launching 3 million tons of shipping per year, fully one-third of the world's output, while the United States was launching merely 200,000 tons annually. Thompson & Sons designed a series of increasingly efficient ships from 1935 to 1940, culminating in Hull 607, *Empire Wave*, whose riveted keel had just been laid in March 1940, and the slightly larger Hull 611, still unnamed and on the drawing boards. Each of them would carry about 10,000 tons of cargo at a speed of 10.5 knots, powered by an old-fashioned but economical coal-fired triple expansion steam engine.[8]

Neither *Empire Wave* nor Hull 611 was yet launched by September 2, 1940, when Cyril Thompson, on the recommendation of the British Admiralty's officer in charge of shipbuilding in the Tyne and Wear, attended a meeting at Admiralty headquarters in London regarding a special mission to the United States to order American-built cargo ships. Ordering ships from the United States was hardly novel; in World War One, the British government used the Cunard Steamship Company to place orders for hundreds of cargo ships at shipyards on both coasts, each yard building its own design. The difference now was that the Admiralty, alarmed by the soaring and unsustainable rate of merchant ship losses in the Atlantic, wanted American yards to build sixty vessels of a uniform type—capable of carrying 10,000 tons of cargo at a speed of 10.5 knots, exactly the type that Thompson's shipyard was already building. The Admiralty impressed upon him the dire situation at sea. Given that British shipyards were already at maximum capacity with wartime construction and repair, the nation's very survival depended on finding a new source of cargo ships. The senior naval officers asked Thompson if he would lead the mission. He accepted the assignment on the spot, requested that his expert marine engineering colleague Harry Hunter accompany him, and immediately began preparations for his trip across the North Atlantic.

Thompson's mission orders were specific in some details and nebulous in others. The Admiralty authorized him to purchase sixty vessels for a total cost of £10 million (almost $6 billion today), with the option for an additional eighteen vessels from Canadian shipyards. Left open was whether the ships would be of American, Canadian, or British design. Unknown to Thompson, chancellor of the exchequer Kingsley Wood had almost put a stop to the program. With Britain now reaching its limits in the Cash-and-Carry program (Lend-Lease was some months off), Wood was determined to allocate the dwindling supply of gold to the most cost-effective purchases abroad. Shipbuilding, Britain's iconic industry, did not seem to fit the bill. "I am not satisfied that it is necessary to place so large a contract as this in America at once," he wrote the Admiralty. He pointed out that it cost twice as much to build a ship in the United States as in Britain. Although Wood was correct that American ships cost substantially more—in fact, they turned out to be three times the cost of comparable British-built vessels—the Admiralty counterargued that the limited shipyard manpower and matériel at home were needed for warships. In the end, it prevailed. The chancellor at least wrung out some savings in the mission, limiting Thompson's per diem to $12.50 a day.[9]

THOMPSON AND HUNTER BOARDED the Cunard liner RMS *Scythia* on September 21. It did not sail in convoy, as the faster passenger ships ("fast" meaning anything above 14 knots) usually crossed the Atlantic alone. In theory, as they zigzagged at high speed, they could not be tracked by submerged U-boats, which could only move at 4 to 8 knots. That would not be the case for the slower cargo ships they would be buying. Those would have to travel in convoy.

The Admiralty of course wanted vessels that could be built in large numbers and in a hurry. This meant they would have to give up on faster ships driven by steam turbine propulsion (like RMS *Scythia*) because of the shortage of engine-builders that could fabricate complex, high-powered turbine engines and associated gears. Instead, they favored slower ships driven by simpler, low-powered triple-expansion steam engines (of which more later), which could be built by more engine-builders at an estimated production rate four times greater than steam turbine engines.[10]

Thompson brought with him copies of the plans for Hull 607 (*Empire Wave*) primarily to show American shipbuilders the kind of vessel they were interested in, rather than to serve as a template for construction like the Rolls-Royce Merlin plans, which were at that very moment being redrawn at the Packard Motor Car Company in Detroit. Thompson and Hunter arrived without incident in New York on October 3. The next day they met with Arthur Purvis of the British Supply Council (BSC), which was still scrambling to sort out all the competing demands for American aircraft, ordnance, and machine tools. The BSC could not spare anyone to join Thompson and Hunter on their cross-country tour of American shipyards, so instead the British embassy and Lloyd's Register provided three technical experts.

Thompson's British Merchant Shipbuilding Mission, as it was known, was now one of several British missions making the rounds in the United States in the fall of 1940, including the Tizard Mission, of which they certainly knew nothing. The first port of call was Washington and the United States Maritime Commission, an independent federal agency in charge of the nation's long-range program. In the fall of 1940 that involved building 500 merchant ships, mostly to standard designs labeled C-type (cargo ships) and T-type (oil tankers). The commission was led by Rear Admiral Emory Land and his assistant Commander Howard Vickery, both of whom had worked together in the navy's design bureau and were widely lauded as effective administrators. Thompson noted in his mission report that the two were "anxious to be as helpful as possible." They nonetheless made it clear to Thompson and his team that American shipyards, which had suffered an even sharper downturn during the Great Depression than those in Great Britain, were now working at full capacity, thanks to orders from the Maritime Commission and navy warship orders—almost a thousand orders were on the books, including 200 cargo ships, 300 warships, and no fewer than twelve aircraft carriers. The best option, they said, would be to reactivate unused shipyards and marine engine-builders, or construct entirely new ones—a contingency that had been discussed back in Britain and deemed the worst option, given how much time it would require. After a trip to Ottawa to add Canadian shipyards and engine-builders to the shopping list, the mission fanned out across the continent, logging 17,000 air miles in a chartered DC-3. In two weeks, they visited eleven locations and over thirty sites, flying and sleeping in the aircraft at night so as not to waste a minute of daylight, returning to New York on November 1.[11]

Even before the mission returned to New York, Thompson had cabled London with the news that he had found no shipyards capable of undertaking the work for them. Most were building C-type cargo ships that were faster, more complex, and more expensive and would take longer to build than Britain needed. However, he added, the "Todd Shipyard Corporation has been practically allocated to us by Maritime Commission," provided the British acted quickly and furnished all of the working drawings for the ships. Todd's co-owned shipyard, established on a barren patch of land in Tacoma, Washington, the year before, had already built two ships while simultaneously creating a whole new shipyard around them. Buoyed by their success, Todd was now proposing to concurrently build shipyards and ships at two undeveloped sites: the first in flat marshlands in Richmond, California, across from San Francisco, and the second on a rocky peninsula in South Portland, Maine.

What impressed the British mission most was not the Tacoma shipyard per se but its co-owner, Kaiser Shipbuilding, and more particularly Henry J. Kaiser himself, whom Cyril Thompson mentioned several times in his diaries and dispatches (barely alluding to the Todd Corporation). Kaiser was already a legend in civil construction—his firm led a consortium called the Six Companies that had built the Hoover Dam, the Grand Coulee Dam, and the San Francisco–Oakland Bay Bridge, among other projects—but knew nothing of shipbuilding until his consortium partnered with Todd Shipyard in 1939 to build ships for the Maritime Commission. Kaiser had risen from photographer's assistant to roadbuilder to head of one of America's largest construction companies, mostly through sheer force of will, self-promotion, and an instinct for developing the right political connections. "His telephone calls were legend; his trips to Washington so numerous that it was easy to believe he slept only four hours out of twenty-four," Emory Land observed in his autobiography. The British mission members were not blinded by Kaiser's salesmanship; "pure theatre," one of them called it. They were, however, convinced that Kaiser's team could bring together the right resources to get the work accomplished in a hurry.[12]

The British mission's instincts were correct. With the blessings of the Maritime Commission and approval from the Admiralty, Cyril Thompson signed provisional contracts with Todd Shipyard Corporation at its downtown New York offices on November 7, 1940, along with representatives from Kaiser and Bath Iron Works, a renowned Maine shipbuilder. The contracts called for the companies to build two shipyards and sixty cargo ships (thirty by each shipbuilder) on behalf of the British government; first delivery in twelve months, all sixty by December 1942, with an option for another sixty by the following year (another twenty-six ships would be built in Canadian yards).

That same day, Todd subcontracted the New York naval architecture design firm Gibbs & Cox, Inc. to handle all ship design and to purchase all material and equipment, effectively designating it as the intermediary between the British mission and the shipyards. Gibbs & Cox was the logical choice for getting the job done, although William Francis Gibbs, the founder, was never trained as a naval architect. Gibbs had grown up in Philadelphia and become fascinated by the passenger liners being built on the Delaware River, but at his father's insistence he attended Harvard, where he studied government and economics (and took a few engineering courses in which he got C's), followed by Columbia Law School. In 1915, while still a practicing lawyer, he and his brother prepared plans for a passenger ship that would be larger than anything on the ocean, and managed to convince both the marine industry and the US Navy to give them serious consideration.

It has never been clear how Gibbs, who struggled with math and had no formal education in naval architecture, developed such a mastery of the field. His technical and legal expertise, however, had made him indispensable at the US Shipping Board, which oversaw merchant shipbuilding. After World War One he leveraged that position to see to it that he and his brother were awarded the contract to convert the German war prize *Vaterland* into the American passenger line *Leviathan*. As the Great Depression loomed, their firm (now called Gibbs & Cox) scrambled to find work as the principal "design agent"—a recent business creation—for shipyards building passenger liners and cargo ships. Gibbs & Cox developed a reputation for exactness and efficiency. In 1934, the US Navy asked them to take over detailed design and specifications for the *Mahan*-class destroyers to be built by Bath Iron Works. By 1940 the firm was handling the detailed design of hundreds of navy ships, and with 1,000 staff on the payroll, they produced not only blueprints and specifications, but also scale models of complex engine rooms, which made arranging the equipment in such a tight space a more efficient and less costly process.[13]

For all that, Cyril Thompson was at first not happy with the arrangement. The very idea of using a design agent ran contrary to Thompson's experience; in Britain, the shipyard itself was responsible for the design, and therefore accountable for any problems in construction or operation. Thompson also had to reluctantly agree to other American practices. With no American designs that would meet British requirements, Thompson's plans for Hull 607, *Empire Wave*, would have to serve as a template for construction, and he left them with Gibbs & Cox to redraw to suit American practices. The most important change was from riveting hull plates to welding them. British yards still riveted their ships, but it was time- and manpower-consuming. Welding, by contrast, was now common in American shipyards. One relatively unskilled welder could join a seam much faster than could a team of five skilled riveters. Welding was relatively new and there were still many doubts about it; welded seams had sometimes failed catastrophically at sea, which helped explain the reluctance to give up tried-and-true riveting. Nevertheless, speed of construction was paramount, and the British mission agreed.[14]

On the other hand, the American shipyards agreed to use the same triple-expansion steam engines that were used in Thompson's British yard (though powered by oil-burning boilers instead of coal). Most American marine engine manufacturers had long since switched to steam turbines. Triple-expansion steam engines look like giant truck engines, with three huge cylinders housing reciprocating pistons that draw the maximum work from the expanding steam. Although low-powered, they turn at the same rate as the propeller (around 70 to 100 rpm), so they can be directly coupled without any gears. Steam turbines, spinning at 2,000 rpm, are more compact and provide greater power but require reduction gears to match the propeller speed. Both turbines and gears required complex manufacturing techniques and took more time to build than reciprocating engines. All the marine engine-builders capable of turning out the gears were flooded with orders for warships. A diesel engine manufacturer, General Machinery Corporation of Ohio, was contracted to build the reciprocating steam engines, while a locomotive builder made many of the boilers. Just as Cyril

Thompson thought everything was in hand, his diary entry for November 16 notes that he received a cable from the Admiralty, which had decided it wanted the slightly larger Hull 611 to serve as the design basis. Thompson had to correct all of the plans and specifications to accommodate the new size ship. "Oh Hell," he wrote in his diary.[15]

The final contracts were signed the evening of December 19, 1940, at Todd headquarters. Cyril Thompson was not there, having arrived in Scotland just days earlier after a harrowing rescue at sea. After completing his corrected plans and specifications, he had left New York for Britain on December 6 aboard the fast passenger liner *Western Prince*, preliminary contracts in his briefcase for final approval by the Admiralty. Like *Scythia*, which Thompson had taken three months earlier, *Western Prince* sailed alone, on the theory that fast ships could outrun U-boats. That theory was exploded by a torpedo from *U-96* on the morning of December 14. Thompson was still asleep in his cabin when the torpedo struck. He later remembered grabbing his briefcase with the official mission papers, and rushing on deck. "I scrambled into one of the lifeboats," he recalled. "As the vessel slid beneath the heaving swell, there came two blasts from her whistle. We were alone in a waste of sea that was dark grey and menacing." Most of the passengers and crew were saved after nine hours adrift. Thompson's first action on arriving ashore was to have his papers retyped before bringing them to the Admiralty several days later.[16]

"Built by the Mile and Cut Off by the Yard"

The final contracts had already been signed before Thompson was able to return to the Admiralty. In addition to the ships they would be producing, the British government now owned two American shipyards. Or rather, they owned the land where they would be built. In December 1940, the Richmond, California, site was a marsh. It swallowed up whole a tractor that was preparing to clear a service road. The South Portland, Maine site, was so rocky that dynamite was needed to blast out the drydocks. Many of Kaiser's team of civil engineers and construction managers had just come off the

Grand Coulee Dam project, whose first dam—from pouring the concrete foundations to completion—was built in just twenty-eight months. They tackled the shipyard construction with the same vigor, filling in 100 acres of Richmond wetland to form the base for the shipbuilding ways in just three weeks, by driving 700 wooden pilings a day and working around the clock to dump a half million tons of crushed rock. Building the ships was another matter; Edward Hannay, one of the superintendents at the shipyard, later testified to Congress that he'd heard one of his team ask, "When do we pour the keel?"[17]

Hence why Kaiser's team leaned heavily on Gibbs & Cox, who were busy recreating the drawings and specifications for building British ships to American standards, though the full plans for Hull 611 (along with plans for engines, equipment, and so forth) would not arrive until later. It was not simply that they had to change hull drawings from riveted to welded. Gibbs's draftsmen found themselves in the same dilemma that Packard engineers did while faced with producing Merlin engines: British drawings simply did not translate to American practice. Details that would have been understood by a British foreman had to be made explicit for American workers. The British manufacturers of the triple-expansion engines, for example, had sent 80 plans to cover their entire construction; it required 550 new plans to build the same engine in American factories. Cyril Thompson soon found reason to recant his previous misgivings about using Gibbs as the shipyards' agent. At first, Thompson "felt very skeptical" about their ability to do tasks normally accomplished by a shipyard, but experience demonstrated that "Gibbs & Cox have been able to do it and have accomplished the result magnificently."[18]

Gibbs and Kaiser moved very fast despite the enormous volume of work. At Richmond, the first vessel of what was called the Ocean ship program, named *Ocean Vanguard*, saw its keel laid (not poured) on April 14, 1941. This was just over 100 days after the first pilings had been driven into the marshy ground. It was launched four months later on August 16 (festooned with British and American flags at the bow) and delivered in October. The first ships built at the South Portland yard followed just weeks behind Richmond. Together the two shipyards soon were launching ships at the rate of one every two weeks.

While construction of the British cargo ships continued apace, the Maritime Commission was contemplating a new Emergency Construction program, which had been ordered by Roosevelt earlier that year, to supplement the long-range program with an additional 200 cargo ships at an expanded number of shipyards. After reviewing many proposals, including building anew World War One–era Hog Islanders, Vickery settled on reusing Thompson's Hull 611 design, since it was both simple to build and easy to operate. In May the ships were designated as EC2 emergency ships, most of them to sail under the American flag as part of the "Liberty Fleet," though some would go to Allied nations under the recently enacted Lend-Lease program. Within weeks, the name "Liberty ship" was being universally applied to these Emergency Fleet vessels; the first Liberty ship, SS *Patrick Henry* ("Give me liberty or give me death"), was launched in September 1941. By then, the British government had sold its two American shipyards back to Todd and Kaiser to help finance its own merchant shipbuilding obligations, which extended well beyond the sixty ships it originally ordered. Many hundreds were built in Britain; Thompson's yard in Tyne and Wear completed his Hull 611, which in a nod to its parentage of the American Liberty ships was named *Empire Liberty*. Hundreds more ships were built in Canada, which also used Thompson's original design. But the American Liberty ship program would become by far the largest part of the Allied merchant fleet. By war's end, it produced 2,700 ships in eighteen shipyards, which came out to one Liberty ship (Figure 14) being launched around the country every sixteen hours—"built by the mile and cut off by the yard," went the common refrain. In one highly publicized case, SS *Robert E. Peary* was built and launched at the Richmond yard in four days fifteen hours.[19]

Kaiser and its affiliated shipyards were so productive in part because they were able to pool their suppliers in order to maintain a steady stream of material and components. A major part of this was due to the women and minority men who came to the shipyards by the millions, taking the place of the white male workforce sent to fight the war. White women were especially sought after by shipbuilders like Kaiser, which during the war maintained seven yards on the Pacific Coast, including the former British shipyard in Richmond, now called Permanente Metals.

The American experience of female shipyard workers stands in direct contrast to the case of Britain, where women were well represented in munitions trades like aircraft and gun production (Figure 24 shows one of the most iconic British paintings of World War Two, *Ruby Loftus Screwing a Breech-ring*, illustrating the construction of a Bofors anti-aircraft gun), but not in the naval and maritime industries. Even when confronted with the slow progress of ship construction, a pace that had led to the British Merchant Shipbuilding Mission, almost everyone from politicians to shop managers to trade unions resisted bringing women into British shipyards. Their attitude was best summed up by director of naval construction Stanley V. Goodall when he told a senior Admiralty officer that "women were not suitable for shipyards; post them into shops and aircraft work so release men for ships."[20]

By early 1943, American women made up 65 percent of new shipyard employees, in part because of the prevailing belief that welded construction required less brute force than riveted construction (though Canadian shipyards, which used riveting throughout the war, employed about the same percentage of women as did US yards). These women did not answer to the term "Rosie the Riveter"—that referred to female workers in the aircraft factories—but rather to "Wendy the Welder" (Figure 15). Kaiser set up large-scale training programs to bring women into the docks and shipbuilding lofts as soon as possible, but there was a high attrition rate. A 1943 Vassar graduate named Augusta Clawson was sent undercover by the United States Office of Education to one of the Kaiser yards in Oregon to find out why this was the case, and wrote a popular best-seller about her experience, *Shipyard Diary of a Woman Welder*, that was published in 1944. Women, she noted, were paid lower wages and resented by the rest of the workers (as their Black counterparts were at Packard in Detroit). Though Kaiser often provided on-site healthcare, and daycare for women with children, those arrangements were often inadequate, and women had to choose between career and family—a familiar situation today. In fact, the worker healthcare system established by Kaiser Shipyards and Permanente Metals, remains the only vestige – Kaiser Permanente – of the once mighty Kaiser Industries.[21]

The remarkable efficiency of Kaiser and its affiliates meant that British shipyards could concentrate on building its naval fleet, leaving most of the merchant ship construction to the United States. Liberty ships made up half of the American cargo ships built during the war, participating in thousands of convoys that shuttled personnel and matériel across the oceans.

With so many vessels built in a hurry, there were bound to be design flaws. But when large cracks begin to appear in the hulls of hundreds of Liberty and other welded ships, including three Liberty ships that actually broke apart at sea, earlier misgivings about welding resurfaced, and suspicion fell particularly on inexperienced welders at American yards. A joint investigation conducted in 1943 by the US Navy and the British Admiralty studied possible causes. Cambridge scientist Constance Tipper discovered that cold weather caused the metal to become brittle and prone to cracking, and she demonstrated that bad design—not bad welding—allowed cracks to form and propagate. British and American engineers developed design and construction fixes, such as employing higher-grade steels and using rounded hatch corners instead of the sharp corners that induced cracking, which largely solved the problem and are still used today.[22]

America Joins the Convoy System

Hull cracking was hardly the chief hazard faced by Liberty ships. By 1942, the greatest danger was of course the U-boats. Surface raiders were no longer a major threat, as Fleet Admiral King had feared; just a month after the Arcadia Conference was concluded in January 1942, the three German warships *Scharnhorst*, *Gneisenau*, and *Prinz Eugen* made their Channel dash to Germany, while *Tirpitz* had already fled to Norway. With all Germany's capital ships now either sunk or bottled up in German and Norwegian waters, the U-boat fleet was the Kriegsmarine's primary weapon, and fleet commander Karl Doenitz unleashed them to attack shipping unhindered along the American eastern seaboard. The US Navy at first resisted tried-and-true British tactics, allowing merchant ships to sail alone unescorted, and did not pressure the government into ordering brightly lit coastal cities, which silhouetted ships against the night sky, to black out. The resulting carnage—over 600 merchant ships sunk and thousands of sailors lost in what the German navy called Operation Drumbeat (Paukenschlag)—forced cities to dim their lights and the American navy to adopt British convoy tactics, at first slowly, then in a full embrace.

By mid-1942, hundreds of convoys were crisscrossing the Atlantic, Pacific, and Indian oceans, composed of cargo ships, tankers, and troopships, each convoy individually tagged by a bewildering array of designators. The North Atlantic trade convoys, which shuttled between US and Canadian ports and Great Britain, were designated by their departure point, and organized as "fast" or "slow" according to the speed of their ships. Thus, "HX" originally designated convoys from Halifax to Britain, and were usually fast. "SC"-designated convoys were generally slow and originally departed from Sydney, Nova Scotia, until HX was moved from Halifax to New York in September 1942, freeing up SC to depart from Halifax. Convoys typically had anywhere from thirty to ninety merchant ships steaming in a dozen or so columns, accompanied by three to nine escort warships—usually a combination of larger destroyers, midsized frigates, and destroyer escorts (DEs), and smaller sloops and corvettes. Each convoy was assigned a prefix and a sequential number, hence the HX 229 and SC 122 convoys, which in March 1943 would be involved in the largest engagement during the Battle of the Atlantic.[23]

The Arcadia Conference, as noted, had established the "Europe first" strategy for the Allies and envisioned an invasion of the continent in 1943. General George Marshall, the US Army chief of staff, developed Operation Bolero in April 1942 to build up American forces in Britain for that invasion. Bolero would require thousands of ships to transport an estimated 1 million Americans and their equipment (including materials for bases and housing) to Great Britain and Northern Ireland, first to expand the strategic bombing of Germany, and then to prepare for a cross-Channel invasion. Marshall leaned heavily on his War Plans Division, led by the fast-rising Major General Dwight D. Eisenhower, to draw up plans for the buildup. The logistical problems were enormous: over 100,000 troops and 5 million tons of cargo would have to arrive monthly, even as British ports like Liverpool were being bombed on a regular basis, halting operations for weeks on end. Operation Torch, the invasion of North Africa that began in November 1942, further complicated matters; troop and cargo convoys planned for Britain had to be redirected to feed into convoys to North Africa (one of which included SS *Patrick Henry*, the first Liberty ship, on its maiden voyage).[24]

Bolero ultimately fell well short of those original goals for the basic reason that plagued all Allied operations during World War Two: there never was enough shipping to meet all the demands. Despite herculean efforts at American and British shipyards, and relentless attempts to scrounge up ships from all over the world, the demand for still more ships never abated. Eisenhower recognized this when he wrote in his diary in January 1942, "We've got to have ships! And we need them now! All we need is ships!" However, it would not be simply a matter of building enough ships or putting them in the right convoys. Those ships and their cargo had to get to their destinations intact, and that meant sinking the U-boats that hounded them.[25]

Finding U-Boats

Inventors had been tinkering with submarines and submersibles since the time of Alexander the Great, with the idea of using them to attack surface ships always at the forefront of development. Indeed, many of the first operational submarines were developed in times of conflict specifically for that purpose: *Turtle* in the War of American Independence, *Hunley* in the American Civil War, and during the Irish uprisings of the late nineteenth century John Holland's *Fenian Ram*, which was the great-grandfather of the first American and British submarines built in 1900–1901, both named *Holland*.

Submarine design advanced rapidly in the early twentieth century, but this was not the case for submarine detection. During World War One, the British Admiralty assessed tens of thousands of wartime inventions, and also established the Anti-Submarine Division (ASD), which in 1917 developed a hull-mounted system, based on French research, that would send out ultrasonic pings underwater and listen for the echoes from submerged U-boats. It was dubbed ASDIC, an acronym that incorporated the initials ASD but was otherwise meaningless. ASDICs came too late to make any impact on the war's outcome, though they saw significant development and were fitted to many destroyers and corvettes in the 1920s and 1930s.[26]

On the other side of the Atlantic in 1915, the inventor Thomas Edison nudged the US Navy to establish what was called the Naval Consulting Board, with Edison as its president. On its face it was similar to the Admiralty's Board, but its real purpose was to promote Edison's own inventions (especially his batteries) for Navy use. The Naval Consulting Board turned its full attention to submarine detection in 1917, after the United States entered the war. After an initial visit from French and British scientists who demonstrated their work on submarine detection, the Americans instead pursued their own version of ASDIC—later named sonar (for "sound navigation and ranging")—which was fitted to US destroyers starting in the late 1930s.[27]

Scientific coordination on anti-submarine warfare (ASW) was haphazard at best during World War One and had little strategic impact on the outcome. That could not be allowed to happen in World War Two. In the intervening years, German U-boats and their tactics had become more advanced and far deadlier. Most significant was the wolfpack tactic, which Karl Doenitz perfected after Germany began secretly rearming in 1935. Having observed firsthand the futility of single U-boats unable to make more than one or two kills on a convoy, he honed the tactic of coordinating large groups of submarines (from three to thirty) to assemble at sea, converge, and make multiple attacks on merchant fleets. The first forays in the early months of the war showed that the submarines at sea could not provide on-site control and coordination, so after the fall of France, Doenitz shifted to a centralized U-boat command (Befehlshaber der U-Boote, BdU) in a headquarters in Lorient, an occupied city on the south coast of Brittany, from which his staff would direct all attacks. To achieve this high degree of centralization, Doenitz relied on almost continuous encrypted radio communications between shore and submarine, and between the submarines themselves.

The need for continuous radio contact left the U-boats vulnerable to three countermeasures by the Allied navies: first, interception and decryption of their communications to learn where wolfpacks were located and where they were headed; second, analysis of their tactics to determine the best ways to search for and attack U-boats; and third, using the U-boat's own radio signals to steer clear or press home the attack. The British led the United States in all three areas, as they did in so many fields of warfare, due to a decade's worth of research and two years of battle experience. To exploit these vulnerabilities and win the Battle of the Atlantic, the Americans would have to learn quickly, and the Royal Navy and the US Navy, despite all the post–World War One rivalries, would have to cooperate more closely than any other services.

Breaking the U-Boat Code

The first countermeasure against U-boats—interception and decryption of communications—was one of the oldest in warfare. Ancient militaries from Mesopotamia to India used codes (substituting words, letters, or numbers) and cyphers (scrambling letters or words using a key) to disguise the contents of messages. George Washington's Culper Spy Ring developed its own codebooks to stay ahead of the British during the War of American Independence. Radio, introduced in the early 1900s, could be intercepted by anyone with a crystal set, hence creating codes and cyphers took on far greater urgency and sophistication, as did the means to decypher them.

World War One and the subsequent peace and armaments negotiations demonstrated the need for systematic decryption, both diplomatic and military, though Britain and the United States took very different paths. Between the wars, Britain established the Government Code and Cypher School (GC&CS, itself a cover name) headquartered at Bletchley Park, a small town north of London, which centralized naval, army, air force, and diplomatic codebreaking. The Admiralty also centralized its Operational Intelligence Centre, which synthesized codebreaking, photo reconnaissance, interrogations, and other sources of information to get the big picture. By contrast, American intelligence was hampered by a hands-off attitude (in 1929, secretary of state Henry L. Stimson shut down the diplomatic intelligence arm, stating, "Gentlemen do not read each other's mail") and a balkanized set of organizations that could not effectively co-ordinate between army and navy, or even between the Atlantic and Pacific theaters. Finally, the two nations not only refused to share intelligence, they had very different priorities. Britain was fixed on the rising threat of Hitler's Germany, while the United States had long focused on Japan to develop its War Plan Orange in the Pacific.[28]

Britain had known since the 1920s that each branch of the German military used a variant of a commercial cypher machine, called Enigma, to shield their communications. Enigma looked like a large typewriter with three cypher wheels and myriad electric connections, which would scramble the text of a message into apparent gibberish that would be radioed by Morse code to the receiver, where it would be unscrambled by a second Enigma. British analysts using hand-based methods had little luck breaking the cyphers until 1939, when replicas of the Enigma machine, created by the Polish Cypher Bureau, were secretly transported to Britain. After the outbreak of war, three of the Polish codebreakers fled to Britain with their "bombes" (the origin of the word is unclear). Bombes were small desktop-sized machines that also used three cypher wheels and electric connections to automate and accelerate deciphering the Enigma codes.

All that winter, British analysts at Bletchley Park braved freezing temperatures inside their little huts to improve upon the Polish bombes. A young Cambridge mathematician recently arrived at Bletchley, Alan Turing, quickly saw shortcomings in the Polish model, and with his GC&CS colleagues designed a larger and more complex bombe that could more effectively attack German naval and U-boat cyphers, which were considered the hardest to crack. Bletchley's first bombes—each weighing a ton—were built by the British Tabulating Machine Company (BTM) and installed in March 1940. Coupled with recent captures of Enigma wheels and codebooks from German vessels, by May 1940 Bletchley was reading U-boat communications traffic, albeit haltingly, for the first time.

As Turing and his team were putting their bombes through their paces, the Americans were trying to break the Japanese diplomatic code, labeled Purple, and the navy code JN-25. The US Navy's attack on JN-25 was led by Agnes Driscoll, already a legend in the Code and Signal Section OP-20-G, using predominantly hand-based methods. She was making some headway when in the fall of 1940 she was reassigned to attack the U-boat Enigma codes. She once again used hand-based methods, the same ones that her British counterparts had long since discarded.

Roosevelt's election to a third term in 1940 opened the opportunity for greater cooperation with Britain, and the intelligence services sanctioned an exchange visit to Bletchley Park by four American codebreakers. In February 1941 they boarded the British battleship *King George V* (escorting convoy BHX 104), bringing with them JN-25 cyphers and two copies of the Purple replica machine the US Navy had just built. During their six-week stay at Bletchley, they were allowed into the inner workings of GC&CS, including a tour of Turing's bombes, arranged at the last minute in exchange for the two Purple replicas. The British gave the Americans full access to Enigma codebreaking—that intelligence was shortly thereafter labeled "Ultra"—and promised actual copies of the bombe when enough were available. But when the American codebreakers returned to OP-20-G with their newfound information, Driscoll staunchly resisted using any of it, insisting that she could crack Enigma without British methods. The head of Bletchley Park came to the United States in August 1941, specifically to offer more information on Ultra, but alas, no bombes just yet. He was brushed off by Driscoll, who told him that her group wanted neither.

For all her experience, Driscoll (and her methods) became the victim of the perceived intelligence failures that led to the attack on Pearl Harbor. In early 1942 she was replaced by one of her former pupils, Commander Joseph Wenger, and a new team of recent graduates from MIT, where they had been research assistants for Vannevar Bush's electronic codebreaking project. Wenger and his team fully embraced machine-led attacks on Enigma. Driven by the ongoing devastation of Operation Drumbeat, he looked to create a sort of Bletchley-on-the-Potomac, building and operating its own bombes. However, the Americans could not rely on the information previously obtained from GC&CS, for in the interim the Kriegsmarine introduced a new four-wheel Enigma for Atlantic U-boat communications (the British code-named it Shark) that required twenty-six times the computing power of the existing three-wheel bombes, making those British bombes effectively obsolete.

This confluence of interests on both sides of the Atlantic meant that Britain needed to give America unimpeded Ultra access, and the Americans needed to share their industrial capabilities with Britain. In July 1942, two American naval officers went to Bletchley Park to learn what they could about the four-wheel bombe design. They returned the following month with complete wiring diagrams and blueprints, which Wenger turned into the Naval Computing Machine Laboratory, a costly operation (a billion dollars by today's equivalent) that would build 360 machines to the British design. In October, GC&CS and OP-20-G signed an agreement that established "full collaboration" on attacking Shark, including all message traffic and technical advancements, and specified that the Americans would provide bombes for British use. The Battle of the Atlantic was to be fought from both sides of the ocean.[29]

The Naval Computing Machine Laboratory was established in the offices of National Cash Register (NCR) in Dayton, Ohio, under the leadership of electrical engineer Joe Desch. NCR was best known, of course, for the ubiquitous cash registers in American stores, but Desch's small laboratory was carrying out advanced electronics research and already had contracts with OSRD to develop electronic counters that would be used in the Manhattan Project. Desch had to give up these contracts and indeed much of his personal freedom to meet Ultra security requirements, notably housing a navy reserve officer in his home to keep tabs on him day and night. The navy also insisted on moving Desch's laboratory from the main NCR campus to an out-of-the-way location—known as Building 26—next to the railroad tracks.

Desch began work on the design in September 1942, and several months later met with Alan Turing, who was sent by GC&CS to the United States to offer assistance, and also to report back to Bletchley whether the Americans could manufacture the bombes. During his month-long visit, Turing realized that Desch's bombe was not simply a copy of his own design, but rather a uniquely American version, much larger and more capable than its British equivalent, with both improvements and flaws in comparison.

Despite Turing's critiques, Britain needed the American bombes; at the time, they had only 50 three-wheel models and no working four-wheel models. The bombe production line, which began in early 1943, was staffed almost exclusively by members of the US Navy women's auxiliary, known as WAVES, who were quartered in Sugar Camp, a rural retreat in Dayton that had originally produced maple syrup and was now owned by NCR. Working at small tables and long benches, 600 WAVES meticulously soldered the Bakelite-and-brass wheels, and assembled wiring harnesses and frames. By then, more efficient codebreaking meant that the number of machines required was greatly reduced; instead of 360 machines, a total of 125 four-wheel bombes (100 for OP-20-G, 25 for GC&CS), each weighing 2.5 tons, were shipped from Dayton at the rate of six per week to the newly established Naval Communications Annex in Washington that would operate the bombes.

The Annex, housed in a former women's school near Tenley Circle in Northwest Washington, would become the Bletchley-on-the-Potomac that Joseph Wenger had envisioned. In both the original Bletchley and the Washington versions, the majority of decryptions were carried out by women; both the American WAVES and the British Wrens (Women's Royal Naval Service) outnumbered their male counterparts by three to one. While BTM built 57 four-wheel bombes for Bletchley Park and its satellite facilities, such as Eastcote just outside London, this was nowhere enough to decrypt the tens of thousands of Shark intercepts, which by mid-1943 were being successfully attacked. The 25 British bombes built by NCR were not shipped overseas. Instead, they were run alongside the 100 American bombes at the Naval Communications Annex.[30]

Every day, Wrens at Bletchley Park, Eastcote, and other facilities sent bombe inputs via secure transatlantic cable to the Naval Communications Annex, from which WAVES operated the bombes (Figure 16). In the space of just a few hours they sent the decoded Enigma messages back across the Atlantic. The combination of American and British decryptions was then sent to both American and British operations centers (such as the Western Approaches Command in Liverpool), allowing them to track U-boat fleets in almost real time. By March 1944, with the imminent invasion of Europe, GC&CS and OP-20-G agreed that Washington would handle all further Shark decryptions, leaving the British (aided by on-site American codebreakers) to focus on other means to decrypt German army and air force messages. Some of these were decrypted by the Colossus code-breaking machines, in reality early forms of electronic computer that British scientists began operating in 1944. But while codebreaking could tell the Allies where the U-boats were headed, it could not predict the best way to attack them. For that, the British and Americans had to develop an entirely new scientific discipline.[31]

"The Proper Use of What We Have Got"

The second countermeasure against U-boats, analysis of tactics, depended upon a relatively new branch of mathematical sciences called operations research, which applies statistical methods to decision-making. Operations research was alluded to in the 2014 film *Imitation Game*, which dramatized the Enigma codebreaking at Bletchley Park, though the film took many liberties for narrative purposes. In addition to leaving out the American contributions to decoding Enigma, the film depicts Alan Turing, played by Benedict Cumberbatch, devising a statistical method to determine how many convoys could be diverted based on Enigma decrypts and how many should be sacrificed to the U-boats, in order not to arouse the suspicions of the Kriegsmarine that its code had been broken. Not only was the entire scene fictional (in real life, both navies almost invariably acted on Enigma intelligence and found ways to disguise the source), but Turing and his team at Bletchley had little to do with this kind of analysis.

Operations research was the province of Britain's other undisputed war-time genius, Patrick Blackett. Blackett had served as a midshipman gunner aboard the battleship HMS *Barham* during the Battle of Jutland in World War One. He demonstrated his wide-ranging intellect by first building and patenting a gunsighting instrument while still a midshipman, then after the war getting accepted to Cambridge, where he studied nuclear physics under the Nobel laureate Ernest Rutherford. Blackett's experimental work using cloud chambers to investigate subatomic particles would later win him a Nobel Prize, but the rising Nazi threat led to his 1934 appointment to Henry Tizard's Air Defence Committee, where he focused on radar and weaponry, before turning his attention to operations research just as the war began.[32]

Robert Watson-Watt laid claim to coining the term "operational research," which he stated was "born of radar," the first of his so-called three steps to victory, as the second logical step. To his dismay, the Americans renamed it "operations research," just as they transmogrified his beloved RDF into radar. The ideas behind it, however, went back at least to World War One when the British engineer Frederick Lanchester developed mathematical models of combat to predict the outcome of aerial battles, and (as mentioned) Rollo Appleyard analyzed convoys to conclude that larger ones were more effective than small ones. At the outbreak of World War Two, Blackett led a team to work with Fighter Command in assessing the best operational use of the Chain Home system. The team—nicknamed Blackett's Circus—demonstrated that simply by rearranging existing anti-aircraft batteries to fit in with available early-warning radar coverage, they increased guns' lethality fivefold. This clear demonstration of using operations research (OR, as it is commonly referred to today) to improve the effectiveness of existing weaponry caught the attention of Air Chief Marshal Philip Joubert, head of the RAF Coastal Command, which was charged with aerial protection of convoys. By March 1941, a new OR group, with Blackett at the helm, was investigating the best ways to attack U-boats from the air.[33]

Blackett's OR group began tackling the most visible (in the literal sense) problem. Coastal Command was not sighting as many U-boats as they should, given their patrol areas. Blackett suspected the U-boats were diving before they were spotted, and upon learning that the Coastal Command aircraft—repurposed RAF night bombers—retained their black paint scheme, which made them stand out against a bright sky, he recommended simply repainting them white for camouflage. Sightings immediately doubled. Another problem they found was that airborne depth charges were not sinking U-boats, even when they made a direct depth charge attack as the U-boat was diving to escape. By speaking with actual (British) submariners and analyzing escape paths, they determined that simply by changing the drop pattern and depth settings of the depth charges from a scattershot method to a concentrated, shallow-depth attack, they saw a tenfold increase in the probability of kill, even with the same number of depth charges dropped.

Blackett's approach, which he summed up as focusing not on the development of new weapons but on "the proper use of what we have got," appealed to the Admiralty, which brought Blackett into its fold in late 1941. There, he and his OR group—his third—examined the myriad problems of defending shipping against U-boats. In particular, they took up the same convoy problem that Appleyard had looked at two decades earlier and came to the same conclusion: larger convoys are safer than smaller ones. Blackett's reasoning, backed up with several years of data, was clear: concentrating merchant ships into fewer but larger convoys meant fewer crossings. U-boats would have more trouble finding targets; and since a larger convoy required a disproportionately smaller increase in the number of screening escorts, more warships could be freed up to attack U-boat targets when sighted. While Blackett's analysis was not the catalyst for larger convoys— that trend had already begun in early 1942—it did confirm the rationale, which gave political cover for the Admiralty to continue doing so. By 1943, the average size of convoys doubled from forty to eighty merchant ships.[34]

As Blackett and his civilian scientists were examining the convoy problem for the Admiralty, an MIT physicist taking a coastal ferry on the other side of the Atlantic saw a tanker, crippled during Operation Drumbeat, limping into Chesapeake Bay in early March 1942. Philip Morse, whose office had been just down the hall from Vannevar Bush, was at that time conducting research for the US Navy on noisemakers that could detonate acoustic mines before they destroyed ships. Morse became dismayed by the apparent lack of scientific efforts directed toward anti-submarine warfare. He voiced his frustrations to a friend, the physicist John Tate at the University of Minnesota, whom he knew was working with the navy and OSRD on acoustics. What Morse could not know, because of security restrictions, was that Tate had already begun exploring the ASW problem a year earlier. He had been one of five scientists who went to Britain in April 1941 as part of the Conant Mission, helping James Conant and Fred Hovde establish the OSRD London Mission office. Tate's job in Britain was to follow up on the exchange of ASDIC information begun with the Tizard Mission a year earlier. During his month-long stay, Tate focused on the technical aspects of ASW, bringing back designs for ASDIC itself (the US Navy eventually adopted the British streamlined dome for its own sonars, though little else), as well as information on underwater sound transmission and anti-submarine weapons.[35]

Americans were also interested in learning from the British experience in ASW operations and tactics. In February 1942, a US destroyer squadron commander, Captain Wilder Baker, spent a month in Britain observing how the Royal Navy and Coastal Command protected Atlantic convoys in the Bay of Biscay, while learning from Blackett how to use civilian scientists in operations research. Baker returned to the First Naval District headquarters in Boston, where he was made head of the newly established ASW Unit for the Atlantic Fleet. Now a Blackett acolyte, he was convinced that the MIT scientists across the Charles River could be key to defeating the U-boat threat. Baker first approached John Tate for recommendations, and Tate immediately pointed him to Philip Morse as the right man for the task. Morse, in fact, knew Blackett from when he was a research fellow at Cambridge, and their shared experience surely helped forge a common viewpoint to solving problems.

Baker asked Morse in March 1942 to organize a scientific task force to help his unit analyze the American anti-submarine effort. Morse later recalled, "It didn't take long for me to accept; this seemed to be the opening I had hoped for." Morse's first task was to recruit scientists, whom he found at MIT, Harvard, Princeton, Berkeley, and Yale, as well as at Bell Laboratories, where he pulled a rising star from the microwave radar division named William Shockley, who became Morse's right-hand man. At first, they numbered three, then seven, then thirteen, at which point they were called "Baker's Dozen," although the Anti-Submarine Warfare Operations Research Group (ASWORG), as it was officially titled, eventually counted more than forty scientists and mathematicians in its ranks.[36]

ASWORG was just one of four operations research groups, based on Blackett's model, that were created by the US Army and Navy early in 1942 (the others focused on sea mines, air defense, and strategic bombing). ASWORG, however, was the only group that did not report directly to the services but instead was under contract with OSRD as Division 6, Group M. This left Vannevar Bush in an uncomfortable position, for despite being a colleague of Morse and an advocate for operations research, he felt that ASWORG belonged with the fleet instead of as part of his R&D organization, whose focus was on developing technology. Despite his opposition, Bush did not interfere with Morse's efforts to place his men in the field with anti-submarine crews so that they could observe firsthand the problems that needed solutions.

Since most of the Allied anti-submarine operations were still taking place on the other side of the Atlantic, in November 1942 Morse and Shockley flew to Britain to establish the first cadre of field personnel, who soon came to be called combat scientists. If Bush was uneasy with ASWORG as part of his organization, his head of the OSRD London Mission, Bennett Archambault, felt decidedly the opposite. He took Morse and Shockley under his wing and made sure they established the right contacts with both British and American forces. Morse marveled that Archambault "seemed to know everyone." He was reintroduced to Blackett (whose direct telephone number was Whitehall 9000 extension 737, according to Archambault's pocket phone book). While Morse remained in London until Christmas to establish a more permanent ASWORG presence, Shockley went to an American ASW squadron newly based in Cornwall to fly in patrols around the Bay of Biscay aboard B-24 Liberators. Despite the risk—as a civilian, he might have been shot as a spy if the plane were downed—he found the experience of combat flying and helping to train aircrews in new methods of ASW deeply satisfying, and spent Christmas Eve typing up his report "Analysis of US Aircraft Attacks on U/Boats."[37]

Even after Morse returned to the United States aboard the converted ocean liner RMS *Queen Elizabeth*, Shockley stayed on for several more months to analyze the operational effectiveness of microwave radar, which he had worked on while at Bell Labs, for European bombing missions. Meanwhile, other members of ASWORG arrived at the OSRD London Mission, where they worked side by side with their British counterparts. Kenneth Thimann, a Harvard plant biologist assigned to ASWORG, was part of Blackett's OR group that analyzed convoy size in early 1943 to conclude that larger convoys were more effective. As more information was gathered by ASWORG combat scientists abroad and reported back to Morse in the United States, he realized that Allies were finding U-boats via radio direction-finding ten times more often than Morse's own calculations predicted. When Morse reported this peculiar observation to a US Navy admiral, the reply came back "with a straight face" that the result was "interesting." The very next day, Morse and his team were let in on Ultra and Enigma and told—as they had already suspected—that the submarine positions came from decrypted German communications, not from superior Allied technology.[38]

By summer 1943 Shockley was back in the United States, spending most of his waking hours leading his research team. That team was developing one of the most important products of wartime operations research: search theories to hunt and destroy U-boats. Back in 1941, the British had captured intact the German *U-570* and were operating it to develop anti-submarine tactics. Two ASWORG scientists attached to the OSRD London Mission interviewed Royal Navy captains who had commanded the captured submarine to learn how they would evade detection. Based in part on those findings, Shockley's team came up with new tactics that increased the probability of a successful hunt; in particular, they developed the "expanding box search plan," by which destroyers followed an initial attack on a convoy by tracing an enlarging, mathematically defined spiral that predicted the likeliest position of the U-boat long after the sub's commander would have thought he was safe from counterattack.[39]

Despite its success in developing effective anti-submarine tactics, Bush remained concerned that ASWORG, by remaining in OSRD, was being kept out of the loop with the navy. In February 1943 Bush told his colleague Karl Compton that he thought operations research would "prosper to best advantage" if the various services did it themselves, rather than feeling that it was "being forced upon them in any way by any outside." By July 1943, Bush saw his chance to transfer ASWORG out of OSRD and into the navy. Fleet Admiral King had established the Tenth Fleet just a few months earlier. It was the only numbered fleet without any ships. Instead, its remit was to consolidate all anti-submarine operations—air, surface, and convoy—under one command, bringing everything to bear on the growing U-boat menace. Both King and his chief of staff of the Tenth Fleet, Rear Admiral Francis S. Low, agreed to the transfer of ASWORG. Low made certain that ASWORG scientists were henceforth kept abreast of all necessary information to do their jobs—he was the admiral who "with a straight face" told Philip Morse about Enigma and Ultra.[40]

Later in July 1943, Bush and Archambault spent three weeks touring British scientific and military facilities, seeing how the British and American scientists were integrated into ASW operations. They stayed aboard Vice Admiral Louis Mountbatten's armed yacht HMS *Sister Anne*, now part of the Royal Naval Reserve (as Bush took pains to point out, the yacht was skippered by Lieutenant Commander Ronald McNairn Teacher of Teacher's Scotch whiskey distillery; he may have been the source for Archambault's legendary ability to supply strictly rationed whiskey for official OSRD functions at Claridge's Hotel). Upon his return, Bush further embedded OSRD directly into the military, creating the Office of Field Service, which placed combat scientists, many engaged in operations research, with troops and aircrews on the front lines to help make their new weapons and equipment work more effectively.[41]

Bletchley Park and the Naval Communications Annex broke the German codes that gave the Allies the position of wolfpacks, while Blackett's OR teams and ASWORG had shown the best ways to search for and attack U-boats. A third countermeasure, high-frequency direction-finding, gave the Allies the means to locate individual U-boats in order to avoid them or pinpoint them for destruction.

Huff-Duff

If codebreaking and operations research achieved their big-screen debuts in *The Imitation Game*, high-frequency direction-finding had its brief moment in the 2020 film *Greyhound*, based on C. S. Forester's 1955 novel, *The Good Shepherd*. It stars Tom Hanks as the commander of a US destroyer escorting a North Atlantic convoy soon after the American entry into the war. At the time the film and novel are set (February 1942), British warships were being equipped with high-frequency direction-finding—HF/DF or Huff-Duff—but American warships were not. A signalman reading a message from the British convoy commander spells out Huff-Duff, with a quizzical expression on his face; the commander impatiently explains, "High-frequency direction-finding. Continue, please," after which the signalman continues, "Huff-Duff reports a German transmission bearing 087 degrees." This exchange concisely depicts exactly what Huff-Duff did: provide accurate bearings to the high-frequency (HF) radio transmitters employed by U-boats, transmitters that they used on an almost continuous basis to coordinate their attacks on convoys.[42]

Watson-Watt claimed HF/DF as the third of his "three steps to victory" and called himself its "proud parent," though as with his two other steps, radar and operations research, he grumbled that the Americans had given it a "pet-name," Huff-Duff. Also like the other two steps, Watson-Watt was not the inventor of HF/DF but was responsible for bringing it into military service. Radio direction-finding as a means of navigation began in the early 1900s, just a few years after Guglielmo Marconi developed wireless telegraphy. During World War One, Watson-Watt, then at the Meteorological Office, investigated radio direction-finding (DF) to track and predict thunderstorms to assist pilots. Lightning strikes emit short-lived radio waves, and Watson-Watt innovated the use of cathode-ray tubes, which left a visible phosphor trace on the screen long after the initial image. By 1926 he had combined this with an Adcock antenna—two sets of dipole antennae set at right angles, to accurately determine bearings—which allowed operators to follow and measure the radio signals on the screen. In 1930 Watson-Watt proposed his system to the Air Ministry as a means of tracking aircraft by their HF voice radios, and during the 1936 Air Exercises, its effectiveness convinced Hugh Dowding to incorporate HF/DF into the Chain Home system.[43]

In 1940, soon after the Battle of the Atlantic had begun, Blackett (then still working on Chain Home) suggested to both Watson-Watt and the Admiralty that a series of HF/DF stations should be located at shore establishments and on ships to find the "talkative U-boats," as Watson-Watt called them. Doenitz was well aware of the dangers posed by his continuous radio communications, but by directing the creation of a short-signal (*kurzsignale*) system that kept coded transmissions under twenty seconds, he was confident that any Allied direction-finders would not have enough time to take accurate bearings. He did not know, and would not find out until after the war, that the Allies were already developing improved HF/DF systems that provided almost instantaneous bearings on the U-boats, helping to seal their fate.[44]

The Admiralty set up HF/DF shore stations in the British Isles, Canada, Bermuda, and other posts around the Atlantic. The position of a U-boat could be determined by mapping where the lines of bearing from two or more stations crossed. Right from the start it was understood that a shore-based system could only provide approximate fixes given the great distances (a one-degree discrepancy over 500 miles is a potential twenty-mile-wide error), and the delay in reporting contacts to convoys meant that evading wolfpacks or locating U-boats to attack was critically hampered. The Royal Navy began equipping convoy escort warships with rudimentary HF/DF systems in 1940. These early systems—notably the FH-3, built by Marconi—performed haphazardly because they were not equipped with still-scarce cathode-ray tubes, meaning the operator had to rotate the antenna and listen through headphones for the null or minimum signal (which sometimes took longer than the German transmission), and also because steel shipboard superstructures were interfering with the antennae themselves. The Royal Navy went through a series of trial-and-error efforts to develop corrections for the problem of ship structures, and by the end of 1942 there were seventy British escorts in the North Atlantic fitted with HF/DF.

The combination of shore-based and shipboard HF/DF allowed 60 percent of early convoys to be routed around wolfpacks. By mid-1943, the newer FH-4 models, now fitted with cathode-ray tubes that allowed the operator to visually fix a bearing on the screen almost instantly, began emerging from the Plessey factory in Ilford (eastern London), which was housed in five miles of disused Central Line Underground tunnels for protection, with over 2,000 women working per shift in conditions that resembled those of coal mines.

THE UNITED STATES NAVY was aware of HF/DF long before Pearl Harbor. In autumn 1940, the American special naval observer in London, Vice Admiral Robert Ghormley, reported back to Washington that HF/DF was important to the conduct of the war, and that the British wanted close cooperation with the Americans on establishing more HF/DF stations around the Atlantic perimeter. A year later, in October 1941, after favorable reports from American Neutrality Patrols convoy escorts, the Navy ordered the development of its own HF/DF system. Once again, Americans turned to overseas expertise for assistance—but that expertise was French, not British. Henri Busignies was an electrical engineer at the International Telephone and Telegraph (ITT) Laboratories in Paris, part of the American conglomerate's growing presence across Europe. He began developing automatic direction-finding equipment for aircraft, after helping Charles Lindbergh correct his compass following his 1927 solo transatlantic flight. In 1938, the French navy approached ITT to develop an HF/DF system to locate U-boats at sea, based on its intelligence that the Kriegsmarine was planning to communicate via short, coded HF transmissions.

Busignies's extensive DF experience led him to create a device very similar to Watson-Watt's, combining an Adcock antenna with a cathode-ray tube to achieve an instant bearing. He had built four working models of the device by June 1940, when the Nazis overran France and occupied Paris. The head of the ITT laboratory, Maurice Deloraine, kept both the British Admiralty and ITT head offices in New York apprised of Busignies's work, and received word that any British ship available would take them to

New York, where they would be welcomed. The two men wrapped drawings and vital pieces of the HF/DF units into seven bundles of brown paper and convinced an unknowing railway worker to hide them in his railroad car. Accompanied by their families and carrying their bundles, Busignies, Deloraine, and two other ITT engineers fled to the American embassy in Lyon, after which they made their way to Lisbon. There they boarded the steamer SS *Siboney*, along with author and pilot Antoine de Saint-Exupéry, film director Jean Renoir, and hundreds of Jewish refugees, and arrived in Hoboken, New Jersey, on December 31, 1940. Coming from war-ravaged France, their first experience in America was the exuberant New Year's Eve celebrations in Manhattan.[45]

ITT wasted no time putting Busignies to work replicating his HF/DF invention. In January 1941, after a brief meeting with the navy, ITT landed a contract to build several land-based sets for testing, designated the DAJ model. That fall, after the navy put in a large production order, ITT ramped up manufacture of the DAJ and added 150 engineers to the original four French ones, extending the HF/DF network with sites along the eastern seaboard from Bar Harbor, Maine, to Jupiter, Florida. The entry of the United States into the war considerably accelerated HF/DF development; in March 1942, Busignies and Deloraine were called to the Naval Research Laboratory (NRL) in Washington to discuss fitting their system to convoy escort warships. They were aware of the interference problems the British experienced with steel shipboard superstructures, so they suggested their HF/DF antenna be located on the highest mast. When told that was where the radar would go, Busignies said, "Then I propose you remove it and place our antenna there instead." (The dilemma was solved by placing HF/DF and radar on separate masts.)

In March, NRL tested both the ITT system—designated DAQ—and a British-supplied FH-3 system side-by-side at sea aboard the destroyer USS *Corry*. The trials demonstrated that the two systems gave "somewhat equivalent performances," though Busignies's system, with its cathode-ray tube offering an instantaneous bearing, had the edge. The equivalent British FH-4 unit was not yet available, so in June 1942, ITT was contracted to produce enough sets of the DAQ model Huff-Duff (it is not clear when that "pet-name" came into use) to equip half of all convoy escort warships, an order that grew to 4,000 sets by the end of the war.[46]

Samuel Eliot Morison, who became the US Navy's official historian with his monumental fifteen-volume *History of United States Naval Operations in World War II*, spoke glowingly of Huff-Duff from personal experience, having pulled convoy escort duty in 1942 aboard the destroyer USS *Buck*. "A convoy is no better than its ears and eyes," he wrote in the first volume. "Radar furnished the convoys with a cat's eyes, sonar with its ears, while the Huff-Duff, picking up from land or ship the radio transmissions of U-boats at sea, acted as highly sensitive and elongated cat's whiskers."[47]

By the middle of 1943, both the American and British navies had significant numbers of all three systems at sea, and were learning to use them in unison during convoy operations. Shipboard Huff-Duff had a range of up to thirty miles, far greater than that of radar or sonar, so it was usually the first to provide indication that U-boats were in the vicinity. Escort warships as well as long-range patrol aircraft—American B-24 Liberators and British Wellingtons, for example—were then being fitted with 10-centimeter (later the more accurate 3-centimeter) microwave radar to find U-boats out to ten or more miles, even when only the periscope was showing. Sonar and ASDIC, whose range was measured in hundreds of yards, then fixed the final position of the submarines. But once the U-boats were found, the escorts still had to sink them.

"An Awful Wallop"

During World War Two, Allied warships sank U-boats using depth charges or variants thereof (aircraft used depth charges, and later in the war acoustic torpedoes). After fixing the position of the submerged U-boat by ASDIC or sonar—mounted near the bow so it could ping and listen ahead of the ship—the crew would run the ship above the target, then drop or throw depth charges from, or near, the stern. These exploded at a preset depth, damaging or sinking the U-boat by underwater shock even when they went off a short distance away from it. The disadvantage of depth charges was that since the warship had to pass over the submarine to sink it, the crew lost ASDIC or sonar contact, often giving the U-boat commander time to evade the attack. Later ASW weapons, with the unlikely names Hedgehog, Mousetrap, and Squid, were more accurate and effective because they were launched ahead of the ship while the U-boat was still within ASDIC/sonar contact.

Due to its early proximity to the U-boat threat, Britain was always ahead of the United States in development of these weapons during both world wars, and helped the Americans jump-start their own efforts to enter the fight. The Royal Navy was building precursors to the depth charge even before the outbreak of World War One in 1914. Since underwater mines were already in common use, the first depth charges were called "droppable mines." Rolled off the stern of a ship, they would sink to a preset depth and explode automatically, using a newly patented hydrostatic trigger that could be depth-adjusted just before launch. The first such weapons were unwieldy, but by 1916 the Type D depth charge, with 300 pounds of TNT, came into standard (and successful) use. When the United States entered the war in 1917, it had only a few puny 50-pound mines, which were set off by a lanyard at a single, fixed depth. That summer, a British exchange engineering officer, Lieutenant Commander Herbert Mock, brought plans for the Type D depth charge to the Navy's Bureau of Ordnance (BuOrd) in Washington, and assisted in the development of an American version, designated Mark II, which had minor differences from the Type D. Six companies were contracted in 1917 to build 10,000 Mark IIs for the US Navy and 15,000 Type Ds for the Royal Navy, with many more ordered before the war ended the following year.[48]

THE TYPE D AND Mark II depth charges became the standard ASW weapon until the beginning of World War Two, but between the wars, both the United States and Britain were improving explosives. TNT was often in short supply, so chemists created explosives like amatol and minol, which combined TNT with ammonium nitrate, and developed entirely new nitrogen-based compounds such as cyclonite, better known by its British cover name Research Department Explosive or RDX. "Research

Department" referred to the establishment at the Royal Arsenal Woolwich, which in the 1930s created a process that combined formaldehyde, ammonia, and nitric acid to form RDX. Two industrial plants began producing RDX at the start of the war, but since it was too sensitive (easily detonated) for direct use, it was combined with TNT and other additives to make explosives such as Composition B and Torpex.[49]

Right away, RDX and its derivatives were caught in a tug-of-war between bombing land targets and destroying U-boats. As the head of the RAF Coastal Command, Philip Joubert, noted to the Air Ministry in September 1941, Torpex was weight-for-weight about 50 percent more effective than amatol. "It seems to me," he continued, "of the greatest importance to have our depth charges filled with Torpex since it would greatly increase our chance of getting kills." Meanwhile, Bomber Command placed "special priority" and "first priority" on Torpex for the massive blockbuster, Tallboy, and bouncing bombs that would destroy German cities, the battleship *Tirpitz*, and Ruhr Valley dams. Long before these bombs and depth charges could become reality, it was apparent that the need for RDX far outstripped Britain's ability to produce it. The United States was the last, best hope for its supply.[50]

American military chemists had experimented with cyclonite in the 1920s but rejected it as too expensive to produce. The Tizard Mission of autumn 1940 brought information on the less expensive Woolwich Arsenal process "to interest United States authorities in the adoption of RDX," as a later Ministry of Supply memo ruefully noted, "but the response was not enthusiastic." That memo was wrong. Unknown to the British at the time, in November 1940 the National Defense Research Committee (soon to be OSRD) had contracted with three American universities to examine the Woolwich Arsenal method and another developed by McGill University in Canada (which used formaldehyde, ammonium nitrate, and acetic anhydride). The organic chemist Werner Bachmann at the University of Michigan soon developed a new process, combining the Woolwich and McGill methods, that promised to greatly increase the output of RDX compared with either. While Bachmann continued his work, Conant went to Britain in March 1941 to formalize US-British scientific ties and establish the OSRD London Mission. The Ministry of Supply, which believed "it would be best to try all means of getting the United States Government to erect these [RDX] plants as part of its own rearmament program," invited Conant to speak with them on the matter, after which he visited the Woolwich Arsenal.[51]

Conant's timing was impeccable. Congress had just approved the Lend-Lease Act, which opened the transatlantic rearmament spigot, while reports reached American ears—notably those of Rear Admiral William "Spike" Blandy, chief of BuOrd—of the powerful new Torpex depth charges. Within weeks of the Conant Mission, a series of meetings in Washington, DC, between representatives of OSRD, the US Navy, and the British Supply Council led to a request for 300 tons of RDX per week, split equally between the US Navy and Britain. In July 1941, Blandy requested Congress to appropriate $70 million ($20 billion today) to build such a plant, to which Congress agreed. But with RDX still being confected in American laboratories only in small quantities, it was not clear how it could be produced at industrial scale.

At that time, Bachmann was fine-tuning his RDX combination process, which used nitric acid, formaldehyde, ammonium nitrate, and acetic anhydride and promised to vastly reduce the quantities needed of the expensive (and limited-supply) chemicals. He was aided by a number of other researchers in Canada and Britain, where RDX factories switched over to the Bachmann process in lieu of the McGill and Woolwich methods. In October 1941, OSRD formally joined these nations in the RDX Committee, whose scientists communicated by coded telegrams: "golf at Ann Arbor" and "golf at Montreal" meant committee meetings, while "ship 1000 lb. golf balls" was a request for RDX samples.

But the Bachmann process was still carried out in batches—the chemical reactions had to finish in one batch before a new batch could be started—which limited its ability to achieve industrial-scale production. Unfazed, OSRD commissioned three companies to establish pilot plants for RDX manufacture. One of them, the Tennessee Eastman Company, had long experience processing acetic anhydride, which its parent company, Eastman Kodak, used in great quantities for its so-called safety film, which was less combustible than nitrate films. Eastman understood that the pilot plant would require a continuous process instead of batch production. In January 1942 Eastman chemists devised a "jeep" reactor, a U-shaped tube that allowed chemicals to be fed into the stream at various stages in the process without stopping the production flow. This became the basis for the small Wexler Bend Pilot Plant, located near Kingsport, Tennessee.

Wexler Bend began operations in February 1942, producing 700 pounds of RDX per day. Encouraged by these results, in June 1942 OSRD contracted with Eastman for the ten-square-mile Holston Ordnance Works at Kingsport, built under the supervision of US Army Corps of Engineers Colonel Leslie Groves, who was also overseeing another Corps project, the construction of the Pentagon, and would soon be in charge of the Manhattan Project. Holston began RDX production in April 1943, generating 20 tons of RDX a day. Factory workers, one-third of them women, then combined it with TNT to produce the less sensitive Composition B, which could be shipped as pellets in fifty-pound boxes with relative safety. From Holston the Composition B went by rail to ammunition depots and loading facilities for filling bombs and munitions. A portion went to factories like the Nebraska Ordnance Plant, where Torpex was made by remelting Composition B pellets and mixing it with aluminum powder to give it more destructive power for depth charges, torpedoes, and other weapons. These were sent to munitions shipping ports such as Yorktown, Virginia, loaded onto cargo ships, and sent overseas. By the height of the war in 1944, Holston was producing 577 tons of RDX per day. To put this in perspective, one week's output from Holston was equivalent to an entire year's RDX production in all of Britain.

Despite having factories running non-stop in the United States, Canada, and Britain, RDX still had to be carefully doled out. In early 1942, with America fully in the fight and no longer just a shadow factory for Britain, a series of five combined boards were established to coordinate the manufacture and allocation of munitions and supplies between the Allies. The Combined Munitions Assignments Board was in charge of distributing RDX, Composition B, and Torpex, assigning 10 percent of US production for British purchase. Torpex was particularly sought after for the Battle of the

Atlantic; one submarine commander remarked that his Torpex warheads "carry an awful wallop." In December 1942, Spike Blandy requested of Fleet Admiral King to use Torpex in all depth charges, despite problems with its susceptibility to exploding when hit by enemy gunfire. King approved the request, agreeing that "some risk might be accepted" given Torpex's proven effectiveness. King's approval came just in time, for a new type of anti-submarine weapon named Hedgehog was just being brought into service. Smaller but more accurate than over-the-stern depth charges, and with contact fuzes that ensured the U-boat was destroyed when struck, it needed the "awful wallop" of Torpex to make it lethal.[52]

The Hedgehog

The Hedgehog anti-submarine weapon was born of two hastily established departments in the British government. Ministry of Defence 1 (MD1), nicknamed, as noted earlier, "Churchill's Toyshop" and just a few miles from his residence at Chequers, created specialized weaponry for the British Army, but also contributed innovations to the other services. The Admiralty's Department of Miscellaneous Weapons Development— DMWD or "Department of Wheezers and Dodgers"—researched and developed weaponry for maritime and naval use. One of MD1's first hires was Stewart Blacker, ostensibly an army officer but better described by the clichéd term "adventurer." He served in the Indian Army, was shot down three times while a pilot in World War One, and organized the first successful flight over Mount Everest. He also invented weapons, notably the Blacker Bombard (he was hardly self-effacing), a lightweight spigot mortar designed for the Territorial Army against invading German tanks. Unlike standard mortars, which fired shells from large, heavy barrels, the spigot mortar was a simple steel pole over which the mortar round—with its own propellant charge—was fitted and fired.

In August 1940 at Chequers, MD1 demonstrated the Blacker Bombard to Churchill, who authorized its production. Several months later, during one of their regular information exchanges, the head of MD1 brought plans for the Blacker Bombard to his counterpart at DMWD, Charles Goodeve, a Canadian chemist who had a hand in producing many British weapons for land and sea. Goodeve immediately saw a naval use for it. The Royal Navy had been wrestling with the concept of an ahead-firing anti-submarine mortar for over a year. The idea was to catch a U-boat ahead of the ship and, while still in ASDIC range, fire a pattern of mortar rounds that would quickly descend and explode on contact with the submarine's hull. The current prototype, the Fairlie mortar, was proving heavy, complex, and unwieldy. Goodeve was convinced that the Blacker Bombard could be adapted to become a simple, lightweight submarine killer.[53]

DWMD calculated the correct angles of the spigots so that the weapon would throw an elliptical pattern of mortar rounds, each filled with 35 pounds of Torpex, about 600 feet ahead of the ship. A boilermaker fabricated the mortar itself, while the mortar rounds were made by Boosey and Hawkes, a musical instrument maker known for its brass trumpets. By March 1941, the device was ready for a demonstration. Goodeve got wind that Churchill was to be shown a new anti-tank bombard near Chequers, not far from where DWMD and MD1 were developing Hedgehog (so named because it resembled the prickly mammal), and contrived to get Churchill to see his weapon as well. After the prime minister witnessed the anti-tank bombard in operation, he looked at his watch and said, "Time for lunch," telling Goodeve he would see Hedgehog another time. Churchill's daughter Mary, who accompanied her father and had been in conversation with one of the naval officers involved with Hedgehog, asked to see the new weapon. "There is plenty of time to do so," she later recalled telling her father, and to everyone's surprise, he relented. Driving to the test site, they witnessed the mortar fire twenty-four rounds through the air and straddle a submarine-shaped target on the ground hundreds of feet away, with several making a direct hit on the target. Churchill asked for a second salvo, then a third.[54]

Word of its success got out quickly. The following day, Goodeve was called into the office of the First Sea Lord, Dudley Pound, who got straight to the point: "This anti-submarine gun of yours . . . how soon can you arrange a trial for me?" Pound threw his weight behind the development of

Hedgehog; by May 1941 it was fitted to a destroyer for trials, and by the end of the year it was being installed on convoy escorts. Over 130 units were deployed before a larger mortar called Squid was put into service.[55]

At the same time DMWD was developing Hedgehog, the US Navy had asked the National Academy of Sciences to study problems in ASW, and in February 1941 they recommended, among other things, the development of ahead-firing weapons. So when John Tate from OSRD went on the Conant Mission to Britain a few months later and returned with plans of the Hedgehog prototype, it caught the attention of the navy. OSRD and the navy tasked the California Institute of Technology (Caltech) to start with the British drawings for Hedgehog and improve the launcher and mortar rounds. During 1941 and early 1942, a consortium of scientists, engineers, and machinists, mostly around Pasadena, developed new rocket motors and created a larger, more streamlined round.[56]

By June 1942, the US Navy had its own version of Hedgehog—officially the Antisubmarine Projector Mark 10—and contracted with Carrier Corporation of Syracuse, New York, to manufacture it. Carrier was hardly the obvious choice; its South Geddes Street plant was already working flat out to build air-conditioning and drying units for the military and the munitions industries. But the company assigned its top engineer, Henry Galson (who later invented the ubiquitous window-mounted air conditioner), and a six-man team to redesign the weapon for production. Despite the secrecy surrounding the project, Galson brought home his drawings every night, after dinner working on them on his dining room table. In the original British design, each launcher spigot was individually mounted and shimmed into position; Galson redesigned a single casting for all the spigots, making the weapon both easier to fabricate and more uniform.

Carrier also chose expediency over secrecy by testing the weapon on a thirty-acre farm in Camillus, a rural town outside Syracuse, New York, that was owned by one of the company's executives. In late 1942, Carrier was building the Hedgehog (Figure 17) at the rate of eighty per month; by the following year it was the US Navy's premier ASW weapon, with 1,501 units deployed across the fleet (a lighter version called Mousetrap was fitted to a few smaller ships). In its most famous series of engagements, in May 1944 aboard destroyer escort USS *England* (DE-635), Hedgehog was credited with sinking six Japanese submarines in twelve days, a record that has not since been equaled.[57]

Winning the Battle of the Atlantic

The Kriegsmarine later referred to it as "die Glückliche Zeit," the Happy Time. Starting in July 1940, after the fall of France, Germany was able to base U-boats, ships, and aircraft in French Atlantic ports such as Brest, Lorient, and Saint-Nazaire. Attacks on British convoys went almost unimpeded until the spring of 1941. Over the course of the first four months of the Happy Time, the German navy sank almost 300 merchant ships with a loss of just six U-boats, none of the capital ships, and the "scourge" Focke-Wulf Condors almost unscathed. The problem for the British was not simply that the German navy enjoyed unfettered access to the Atlantic Ocean, instead of passing through the chokepoints around the North Sea. Since the mid-1930s, the Kriegsmarine radio intelligence bureau Beobachtungs-Dienst (B-Dienst) had been successfully decrypting the British naval codes and ciphers. Naval Code, used for merchant shipping, was broken in 1935, so the Kriegsmarine knew exactly where to hunt for convoys just days after the war began. Naval Cypher Numbers 1 and 2 were largely cracked by early 1940, allowing Germany to respond to the planned Anglo-French invasion of Norway. Like their German counterparts, the Admiralty had full faith that its codes and ciphers could not be decrypted, and sought other reasons for the German successes.

Those reasons were not hard to identify. GC&CS was unable to break more than a fraction of the German naval and U-boat cyphers, even with the new bombes installed at Bletchley Park, leaving Admiralty intelligence well astern of the Kriegsmarine. HF/DF was still primarily used from shore stations, which gave less-than-accurate fixes, and the few convoy escorts equipped with shipboard HF/DF were ironing out the kinks in getting it to work aboard a steel vessel. The mid-Atlantic gap, where convoys received no air cover to spot and attack U-boats, seemed stubbornly unbridgeable.

When convoys did have air cover, the few airborne radars in service were unreliable—the cavity magnetron was still a laboratory experiment—and even when U-boats were located, attacks with depth charges were often unsuccessful due both to ineffective tactics and to inadequate explosives. Despite British and Canadian shipyards running at full tilt, they could not build escort warships and merchant ships fast enough to keep up with the losses and meet the increasing demands for more convoys, while the convoys themselves remained small and insufficiently protected.[58]

The Kriegsmarine lost some of its advantage during 1941. The death of its top three U-boat aces in March coincided with Churchill's proclamation of the Battle of the Atlantic, which signaled a more aggressive approach—if more in rhetoric than in practice. The mid-Atlantic gap was slowly being narrowed with more long-range bombers, equipped with better radar and powerful Leigh lights for targeting submarines at night. *Bismarck* was sunk and other German capital ships were put out of action. The capture of several U-boat Enigma machines gave Bletchley codebreakers a boost.

It was therefore the greatest of ironies that the American entry into the war marked the Kriegsmarine's second Happy Time, with Operation Drumbeat deploying U-boats along America's eastern seaboard, with similar operations in the Caribbean and Gulf of Mexico. Despite the fact that the Arcadia Conference had established the Battle of the Atlantic as the Allies' top priority, Fleet Admiral King had his eye firmly on the Japanese threat in the Pacific, and refused to transfer even a small number of escort warships from the West Coast for Atlantic convoy duty. In King's eyes, unprotected convoys were more inviting targets than individual ships, so he resisted British recommendations for even minimal convoy protection, despite hundreds of sinkings every month.

This problem was exacerbated by the fact that the Kriegsmarine knew when and where American merchant ships were sailing, because B-Dienst had broken the Combined Naval Cypher No. 3, allowing them to eavesdrop on all Allied shipping communications (GC&CS, through its own code-breaking, had early indications of the breach, but it was not until confirmation by OP-20-G the following year that Cypher No. 3 was replaced). At the same time, the Germans switched from the three-wheel Enigma to the four-wheel model, rendering Ultra almost deaf, which the new shipboard Huff-Duffs only partially made up for. By July 1942, American losses had become so untenable that Roosevelt himself ordered King to instate an interlocking convoy system that stretched from Brazil to Newfoundland. Darkened coastal cities also became the norm.

March 1943 marked the largest convoy battle of the war. Slow convoy SC 122 left New York on March 5 with sixty mostly British merchant vessels. HX 229 left three days later with forty merchantmen, including seven Liberty ships. Both convoys handed off escorts en route. Awaiting them were three lines of wolfpacks with a total of thirty-eight U-boats, alerted to the sailings by B-Dienst intercepts of Naval Cypher 3. GC&CS was temporarily unable to decrypt Shark to provide a warning, and HF/DF gave only the approximate position of one U-boat. The wolfpacks caught HX 229 first on March 16, sinking eight ships in as many hours. The next day they sighted and attacked the nearby SC 122, sinking another five ships. The convoys soon converged on parallel courses, engaged in a running battle with the U-boats. By March 19 Doenitz called off his wolfpacks, having sunk twenty-two merchant ships with the loss of only one U-boat.

Yet this climactic German victory signaled the beginning of the end of the U-boat threat. That month, the Atlantic Convoy Conference in Washington established new anti-submarine measures and increased mid-Atlantic air coverage by long-range bombers and escort aircraft carriers, setting the stage for the remainder of the Battle of the Atlantic. The Allies, led by the United States' Liberty ship program, were launching cargo ships faster than they could be sunk, and those were sailing in ever-larger convoys. The first American bombes, combined with the British ones, were successfully attacking tens of thousands of Shark intercepts, while Naval Cypher Number 3 was retired and replaced with a new cipher that rendered B-Dienst effectively deaf. The US Navy's Tenth Fleet was established, with ASWORG as its flagship arm to advise on the best ways to find and sink U-boats. Those U-boats were being located by microwave radar and Huff-Duff, and attacks using a combination of Torpex-filled depth charges and Hedgehogs were proving ever more lethal.[59]

The combination of Allied tactics, weapons, and intelligence dramatically changed the fortunes of the opposing forces in the North Atlantic. In all of 1942, 1,100 merchant ships were lost in and around the North Atlantic, compared with 86 U-boats sunk (a twelve-to-one ratio). From September to December 1943, 67 merchant ships were sunk, against 64 U-boats. This nearly one-for-one exchange was untenable for Doenitz, who could not replace the lost submarines since shipyards and factories were also being smashed by bombing raids, while the fortified submarine pens along the French seaboard were subject to weekly attacks. He reacted to this reversal of fortune by shifting his U-boat operations from the mid-Atlantic to the Western Approaches, where they were in range of support from the naval air arm of the Luftwaffe. Doenitz could not afford to let up in his efforts to cut off the Allied supply line. German leaders guessed that the Allies would attempt a cross-Channel attack sometime after February 1944, probably in the spring, but they had no doubt that the invasion was imminent.

The experience of convoy SC 154 and the sinking of *U-845* best illustrates how the combination of British and American science and engineering won the Battle of the Atlantic. SC 154 departed Halifax on February 28, 1944, with thirty merchant ships including *Ocean Courier*, one of the first Todd-Kaiser ships built for the British Merchant Shipbuilding Mission. Nine Landing Ship, Tanks (LSTs) carried troops, fuel, general cargo, and explosives, much of which would have been Torpex and Composite B. The Allies knew, from Shark decryptions carried out at the Naval Communications Annex and relayed to Bletchley Park, that a wolfpack was attempting to intercept SC 154 and other nearby convoys, so they ordered two escort groups of destroyers and corvettes to hunt them down.

At 1400 (2:00 p.m.) on the afternoon of March 10, *U-845* sighted convoy SC 154 and radioed the information to the central U-boat command, BdU. One of the Canadian destroyers in the escort group, HMCS *St. Laurent*, picked up the transmission on Huff-Duff and headed for the U-boat in the company of Canadian corvette HMCS *Owen Sound* and British destroyer HMS *Forester*. They sighted *U-845* at 1630 (4:30 p.m.) but lost it when it dove. Taking its last known position as the center of a two-mile square, the groups carried out an expanding box search plan originally developed by

ASWORG, circling in a clockwise pattern. They reacquired the submarine on ASDIC at 1650. The report of the forty-five surviving U-boat crewmen, as annotated by the Admiralty Intelligence Division, picks up the story:

> Some time elapsed before the depth charges began to explode. *U-845* dived to about 180 metres (590 feet), and the first pattern exploded well above her, doing no harm. HMCS *Owen Sound* fired a pattern of depth-charges at 1657, HMCS *St. Laurent*, 20 depth-charges at 1704, and Hedgehog at 1715. At 1926 HMS *Forester* commenced firing a creeping attack pattern of 22 depth-charges with deep settings. . . . Suddenly the batteries went dead. The [commanding officer] decided to attempt escape on the surface. At 2234 the U-boat surfaced, and fire was opened with all weapons that would bear. At 2315 the U-boat was observed to be down by the stern, and was taking violent evasive action. *St. Laurent* fired a 10-charge pattern. She observed that the forward gun was hanging over the side, and that the U-boat appeared to be on fire internally at the base of the conning tower. At 2338 the U-boat sank.

The final toll of that convoy battle was one Allied tanker and four warships lost, against ten U-boats sunk. SC 154 arrived in Liverpool on March 15, adding its cargo to the millions of tons and troops already in Britain. All nine LSTs would go on to take part in Operation Overlord.[60]

By June 1944, the Allies had opened and maintained the 3,500-mile stretch of water across the North Atlantic, allowing the massive buildup of men and material in the British Isles. Now the invasion of Europe and ultimate victory depended upon opening and maintaining a 150-mile stretch across the English Channel and, most urgently, crossing the last few hundred yards of surf to land troops, armor, and equipment on the beaches of Normandy.

CHAPTER 6

FIGHT ON THE BEACHES

THE BLITZ ENDED with a bang the night of May 10–11, 1941. That night, German bomber crews flew over 500 sorties, resulting in the greatest devastation that London had seen in the war. Over 1,400 died, thousands more were injured, and the destruction included the whole of Westminster, with the House of Commons itself in flames. This raid was followed by almost total silence. Week after week, no German bomber was seen over London. Newspapers continued reporting the war headlines—the battle-ship *Bismarck* was sunk, Germany invaded Crete—but only on June 5 did they report the first air raid in twenty-six days, with just a few bombers, and it resulted in "no extensive damage." No public explanations for this lack of activity were offered, until a week later when the papers proclaimed what Churchill and his closest advisors, alerted by Bletchley Park codebreakers and numerous other sources, already knew: "German armies on Stalin's frontier." With those armies came the German bombers that had previously filled the skies over London.[1]

Stalin had received warnings months earlier of the impending German attack, even from Churchill himself, but he mistrusted not just the message but the messenger. He was therefore blindsided on June 22, when Hitler launched Operation Barbarossa with three army groups that swept toward Leningrad, Moscow, and Kiev. Although Stalin's forces outnumbered the Germans on paper, they were outclassed and overrun by the speed and mass of tanks and aircraft thrown at them. Soviet troops fell back many hundreds of miles in just days; whole cities and entire industries were evacuated behind the Volga River and Ural Mountains.

A month later, Stalin was asking Churchill for relief in the form of a second front in northern France, which he argued would "not only divert Hitler's forces from the East, but at the same time would make it impossible for Hitler to invade Britain." Churchill was never going to fall for that ploy; he already knew that the window for Operation Sealion (the Nazi cover name for the planned invasion) had come and gone back in September 1940. In any event, his Chiefs of Staff had examined the problem and concluded they did not have the forces needed to mount a major amphibious assault against France, of the size needed to produce "useful results." He reported this to Stalin on July 20. The Germans, he wrote, had forty divisions in France and the coast "bristled" with fortifications.[2]

This would be the earliest of increasingly insistent petitions to open a second front on the beaches of France, not just from Stalin but later from Roosevelt. What Churchill could not tell Stalin at the time, and what he eventually had to confide to Roosevelt, was that Britain and the Allies did not yet have the proper types of ships that could land tanks and heavy equipment on the beaches, without which any invasion would be doomed. Churchill knew this because his own career had been nearly wrecked by this lack twenty-five years earlier during World War One, on the beaches of Gallipoli.

The Problem of Amphibious Assaults

Appalled by the stalemate and slaughter on the Western Front at the end of 1914, Churchill, then First Lord of the Admiralty, had slowly warmed to the strategy of bringing a combined French-British fleet through the Dardanelles Straits, in modern-day Turkey, to destroy the Ottoman fortifications along the Gallipoli Peninsula. This would open up the Dardanelles and the Black Sea, allowing Britain to assist its ally Russia. It would also cut off the Ottoman Empire from its own ally, Germany, and potentially end the war. The initial attacks on March 18, 1915, ended in catastrophe for the French and British. Older British and French battleships shelled the forts to little effect, but some were themselves sunk or damaged by a combination of shore gunfire and sea mines. The most tragic loss was the French battleship *Bouvet*, which was struck either by an artillery shell or by a mine and capsized in fifty seconds, taking 650 men with it. Unable to sustain a naval attack, the French and British instead opted for an amphibious assault on Gallipoli to capture the forts.[3]

As horrific as was the loss of *Bouvet*, the carnage during the ensuing eight-month-long Gallipoli Campaign was mind-numbing, the losses to both the invading Australian and New Zealand Army Corps (Anzac) and the defending Turkish troops today seared in their national consciousnesses. The first assaults began April 25, with 25,000 Anzac troops establishing a beachhead near Ari Burnu, immediately nicknamed Anzac Cove. The Royal Navy had no specialized craft for this; most of the troops were conveyed in unseaworthy rowboats that were initially towed by steam tugs but had to be rowed the last 300 yards. With no protection, the soldiers were easy targets for the German-built Ottoman guns as they struggled to clamber over the sides of the boats. At another beach, a converted troopship was intentionally run aground, only to have 700 troops mowed down by artillery and machine gun fire before they could even leave the ship. Further landings and massed assaults resulted in exactly the kind of stalemated trench warfare the British and French had tried to avoid.[4]

Roundly blamed for the Dardanelles and Gallipoli failures, Churchill resigned as First Lord in November, even before the campaign was halted, leaving half a million casualties on both sides. Disgraced though Churchill had been, the experience led him to imagine a scheme, as he wrote in his memoir *The Second World War*, of "using tanks to run ashore from specially-constructed landing craft on beaches." This was surely based on

the shallow-draft boats called X-lighters, designed by a civilian naval architect and fitted with a bow ramp for troops and pack animals, that were used
during later Gallipoli landings. Although his idea of tank-carrying landing
craft never was employed during World War One, Churchill filed the idea
for future use.[5]

"Large Armoured Irruptions"

That future use materialized in World War Two, when the concept of
tank-carrying landing craft was revived just after the Dunkirk evacuations.
During Churchill's tenure as First Lord of the Admiralty under Neville
Chamberlain, the Royal Navy had embarked on several commando raids
that attacked targets in France, and (with French and Polish forces) carried
out amphibious assaults in Norway. These latter were ultimately repulsed,
forcing the Allies to abandon their goal of capturing the critical port of
Narvik. For these raids, commandos and marines had used small craft built
by Thornycroft shipyards, which could carry a few dozen troops and light
vehicles, but no heavy equipment.

The need for landing craft that could also transport heavy tanks and
vehicles became apparent at Dunkirk, which, in a certain sense, was an amphibious assault in reverse. The evacuation of 338,000 troops was accomplished in part with craft little removed from the rowboats at Gallipoli, but
as already noted, it left tens of thousands of tanks, artillery, and vehicles
behind. Churchill, now of course prime minister, realized the lack of any
vessels to transport armor and equipment from the French beaches had
left Britain almost defenseless. He also realized that such vessels would be
needed to recapture France and Europe.

On June 6, 1940, Churchill revived his quarter-century-old idea of tank-
carrying landing craft in a carefully crafted minute to his chief of staff, Pug
Ismay, ordering him to submit proposals "for a vigorous, enterprising and
ceaseless offensive against the whole German-occupied coastline." In particular, Churchill wanted "flat-bottomed boats," out of which tanks and
armored vehicles "can crawl ashore, do a deep raid inland, and then back."

Over the next several weeks, not quite certain if the Admiralty or the Ministry of Supply should be in charge, he continued to hound both Ismay and his minister of supply, Herbert Morrison, for details on "what is being done about designing and planning vessels to transport tanks across the sea" and land them on beaches.[6]

At first, it would be neither. In July, Churchill created the Combined Operations Command, tasked with carrying out amphibious raids on the Continent using navy, army, and commando forces. This was simultaneous with the creation of the Special Operations Executive, and though both initially accomplished similar goals of laying the groundwork for a major assault, as outlined in the previously mentioned Appreciation of Future Strategy paper, the Special Operations forces were often parachuted into enemy territory, while Combined Operations focused on coastal assaults. The first director of Combined Operations was Admiral of the Fleet Roger Keyes (replaced in 1941 by Louis Mountbatten), who began expanding Britain's amphibious capabilities from small-scale raids to "large armoured irruptions" on the Continent, as Churchill noted in *The Second World War*. Keyes took charge of the landing craft project, instructing his staff to work with the naval architects at the Directorate of Naval Construction to turn Churchill's ideas into actual vessels.[7]

The naval architect who forged Churchill's concept into steel was Rowland Baker, a member of the Royal Corps of Naval Constructors, RCNC (which is how the Admiralty referred to its naval architects). Baker (Figure 18) was born in 1908 at Upchurch in Kent, within sight of the river Medway, the son of a bargeman from whom he claimed to have inherited "an almost infinite degree of patience," though his colleagues often found reason to dispute this claim. He had been working on small warships since joining the RCNC in 1932. In mid-July, three days after he received Keyes's requirements—carry three heavy tanks at a speed of 10 knots across the short distance of the Channel or North Sea, and land them in 2.5 feet of water—he had designed an open-decked vessel, known as a "Landing Craft, Tank" or LCT, of about 370 tons. Knowing that simplicity was the key to mass production, Baker insisted on slab-sided hull sections that could be fabricated by bridge-builders instead of shipyards, and also made certain the craft could use aircraft engines or locomotive diesels, more readily available than marine engines. By November, the first of these vessels were in the water, and by the end of the war, over 2,800 LCTs, based on Baker's initial designs, would be built on both sides of the Atlantic.[8]

Churchill's Concept of the Tank-Carrying Landing Ship Is Born

In September 1940, while Baker was beginning construction of the LCTs, Keyes and Churchill were developing a plan to land General Charles de Gaulle's Free French Forces at the strategic port of Dakar in Vichy-held French West Africa, where de Gaulle believed he could rally colonial forces to the side of the Allies and establish a base for further African operations. Operation Menace, as it was called, turned into a disaster. The plan was to land troops at a beach a few miles from the city, from where they would advance to capture the port, which would then be used to debark tanks and other heavy equipment from conventional cargo ships. The initial assault began September 23, but heavy fire kept the troops from even landing on the beach, and the assault was called off just two days later. British war planning for invading Europe had initially assumed that troops alone could capture a major port. Dakar proved to the British military that tanks were indispensable to capture a port. Moreover, these vehicles would have to be transported a long distance across the ocean, to be landed directly upon a beachhead.[9]

A month after Operation Menace, Churchill met with his Joint Planning Staff (composed of planning directors from each of the services and Combined Operation Command) to take the lessons from Dakar. The two-hour meeting took place on the evening of Sunday, October 27, 1940, in The Barn, an underground bunker in the disused Down Street tube station (in Mayfair just off Piccadilly) that Churchill and his cabinet employed as a temporary office while the Cabinet War Rooms were being reinforced during the Blitz. The problem, Churchill argued, was a vicious circle: it was necessary to capture a port to land the armor, but the port itself could not be captured without the use of tanks. However, there were no extant ships capable of carrying tanks on a long sea voyage to assault distant shores in Africa and southern Europe, since LCTs were too small and did not have the range. This problem, Churchill further argued, would constantly recur, and no offensive operations would be possible there until it was solved. According to the meeting minutes, Churchill directed the Admiralty's planning director, Captain Charles S. Daniel, to harness "the best engineering brains in country" to the problem of finding a way of landing tanks on a beach in 10 feet of water."[10]

When it came to the design of amphibious ships, Daniel knew that "the best engineering brains in country" were at the Directorate of Naval Construction (DNC), which was led by Stanley V. Goodall, who as mentioned had worked in the United States during World War One. Goodall assumed leadership of the DNC in 1936, and in 1939 oversaw the move from the Whitehall government offices in London to the Grand Pump Room Hotel in the city of Bath, made famous by Jane Austen's novels, among others. Although Bath was ostensibly safer than London, Goodall's diary entries made constant reference to day-and-night air raids, while lamenting that the distance kept him out of regular touch with the Whitehall naval staff.[11]

Goodall was on leave the day of Churchill's meeting at The Barn, and for a week afterward. On Sunday, November 10, he received a message from his boss, Third Sea Lord and controller of the navy (responsible for all matériel) Vice Admiral Bruce A. Fraser, about "big tank landing" ships. The next day, Goodall and the Admiralty staff discussed Churchill's concept of the tank-carrying landing ship, which would have sufficient range to get to Africa, the Mediterranean, and the Middle East, be big enough to carry an entire regiment of sixty tanks, and be able to land them on a shallow beach. The trade-off was that these ships needed a deeper draft to cross the ocean, which was not compatible with the shallow draft for beaching.

Goodall thought that a single, sixty-tank landing ship (nicknamed "Winston") would be too cumbersome, and suggested that the tanks instead be carried on three smaller, twenty-tank ships, which were immediately dubbed "Winettes." He took Baker off the LCT project (which had already launched its first craft) and had him develop designs for each concept. By December 10, Baker had sufficiently developed both designs to support the Winette concept, with Goodall's approval. On December 14, Captain Daniel submitted the three-Winette program to a Combined Operations planning conference, and after much deliberation, on December 19 the controller "told staff to make up their minds" regarding which concept to go with. They apparently did so quickly, for the following day, December 20, Goodall told his director of contract works to order the three Winettes.[12]

Goodall estimated that it would require up to two years to design and build the new ships (i.e., by late 1942). However, Britain lacked the industrial capacity to produce them in large numbers. On December 24, the controller approved the construction of Winettes in overseas shipyards in Canada or the United States. The bigger problem was that tank landing ships were needed for operations planned for mid-1941—just months away—which was not enough time for a new ship to be designed and built. Another solution that modified existing ships would have to be found. Goodall assigned one of his naval architects, Alfred T. S. Sheffer (who was on loan from Lloyd's Register, a leading ship classification society, but separate from the Lloyd's insurance syndicate), to convert three shallow-draft oil tankers that were in commercial service on Lake Maracaibo in Venezuela. Sheffer determined that these three ships, *Bachaquero*, *Misoa*, and *Tasajera*, could be converted to landing ships by having a "nose job," that is, cutting off part of the bow and fitting bow doors and a loading ramp. On Christmas Day 1940 the ships were transferred to the Admiralty, and by July 1941 they were converted to tank-carrying landing ships.[13]

Baker, meanwhile, had finished the initial plans and specifications for the three Winettes at the end of December 1940, which were then sent to Harland & Wolff shipbuilders of Belfast. They were now designated as Landing Ship, Tank (LST), and named *Boxer*, *Bruiser*, and *Thruster*. The Royal Navy, however, already knew that these three LSTs, plus the three converted tankers, would not be enough to carry out its proposed operations. It also learned that Canadian shipyards were too busy with repairs and building warships to take on new orders. That left only American shipyards as a potential source for LSTs, but the United States was not yet in the war, of course, and its shipyards and factories would need convincing to build these as-yet-untried ships. The queue for access was already long and growing. In Washington, DC, the British Supply Council in North America was already coordinating dozens of bodies like the British Merchant Shipbuilding Mission, now negotiating for what would become the Ocean and Liberty ship programs. In London, Captain Alan Kirk and Rear Admiral Robert Ghormley were working from cramped, understaffed attaché offices in the American embassy to sort out competing British demands.

Britain Asks America to Build Its LSTs

One US Navy engineering officer, Captain Edward L. Cochrane, saw firsthand that what the British were asking for today, the Americans would need tomorrow. In November and December 1940, he had an office at the DNC in Bath, at the agreement of Goodall, whom he had known when Goodall was assigned to the US Navy in World War One. Cochrane took note of how the British were fighting U-boats and preparing for amphibious assaults, certain that America would soon be doing the same. In early 1941 he returned to become assistant head of the ship design division at the navy's Bureau of Ships (BuShips). Once there, he began planning for anti-submarine destroyer escorts, based on the British *Hunt* class. His timing was flawless: on March 11, 1941, Roosevelt signed into law the Lend-Lease Act. The Royal Navy wasted no time in taking full advantage of this. Even before the act was signed, a new British Admiralty delegation, one that would report directly to First Sea Lord Admiral Dudley Pound, was on its way to Washington to coordinate Lend-Lease shipbuilding. American shipbuilding would turn out to be key to British naval strategy; by the end of the war, one-third of all Royal Navy ships would be built in the United States.[14]

Once the delegation was established in the offices of the British Supply Council, they began negotiating for a hundred American-built destroyer escorts. After some back-and-forth between the British delegation and the American chief of naval operations, Admiral Harold "Betty" Stark, in August 1941 Roosevelt approved the sale of fifty new destroyer escorts to be built at four shipyards, one of which was the small inland yard of Dravo Corporation in Pittsburgh. Cochrane, who as noted based his destroyer escorts on the British *Hunt* class, now modified the design to British standards, assisted by Albert P. Cole, a British naval constructor who had a desk in his bureau. Gibbs & Cox—now familiar with British standards from the aforementioned Ocean ship program—became the design agent. The next British request was for seven *Boxer*-class LSTs, once again with Gibbs & Cox as design agent. In September 1941, contracts for these were placed with Newport News Shipbuilding and Drydock Company, where they would likely be unnoticed among the aircraft carriers and cruisers already under construction.[15]

Just as these contracts were being signed, however, the Admiralty changed its mind and decided it needed a different type of ship than the *Boxer*-class of LSTs it had requestioned. Although *Boxer* was not even on the shipbuilding ways, a new analysis by the Admiralty staff determined that these ships, although having a draft of just 10 feet, were nevertheless still too deep to land tanks on the very shallow beaches in northern France, which were already being identified for the future D-Day landings. It also determined that the Royal Navy would need hundreds of LSTs, not just the handful they had on order.

On September 13, 1941, Whitehall sent a new set of requirements to the technical head of the British Admiralty delegation, Rear Admiral James W. S. Dorling. Dorling recorded in his journal, "A British Staff Paper was received showing the estimates of force required. . . . [A]mong the long list of requirements were mentioned seagoing landing craft for tanks and vehicles, 1300#." Two days later, a joint British-American statement reduced the number of LSTs from 1,300 to 819. Nonetheless, the biggest problem remained—that of designing a ship that was both deep enough to cross the ocean yet shallow enough to land tanks on French beaches. After several weeks of refining the requirements with the Admiralty, Dorling was given permission to ask BuShips to make a "sketch design" of such a ship.[16]

On November 3, Dorling discussed the idea with Captain Cochrane. The following afternoon, Cochrane sat down at the desk of his civilian head of the Preliminary Design Branch, John C. Niedermair Jr. (Figure 19), and showed him a "dispatch from the British" that briefly outlined their requirements. The only information given to the Americans was a desired speed of 10 to 11.5 knots (about that of the Ocean-type cargo ships then under construction) and a cruising radius of 10,000 miles (which would allow them to get from Britain to Africa and the Middle East) while carrying a military load of "at least ten big tanks over 30 tons each." The biggest challenge was that the Admiralty also wanted this seagoing vessel to have a draft at the bow of less than 5 feet when beached—"so shallow," Niedermair was told, "that the British had a good deal of doubt as to whether a satisfactory design could be achieved."[17]

In just over two hours, Niedermair sketched out the concept and a few calculations on a small sheet of paper (Figure 20) that, with few alterations before construction, would become the American LST. Niedermair's ship featured ballast tanks, used in submarines but never before considered for landing ships. While the ballast tanks were empty, the ship would displace 1,400 tons with a draft at the bow of just 3.5 feet, shallow enough for the French beaches. But in seagoing condition, it would take on another 1,300 tons of ballast water, bringing it down to a 9-foot draft, deep enough to weather heavy seas. At the end of the workday, he put his sketch in his briefcase and hurried to his carpool—one of its members, future father of the nuclear navy Lieutenant Commander Hyman Rickover, was even then cantankerous about schedules—and went home to work on the design that evening.

John Niedermair, born in 1893 to German-speaking parents, spent his youth on Staten Island, where he could look down from the bluffs and see the ships in New York Harbor. In 1914, age twenty-one, he took advantage of the fully paid scholarships offered by Webb's Academy in New York (today Webb Institute) to get his bachelor's degree in naval architecture. After the end of World War One, he worked in the New York Navy Yard in Brooklyn. In 1925 he was technical advisor for the salvage of the submarine S-51, which had sunk after a collision, and two years later helped salvage another submarine, S-4, after another accidental ramming. During the Depression, he moved to the Preliminary Design Branch of what would become BuShips, in the Main Navy Building on the Mall in Washington, while commuting to New York on weekends to be with his family. In 1933 they moved to nearby Chevy Chase, while he rose to become head of the branch. Though most of his work concerned battleships and aircraft carriers, his early experience with submarines—which his British counterpart Rowland Baker lacked—led him to the insight about ballasting that made the American LST possible.[18]

Niedermair redrew his plans for the LST at a larger scale in his home studio on the evening of November 4, 1941. The following day, Cochrane had the plans and calculations copied and sent by courier to the Admiralty, where Niedermair's design was "met with immediate approval." British naval staff began drafting the full specifications, while the newly formed British Landing Ship Mission, which included Rowland Baker, as well as Commander Robin C. Todhunter and Captain Thomas A. Hussey of the Combined Operations Command, flew to Washington, DC, to begin negotiating for construction of 200 of Niedermair's LSTs, along with hundreds of smaller landing craft. On Friday, November 28, members of the Admiralty delegation and the Landing Ship Mission sat down with representatives from BuShips (including Cochrane) in Admiral Stark's office at the Main Navy Building. After a lengthy discussion, in which Cochrane argued that LSTs could be built in the smaller inland shipyards so as not to interfere with more pressing construction such as the Liberty ships, Stark put off any decisions for a week while he examined their proposals.

The British took advantage of the delay for a weekend visit to the New Orleans boatyard of Andrew J. Higgins, the designer and businessman who was building small landing craft (known as LCVPs and almost immediately called "Higgins boats") for the navy and marines. The British wanted 150 of them. Higgins was initially wary of Baker, but once he realized that Baker "was the one person in the world who knew as much about landing craft as he did himself," according to Todhunter, "they got on like a house on fire." Higgins agreed to the contract even with changes ordered by Baker. Most of the British returned to Washington by December 2, but Hussey had been alerted to a modular pontoon system for beaching operations pioneered by Commander John N. Laycock, and flew to Rhode Island to see it.[19]

Niedermair had already received the new British staff requirements for his LST, and his engineering staff was working with Baker, who was given a desk in the branch to help with the design. On Friday, December 5, Admiral Stark met with Hussey and the heads of the British Admiralty delegation to inform them that he did not support building British LSTs in America. He told them that they needed a navy "twice the strength of your present one," not more landing ships. Not easily rebuffed, Hussey got in a telephone booth outside the Main Navy Building and called Supreme Court justice Felix Frankfurter, using their mutual friends back in Britain as the introduction. At tea that afternoon, Frankfurter arranged for Hussey to meet with Harry Hopkins, Roosevelt's advisor, the following day. On Saturday afternoon, December 6, Hussey, along with Dorling, met with Hopkins at the White House and told him the whole saga. Hopkins said he would try to arrange a meeting with the president on Monday, December 8, to make the case for Lend-Lease LSTs.[20]

About 2:30 p.m. on Sunday, December 7, the news of Pearl Harbor began to flash across the wires. Dorling was at home with his wife listening to the radio when he heard the news; Todhunter heard it in his hotel; Hussey heard it over the radio in a taxi (which surprised him, as British taxis did not have radios); and Baker was at the cinema when the announcement was made over the auditorium speakers. Niedermair and his wife, Ethel, were at a brunch given by friends. Their children were at home when they heard the radio broadcast, and the phone began ringing constantly as they took message after message from senior navy officials. When their parents walked through the door at 5 p.m., their daughter Patricia gave them the news. "Dad's face was ashen," she recalled, "and mom sat on the stairs and cried. Dad went upstairs to return calls. He came downstairs twenty minutes later with his attaché case and a suitcase, and said to Ethel, 'I don't know when I'll be back.' And out the door he went." A government car waiting outside his home took him to the Main Navy Building, which was already a hive of activity as personnel streamed in. The following day, Roosevelt and Congress formally declared war on Japan. Three days later, the United States was allied with Britain in the war against Nazi Germany.[21]

America Takes Over the LST Program

Even with the entry of the United States into the war, the navy did not immediately embrace the LST, given its focus on regaining warship dominance in the Pacific theatre. Negotiations with the Maritime Commission to build Niedermair's design dragged on through December, while the Lend-Lease contracts for the seven *Boxer*-class ships were put on hold and eventually diverted to other amphibious ships. By this point, Churchill was already aboard the battleship HMS *Duke of York*, crossing the Atlantic to see Roosevelt again, just four months after their Atlantic Charter meeting in Placentia Bay, Newfoundland. *Duke of York* arrived at the Norfolk Navy Yard on December 22, and Churchill flew straight to Washington for a series of strategic talks at the White House, talks that lasted until mid-January. At the same time, the Arcadia Conference was held between senior military officials, confirming, as noted, the "Europe first" strategy agreed to by the United Nations (Roosevelt's term for the Allies). For Churchill, this meant landing ships were needed immediately, and he repeatedly pressed Roosevelt on the issue. On January 7, 1942, Roosevelt approved the construction of 200 LSTs for Britain and another 200 for the United States.[22]

The Bureau of Ships moved into high gear to get the LST into production. Small-scale model tests of the hull were completed in record time at the David Taylor Model Basin in Carderock, Maryland, while the overall design at BuShips was carried out with the on-site help of Baker and other British naval constructors, who "gave us the benefit of their experience," as Niedermair later recalled. Design time was cut by including the lead shipyard, Dravo Corporation, and its design agent, Gibbs & Cox, who paralleled Baker's ideas of using slab-sided hull sections and locomotive diesel engines for speed of construction. The last of the contract plans were signed on March 10, 1942.[23]

The political foundations of the LST program, on the other hand, were crumbling fast and needed shoring up. In January 1942, landing vessels of all types were eighth in the navy's Shipbuilding Precedence List, and by March 31 had fallen to tenth place, due to the U-boat menace demanding more destroyers and destroyer escorts. In early May, the British Admiralty delegation made the case directly to the White House that LSTs had to be prioritized above any other shipbuilding for any invasion of Europe. A study by Major General Dwight D. Eisenhower agreed. On May 15, Roosevelt told his Joint Chiefs of Staff to get LST production "under way as quickly as possible." Within weeks, the navy raised it to number one on its priority list, even delaying by several months the construction of two aircraft carriers to build two dozen LSTs.[24]

Over 1,000 LSTs would be built during the war, of which only 113 would eventually go to the Royal Navy, which ordered them in the first place. The ships had no names, only numbers. They were equally nondescript: a 50-foot-wide box the length of a football field, with a set of clamshell bow doors that enclosed a drop-down ramp for beaching. Inside, they could carry twenty medium tanks, such as the American Shermans, or eighteen heavy tanks such as the British Churchill. On the main deck they could carry trucks and light vehicles, or even small landing craft. They were built in sixteen shipyards around the country, including five midwestern yards like Dravo, where they had to compete for shipways and manpower with the hundreds of destroyer escorts being churned out for the two Allied navies. Sailors did not like them while at sea; they called them "Large, Slow Targets." LSTs had an uncomfortable, snappy roll, and they pounded heavily when the waves turned rough. And although these British-inspired, American-built ships were intended to land tanks on the invasion beaches of France, they would not be able to do so without the use of one more innovation, one that was also the result of close British-American cooperation.[25]

Bridging the Gap

When Captain Thomas Hussey of the British Landing Ship Mission flew to Rhode Island after visiting the Higgins boatyard in December 1941, it was to see the modular pontoon bridges invented by Captain John Laycock, a Civil Engineer Corps officer at the Navy's Bureau of Yards and Docks. Laycock did not invent the modular pontoons as causeways; he envisioned them as a means of building naval bases in remote locations in the Pacific.

However, Hussey saw their potential for amphibious operations, and filed away the idea for future use.

He saw that opportunity just over a year later. In early 1943, Hussey and his commanding officer at the Combined Operations Command, Louis Mountbatten, were planning for the invasions of Sicily and Italy. They had read reports about the Operation Torch amphibious landings in North Africa, which had taken place just a few months earlier, in November 1942. There, the British *Bachaquero*-class LSTs could not directly unload their tanks onto the beach. Instead, they had used the US Army Corps of Engineers' floating causeways to "bridge the gap," as they termed it, between the ship and the shore. Hussey and Mountbatten alerted Eisenhower that even the shallow-draft American LSTs would likely not be able to get all the way to the beach. Hussey was directed to go to the United States to press the navy to develop either the Laycock pontoons or the army's causeways to create a floating bridge for this purpose.

When Hussey arrived on March 4, 1943, to bring this up with Fleet Admiral Ernest King (who had replaced Stark the previous year as chief of naval operations), he found no one in King's office who knew anything about Laycock's pontoons. The British, it appeared, were better informed than the Americans; after Hussey arranged for a few phone calls to Laycock and Rear Admiral Alan Kirk, commander, Amphibious Force, Atlantic Fleet (whom he knew from Kirk's days as assistant naval attaché in London), he was able to secure both a series of pontoons and floating army causeways (known as treadway bridges), as well as two newly built LSTs. They had decided to test the combination of LSTs and causeways in what they called the "Bridging the Gap" trial, using the shallow beaches of Quonset Point, Rhode Island, for their similarity to the invasion beaches in northern France and the Mediterranean.[26]

On the day of the "Bridging the Gap" trial, March 18, 1943, the British-American Combined Chiefs of Staff, including King, were aboard the LSTs. Niedermair directed the helmsman for the actual beaching operation. The first LST tested Laycock's pontoons. The vessel ran aground about 300 feet from the shoreline, and allowed the pontoons to run ahead and hit the beach. "We had the ramp down a bit and we pulled the roadway over, dropped the ramp on it," Niedermair later recalled. "The beach was so perfect that I didn't have to do any ballasting in the roadway to bring it down solid on the beach." It took eight minutes to deploy the pontoons, and another eight minutes for the tank to get to the beach. This was faster than the subsequent test with the second LST towing army treadways. "Ernie King and all the Combined Chiefs were tickled to death," claimed Niedermair, and the next day the navy ordered pontoons for the upcoming Operation Husky, the invasion of Sicily.[27]

The combination of the LST and pontoons would prove vital to the invasion of Europe, yet the planners of D-Day knew they would be wholly inadequate for the initial assaults. Churchill had not been exaggerating when he told Stalin that Hitler's Atlantic Wall along the French coastline "bristled" with defenses. In the ten or fifteen minutes between an LST hitting the shore and its tanks landing on the beach, German artillery and machine guns could mow down the troops every bit as effectively as at Anzac Cove three decades earlier. These German weapons would have to be neutralized by heavy firepower early in the landing, which required tanks that could swim—a counterintuitive idea for such heavy machines. Fortunately, by this point in the war the Allies had already cooperatively developed and fielded a very effective tank, the M-4 Sherman, which could be modified for this unusual purpose.

Developing the Sherman Tank

Long before Winston Churchill came up with the idea for the Landing Ship, Tank, he conceived of the tank itself. In 1914 during the early days of World War One trench warfare, Churchill proposed the concept of the "landship" to cross trenches and provide heavy mobile firepower. He was in part inspired by the 1903 short story "The Land Ironclads" by his friend H. G. Wells, which imagined a handful of hundred-foot-long armored vehicles defeating an entire army. When Churchill did not think that the army was pursuing the idea "with sufficient vigour," as he later wrote, he overstepped his authority as First Lord of the Admiralty and ordered his director of naval construction, Eustace Tennyson d'Eyncourt, to head the Landships Committee that would design and develop these machines (which is why tanks have naval-sounding "hulls" and "turrets"). To keep the machines a secret during their transport to the front lines, the Committee at first called them "water-carriers for Russia," then settled on "tanks."[28]

Churchill, of course, was not the only one to envision armored trench-crossing vehicles; in France, the *char* (chariot) had been proposed as far back as 1903, and similar ideas had been moving in British circles since the beginning of the World War One. The tank, which was initially used to support infantry assaults, came too late in the war to be decisive, although it played significant roles in the summer 1918 Battles of Soissons and Amiens, which marked the beginning of the final Allied offensive.

During the interwar period, Britain, France, United States, Germany, Italy, and the Soviet Union all evolved and diversified the tank, from infantry support to multi-role vehicles that could operate independently to provide mobile firepower. Tanks were generally divided by weight class— light, medium, and heavy—with differences in speed, armor, and gun caliber emphasizing different aspects of each nation's doctrine and tactics.

With Hitler's rise to power in 1933, Germany, which had been prohibited from building tanks by the Versailles Treaty, saw its tank production catch up with and significantly outpace that of France and Britain (though the two allies would regain their numerical advantage by 1940). More importantly, the German army brought tank warfare to new levels of lethality with its maneuver warfare doctrine, popularized by the press as "blitzkrieg" or lightning war. Despite witnessing the German blitzkrieg attacks launched against Poland in 1939, the French and British armies were wholly unable to stop a similar assault in May 1940. After Dunkirk and with France out of the picture, Britain had fewer than 300 tanks to fight Nazi Germany, which had over 1,600 tanks still on hand, with the number growing by the day.[29]

Britain looked to the United States to help rebuild its armored formations. Unlike its relatively open embrace of American aircraft production, the British military was hesitant about buying American tanks. The two nations were familiar with each other's fighting vehicles. George Patton's original World War One Tank Corps employed British tanks, and between the wars the US Army Ordnance Department built its first tanks, based on British Vickers designs, at the Rock Island Arsenal in Illinois. The British, for their part, believed they knew what the Americans could do when in 1936 they bought two prototypes, built by automotive engineer J. Walter Christie, that had been the basis for some early army light tanks before being rejected.

Familiarity bred more contempt than admiration; by the beginning of the war, the prevailing opinion was that the British first designed a turret and gun for fighting, then built the hull, engine, and automotive components to carry it, while the Americans started with a reliable engine and only afterward shoehorned in the gun and turret. A more nuanced view was expressed after the war by George Marshall (as mentioned earlier, the U.S. Army Chief of Staff), which helps explain why there was mutual disapproval when the British Tank Mission arrived in New York in late July 1940. American tanks were "the most mobile, most perfectly controlled of all the tanks," he said, but "deficient, very decidedly, in their fighting qualities." The British "had it right on the fighting part" and the Americans "had it right on the mobility of tanks." The difference was that the British had actually faced battle and knew that the "fighting part" counted for more.[30]

The British Tank Mission was led by Michael Dewar, an industrialist who headed the British branch of the American bearing manufacturer Timken Company. On Churchill's recommendation, the minister of supply, Herbert Morrison, requested that Dewar, along with tank engineer L. Edward Carr and Brigadier Douglas Pratt (who had commanded a tank brigade in France that recently fought the Nazis), negotiate for building medium tanks—specifically the models called Matilda and Crusader—in American factories. After a brief meeting in New York with Arthur Purvis's British Purchasing Commission, Dewar realized that the right people were in Washington, and set up shop in the Carlton Hotel, where many government officials also had rooms.[31]

Despite the considerable engineering and battle experience that the British Tank Mission brought to bear, it could not convince American officials that its tank designs were superior to theirs. At a crucial meeting on August 6, 1940, with Bill Knudsen, head of the Advisory Commission on National Defense, they were told that American industry would not supply them with British-unique products, but instead they would have to buy vehicles like the M3 medium tank, which was just coming into production. In the event that Britain fell to the Nazis (which at the time appeared quite likely), the US Army could then simply appropriate them for their fighting needs.

The Tank Mission soon discovered what buying American would mean for the British Army: upon viewing a wooden mockup of the new M3 at the Aberdeen Proving Grounds, Pratt pronounced it "as high as the Tower of Babel," making it vulnerable to enemy fire. The Americans, for their part, were happy with the M3's drive train and chassis, and had only disparaging remarks for a British Matilda tank that was shipped to Aberdeen for trials (cramped and underpowered was their verdict).[32]

Despite misgivings on both sides, the British knew they had little choice but to settle for the American tanks. On August 18, Dewar cabled the Ministry of Supply that British orders must be given within a few days, or the Americans would go ahead alone. The ministry acceded and on August 22 authorized Dewar to order 1,500 M3s, which Dewar promptly doubled to 3,000. At the same time, the British Purchasing Commission began looking for factories to produce the tanks. In October 1940, it signed deals with the American Locomotive Company, with underused plants in Schenectady, New York, and in Canada (Montreal Locomotive Works), to begin manufacture. Meanwhile, Pratt and Ted Carr of the Tank Mission were hard at work developing modifications for the British M3 turret (also used by the Canadians) that would make it more acceptable for combat use, notably lowering the profile and casting it as a single piece with improved armor protection.

The signing of Lend-Lease six months later, in March 1941, confirmed the choice to have British and American variants of the M3, even with different turrets, share a common hull. The tanks would be built side by side at American Locomotive, as well as at the Baldwin Locomotive Works in Pennsylvania, the Lima Locomotive Works in Ohio, and other manufacturers. The first American-variant M3s (named Lee for the Confederate general) came off the Schenectady line in April 1941, followed by the British variant, Grant (for the Union general and former president) in July. These distinctions soon became immaterial; many American Lees later incorporated Grant turret features, and the British army used both variants. The first Grants were shipped to the British Eighth Army in Egypt in November 1941. When they were first used in the North Africa campaign in May 1942, the gunnery, armor, and reliability of the M3s proved a match for the German Panzers, although by July, Erwin Rommel's Africa Corps had pushed the British forces from Libya deep into Egypt, indeed all the way to El Alamein, located on the borders of Cairo.[33]

Even as the M3s were in production, American, British, and Canadian engineers knew their armies needed a better tank. Pratt's denunciation of the turret height was just the start; the main 75 mm gun, though powerful, was encased in a hull sponson that made it too low for uneven terrain and limited its firing arc. The riveted hulls were vulnerable to damage. The list went on, with engineering changes coming in at the rate of 3,000 per month. The Canadians had gone some way toward rectifying these problems with their Ram medium tank, but the Americans wanted a new tank that retained the M3's reliable chassis and drive train, yet completely redesigned the hull armor and gun turret to be more effective in battle.

In April 1941, the Aberdeen Proving Grounds and Rock Island Arsenal began producing prototypes for what would become the M4 Sherman (named by the British for the Union general), with the hulls either welded or cast steel, and the main 75 mm gun now in a rotating armored turret. The British Tank Mission actively participated in this development, providing recommendations when visiting the early wooden mockups at Aberdeen Proving Grounds that summer, such as placing the radio set in the turret bustle instead of the hull. The first production line for the Sherman was established at the Lima Locomotive Works (soon to become the Lima Tank Depot), which began delivering the tanks in February 1942. The first one went to Aberdeen for testing; the second was shipped to Britain, bearing a brass plaque engraved with the name Michael, in honor of Michael Dewar, head of the Tank Mission.[34]

The Sherman tank would ultimately become the mainstay of both British and American armored units. The Shermans were first shipped to the British

Eighth Army in Egypt and fought in the Second Battle of El Alamein, which began in October 1942 and subsequently drove Rommel back across the Libyan desert to Tunisia ("the end of the beginning," declared Churchill). This coincided with the Operation Torch landings to the west, which trapped Rommel between two Allied armies and ultimately drove him out of North Africa, giving the Allies a staging point for invading southern Europe in 1943. By that time, Shermans was being built at the rate of 1,200 per month in ten plants including those operated by Ford and Chrysler. They came in a bewildering array of variants according to gun, engine, and hull type. Many were fitted with weapons like howitzers and rockets, or converted by Royal Ordnance factories to carry British guns (such as the Firefly, which was fitted with a larger 76.2 mm gun that could more effectively defeat German tanks). The British 79th Armoured Division, led by Major General Percy Hobart, was famous for developing a series of specialized tanks, collectively known as Hobart's Funnies, in preparation for the D-Day assault. Among the varieties of mine-clearing flail tanks, engineering tanks fitted with bulldozer blades and assault bridges, and flame-throwing tanks, one of the most important was the amphibious or Duplex Drive (DD) tank.

Tanks That Can Swim

The concept of the amphibious tank, which could either ford rivers or swim from the sea onto the shore, was almost as old as the tank itself. Britain experimented with a tank equipped with side floats just as World War One drew to a close. In the United States, J. Walter Christie's 1920s prototypes for a Marine Corps amphibious tank were rejected even before the Army Ordnance Department rejected his light tank designs (instead the Marines adapted a commercial amphibious tractor, which became the LVT or am-trac, to carry troops ashore).

The first successful trials of amphibious tanks were carried out in Britain by the Hungarian-born automotive engineer Nicholas Straussler, who had developed a series of cumbersome strap-on buoyancy devices before hitting upon the idea of a collapsible flotation skirt. The issue with any amphibious vehicle is that in order to float, its buoyancy (the water it displaces) must be equal to its weight. Tanks, as noted, are heavy, so providing the needed buoyancy was problematic, as was giving it enough propulsive power to swim in the ocean. Straussler's solution was twofold: first, equip existing tanks with collapsible, waterproof canvas screens that could be raised with pneumatic tubes to the correct height to keep water from entering, then mechanically locked into place; and second, fit the tanks with one or two retractable outboard propellers that hinged up when on dry land but in the water made use of the tank's engine to drive them through a gearbox—this was the so-called Duplex Drive.[35]

During the 1930s, Straussler's company had been developing tank equipment with the armaments manufacturer Vickers-Armstrong. It was through those connections that he was provided a light tank for trials. In June 1941 the little tank with a bolted-on outboard motor swam into the Brent Reservoir in Hendon, North London. These trials were witnessed by Churchill's chief of staff, General Alanbrooke, who after witnessing a series of saltwater trials gave the green light for its further development. Straussler began work in September to fit his flotation screens to the larger Valentine tank and connect the propellers to its gearbox aft. Its first trials in May 1942 were inconclusive, but the British Army's need for a swimming tank was so pressing that in July, the Ministry of Supply contracted with Vickers subsidiary Metro-Cammell of Birmingham to build 450 Valentine tanks to the DD configuration, with further testing to continue until the start of production in March 1943.

Meanwhile, across the Atlantic, the US Army Ordnance Department was developing deep wading kits for Sherman tanks (waterproofing the hulls and adding raised air intake trunks), which were used effectively during Operation Torch. At the same time, the army was investigating how to deploy tanks from further offshore, and coordinated with OSRD Division 12 (Transportation) to study methods to float tanks. The division leader, Hartley Rowe, traveled with members of the OSRD London Mission office to examine Straussler's device, reporting that his first DD experiments were "unsuccessful." Although the invasions of Sicily and Italy (July 1943–January 1944) continued to demonstrate the utility of deep wading tanks, those beaches were not as fortified as the Atlantic Wall that defended the Normandy coastline. Now the American planners for the invasion realized that the need for a swimming tank to breach those defenses, prior to the troops coming ashore, was more urgent than ever.[36]

Despite Rowe's initial assessment, Eisenhower's staff contacted the Ordnance Department in early November 1943 about using Straussler's DD concept to equip Sherman tanks for the D-Day assault. The Allies, in response to increasing pressure from Stalin to open a second front, had set May 1, 1944, as the date of the operation. Since General Omar Bradley's First Army would lead that assault, the British arranged a demonstration of a DD Valentine for him and his staff on November 17. The approval to build DD Shermans was rushed through George Marshall's office eleven days later. Straussler and Metro-Cammell had already converted some Shermans to a prototype DD arrangement (unlike Valentines, Shermans had their gearbox forward, so the propellers were instead driven from the tread idlers). This demonstrated that converting existing tanks would be slow and cumbersome. Production of DD Shermans was instead assigned to the Lima Tank Depot and bumped up to AAA priority status (the equivalent of the Manhattan Project). In early December, Marshall requested Straussler to provide plans, parts, and above all a technical expert to Lima to expedite production. Straussler chose his factory manager, John E. Whatmough, for the task.[37]

In an almost exact repetition of the saga of Rolls-Royce's Merlin engine being sent to Packard three years earlier, Whatmough arranged for Metro-Cammell to pack up and ship twelve crates of DD components, weighing 1,200 pounds. On December 12, they were placed on the 11:10 p.m. train from Birmingham to Glasgow, accompanied by military police and two American officers as couriers. The following morning, an armed truck convoy brought them to the mouth of the river Clyde, where they were taken by tender to a special room aboard the converted ocean liner RMS *Aquitania*, its Cunard–White Star black-and-white livery now a uniform haze gray, as befitted a wartime troopship. It sailed on December 22, arriving in New York without incident on the thirtieth. A further seven crates were carried aboard a Liberty ship in convoy TU 5, which arrived New Year's Eve, having narrowly avoided a thirty-boat wolfpack. Whatmough himself departed aboard the "Grey Ghost," RMS *Queen Mary*, on January 3, with another six crates of components in the hold and the duplicate DD plans in a briefcase handcuffed to his wrist when he was out of his cabin.

By mid-January 1944, Whatmough, along with the DD plans and the parts, were at the Lima Tank Depot. Using the British-supplied components, Lima built a prototype DD Sherman in just a few weeks, and on January 24 sent it for testing on the beaches of Fort Story, Virginia. The trials went well enough (though the tank eventually sank) for production to begin. Firestone Tire & Rubber Co. built the skirt, and other Ohio contractors supplied mechanical parts. Whatmough and Straussler continually exchanged drawings, correspondence, and cables as the design evolved. Some changes were obvious—replacing British Standard screws with American ones—and some less so, such as the complete redesign of the underwater breathing apparatus for the crew to escape in the case of sinking.

The first batch of production DD Shermans (Figure 21) left Lima on February 24 and arrived in Britain on March 10, divided between American and British forces. Within a month, Lima was turning out fifteen tanks a day, and by mid-March had completed the 350 DD tanks ordered. Metro-Cammell, meanwhile, was only able to convert 150 Shermans by April, so American-built models were allocated to British and Canadian battalions, alongside their Valentine DDs. All DD tank crews did their first training in calm, freshwater lakes in Suffolk, including practice with their escape apparatus, before moving on to realistic exercises on the shores of Scotland and southern England. These exercises would have to be carried out in a great hurry and with great secrecy, for the D-Day invasion of Europe, already postponed from May 1 to June 5, 1944, was now just weeks away.

CHAPTER 7

FIGHT IN FRANCE

W HEN ROOSEVELT APPOINTED Eisenhower in December 1943 to command the invasion of France, both the general and the Allies had already accumulated an abundance of experience in planning for and conducting amphibious assaults. Even though he was an army officer, Eisenhower's time in the War Plans Division in early 1942 had taught him to recognize the critical importance of ships and shipping both during the buildup of forces and for the invasion itself. He gained further experience over the next eighteen months as overall commander for three major Allied amphibious assaults, Operation Torch in North Africa, Operation Husky in Sicily, and Operation Avalanche in Italy. During this same period, Americans also learned to attack heavily defended beaches in island-hopping campaigns in the Pacific Ocean. British forces, meanwhile, had honed their skills in amphibious operations as close as Dieppe in France and as far away as Madagascar. Each operation provided valuable lessons that would help the Allies plan and carry out the invasion of France, under the cover name Operation Overlord.

Learning the Lessons of Amphibious Assaults

Operation Menace, the aforementioned assault on Dakar in September 1940, gave the British their first hard-won lesson in amphibious warfare, that heavy armor needed to be carried by ship and landed directly upon a beachhead. The LST, of course, was the result. Britain's first operational employment of an LST occurred during Operation Ironclad against Vichy-held Madagascar in May 1942, intended to deny the Indian Ocean island to the Japanese. HMS *Bachaquero*, one of three oil tankers converted to LSTs, was assigned to a follow-on echelon after the initial assault by troop landing craft, where it carried trucks and artillery to shore. The ship's commanding officer, having identified an appropriate landing site, rammed the ship through a sandbar to bring it directly onto the beach. Within ninety minutes, the LST was offloaded and refloated, helping make Operation Ironclad a success.[1]

The Allied raid on Dieppe in August 1942 (Operation Jubilee) proved far less successful than Operation Ironclad. This cross-Channel attack made use of the smaller LCTs, which carried heavy Churchill tanks to shore. However, the beach conditions made it almost impossible for the tanks to proceed inland. Under heavy fire from German ground and air forces, the tanks were destroyed, the raid faltered, and the Allied troops were forced to evacuate after just ten hours, with almost two-thirds captured, killed, or wounded. The shock of the failure at Dieppe forced the Allies to reconsider their amphibious doctrine, especially the need for better planning and for increased emphasis on naval and aerial fire support prior to the landing.[2]

Operation Torch in November 1942 was the Allies' first major amphibious operation, which dislodged the Vichy French from Morocco and Algeria and replaced them with Free French forces, while also surrounding and defeating the German and Italian armies in Tunisia. Employing some of the lessons from Dakar and Dieppe, including careful planning of landing zones and selective shore bombardment, the Allies carried out simultaneous assaults along the North Africa coast, centered on Casablanca, Oran, and Algiers. All three converted British LSTs participated in the operations. On November 8, HMS *Misoa* and *Tasajera* disembarked American tanks of the 1st Armored Division onto the beach near the Algerian port of Oran. Several days later they were joined by HMS *Bachaquero*, and the three ships together ferried tanks, trucks, and artillery to the beach. This was where the three LSTs had used the US Army Corps of Engineers' floating treadways to "bridge the gap" between ship and shore, which, as mentioned, was the impetus for Captain Thomas Hussey to propose using pontoon bridges in conjunction with LSTs. A further improvement (also mentioned earlier), wading kits for the Sherman tanks, allowed deeper-draft landing craft to land the tanks in shallow water, from where they crawled the several hundred yards through the surf to the beach.[3]

Operation Torch had given the American and British a toehold in North Africa, whence they would launch invasions across the Mediterranean Sea on Sicily and Italy, "the soft underbelly of Europe," as Churchill often termed it. Operation Husky was the first of these invasions, a combined assault on Sicily in July 1943. By then the three *Boxer*-class LSTs were in operation, along with hundreds of American-built LSTs and their pontoon bridges that were in service in both the US Navy and the Royal Navy. As they crossed the Atlantic, they rolled and pounded the entire way. Vomit bags were quickly exhausted, so soldiers used their helmets, and even the hardiest sailors regularly puked over the railings.[4]

On July 10, American, British and Canadian forces attacked in a wide swath around the southern part of the island, from Syracuse to Licata. The early morning assaults went so smoothly that Mountbatten later said it "looked like a rehearsal." That afternoon, however, the follow-on landings of over seventy LSTs were made more difficult by high winds and heavy surf. Nevertheless, the combination of LSTs and the Laycock pontoons, which as mentioned had been requisitioned just four months earlier, allowed most of the equipment to be landed by the end of the day (Figure 22). Operation Husky, according to Major General Lucian Truscott Jr., the commander of the 3rd Infantry Division, which landed at Licata, was "the first real test of shore-to-shore operations under actual conditions of war with adequate equipment."[5]

The Sicily campaign demonstrated the versatility of the LSTs. Depending upon which zone they were assigned to, the ships delivered tanks, trucks, infantry, fuel, fresh water, and supplies. Some of them were fitted with stalls for burros to carry ammunition over Sicily's mountainous terrain. Other LSTs were modified to serve as repair depots and hospitals, or to transport prisoners of war and evacuate casualties. The experience of *LST-386* was emblematic of the variety of missions they accomplished. During Husky, it was fitted with a runway to launch small aircraft for reconnaissance. It next served in Operation Avalanche, the invasion of Italy around Salerno in September 1943. This was a far more difficult campaign than at Sicily, with many more casualties. *LST-386* struck a mine, which killed several men, punched a 48-foot hole in the side, and knocked out one of its engines. The tank deck was flooded, so it could not successfully beach, but even so, the tough ship and even tougher crew successfully offloaded its cargo and vehicles onto another landing craft before returning to North Africa for repairs. From January to April 1944, it was part of Operation Shingle, which established a beachhead at Anzio to support the Allied campaign in central Italy.[6]

LSTs were also critical to the Pacific island-hopping campaigns, though they were used in an entirely different way. Operation Galvanic aimed to capture the major Gilbert Islands, which straddled the equator. In November 1943, a sizeable Marine contingent assailed the heavily defended Tarawa atoll, intending to use the shallow-draft LCVPs (Higgins boats) to carry the troops over the coral reefs that encircled the island. The tides were unexpectedly low that day, so even the Higgins boats could not cross the reefs; only the shallower LVT tractors (amtracs) could do so, either by swimming over them or crawling along the tops of the coral. The Marine Corps, true to its history of discovering new ways to adapt, quickly turned to the LSTs as the means of launching the assault. During Operation Flintlock in January–February 1944, groups of a dozen or more LSTs mustered outside the reefs of Kwajalein Island, each LST crowding seventeen amtracs into its tank deck. Instead of hitting the shore, they hove to while the bow ramps dropped. One by one, amtracs (each carrying twenty marines) drove off the ramp into the ocean, then marshaled on the lee side of the ship. In just fifteen minutes, the first of three waves swam over the reefs and onto the shore, 3,000 marines in each wave, which overwhelmed the Japanese defenders.

Planning Overlord

Eisenhower's appointment in December 1943 to command the invasion of France was the culmination of the planning that had begun back in September 1940. It was then that Britain, as noted, developed its Appreciation of Future Strategy paper that largely guided the future Allied efforts. The final step, after strategic bombing, sabotage, opening the transatlantic supply lines, and conducting amphibious assaults on the peripheries, was to "provide a striking force on the Continent when the morale of the enemy forces has been considerably weakened," inflicting the final blows against Germany itself.[7]

Each of those steps so far had been made possible by the strong partnership between the United States and Britain, and in particular their engineers and scientists. The strategic bombing raids in 1943–1944 against Schweinfurt, during Operation Pointblank and the Big Week, made possible by H2S and H2X radars and the Merlin Mustang, had dislocated German aircraft production and decimated Luftwaffe pilots to such an extent that the skies over Normandy on D-Day were completely dominated by Allied aircraft. Rebecca and Eureka made SOE infiltration and sabotage operations possible, long before they were used by pathfinder paratroopers. Liberty ships, along with Allied advances in codebreaking, ASW tactics, and weapons, kept the transatlantic sea lanes open; from 1942 until just before D-Day, Bolero and subsequent operations brought over 1.5 million American troops and aircrews, along with their aircraft, vehicles, and weapons, now cantoned in the four corners of England and Northern Ireland.[8]

The plans for the invasion and occupation of France had undergone many variations under different cover names: Roundup, Roundhammer, and Sledgehammer in the early days, with Operation Overlord finally being settled on in August 1943. Overlord itself would comprise several other operations, including Neptune for the amphibious and air assaults on D-Day. One of the most important of those operations was Bodyguard, a carefully coordinated series of countermeasures to fool the Germans and reinforce the Nazi high command's belief that the main attack would be at Calais, not

Normandy. The Allies had been deploying an intricate series of deceptions for over a year, from double agents, misleading radio traffic, and false documents planted on a corpse to General George Patton's fictitious First Army Group (complete with inflatable decoy tanks) at Dover, just across the Channel from Calais.

The planning for the invasion accelerated after the final command structure for Overlord was established in mid-January 1944. Eisenhower's commanders included General Bernard Montgomery as head of the Allied ground forces and Rear Admiral Alan Kirk in charge of the Western naval task groups. By February, however, Eisenhower and his staff had to acknowledge that the lack of ships, specifically LSTs, meant that the proposed date for the invasion, May 1, 1944, would have to be pushed back to late May, then to June 5.[9]

This was becoming all too much for Churchill, who had conceived of the LST as the way to solve the Allies' greatest logistical problem, only now to see it as the weak link in their planning. He recognized that the Allies had enough troops, aircraft, and equipment, but now "all turned upon LSTs." In an April 16, 1944, telegram, Churchill grumbled to George Marshall, "The destinies of two great empires . . . seemed to be tied up in some goddammed things called LSTs."[10]

As troops, ships, and equipment gathered across Britain in the final buildup to D-Day, training became more intense. Some of the largest exercises took place at Slapton Sands in Devon, where the beach is not sand but shingle, with small cobbles and pebbles that resembled Utah Beach. Evacuated of its residents, it hosted a series of increasingly realistic exercises, code-named Duck, Fox, Beaver, and Tiger, the last being a full-scale dress rehearsal for the landings. Hundreds of LSTs were taken through the paces of loading troops and equipment, then landing them on the beaches. Operations with DD tanks were given special attention, with over 1,200 launches from LCTs.

There were many casualties during the exercises—accepted as the cost of war, but also as lessons to be absorbed for the actual assault. During Exercise Fox, two DD Shermans sank with three crew lost, resulting in changes to skirt and engine exhausts; in another exercise, six DD Valentines were lost in rough seas, spurring the British to launch closer to the shore during poor conditions.

Exercise Tiger saw the most horrific attack of the buildup. In the morning darkness of April 28, a convoy of eight LSTs in Lyme Bay was sighted by nine German torpedo boats. When tracer rounds flew past, the American crews thought it was a drill, until the first torpedo struck *LST- 507* amidships, turning it into a fireball. More torpedoes struck other ships; in all, 750 servicemen perished, two LSTs sank, and one was seriously damaged. Eisenhower was appalled, not just by the casualties but also by the loss of precious LSTs and the possibility that the Germans were tipped off to the invasion (they were not). At the same time, the D-Day operational plan was again altered to include rescue craft to pick up survivors.[11]

D-Day

On June 4, one day before the planned invasion, Eisenhower was forced to postpone the operation due to bad weather. The following day, he was faced with the possibility of using a predicted break in the storms on June 6 or having to accept a two-week postponement. At 4:00 a.m. on June 5, in the morning twilight, Eisenhower made the final decision—"OK, we'll go." That evening while it was still daylight, the invasion fleets began steaming out from ports in southern England. Minesweepers went first, sweeping lanes for the rest of the fleet to follow. Just after midnight on June 6, the 6,000 ships, vessels, and craft were assembling in mid-Channel at a site nicknamed Piccadilly Circus, their crews and troops unaware that on either side of them, bombers were delivering chaff, while other aircraft brought paratroopers and gliders to carefully selected landing zones. The Channel was running with moderate seas at four to six feet, easily handled by seagoing ships but very hard on low-freeboard LCTs, as well as the personnel landing craft (Higgins for US troops, Thornycroft for British and Canadian), which were deployed from their transports starting around 2:30 a.m. Battleships and cruisers were scheduled to begin shore bombardment about 5:30 a.m. At the same time, bombers were due to begin striking their targets, despite the low cloud deck and heavy winds that restricted their operations.[12]

The first combat operations of D-Day, however, did not involve amphibious landings or bombardment, but rather the final phases of Operation Bodyguard. While that campaign of deception had worked so far—Hitler's Atlantic Wall and its supporting army divisions were strongest in the Pas-de-Calais region—the Germans' attention had to be held at that point while 150 miles to the south, the great Allied invasion fleet was making its way across the Channel to Normandy. Furthermore, their attention had to be kept there even after the landings had begun at the five invasion beaches arrayed from the Cotentin Peninsula to Caen—Utah and Omaha (American), Gold, Juno, and Sword (British and Canadian).

On June 5 at 11:00 p.m. British Double Summer Time (which was the time used throughout the operation, and was two hours ahead of Greenwich Mean Time), a series of bomber flights took off from southern England and the Midlands, despite the fact that winds were still gusting heavily. These aircraft did not carry explosives, but rather enormous loads of aluminum chaff. The brainchild of Robert Cockburn at TRE, the idea was for the bombers to fly continuous elliptical relays over the English Channel while deploying clouds of chaff, so that the overall pattern of radar reflection dropped by each succeeding bomber group appeared to be slowly moving across the Channel at a speed of 5 to 10 knots, that of an advancing armada of ships.

The demands placed on the pilots flying through the buffeting winds were enormous, even though the crew made extensive use of the Gee navigation system; each bomber had to fly a precise, predetermined pattern at 200 knots in order for the entire group to simulate a 5- to 10-knot forward motion of the chaff clouds. One set of bomber groups deployed chaff toward Calais and Boulogne (Operation Glimmer), another toward Le Havre and the mouth of the River Seine (Operation Taxable). Meanwhile, small craft fitted with radar reflectors and repeaters bobbed through the rough seas under the bomber streams, to deceive German radars (Operations Big Drum and Moonshine). The ruse certainly convinced the Nazi leaders that an attack at Calais was imminent; scarce night fighters were sent out to chase the ghostly images, a report from Luftwaffe High Command spoke of "ships assembling off Calais and Dunkirk," and an invasion alert was declared for the Pas-de-Calais region.[13]

The deception operations continued between Calais and Le Havre and elsewhere, as hundreds of cloth dummies were parachuted into the countryside in an effort to draw off German divisions from the invasion site. The real paratroopers were already being dropped behind Utah Beach (American 82nd and 101st Airborne Divisions) and Sword Beach (British and Canadian elements of the 6th Airborne Division), followed by gliders. Their immediate missions were to secure the flanks of the invasion, cut off roads and bridges and destroy artillery to prevent German counterattacks, and capture major routes for the invasion force to exit the beachheads.

Each parachute drop and glider landing was preceded by teams of pathfinder paratroopers who arrived thirty minutes to an hour beforehand. The pathfinder aircraft (both the British and Americans used C-47 Dakotas) were equipped with Gee navigation to pinpoint the drop zones, a task made far more difficult by high winds and low clouds. The pathfinders themselves jumped from the aircraft at altitudes as low as 300 feet, each paratrooper stick equipped with two Eureka radio beacons (the new AN/PPN-1 version, just 25 pounds with a spring-loaded antenna), as well as colored signal lights that would be arranged into a T shape to provide visual reference for the drop or landing zone. The American 82nd and 101st each had three 3-plane pathfinder elements, while the British 22nd Independent Parachute Company had six aircraft that carried the pathfinders for all the British and Canadian drops and landings.[14]

The first pathfinder to land in Normandy was Captain Frank Lillyman of the 502nd Parachute Infantry Regiment of the 101st. At 12:15 a.m. on June 6, he and his sticks landed in a small field near the coastal town of Saint-Germain-de-Varreville behind Utah Beach, about a mile northeast of their objective. The pathfinders quickly regrouped at the church, then headed through the hedgerows to set up the landing aids in a suitable field. By 12:25 a.m. they assembled three Eurekas and seven signal lights for the incoming paratroopers, who began arriving a half-hour later.

Sixty miles away near Merville behind Sword Beach, the first British pathfinders under Lieutenant Robert E. V. de Latour touched ground at 12:20 a.m., just five minutes behind Lillyman, and set up their Eureka beacons and landing lights at 12:35 a.m. The first waves of aircraft carrying what would be almost 20,000 Allied paratroopers, along with 600 gliders, now began following the signals on their Rebecca receivers to guide them to their drop and landing zones. Despite high winds, low clouds, and enemy flak, most of the pathfinders were successful; though many aircraft were dispersed, only 2 percent were completely lost, with 80 percent landing within five miles of their intended drop or landing zone. One-quarter of all aircraft were guided in by Rebecca/Eureka alone, with no help from the signal lights for fear of being detected by nearby German troops.[15]

Even so, many of the drops and landings went terribly wrong. Scattered sticks, even when dropped just a few miles from the target, had trouble regrouping in the hedgerow country. Occupying German forces had deliberately set many obstacles, such as by flooding fields, which trapped and drowned some paratroopers, and "Rommel's asparagus"—large wooden poles that wrecked several gliders. But the paratroopers and glider troops improvised their way to their objectives even before first light; British glider troops, for example, quickly captured the Bénouville (later renamed Pegasus) Bridge over the Caen Canal, while American paratroopers occupied the vital crossroads at Sainte-Mère-Église behind Utah Beach. Time was of the essence, for the first amphibious landings were set to begin at 6:30 a.m., between low and high tides, to avoid some of the underwater obstacles for the landing craft while giving the troops a minimum distance to cross the beach to gain cover.

THE ACTUAL LANDINGS LARGELY went to schedule, led by armored assaults using DD tanks. A total of 290 DD Shermans and Valentines were launched from their LCTs half an hour to an hour before the troop landings, to give them time to swim ahead and provide armored support to destroy German gun emplacements. At the British and Canadian beaches, the lessons from Slapton Sands of launching DD tanks in rough seas were taken to heart, and most of the LCTs approached within 1,500 yards of shore before they launched their tanks in shallower, somewhat calmer water, so most of the tanks arrived successfully to provide much-needed firepower. On Utah Beach, the LCTs got within 1,000 yards before launching, and also generally arrived successfully.

But the Americans at Omaha Beach, which had shorter and steeper seas than any of the other beaches, launched their DD Shermans more than 5,000 yards out to avoid German artillery. The results were disastrous, with the 741st Tank Battalion suffering the worst; one company lost all sixteen tanks sunk with their crews immediately upon launch, while others came ashore at the Easy Red and Fox Green Sectors with just one or two tanks intact, leaving the soldiers of the 1st Infantry Division to face German machine guns and artillery with just their small-arms weapons (this was the inspiration for the horrific opening scene in the 1998 film *Saving Private Ryan*, where Tom Hanks's character, Captain Miller, radios, "We got no DD tanks on the beach. Dog-One is not open!"). However, across the whole of the Normandy invasion, almost three-quarters of all DD tanks made it to shore, either swimming, wading, or landing directly, and brought the fight to the enemy. One American infantry commander said of the DD Shermans, "[They] saved the day. They shot the hell out of the Germans and got the hell shot out of them."[16]

LSTs did not go ashore in the first assault waves; they were both too valuable to be exposed to concentrated German artillery and too vulnerable should they be disabled and incapable of pulling away from shore, taking up precious shoreline that was needed for further waves of amphibious forces. Instead, many LSTs anchored several miles from the beaches, then painstakingly offloaded their vehicles onto Rhino ferries, each of which was a series of Laycock pontoons connected together to form a large raft, fitted with twin outboard motors to propel them to shore. Those Rhinos carried the jeeps, trucks, half-tracks, bulldozers, and other specialized vehicles needed by the troops during their initial assault and breakout from the beach.

On Gold, Juno, and Sword Beaches, those vehicles included Hobart's Funnies, which cleared mines and obstacles and attacked fortified emplacements. On Utah and Omaha, two of the oddest-looking American

Figure 18 Rowland Baker, undated (David K. Brown)

Figure 19 John C. Niedermair Jr. at his drafting table at the Main Navy Building in Washington, DC, undated (Office of the Curator of Models, Naval Surface Warfare Center Carderock Division)

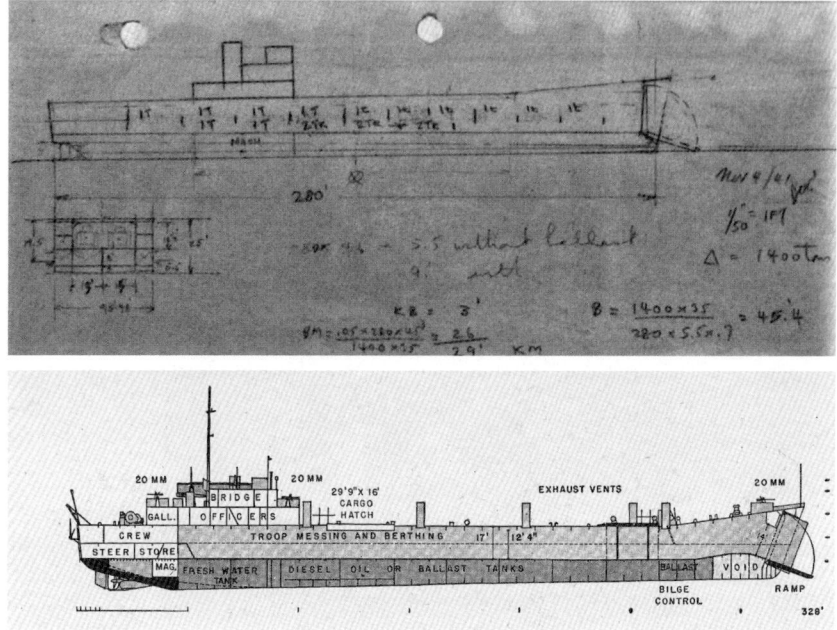

Figure 20 *Top:* Original pencil sketch of the LST concept, drawn by John Niedermair on November 4, 1941 (Webb Institute of Naval Architecture). *Bottom:* Schematic of a production LST (Naval History and Heritage Command). It is noteworthy that the LST was built almost exactly as Niedermair's initial sketch had shown.

Figure 21 Duplex Drive (DD) Sherman tank, undated (Tank Museum, Bovington)

Figure 22 LST offloading trucks across Laycock pontoons during Operation Husky (invasion of Sicily), July 1943 (Naval History and Heritage Command)

Figure 23 LSTs offloading equipment at Omaha Beach in Normandy, during Operation Overlord (invasion of France), June 1944 (Naval History and Heritage Command)

Figure 24 Laura Knight, *Ruby Loftus Screwing a Breech-ring*, painted at the Royal Ordnance Factory, Newport, Wales 1943 (Imperial War Museums)

Figure 25 Merle Tuve at his desk, c. 1945 (The Johns Hopkins University Applied Physics Laboratory LLC)

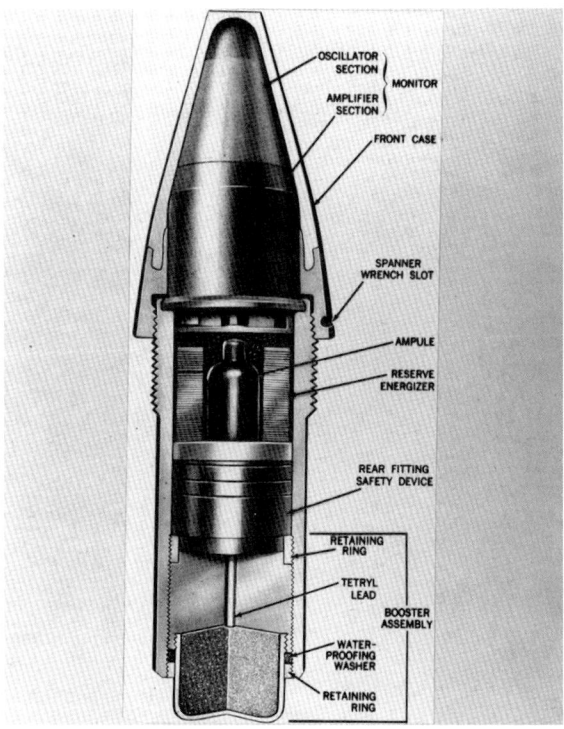

Figure 26 Cross-section of a proximity fuze (Naval History and Heritage Command)

Figure 27 Churchill crossing the Roer River over a Bailey Bridge, March 3, 1945. *Front row, left to right:* Alan Brooke, Winston Churchill, Bernard Montgomery, William Simpson (Imperial War Museums).

Figure 28 "Thanks to Penicillin, He Will Come Home." Magazine ad for Schenley Laboratories, 1944 (Wellcome Collection)

Figure 29 The Alsos team dismantling an experimental uranium pile in a cave at Haigerloch, Germany, April 1945 (Brookhaven National Laboratory/AIP Emilio Segrè Visual Archives)

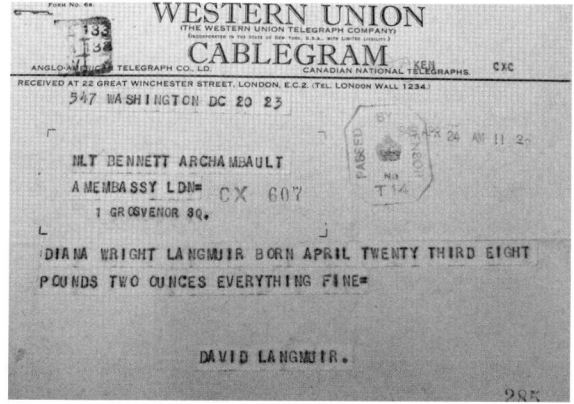

FORM No. 68.
WESTERN UNION
(THE WESTERN UNION TELEGRAPH COMPANY)
CABLEGRAM
ANGLO-AMERICAN TELEGRAPH CO., LD. CANADIAN NATIONAL TELEGRAPHS. CXC
RECEIVED AT 22 GREAT WINCHESTER STREET, LONDON, E.C.2. (TEL. LONDON WALL 1234.)

547 WASHINGTON DC 20 23

1945 APR 24 AM 11 2

NLT BENNETT ARCHAMBAULT
AMEMBASSY LDN= CX 607
1 GROSVENOR SQ.

DIANA WRIGHT LANGMUIR BORN APRIL TWENTY THIRD EIGHT POUNDS TWO OUNCES EVERYTHING FINE=

DAVID LANGMUIR.

Figure 30 Western Union cablegram from David Langmuir to Bennett Archambault, announcing the birth of Diane Langmuir, April 24, 1945 (National Archives and Records Administration)

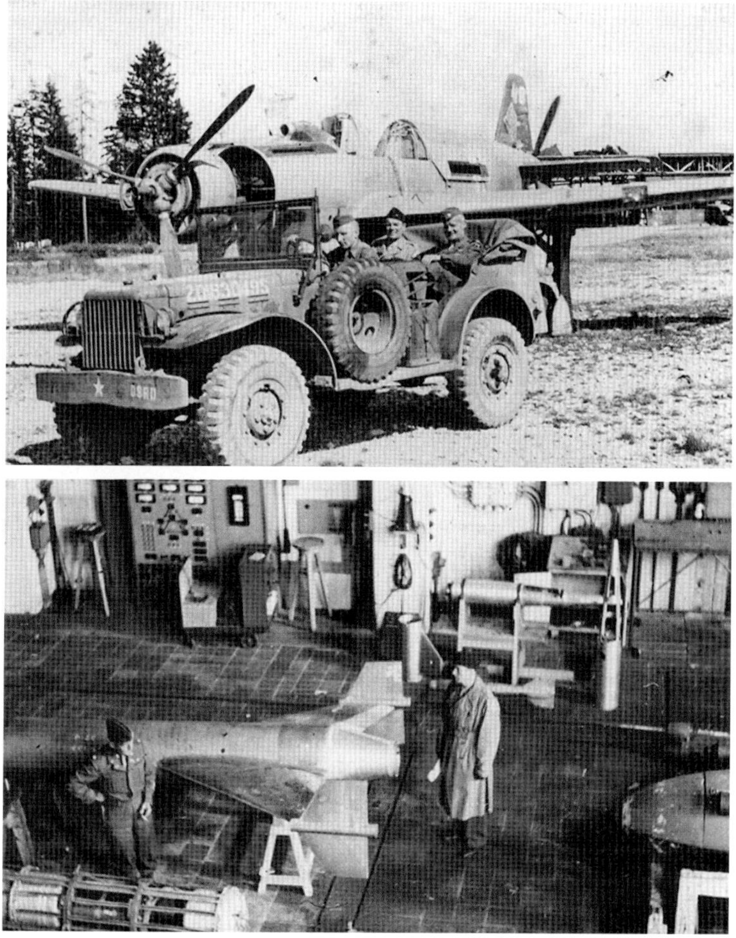

Figure 31 OSRD London Mission visiting German sites around Munich, Germany, June 1945. *Left:* In front of a Dornier Do 335 Pfeil experimental fighter; Bennett Archambault is in the backseat of the jeep, on the left. *Right:* German rocket laboratory (Michele Archambault).

Figure 32 The Langmuir family, 1945. *Left to right:* Nancy, Diana, David (Jean Langmuir).

Figure 33 Author in front of a Bailey-panel bridge, Oahu, Hawaii, 2021 (Mirna J. Ferreiro)

vehicles to drive off the Rhinos—the M-29 Weasel and the DUKW—had distinctly British roots.[17]

The M29 Weasel cargo carrier was the brainchild of Geoffery Pyke, a British journalist and inventor. Better known for his Habakkuk (a proposed artificial iceberg-cum-aircraft carrier, never built), Pyke was prompted by Germany's 1940 occupation of neutral Norway to envision Project Plough, which would bring commandos into Norway along with small, air-transportable vehicles that could transport them across the snow for special operations. In early 1942, Mountbatten and Churchill were made aware of the possibilities of Project Plough (disabling heavy-water production at the Vemork Norsk plant in Telemark was one obvious mission), and they in turn convinced George Marshall to fund development of Pyke's vehicle. OSRD Division 12 and the army took over the project, with Pyke as consultant. After many prototypes, the M29 Weasel was built by the Studebaker Corporation. It was a light tracked vehicle with a watertight hull that could go through snow, mud, and swamps, and could even ford rivers. Although Project Plough was disbanded, the US Army and Marines, as well as the British Army, found the M29 indispensable to get troops and supplies to hard-to-reach locations in Europe and the Pacific.

The amphibious DUKW (the initials designate that it was an all-wheel-drive utility vehicle) was also co-developed by OSRD Division 12 and the army in 1942, but its inventor was a British-born naval architect named Dennis Puleston who had been living on Long Island, New York, for several years. The DUKW (built by General Motors) was intended to ferry supplies from ship to shore after the initial amphibious assault, but like the Weasel, its versatility made it almost indispensable across many theaters of operations.

The main assaults at Normandy were staggered according to tide schedules. On Utah and Omaha Beaches, hundreds of Higgins boats hit the beaches at 6:30 a.m. On Gold, Juno, and Sword, Thornycroft boats arrived an hour later. On all beaches, tens of thousands of soldiers scrambled to get to the first line of German defenses, intent on blowing them up to begin the breakthrough from the beachhead. Many of them used some form of the Bangalore torpedo to help achieve this. It was (and is) a long series of metal pipes filled with explosive charges, developed by a British officer in Bangalore, India (today Bengaluru), in 1912 to detonate booby traps. During World War One, the British used them to blow holes through barbed wire defenses, and while the Americans tested the concept, they did no further development until 1941, when the US Army Corps of Engineers began looking for ways to demolish bridges. They soon hit upon the Bangalore and, with additional British and Canadian assistance, developed a production model, manufactured in Ohio by Republic Steel, that could also blow a path through minefields or beach obstacles. The difficulty of breaching these defenses varied from one section of Normandy to the next. On the Canadian and British beaches, inland objectives were captured by midafternoon; on Omaha Beach, the most heavily defended section, which also saw the highest casualties, the inland foothold was still tenuous at nightfall. But the Allies now held all the beaches, clearing the way to bring follow-on echelons and build up forces ashore.[18]

THE D-DAY LANDINGS WERE the opening act of what would turn into a two-month-long battle to break out of the Normandy region and begin the re-conquest of Europe. This would be a marathon, not a sprint; the first assaults were followed by wave after wave of LSTs landing on the beaches and offloading more tanks, more artillery, more equipment, food, ammunition, and supplies, constantly building up and moving inland against the German counteroffensive (Figure 23). The experience of the aforementioned *LST-386* was typical. The ships and its commanding officer, Lieutenant David Allen Pace, were already veterans of the amphibious assaults of Sicily and Italy. *LST-386* hit Juno Beach on June 7, D+1, offloaded without incident, and returned to Britain, also without incident. The following supply runs were equally uneventful until June 19, when they "had the misfortune to arrive off [our] assigned beach during the most violent storm ever to hit the English Channel," recounted Pace. He was loath to take his wallowing ship into the pounding surf off Juno Beach, but this particular load of ammunition was vital to Montgomery's campaign to capture Caen. Pace managed to beach the ship and offload the ammunition, but the action of the waves lifted the ship bodily and smashed it down again on the beach, damaging the propeller and rudder and visibly bending the hull. He cautiously drove the ship back to the Thames and limped it into drydock, where during its repair it was nearly struck several times by V-1 buzz bombs.[19]

Meanwhile, another 235 LSTs, two-thirds of those available worldwide at the time, took up the slack to keep the advancing Allied forces supplied. On just a single day in June, over 20,000 men, 3,500 vehicles, and 10,000 tons of equipment were deposited on the beaches of Normandy. Over the summer, LSTs were fitted as floating hospitals and transported over 40,000 casualties back to British shores for treatment. Many of those troops would be patched up and sent back to Europe as the Allied armies fought to break out of western France and begin their march toward Berlin.

CHAPTER 8

FIGHT IN THE HILLS

BACK IN BRITAIN, members of the OSRD London Mission followed the news of the D-Day invasion with a mixture of hope, anxiety, and some measure of pride. The intense pace of work over the past four years, keeping the Allied technical and scientific partnership on track across hundreds of different programs, seemed now to be bearing fruit. David Langmuir, the second-in-command in the London Mission, worked directly with Eisenhower's staff on the planning for Overlord. As he was responsible for Operation Moonshine, part of the deception campaign to deceive German radars, he had received BIGOT clearance, the highest level of security, given only to personnel needing direct knowledge of Overlord. Both the responsibility for the task and the need for absolute secrecy weighed heavily on him, and at times he felt overwhelmed by the vast scale of the conflict. He tried to explain this in a letter to his colleague Carroll Wilson back at OSRD headquarters in Washington, whom he wrote on July 4, just a month after D-Day:[1]

I'd hate to have to prove to anyone that one single thing I did during these two months specifically helped the invasion. I have the vague memory of moving around, carrying the burden of some terrifying secrets, trying to keep the ball rolling, attending meetings where a superman probably could have accomplished a lot but where I felt capable of doing nothing more than sit and listen.

In the same letter, Langmuir mentioned the German V-1 missiles (buzz bombs, which the Germans called *Vergeltungswaffen* or "vengeance weapons"), which had started hitting London the week after D-Day:

> Everyone is talking about them. They are undoubtedly interfering seriously with work, as the whole office staff spends most of the day hanging out the window looking for the things. After several days I began to show a lot of will power, and to work right through without moving even when a buzz was approaching. . . . Personally I wish the bombs would stop, but I can't get sufficiently frightened to change my way of life.

By June 1944, Langmuir had already endured three years of intermittent German bombings—the so-called tip-and-run raids after the Blitz—which is why, like most Londoners, he refused to change his way of life. Air raid warnings sounded so frequently, he wrote Wilson, that "everyone walks around the streets with almost complete disregard of whether there was an alert or not." Often the danger was not the German bombers but the "friendly" fallout of British anti-aircraft (AA or "ack-ack") guns. Langmuir described to his wife, Nancy, one such incident that happened in January 1943 as he, his friend and boss at OSRD London, Bennett Archambault ("Arch"), and Arch's date Dilys Charlton were at the cinema:[2]

> The show was *Casablanca*, and it is a swell film. Humphrey Bogart does a swell job, Ingmar Bergman is about the most beautiful woman on the screen. . . . The plot is exciting and subtle in spots. While gripping the seat to see how the heroine was going to get out of her dilemma a notice was suddenly flashed on the screen:
> THE ALERT SIGNAL HAS SOUNDED
> PERFORMANCE WILL CONTINUE

A good hearty chuckle seemed to be the reaction to this. About five minutes later there was the distinct sound of explosions in the distance . . . which became more frequent and closer. Then the sound took on a real crescendo. I reacted in proportion until Dilys remarked, "Those are just the new AA guns in Hyde Park, aren't they? I haven't heard a bomb drop." Lots more people left. We sat through. . . . After the show we merged into the street. It was beautiful and thrilling and terrifying to hear an ack-ack barrage go off, then see myriad pinpoints of light flash in the sky, followed by falling fragments, which punch holes in the roofs, and often are lethal when they hit humans.

By this point in the war, Langmuir's primary worries were not bombs or ack-ack. He had begun working at OSRD London Mission in April 1942, and married that July during one of his infrequent returns to the United States. Since then, he had spent most of his time at OSRD London and ABL-15 in Great Malvern, while Nancy was back in New Jersey. He was continually torn between the need to continue his war work and his desire to be home. His airmail and V-mail letters are filled with longing, and a constant debate over whether she should come to London: "There is a risk involved," he told her, "to life and limb." He went so far as to send her telegrams coded in poetry references to avoid the British censors, until the American embassy's security personnel called Archambault, telling him, "That is a security violation," forcing Langmuir to admit they were love letters. Langmuir somewhat envied his friend Arch's situation; as a single man in London, he could focus on the job at hand, and even see its absurdities. "Arch has come to the conclusion," Langmuir wrote his father in April 1944, "that the more he sees of the war, the more convinced he is that no one should take it too seriously. Any individual who thinks his presence or absence could make any noticeable difference to the big show has a funny idea of himself."[3]

The Problems of Shooting Down Aircraft

The "big show," as Archambault put it to Langmuir, had shifted dramatically by July 1944 from Britain to the Continent, as the Allies broke out from their German encirclement at Normandy, liberated Paris on August 26, and began the relentless drive toward Berlin. The Germans fiercely counterattacked at every turn, often by air; even if the Luftwaffe was barely present during the initial D-Day landings, it remained a lethal force against the advancing Allied armies. By this time in the Pacific theater, Japan had lost most of its aircraft carriers, but its land-based fighters and bombers still attacked Allied navies. Britain and the United States had together been developing, since the beginning of the war, a series of increasingly effective anti-aircraft guns that their armies and navies put to the test as the final battles intensified.

The Hyde Park anti-aircraft guns that Dilys Charlton recognized were Vickers 3.7-inch mobile batteries belonging to the 1st Anti-Aircraft Group, operated principally by the men and women of the Home Guard volunteers. They were among the most effective AA guns in the world, comparable to the German 88 mm and the American 90 mm, but none of them were very good. All large-caliber AA guns had in common three problems.

The first problem was that they were generally used for higher-altitude bombers and fighters, so their shells had fuzes (the trigger mechanisms) set to explode automatically at a certain height using time delay, or on contact with the aircraft. Neither method was likely to result in a kill, often requiring tens of thousands of rounds to bring down a single aircraft, which is why Langmuir, in the aforementioned letter to his wife, took special note of falling fragments as posing a greater danger. The second problem was that heavy guns had a slow rate of fire, about one round every two seconds, so tracking fast, low-level enemy fighters and dive-bombers was extremely difficult. The third problem was that gun-laying (aiming the gun at the target) was primarily done with optical sights, a method that became increasingly inaccurate as airplanes became faster and which was almost impossible to use in darkness or overcast conditions. Each problem would have to be successively overcome to win the anti-aircraft war.[4]

The third of these problems, accurate gun-laying of large-caliber weapons, was addressed by the introduction of radar. By the beginning of the war, several nations were using sophisticated fire-control systems that employed analog computers (alternatively called "predictors" or "directors") to aim the gun where the target aircraft would be when the shell arrived. In the United States, Sperry's M7 Director was used for the 90 mm gun, while the Vickers No. 1 Mark III Predictor aimed the 3.7-inch gun. Both systems operated along the same basic principles. Observers using optical sights fed inputs of the target range, elevation, and azimuth into the computer—actually a complex set of gears that adjusted for information such as wind speed and gun ballistics—to provide the gun operator with the proper azimuth and angle of elevation to fire the gun, and the fuze time delay in the case of exploding shells. But gun-laying was still subject to the limits of human eyesight and judgment at a time when the difference between success and failure was measured in a few seconds.

Early-warning radars helped focus the efforts of the gunners on specific sectors of the sky, but it was not until the invention of the cavity magnetron in 1940 (which, as noted, was initially introduced by the Tizard Mission but further developed by the MIT Rad Lab) that reliable gun-laying radars, which could accurately track aircraft even in overcast or darkness, were made possible. The most successful was the SCR-584 radar tracking unit, which was used to direct the elevation and azimuth of the guns. It combined a 10-centimeter radar, employing the cavity magnetron, with a Bell Labs electromechanical computer that coordinated radar and optical data in order to keep the guns on target. Its MIT designers, Ivan Getting and Louis Ridenour, spent 1942 and 1943 traveling back and forth between Bell Labs, the Rad Lab, and its British branch BBRL, building and integrating the various components. The first completed units arrived for testing at Great Malvern in October 1943, though they did not "draw first blood," as Getting later put it, until February 1944, when they directed the downing of German fighters over Essex and at the invasion of Anzio.[5]

The second of the problems mentioned above, the slow rate of fire against low-level aircraft, had long been recognized by warring nations. This is why, as early as World War One, small-caliber weapons had been introduced, such as the .50-caliber Browning machine gun, along with quick-firing artillery like British 1- and 2-pound pom-poms, and later the American 1.1-inch and 37 mm guns (Britain sometimes measured shells by weight, while Americans and Europeans usually measured by diameter). Though having shorter range, these guns could put up far more shells against low-flying aircraft. Between the wars, the British and American militaries—armies and navies both—recognized that their light AA guns suffered from problems with reliability and accuracy, and took note of developments abroad.

The most promising of these weapons seemed to be the 20 mm gun made by Oerlikon of Switzerland and the 40 mm Bofors gun from Sweden. The outbreak of World War Two made it impossible to buy them even from neutral countries; the Allies would have to build them instead. It took a series of cloak-and-dagger missions, which even Ian Fleming (then with the Admiralty's Naval Intelligence Division) would have dismissed as too far-fetched for his later James Bond novels, to smuggle out the drawings and parts and get them to British and American factories, where the guns would be built by the thousands for use around the world.

Smuggling the Oerlikon

The Oerlikon Machine Tool Works in Zurich had been famous for its precision engineering since the nineteenth century. After being taken over by the German-born industrialist Emil Georg Buehrle in 1929, it began producing armaments, of which its aircraft-mounted 20 mm machine cannon was the most widely sold. In 1935 Buehrle was introduced to Austrian engineer and salesman Antoine Gazda, who was on his way to Japan on behalf of a French client. They struck a deal whereby Gazda also sold Oerlikon machine cannon to the Japanese navy, which fitted them to their Zero fighters, among others. While in Tokyo, Gazda's wife, Leopoldine, met the British naval attaché Lieutenant George Ross at a diplomatic social event. "Her blonde hair fell over her shoulders" was what Ross remembered most vividly, even though she was a highly qualified engineer. She introduced him to her husband, and together they spoke of the Oerlikon's performance and later arranged for Ross to visit the Oerlikon works.[6]

Ross then brought the matter to the attention of Louis Mountbatten, at the time in the Naval Air Division of the Admiralty. Mountbatten, after meeting Gazda and seeing the gun demonstrated, recognized its value in the anti-aircraft role (compared with its competitor the Hispano-Suiza, Oerlikon barrels could be easily changed out when they overheated). It took until 1939 for Mountbatten to convince the Admiralty to purchase it. Gazda, meanwhile, tried unsuccessfully to sell the gun to the US Navy and War Department. In July 1939, with war looming, the Admiralty ordered 1,500 Oerlikon 20 mm guns and placed Commander Steuart Mitchell as the Admiralty purchasing officer in Zurich to oversee the contract.

After war broke out in September, Mitchell tried to hold Oerlikon to its promised delivery, but production quickly fell behind; by May 1940, when Germany began to overrun Western Europe, only 109 guns had been shipped and mounted on British vessels. Mitchell realized that no more guns were forthcoming when on May 24 Oerlikon's management gave him all the technical drawings required for manufacture. Buehrle, knowing that the Nazis would prohibit any export of his gun, had made his intent clear to Mitchell: he was to smuggle the drawings out of the country in order to have the guns built in Britain. Both men certainly knew this was possible because the British government, which depended upon Swiss industry for arms, machine tools, and precision parts, had already established a complex smuggling operation in the event of a German blockade or even invasion of Switzerland. Smaller items were secreted out in the clothes and luggage of diplomatic couriers, while for larger goods, substantial bribes ensured that the right officials turned a blind eye. But the stakes were too high to entrust this shipment to anyone else; Mitchell would have to become a smuggler himself.

After ensuring his wife made it safely out of Zurich, Mitchell loaded his car with drawings and precision parts on the night of June 16, 1940, and set out for Spain through newly occupied France. Managing to pass across the Swiss-French border, he was driving along the Rhône Valley near Lyon under an almost full moon, when, as he remembered, he had a premonition of danger and stopped the car. Scrambling down a moonlit slope, he saw a squad of Wehrmacht motorcycle troops dismount on the bridge below and take up positions. With his only way to Spain now blocked, he returned to Zurich and planned an alternative escape to the east. Over the course of the next three weeks, he somehow made the risky journey (whether by car, airplane, or train, he never specified) through the Balkans to Turkey, then through British-held Palestine and Egypt, where he was able to board an aircraft at Cairo to take him and his trove back to Britain.

With the Oerlikon drawings safely in Britain, it was now a matter of finding a factory to build them. Gazda had signed an agreement with the Admiralty in 1939 to establish a British shadow works at Brighton, but that was now moot. The Admiralty assigned the task of setting up an Oerlikon factory to Commander Charles Goodeve, the Canadian chemist who would soon become involved in the development of Hedgehog. Goodeve had just come off another pair of assignments, creating a magnetic mine-sweeping system and methods to demagnetize warships against mines. Goodeve first conferred with Mitchell, then both went to the government departments responsible for setting up factories and obtaining machine tools. The first department told them they could not get a factory without having machine tools; the second would not release machine tools without a factory to put them in. Goodeve cut this Gordian knot by going straight to First Sea Lord Dudley Pound (who, as mentioned, later helped him solve a similar problem with Hedgehog), who gave him his backing.

Armed with Pound's assurances, Goodeve first commandeered a new but underused London Underground maintenance depot in the town of Ruislip, outside London, by telling them he had 250 machine tools but no factory. He then went back to the ministry responsible for machine tools, telling them he had an empty factory that now needed machine tools, which they granted. Having bluffed his way into establishing a fully functioning factory, he spent the summer and fall of 1940—in the middle of the Battle of Britain and the Blitz—gearing up for production. The first gun was not delivered until April 1941, but by the following October, the Ruislip factory was delivering 1,000 guns per month, with another 1,500 guns monthly from other shadow factories in the west of England. This, however, was not nearly enough for army and navy requests; they needed shadow factories in the United States to meet the enormous demand.[7]

When Goodeve had set up the Oerlikon Gun Factory at Ruislip in October 1940, Mitchell was in Washington as part of the British Purchasing Commission, trying to interest the US Navy in building the Oerlikon gun for themselves as well as for Britain. Mitchell approached Captain William "Spike" Blandy, in charge of AA guns at the navy's Bureau of Ordnance, about the advantages of the Swiss gun. Blandy knew that the navy had turned down Gazda's offer back in 1935 because of poor performance. Mitchell impressed upon Blandy the improvements that Oerlikon had made since then. Further, said Mitchell, he could demonstrate the gun the next day at the Dahlgren Naval Proving Ground, fifty miles south of Washington DC. He contacted the Oerlikon agent in Providence, Rhode Island, to send by truck his only working model of the 20 mm cannon. True to his word, the following day Mitchell set up the gun and demonstrated it. According to historian Gerald Pawle, who later interviewed Mitchell, he then asked Blandy to try it for himself. Mitchell strapped Blandy to the gun harness and told him to write the letter B in the sky. "Captain Blandy began a little gingerly," he recounted, "but he quickly warmed to his work as he neared the lower half of the letter B. When he unbuttoned his harness, he was grinning broadly. 'Well, Commander,' he said, 'I guess we'll buy that!' "[8]

THE OERLIKON AGENT IN Providence was none other than Antoine Gazda. He and Leopoldine, with Oerlikon drawings and power of attorney in hand, had landed in New York City back on May 26, 1940, having departed days before Mitchell received duplicate drawings of the gun to be smuggled out of Switzerland. Oerlikon's owner, Buehrle, was clearly hedging his bets by arranging for manufacture in both Britain and America. He also sent a prototype gun and ammunition to be shipped to the United States. When that gun was captured aboard ship at Bordeaux by the Germans, Gazda arranged with the Admiralty for a British destroyer, en route to the United States, to dismount one of its precious Oerlikon guns (which had proved themselves in the Battles of Narvik) and give it to him for demonstration purposes.

Gazda, meanwhile, was trying to impress potential clients to win Oerlikon contracts. He and his wife stayed at the Waldorf-Astoria Hotel, entertained lavishly, and traveled across the country in an attempt to woo politicians, bankers, and industrialists. In August, he met with Arthur Purvis, head of the British Purchasing Commission (BPC), and promised that he would form a company to build 150 guns per month. Gazda negotiated with Rhode Island governor William Vanderbilt III and New York investment banker Karl Behr (a survivor of *Titanic*) to form the company American Oerlikon Gazda (AOG), headquartered in Providence, Rhode Island, to manufacture the Oerlikon gun under license from its parent Swiss company. The BPC approved purchase of the AOG guns on September 21, but within two days it ran headlong into the same problem that the British Tank Mission was already experiencing: government policy required American industry to supply to the British only products already being manufactured for the US military. The Oerlikon gun first had to be accepted by the US Navy, or none would be built at all. This explains why the following month, Mitchell was so anxious to have Blandy write out his initials in 20 mm script.

Blandy's recommendation of the Oerlikon was influential in the Bureau of Ordnance (BuOrd, which he would command three months later), but the final decision would be political, not technical. In early November, Purvis wrote secretary of the navy Frank Knox, urging him to adopt the Oerlikon as a standard navy weapon. Knox, who would later support Lend-Lease by telling Congress that the roots of American life "lie embedded in British soil," agreed that a common weapon would best serve both nations. Knowing of Blandy's recommendation, Knox directed BuOrd to work with BPC (which had the licensing agreement with AOG) to order 5,000 guns, 4,000 for the Americans and 1,000 for the British. The fact that the Swiss government denied AOG's license did not deter either the BPC or BuOrd; the gun was too important to both nations to worry about breaking a few international rules. When Lend-Lease was signed in March 1941, the British simply turned over their agreement to BuOrd, which in August formally contracted with AOG to produce 200 guns per month for British and American use.

AOG was already manufacturing guns during these negotiations. Gazda had been directed by Governor Vanderbilt to a disused textile mill in Pawtucket, which soon became AOG's assembly plant. Dozens of smaller companies in the northwest corner of Rhode Island manufactured parts for the gun. The first US-built Oerlikon was test-fired in June 1941, two months before the official contract was signed. BuOrd, however, was not content with the relatively meager output offered by AOG, so it signed additional contracts with two Detroit-based car companies, Pontiac and Hudson. As with Packard's experience with the Merlin engine, engineers had to take apart the gun, remeasure it to convert from metric to English units, and completely redesign it for American mass production. Unlike the Merlin, however, British and American versions of the Oerlikon were virtually identical. The guns at first were slow to come off the assembly lines; by the time of Pearl Harbor, there were only 379 mounts available—264 from AOG and 115 from Pontiac, with Hudson's first model was still weeks away.

Gazda, meanwhile, was facing growing problems that had nothing to do with manufacturing. When BuOrd contracted with AOG for the guns, it was on the condition that Gazda, as a foreign national, be removed from the company. Gazda then formed a separate engineering company that made parts for the gun as well as aircraft components. He then found himself locked in legal disputes with Oerlikon's original (prewar) US agent, Alfred Altman, a New York–based importer/exporter of everything from dairy products to barbed wire. Since Gazda had no intention of paying Altman's 5 percent commission, they and the Swiss parent company sued and countersued each other and the government—even as the war was raging and indeed long afterward—in lawsuits extending to the state and federal courts.[9]

Then on December 11, 1941, a post–Pearl Harbor sweep by the New York office of the FBI rounded up Gazda, along with hundreds of other German, Austrian, Italian, and Japanese nationals, and imprisoned them on Ellis Island. Unlike that of most of his fellow detainees, Gazda's confinement drew attention at the highest levels of state and national governments. The Navy Department had had him followed before his detention, and afterward John McCloy, the assistant secretary of war—who surely had more important things to worry about—received regular calls about Gazda from AOG's banker Karl Behr, and fielded entreaties from the likes of Louis Mountbatten, arguing for his freedom. After several months Gazda was released under the recognizance of the new governor of Rhode Island, Howard McGrath, and allowed to continue working under twenty-four-hour army guard in Suite 1009 of the Providence Biltmore Hotel.[10]

Despite Gazda's travails, production of the Oerlikon gun at the three American factories steadily increased during 1942 and 1943, until at their peak they were producing 5,000 guns per month. The British factories at Ruislip (which, despite its proximity to London, was never bombed) and in the west of England added another 2,500 guns every month, for a total of over 150,000 guns by war's end. Being light, easy to handle, and pointed by hand using a fixed gunsight, the 20 mm Oerlikon became the standard short-range (about 1,000 yards) AA gun on almost every type of Allied vessel, from single and twin mounts on PT boats to several dozen guns on troop transports to battleships bristling with eighty mounts.

In the Pacific Theater prior to 1944, Oerlikons accounted for over one-third of Japanese aircraft downed. Armies and air forces of both nations adopted Oerlikons for AA defense of their bases, and the AA batteries that ringed London and extended out toward Kent and Sussex were festooned with Oerlikons. As the war progressed, however, it became clear that the lightweight Oerlikon did not have the stopping power needed for the increased threats from German and Japanese aircraft, especially the kamikaze attacks that began in late 1944. That was where the heavier Swedish 40 mm Bofors gun demonstrated its worth.

Building the Bofors

The story of the Bofors gun, like that of the Oerlikon, involved unexpected encounters, skullduggery, and a complete flouting of international laws. The Swedish company AB Bofors was transformed in the 1890s by Alfred Nobel (inventor of dynamite and founder of the prizes) from a steelmaker to an armaments manufacturer. In 1934 it developed a light but powerful 40 mm gun that could be used against aircraft and small ships. The Swedish and Dutch navies were the first to buy it, but both naval and land models soon became popular around the world, with Allied and Axis powers alike.

British Army observers were impressed by the weapon, and in 1936 the War Office ordered 100 guns, with a licensing agreement to build more in shadow factories at Coventry and in Newport, Wales (where Laura Knight painted the aforementioned *Ruby Loftus Screwing a Breech-ring*, Figure 24), as well as in Canada in factories in Vancouver, British Columbia, and Hamilton, Ontario. Converting from Swedish to British manufacturing practices and metric to English units meant that the first guns did not start coming off British production lines until mid-1939, and not until fall 1940 for Canada. Even then, production numbers were paltry (a few dozen per month). Sweden, which had declared itself a non-belligerent nation soon after the outbreak of the war, cut off all further arms exports to Britain and its Commonwealth, so all eyes now looked to the United States.[11]

US military attachés had been sending reports of the Bofors gun's excellent reputation—it had been used by the Republicans in the Spanish Civil War, and by the British during the evacuation at Dunkirk—but it took the unlikely intervention of a well-connected civilian to jump-start American interest. Henry Howard, a retired engineer and businessman in Newport, Rhode Island, had been head of several chemical companies that manufactured explosives. He was an avid yachtsman, and his regattas and voyages to the Caribbean acquainted him with European aristocrats and industrialists, including the Swedish financier Axel Wenner-Gren, a fellow yachtsman who also owned a controlling interest in AB Bofors. In June 1939 at Wenner-Gren's invitation, Howard (who was attending a business convention in Copenhagen) took a side trip to Stockholm to witness a demonstration of the Bofors gun. On his return, Howard wrote to BuOrd (presumably his chemical companies had had previous business with them), impressing upon them its advantages over other AA gun models.[12]

HOWARD'S MISSIVES, WHICH ARRIVED just as war broke out in Europe, convinced BuOrd to more closely study its anti-aircraft needs, specifically identifying the requirements for a low-level gun that had greater range and stopping power than a machine gun, but with higher rate of fire than the heavier AA batteries. By early 1940 it decided to purchase a Bofors model for testing purposes. Working through the naval attaché in Stockholm,

BuOrd purchased in July a double-barreled 40 mm gun and 3,000 rounds of ammunition. Getting it to the States would be far more difficult than buying it, as Germany had just launched its blitzkrieg across Europe and invaded neutral Norway.

Roosevelt, though, had ordered the US Army troopship *American Legion* to sail to Petsamo in northern Finland (at the time in an uneasy truce with both Germany and the Soviet Union) to evacuate American diplomatic personnel, along with Norway's Crown Princess Martha and her family, as well as refugees from across the region. As the ship sailed into the fjord on August 6, a truck convoy carrying the Bofors gun and its ammo was making the 1,000-mile journey from the Bofors plant in Karlskoga through Sweden and Finland to where *American Legion* was moored. The gun and ammo were surreptitiously loaded onto the vessel before it departed on August 16, 1940. Germany was permitting safe passage of the army troopship, the last time it would do so. The ship arrived uneventfully in New York on August 28, after which the Bofors was shipped to the Dahlgren Naval Proving Grounds.

While *American Legion* was crossing the Atlantic with a Bofors in its cargo hold, another Bofors gun was being shown to the Americans by the Dutch navy. But the gun was not what the Dutch were trying to sell to the Americans. In early August 1940, the Dutch naval attaché in Washington, DC, approached Spike Blandy about buying the Royal Netherlands Navy's new fire-control system, based on a German design, which directed the aim of the Bofors gun (Blandy, who would have known of BuOrd's purchase of a gun in Sweden, was not yet involved with the Oerlikon). Together they arranged for a demonstration of the system in the Caribbean waters off the British colony of Trinidad. Blandy convinced Admiral Harold Stark, then still chief of naval operations, to order the heavy cruiser USS *Tuscaloosa*, then in Guantanamo Bay, Cuba, to sail to Trinidad so that its reconnaissance floatplanes could tow aerial targets for the demonstration. Blandy flew down separately.

On August 20, *Tuscaloosa* rendezvoused off Trinidad with the Dutch warship HNLMS *Van Kinsbergen*, which mounted the Bofors gun and the fire-control system. "The demonstration was about as international an

254 ≡ CHURCHILL'S AMERICAN ARSENAL

affair as it could be," recalled Blandy. "American planes towed targets for a Dutch ship firing Swedish guns with a combined Dutch-German fire control system, the whole taking place in the Caribbean Sea off a British port." Blandy was unimpressed with the Dutch fire-control system but almost instantly decided that the US Navy needed the Bofors gun.[13]

Soon after Blandy returned to the United States, the Bofors gun that had arrived aboard *American Legion* was mounted at the Dahlgren Naval Proving Grounds, alongside American 1.1-inch and 37 mm guns and British 2-pound pom-poms. In September and October 1940, a series of side-by-side tests demonstrated that the Bofors was superior to the American guns (it fired heavier shells, thus had greater stopping power), and also that its ammunition was compatible with American propellants, which the British pom-poms were not. Army observers present at the Dahlgren test firings were also impressed and arranged further trials at their ranges in Aberdeen, Maryland, and Fort Monroe, Virginia. By April 1941, both the US Army and Navy agreed to adopt the Bofors as a standard low-level AA weapon. And this made them available for Lend-Lease purchase by Britain.

BuOrd now had a model of the gun but not its drawings, so Blandy asked the Dutch naval attaché (who must have gotten over his disappointment about the fire-control system) to arrange for Bofors drawings located in Surabaya, Dutch Java, to be microfilmed and sent to Washington, DC, where they were translated and converted to English units. Other drawings came from the Bofors plants in Canada. In June 1941, BuOrd completed a contract with AB Bofors on behalf of both the army and navy to manufacture under license single-, dual-, and quadruple-mount guns (one difference was that the navy's gun barrels were water-cooled, while the army's were air-cooled) plus ammunition.

Not long after the contracts were signed, AB Bofors realized that US manufacture included Lend-Lease sales of its gun to the British. This was something to which it did not agree. Sweden's neutrality was hanging by a thread; Germany had invaded neutral Norway on the pretense of British influence, and so the Bofors deal might precipitate another such attack on Sweden. AB Bofors's New York representative, Alexander Proudfit, wrote a cease-and-desist letter to Harry Hopkins, in charge of Lend-Lease. Hopkins, using

Roosevelt's term "United Nations" for the Allies, replied in a letter on White House letterhead dated January 21, 1942:[14]

> Sir:
>
> I have your letter of December 30 [1941] telling me to tell the Army and Navy to stop manufacturing Bofors guns for use of the United Nations in the defeat of Germany and Japan.
>
> I can only say that if I had a client who asked me to do what you are asking your Government to do I should tell him to jump in the Lake.
>
> Very truly yours,
> Signed, Harry L. Hopkins

Although the navy and army agreed on the Bofors gun, they did not agree on who would build it. In June 1941, the navy had contracted with York Safe and Lock in York, Pennsylvania, which had been making AA guns for several years and had even begun license negotiations with AB Bofors prior to the navy's interest. That same month, the army contracted with Chrysler in Detroit, followed by Pontiac. As with the Oerlikon gun and Merlin engine, engineers had to take the Bofors apart, measure and study each piece, compare them with the plans, and then redesign the entire apparatus to American units and for mass production, including substituting widely-available steel instead of precious brass in many of the fittings.

Right from the start, there were problems with the interchangeability of parts between the army and navy models; for example, York translated its drawings into decimal inches, while Chrysler used imperial fractions. The matter was settled in November 1941 when Rear Admiral Blandy—now chief of BuOrd—decided that Chrysler's drawings would be the standard for all manufacturing. The number of differences between the army and navy models dropped from 200 to 10, and those mostly involved the gun barrel cooling, as noted above. Chrysler soon took over much of the navy manufacturing, eventually coordinating a dozen factories with thousands of subcontractors. Full series production began in February 1942, and within eleven months, almost 8,000 guns (plus carriages for mobile army mounts) were produced, of which Britain got 2,334 under Lend-Lease. By the war's end, over 50,000 Bofors guns were built in American factories, split roughly fifty-fifty between army and navy, with Britain getting roughly 10 percent of that total to supplement their domestic and Canadian production.

Aiming the Bofors

The Bofors 40 mm gun had more stopping power than the Oerlikon and greater range (about 3,000 yards, almost 2 miles), but unlike the Oerlikon, it could not simply be pointed by hand using a fixed gunsight. Without an adequate fire-control system, the Bofors gun would be almost useless. Neither Sperry's M7 Director nor Vickers's No. 1 Mark III Predictor, both designed for high-altitude bombers flying with a relatively small angular rate of motion, was adequate for the job. Aircraft that flew lower down, like dive bombers and fighters, presented a much more difficult targeting problem; the angular rates of motion were high, while engagement times were meas-ured in seconds, so it was almost impossible for the human gun operator to keep up with the changing azimuth and elevation commands being spit out from the analog computer. Blandy, as noted, had been unimpressed with the Dutch fire-control system he saw in Trinidad. However, while he was re-turning home from the trials, the British Tizard Mission was on its way to the United States with a solution.

Soon after the British War Office ordered its first Bofors 40 mm guns in 1936, it tasked Albert V. Kerrison, an army artillery colonel, to develop a fire-control system for it. Each gun mount would be aimed by its own predictor, which would automatically drive the hydraulic transmission that trained and elevated the guns. This removed the time lag of the human operator while allowing the gun to continuously track the target. Kerrison was transferred to the Admiralty Research Laboratory at Teddington, outside London, where his team spent two years developing what became known as the Kerrison Anti-aircraft Predictor No. 3. Weighing 500 pounds, it was nonetheless built with the precision of a Swiss watch. The success of the firing trials in autumn

1939, soon after the outbreak of the war, led to its immediate full-scale production by the laboratory (reaching about 5,000 units during the war).

By August 1940, the British government had such confidence in the Kerrison Predictor that the Tizard Mission offered it to the United States, along with the cavity magnetron, in the hopes of opening the doors of Allied scientific cooperation. That fall, at the request of OSRD and the US Army, a model of the Kerrison was shipped via Canada to Fort Monroe, and after a British crew demonstrated it with the Bofors gun, it was given to the Americans without cost or consideration about patent rights. The Kerrison was then sent to Frankford Arsenal near Philadelphia, where engineers took it apart to measure and draw each piece. In December 1940, as the army was nearing the decision to adopt the Kerrison, a team from the Singer Manufacturing Company in Elizabeth, New Jersey, was at the Frankford Arsenal to examine the feasibility of building it.

Despite the incongruence of a sewing machine maker turning out precision fire-control systems, Singer turned out to be a good fit. It was already winding down its sewing machine production due to lack of materials (which were being diverted to war work), so they had on hand a large, capable workforce; further, Sperry was backlogged with orders for its M7 Director and could not take on more work. Singer agreed to a contract to produce annually 1,700 M5 Directors (the US Army's designation for the Kerrison), though its management worried that doing so would be "overwhelming." Frankford handed over the first of 600 drawings in early 1941, while Singer broke ground in March on a new factory. Within a year, America was at war and Singer was now asked to produce 1,500 M5 Directors per month, even though that number was ten times larger than their previous target, which was already considered "overwhelming".. Singer's workers, as with those in so many American factories, found novel ways to rearrange and improve tooling and production in order to meet the demand. The first models were in use by February 1942, the 1,000th by July, and by the end of the war, 25,308 units had been produced and shipped out for the US Army and, under Lend-Lease, used for stationary and mobile Bofors and other AA guns.[15]

The first American Bofors guns were installed on existing battleships and destroyers in June 1942, replacing some 5-inch gun mounts with either a quad-mount or two twin-mount 40 mm guns. Newly built ships like LSTs had Bofors as standard AA equipment, along with Oerlikons. Naval Bofors guns did not use the Kerrison Predictor, which was too large and unwieldy for shipboard installation and was not accurate on a rolling, pitching platform. Instead, the much smaller Mark 14 gyroscopic gunsight (developed by MIT and built by Sperry) aimed the Bofors mounts as well as many Oerlikons. In the fall of 1944, the first kamikaze attacks against American ships in the Pacific precipitated a flood of demands for the 40 mm Bofors, especially quad mounts, because the 20 mm Oerlikons were seen as having insufficient range and stopping power to deal with this new threat. Aircraft carriers were specifically targeted by the Japanese pilots, so by 1945 they were fitted with up to nineteen quad-mounts, exhausting all available deck space. In the 1944–1945 period, nearly half of all Japanese aircraft downed were credited to the Bofors gun.[16]

"The Funny Fuze"

When David Langmuir in London had told his wife in 1943 that her coming would involve a risk "to life and limb," high on the list was the danger of being struck by friendly fire from heavy British AA batteries. Though the batteries had increasingly accurate fire-control systems, the time delay and contact-fuzed shells were irredeemably inaccurate. The first problem of large-caliber AA guns was described earlier—they had to fire tens of thousands of rounds to achieve a single kill, both limiting their effectiveness against enemy aircraft and endangering civilian populations below. The solution, most artillery experts already knew, was to develop a fuze that could detect the aircraft and explode the shell in close proximity to the target. This would require inventing entirely new technologies almost from scratch, even as the urgency for such a weapon grew daily.

The first ideas for a proximity fuze grew out of Henry Tizard's Air Defence Committee. One of the committee's early ventures was known as the "bomb-the-bomber" concept, by which obsolete biplane fighters would drop bombs on more modern enemy bombers below them. In August 1937, Patrick Blackett proposed a fuze for this bomb that would use either a photoelectric or acoustic device to detonate automatically when it got near the enemy aircraft. The Ministry of Supply's Experimental Establishment began trials the following year, but these proved disappointing. The photoelectric fuze was spoofed by the sun and clouds, and of course unusable at night. The acoustic fuze showed more promise. However, it could be prematurely detonated by the sounds of anti-aircraft shells bursting nearby. Both were abandoned in 1940 in favor of the radio proximity fuze, which would use a miniature radar to trigger the explosion.[17]

Radar (RDF at the time, of course) was still in its infancy, with the Chain Home system being its largest application to date. One of the scientists working on Chain Home, William Butement, turned his attention to proximity fuzes. In October 1939, he proposed to the Air Defence Committee to fit artillery shells with radio fuzes that transmitted and received signals using the Doppler effect, whereby approaching objects reflect back radar returns but with shortened wavelengths. By May 1940, Butement's small team had built and tested a laboratory model of the fuze, then mounted it on a tower and flown aircraft past it to determine at what distance the fuze would be triggered. At about the same time, two British electronics companies, Pye Ltd. and General Electric Company (GEC), were also building and testing prototype radio proximity fuzes.

Encouraged by these results, in July, John Cockcroft began work on miniature radio vacuum tubes that could withstand the enormous acceleration forces (upward of 15,000 g) from being fired from a gun, and the centrifugal forces from the spinning (20,000 rpm) shell. Knowing that American companies RCA and Western Electric were developing miniature vacuum tubes for hearing aids, his team quietly ordered 20,000 units for development of proximity fuzes. In August 1940, Cockcroft was selected as a member of the Tizard Mission to the United States, and began packing up the latest proximity fuze research, alongside the cavity magnetron and the Kerrison Predictor, as an offering to the Americans to spur scientific cooperation.

———————

EVEN BEFORE THE TIZARD Mission had arrived in the United States, American scientists were already working on proximity fuzes, and indeed knew that the British were developing them, too. Soon after the NDRC (later OSRD) was formed in June 1940, Vannevar Bush's committees, as noted earlier, began recruiting scientists and engineers from around the country. Bush tapped one of his own scientists at the Carnegie Institution, Merle Tuve (Figure 25), to help lead the search. Tuve was at the Department of Terrestrial Magnetism, which studied electricity, magnetism, and high-altitude meteorology (they had recently discovered the ionosphere) in well-appointed laboratories in the Chevy Chase suburb of Washington, DC. Tuve's work was becoming known internationally. Earlier in the year, he had hosted A. V. Hill during his American tour to drum up support for transatlantic technology exchange. Tuve would use his growing promi-nence to persuade others to join the government. One of his early recruits, Danish-born Caltech physicist Charles Lauritsen, alerted Tuve in late July to the intelligence reports that the British had ordered 20,000 miniature radio vacuum tubes from RCA and Western Electric, and correctly deduced they were working on proximity fuzes.

Tuve soon learned that the US Navy was also interested in proximity fuzes, though they had no idea how they could be built. On August 12, 1940, Bush convened a meeting between the NDRC and the Bureau of Ordnance to help determine which research activities the NDRC should undertake. One of the BuOrd members present was none other than Captain Spike Blandy, who had been thinking about "influence fuzes" (as he termed them) ever since he was a junior gunnery officer in the 1920s. Blandy told the assembled group (which included Tuve and Lauritsen) that he hoped for the development of a proximity fuze, because "every artillery man realized that the anti-aircraft fuzes that were available ... were almost useless," and that the only thing that would work was a fuze that was influenced by the proximity of the target to detonate the warhead. Blandy later recalled of the meeting, "The how was left entirely to NDRC. My attitude was, here is something the

Navy badly needs. Please go out and get it for us. The field is wide open. We don't know how you are going to do it. If we did—we'd have done it."[18]

Nothing much happened for several weeks after that meeting. Tuve and his family went to Minnesota to visit with his in-laws. It was not a relaxing time for him; as the grandson of Norwegian immigrants, he was keen to find a way to help America turn back the German invasion of Europe and liberate his ancestral home. Even while he was investigating cosmic rays and lightning at the Carnegie Institution, he had been thinking of how to stop the Nazi advance. When Tuve returned to Washington later that August, it was to a new assignment as head of NDRC Section T (which Bush named for Tuve) with the remit to perform "preliminary investigations" of a proximity fuze. Section T began with just a few physicists already at the Department of Terrestrial Magnetism, such as Richard Roberts and James Van Allen, who were studying nuclear decay. Tuve brought in new talent, such as Edward O. Salant, associate professor of physics of New York University ("anxious to serve," Tuve told Bush), though he was often hamstrung by the security clearance process.

As with his British counterparts, Tuve set up his laboratories to build three types of proximity fuzes—photoelectric, acoustic, and radio. Like the British, his team soon discarded the first two, and focused all further efforts on developing the radio proximity fuze. They also investigated whether vacuum tubes could withstand the shock of being fired from a gun. Since Section T did not yet have access to military equipment or facilities, Tuve bought explosives from a nearby florist who sold gunpowder as a side business, then obtained from the army a World War One–era French 37 mm howitzer, and made use of a friend's farm in Fairfax County, Virginia, to conduct his experiments.[19]

As Tuve was running his first experiments, the Tizard Mission was already in Washington, giving Section T an early leg up on the fuze design. Several times between September 12 and 17, 1940, Cockcroft briefed the army, navy, and NDRC on their efforts with radio proximity fuzes in artillery. The British were also examining using such fuzes in bombs and rockets, because detonating a warhead a short distance above the ground was more devastating than a direct impact, since the blast was not absorbed by the earth. On the nineteenth, Cockcroft was in Tuve's home in Chevy Chase, showing him Butement's circuit diagram of the Doppler radio fuze. Tuve copied it into his notebook and the next day asked Richard Roberts to build it. The prototype circuit was far too big to fit in a shell, but it performed so well against a simulated target that "it became the prime mode of operation" for all future proximity fuzes. While the British circuit design had given the Americans a jump start, it did not solve the biggest problem that both nations faced: building miniature vacuum tubes rugged enough to survive being shot from the barrel of a gun.[20]

Tuve organized Section T into five divisions, each focused on a different aspect of the fuze, and, like the British, expanded its application to bombs and rockets. As Section T grew in both scope and size (it eventually had 800 staff), Tuve transformed himself from a bench scientist carrying out experiments to a hard-driving manager up against an impossible-to-meet deadline. Tuve developed a set of running orders to guide his personnel. Rule Number 1 was "I don't want any damn fool in this laboratory to save money. I only want him to save time." Rule Number 2 was "We don't want the best unit, we want the first one." His closing admonitions were "Run your bets in parallel, not in series. This is a war program, not a scientific program," and "The final result is the only thing that counts, and the only criterion is: Does it work then?"[21]

Tuve worked incessantly and demanded that his staff do the same. At least one scientist quit under the strain, which was worsened by the fact that Tuve's jury-rigged testing facilities were proving wholly inadequate to the task. The 37 mm howitzer was nowhere near powerful enough to replicate the forces from larger artillery pieces, and his friend who owned the farm was growing anxious that all the ballistics testing there would interfere with the hay crop he was expecting. Tuve asked the navy for a larger gun and a test range. The team was soon firing shells with experimental fuzes from a 57 mm gun at a location near a navy site in Indian Head, Maryland. The shells dug a barely visible four-foot hole in the ground, so the resident Chesapeake Bay retriever, Curly, found most of them.

On April 20, 1941, one shell with a vacuum tube fitted with special tungsten filaments, but rigged with a radio transmitter instead of a fuze, was shot into the air. The ground crew heard the radio signals coming from the shell as it flew, proving that it was possible to build a vacuum tube rugged enough to survive the initial blast and high-speed rotation. Further tests at Dahlgren on May 8, attended by Tuve, Lauritsen, and Roberts, who sat in a boat listening through headphones for the radio beeps, also showed that the tungsten vacuum tubes survived being fired from a larger (5-inch) gun. A radio proximity fuze was indeed feasible.

JUST AFTER THE DAHLGREN tests showed the feasibility of the radio proximity fuze, Tuve dispatched Charles Lauritsen to the OSRD London Mission to coordinate research and testing activities with the British, although their lack of progress was such that he found himself far more involved with a recent British study on the possibilities of using uranium to create an atomic bomb (of which more in Chapter 9). Cooperation on the proximity fuze continued, however, with the British Central Scientific Office in Washington becoming the conduit for exchange of technical reports as well as samples of the experimental fuzes, chemicals, and explosives as they came out of the production facilities.

This transatlantic cooperation extended to Canadian researchers at the University of Toronto, where a team under the physicist Arnold Pitt made great strides in rugged batteries that could survive being fired from a gun. Section T, meanwhile, had contracted with Raytheon to begin building prototype vacuum tubes—2,000 to start—for wide-scale testing, and sent a shipment to Cockcroft's team for their use. But British efforts were set back when Mark Benjamin, a British scientist assigned as liaison with Section T who was ferrying samples of the Raytheon tubes, was killed in a plane crash in Scotland that also destroyed the shipment.

Section T plowed ahead, now under OSRD, which had far more authority and funding than the NDRC it had subsumed. Initial tests of the Raytheon fuzes at Dahlgren in August 1941 demonstrated that the basic concept worked; one shell fired from a 5-inch gun was triggered by the proximity fuze and burst fifty feet over the water. But nine other shells failed, showing that they still had a very long way to go. As fall turned to winter, the situation only grew worse. The quality of the Raytheon vacuum tubes was declining, and OSRD London was reporting that the British were increasingly frustrated by a lack of coordination with the Americans. Tuve, discouraged by the lack of progress, wrote a memo outlining why Section T needed its own dedicated laboratory. "Time is shorter than we think," he noted. The date on the memo was Saturday, December 6, 1941.[22]

The following day, Spike Blandy—now promoted to rear admiral and the head of BuOrd—was at Griffith Stadium in Washington, watching his home team play the Philadelphia Eagles. Halfway into the first quarter, he was stunned to hear his name called over the stadium loudspeaker, asking him to return to work. Soon other names were announced with the same request—J. Edgar Hoover of the FBI, army colonels, navy admirals. After the initial shock of Pearl Harbor had worn off, Blandy made certain that the proximity fuze received top priority. On December 10, one of Blandy's staff called Tuve to tell him that "it is most urgent to concentrate every possible effort" on the fuze. This was followed by a sudden infusion of cash from OSRD and the navy. Further testing in January 1942 showed a marked improvement in the fuze performance. Still, Tuve needed more than just money to speed up development and production.

In March 1942, Section T moved to a new facility at Johns Hopkins University with the innocuous-sounding name Applied Physics Laboratory. They converted a two-story car dealership on Georgia Avenue in Silver Spring, Maryland, to serve as laboratory, quality control facility, and office space. Several navy proving grounds geared up for round-the-clock testing. By now Section T was focused solely on artillery fuzes, having hived off the proximity-fuzed bomb and rocket projects to other parts of OSRD.[23]

In mid-1942, Section T's priority list for the fuze was, in order: US Navy, Royal Navy, British Army, US Army. Japanese planes had already sunk two American aircraft carriers and a half-dozen cruisers in combat, while the earlier losses of HMS *Prince of Wales* and HMS *Repulse* in the South China Sea came as an utter shock to the British. The proximity fuze was seen as the quickest way of evening the odds, though it had yet to work against a moving aircraft. On August 11, 1942, the newly built cruiser USS *Cleveland* was in Chesapeake Bay, its 5-inch guns armed with Section T's proximity fuzes (Figure 26), and embarking radio-controlled model planes to serve as targets. These were small and almost impossible to hit, but *Cleveland*'s gunners brought down all three model planes with their first salvoes, at distances of over 1,000 yards. "Three runs, three hits, and no errors," Bush crowed in a telegram to his friend James Conant.[24]

BuOrd immediately expedited contracts for fuze production, eventually totaling more than one hundred companies, including radio firms like Crosley Corporation and even musical instrument maker Wurlitzer (best known for its pipe organs), which together built over 22 million fuzes by the end of the war. In September, proximity fuzes were shipped to Hawaii for further testing. then on to the South Pacific theater for distribution to warships, where gunnery crews were trained under the watchful eyes of the combat scientists of OSRD's Office of Field Service, notably James Van Allen, who was awarded four battle stars for his work. On January 5, 1943, off Guadalcanal, the cruiser USS Helena shot down two Aichi "Val" bombers. This was the first use of the proximity fuze in combat, and during that year alone, the fuze was credited with half of all Japanese aircraft downed.

By this point, David Langmuir had taken over the proximity fuze liaison duties at OSRD London, in addition to his other work. He noted in his reports back to Washington that Section T was so far ahead of the British in proximity fuze development (for which both sides used the cover name VT, or variable timing fuze) that the exchange of information was now essentially one-way, from Washington to London. Even John Cockcroft admitted that his British team "continually struggled to overcome the disabilities due to poor industrial development facilities." Britain's policy was now simply to get as many American models as possible.

In May 1943, Ed Salant and his team arrived at OSRD London to oversee the testing of new Section T fuzes built to British requirements. Both British navy and army guns fired smaller-diameter shells than the US Navy guns did, so Salant's group had been designing and building smaller fuzes to suit. Early work in Canada and at Dahlgren had demonstrated their feasibility in British 3.7-inch army and 4.5-inch navy guns, but differences in British gun design practices required more testing. Salant's team brought fuze samples for the Royal Navy guns (by then designated as top priority), which were successfully tested against targets at the artillery range in Shoeburyness, Essex, and at sea aboard a cruiser. Meanwhile, various components like the batteries were put through "rough usage" trials to ensure they could survive conditions aboard naval ships. To enhance their explosive power, navy AA shells were filled with RDX instead of the usual TNT. That winter, Royal Navy ships recorded their first kills against German aircraft using the proximity fuze.[25]

While Salant was still in Britain in early August 1943, John Cockcroft arranged a meeting between him and General Frederick Pile, in charge of all anti-aircraft defenses in Britain. Pile impressed upon Salant the urgent need for proximity fuzes for his stationary and mobile AA guns. Although the Luftwaffe's tip-and-run raids were no longer as deadly as in the past, what Pile apparently could not reveal to Salant was the growing number of intelligence reports indicating that the Nazis were developing a flying bomb, the V-1, which was likely to be used against London. Salant brought Pile's informal request back to Section T, which raised the level of priority for producing fuzes for the British Army's AA guns. Fortunately, this coincided with a US Army request to develop proximity fuzes for its 90 mm AA guns and for howitzer fuzes to provide air bursts against enemy ground troops, given that they had more lethal effect. The fuze for the British guns was not very different from the one used for the American guns, so Section T began producing 250,000 fuzes for General Pile, though the priority was still behind American fuzes.

Toward the end of 1943, OSRD London Mission passed along British intelligence, obtained through French and Danish sources, on the characteristics of the V-1. Section T built models of the V-1 and successfully tested the 3.7-inch fuze against it, though these reports did not reach Pile until the spring of 1944. At Pile's "urgent request" (British intelligence now estimated that V-1s would be ready in just weeks), Section T immediately placed British Army fuze production at top priority—even at the expense of US Army and Navy fuzes. In London, Churchill's war cabinet Crossbow Committee, which had been established to counter Nazi "vengeance weapons," instructed the Flying Bomb Subcommittee to coordinate all anti-air activities against the V-1. Bennett Archambault, head of OSRD London, was an active member of that subcommittee, while OSRD scientists Langmuir, Guy Stever, and John Trump helped British forces with radar tracking and fire control. Britain rushed to ready its air defense against the arrival of the V-1s even as it was preparing for D-Day. They were now both days away.[26]

London and Antwerp Under Attack

Of all the British nicknames bestowed on the V-1s ("buzz bombs," "doodlebugs," "divers"), surely the most incongruous was "Bob Hopes," as in "bob down and hope for the best." In the predawn hours of June 13, 1944—one week after D-Day—four V-1s (out of ten launched that day) sped low at over 350 mph from the southeast and toward London, chuffing like diesel trucks going uphill, until suddenly falling silent as the pulse-jet engines cut off and the bombs fell to earth. Most landed on farms; only one struck a populated area, Bethnal Green, its 1,000-pound warhead detonating on a railroad bridge, killing six people and wounding twenty-eight. The following day, an RAF fighter intercepted and shot down a V-1 over the English Channel. On June 15, residents of Kent, Surrey, Sussex, and London began hearing the almost incessant booming and clatter of AA guns as nearly 100 V-1s crossed the Channel daily.[27]

The British had already established an elaborate defense system against the V-1s. Its first element consisted of bombing and strafing the V-1 launch sites in northern France. The next employed the squadrons of RAF fighters (mostly Spitfires and Mustangs) that patrolled the English Channel, flying above the 2,500-foot flight path of the much faster buzz bombs, so they could build up speed by swooping down on them, either shooting them or tipping them over with their wingtips. After that were the anti-aircraft sites—called Gun Belts—set in a ring to the southeast of London. Many were established on hills and high terrain for the maximum field of view, such as those in Kent along the North Downs and Dover Heights. The sites typically consisted of two to four 3.7-inch guns, an SCR-584 radar tracking unit, and a half-dozen or more Bofors 40 mm guns. Closer to London, barrage balloons would snag the odd buzz bomb, while individual factories and military sites were defended by Oerlikon 20 mm cannon. The first two weeks of attacks saw 1,000 buzz bombs cross the Channel, half of which struck London. Fighters downed 300, while only 142 were brought down by AA guns.[28]

Despite the nonchalant nicknames given to the V-1s, the frequency and randomness of the bombings began to take a toll on British and Americans alike. By the end of June, almost 3,000 British residents were dead, another 8,000 wounded; for security reasons, those numbers did not include Americans. The single largest American loss of life (sixty-six men, which went unreported at the time) was from the early-morning July 3 attack on the Chelsea district of London, where servicemen from the Army's Chemical Warfare Service were billeted, The inhumanity of the bombs haunted popular and private imaginations. The British writer Evelyn Waugh, who witnessed one such attack, described V-1s in his novel *Unconditional Surrender* as "impersonal as a plague . . . enormous, venomous insects." The OSRD London Mission, desperate for more men to take on the mountain of work, found it impossible to recruit American scientists, for fear of the "robot bombs" in the newspaper reports.[29]

After several weeks of relatively ineffective performance of the AA batteries (they were downing only 10 percent of the V-1s that escaped the fighters), General Pile convinced Churchill and the RAF to allow him to move his batteries to the coastline, where they had greater freedom of fire and less chance of "friendly" fallout. On July 14, Pile initiated a wholesale uprooting of the Gun Belt, in a matter of three days moving hundreds of guns and thousands of troops to create a new Diver Belt (aka "buzz bomb coast"), extending from Eastbourne to Dover. US Army 90 mm guns supplemented the British ones, while the first proximity fuzes, which had arrived in Britain in early July 1944, were now being screwed into the noses of the shells. Special flights of Lancaster bombers transported more fuzes directly from factories in the United States. A Pan Am flight brought Ed Salant back to OSRD London, where he and other scientists joined General Piles's staff to help instruct the gunners to use the Section T fuzes.

The results of the new gunnery arrangements were remarkable. In the first few weeks, Diver Belt gunners downed 17 percent of V-1s, then 24 percent, then half. The burst patterns looked markedly different from regular ack-ack; instead of a wall of black clouds appearing all along the flight path, the proximity-fuzed shells—which did not detonate unless triggered—erupted in a small, focused cluster in one part of the sky. By the end of August 1944, three-quarters of all V-1s were being shot down by the guns; on August 28, three days after Paris was liberated, gunners downed ninety out of ninety-seven buzz bombs, and only four actually got through to London. By September 1944, with Allied troops overrunning V-1 launch sites and proximity-fuzed guns taking out the few that were launched, the V-1 threat to London effectively disappeared. General Piles sent a copy of his report on the V-1 campaign directly to Vannevar Bush, with a handwritten dedication on the cover: "With my compliments to OSRD who made the victory possible."[30]

THE END OF THE London campaign did not spell the finish of V-1 attacks, nor the use of proximity fuzes in Europe. On September 24, British troops captured almost intact the Belgian port of Antwerp, a vital hub to keep Allied troops resupplied as they advanced toward Berlin. Germany began launching a hundred V-1s daily at Antwerp from repositioned sites a month later; fear of proximity fuzes falling into enemy hands prevented their use for several weeks. Meanwhile, the US Army had been testing the fuze in air-burst artillery, first at Fort Bragg, North Carolina, and then (with the assistance of Salant and other OSRD scientists) at the Royal Artillery grounds at Larkhill, within sight of Stonehenge. The results of the tests showed its devastating power—lethal fragments shredded wooden boards that represented enemy troops. On October 25, the Combined Chiefs of Staff approved the use of the proximity fuze on the Continent, and it would be deployed everywhere, all at once, to utterly surprise the enemy. In mid-December, with technical assistance from OSRD scientists, American 90 mm guns firing proximity-fuzed shells started downing V-1s at an astonishing rate, 90 percent right from the start, which continued well after the New Year and into 1945.

The use of the AA proximity fuze at Antwerp coincided with the Battle of the Bulge, Germany's last major offensive against the Allies. The surprise advance was intended to push Wehrmacht forces through the Ardennes, recapture Antwerp, and split the Allied lines. Although the Germans launched a major encircling offensive against the American First Army just before Christmas, they were met with a barrage of air-burst artillery that stopped them in their tracks, shredding bodies and machines like nothing they had seen. The barrages and counterattacks continued until Lieutenant General George Patton's Third Army was able to break through the siege the day after Christmas, 1944. By this time, OSRD London had established a field office in Paris, from where Ed Salant ventured out to the front to help artillery troops make the proximity fuze even more effective. Patton immediately recognized the importance of Section T's work; on December 29, he wrote the War Department, "The new shell with the funny fuze is devastating," and later told Salant, "The funny fuze won the Battle of the Bulge for us."[31]

CHAPTER 9

FIGHT IN THE FIELDS AND IN THE STREETS

B Y THE BEGINNING of 1945, Patton's Third Army was just one of four Allied armies advancing toward Nazi Germany's heavily defended Siegfried Line, which they had to overcome before arriving at the Rhine River, the last major barrier to Berlin. Given that the retreating Germans blew up existing bridges, those armies needed robust, easy-to-construct temporary bridging to cross the Rhine and hundreds of other waterways. On the other side of the world, Allied troops fighting in the Pacific also found themselves needing thousands of temporary bridges. In both theaters, the Bailey Bridge would prove to be a vital link for bringing troops across Europe and the Pacific. And as those troops advanced along the roads and streets and across the woodlands and fields, a newly developed antibiotic, penicillin, would help ensure that they would also come home.

No Bridge Too Far

About halfway through the 1977 film *A Bridge Too Far*, which is about Operation Market Garden (the ultimately unsuccessful Allied attempt to invade Germany via the Netherlands), is the following exchange:

> Colonel Robert Stout (based on Robert Sink, played by Elliott Gould): "Hey, that Bailey crap. You got it amongst this stuff?"
>
> Lieutenant Colonel J. O. E. Vandeleur (played by Michael Caine): "When you refer to Bailey crap, I take it you mean that glorious, precision-made, British-built bridge which is the envy of the civilized world."

This exchange does not appear in the eponymous book by Cornelius Ryan (who also authored the D-Day classic *The Longest Day*). It was wholly invented by the screenwriter William Goldman, who had a way with the turn of a phrase (he later wrote the cult favorite *The Princess Bride*). He did not always have a way with the facts. The Bailey Bridge was hardly precision-made the way Rolls-Royce and Packard fabricated their Merlin engines, with an accuracy to a ten-thousandth of an inch. Each bridge was created from a few standard, mass-produced parts that were endlessly interchangeable, and whose construction allowed them to survive twisting and bending through rough handling, battle damage, and being banged up by crossing tanks.[1]

Temporary bridging across rivers and waterways had been a staple of military engineers since at least the time of Xerxes I (whose spanning of the Dardanelles in 480 BCE led to taking part of Greece) and Julius Caesar (across the Rhine in 55 BCE). During the Crimean War (1853–1856), the British Corps of Royal Engineers ("Sappers") developed standardized pontoon bridges, whereby wooden or metal boats were connected side by side across a body of water, with a wooden roadway laid over top. The US Army Corps of Engineers did much the same a decade later, during the Civil War. The introduction of tanks in World War One spurred cooperation between Britain and the United States in the development of new military bridging, including floating treadways (like those used in the LST landing trials in

Rhode Island, previously mentioned) and the portable box girder bridge, which was assembled from prefabricated steel units to form a continuous span over a river or canal. During the late 1930s, tanks grew rapidly in dimensions and weight (some as large as 30 or 40 tons were being contemplated), forcing both nations to rethink their military bridge designs.

Donald Bailey was the sole civil engineer in the Experimental Bridging Establishment (EBE), an agency under the Ministry of Supply that designed military bridging for the Royal Engineers. Despite its name, the EBE barely had enough money for experimentation and could only pay Bailey an annual salary of £400 (about $1,600 at the time, compared with the amount received by John Niedermair, the previously discussed American naval architect, who made $5,600 per year). In late 1940, after Churchill's Chiefs of Staff, in their Appreciation of Future Strategy, had outlined the plan to retake the Continent, the army was faced with the wholesale rebuilding and modernization of its equipment, including bridging. That November, Bailey and other EBE members had witnessed an unsatisfactory demonstration of a prototype upgrade to some existing military bridging, and were returning to their home office in Dorset in a Humber sedan staff car (the type preferred by General Montgomery). The current bridge models, they knew, were laborsome to put together—a deadly sin to engineers toiling under enemy fire—and could not be easily strengthened, should tanks grow even larger than currently contemplated. Bailey already had been thinking for some years about the requirements for a combat bridge. On the spur of the moment, he later recalled to his biographer Brian Harpur, he pulled out an envelope to sketch a new bridge concept, while still being jostled in the staff car.[2]

Bailey's car-ride insight was that combat bridges had to be assembled in the field from the fewest pieces possible with the fewest connections possible. Many older temporary bridges were stick-built, requiring every girder, beam, and brace to be brought to the site in a prefabricated bundle, then assembled and bolted together. His back-of-the-envelope sketch showed the concept of constructing modular, standard-sized panels that could be quickly pinned together to form bridge sections, even in the dark or under fire. From that basic idea came several more: each panel could fit in a standard three-ton truck and be carried by just six men, so they could be assembled without cranes or heavy equipment; the panels could be arranged in different ways to create different types of bridge sections, including pontoon and continuous span; the assembled sections could telescope out like a firefighter's ladder, to create bridges of different lengths; and the bridge sections could be strengthened at will, simply by attaching more panels at the sides.

Bailey's concept was firmed up over several weeks, and on February 14, 1941, the Ministry of Supply requested he undertake a full-scale trial of his complete bridge by May 1. In the meantime, Bailey's little office had grown from a few dozen to several hundred personnel, with him now the chief engineer, though with a paltry rise in salary to just £549 (still only half what Niedermair was making). Even given such a simple design, building the bridge involved hundreds of little decisions. To meet the six-man carry, truck load, and strength requirements, each panel would be 10 by 5 feet, be cross-braced, and weigh 600 pounds. So that even the most unsophisticated steel company could build the bridge sections, the simplest and most common structural shapes were used, made from widely available alloys. To ensure that all parts were interchangeable regardless of the manufacturer, a special set of fabrication gauges (dimensional templates) were sent to each factory.

Bailey carried out his full-scale tests in May 1941, more or less on schedule. The first demonstration showed that a seventy-foot bridge could be constructed by a team of Sappers in just under forty minutes (compared with three to four hours for other models of the same length). A rather spectacular static-load test was then conducted by driving a World War One–era heavy tank onto a bridge section, loading it with pig iron, then driving two light tanks on top of the first tank. The bridge held.

WHILE OVER 650 DIFFERENT steel companies began full-scale production of these bridges in the summer of 1941, a US Army Corps of Engineer officer, Frank S. Besson, was in Britain to the evaluate the "modification of the British Bailey Panel Bridge to fit standard U.S. sections," as part of a larger program to overhaul the Corps' bridging systems. Besson came back with plans for the Bailey and the firm conviction that it was the answer to many of the army's needs. The Corps agreed with Besson's assessment, and asked one of its civil engineering firms, Sverdrup and Parcel of St. Louis, to modify the British plans for American use.[3]

Three weeks after Pearl Harbor, the Corps began work on a prototype bridge, and in February 1942 issued contracts to build the Baileys. Three midwestern firms, none of them bridge-builders, were given the task of redesigning and building M2 Bailey Type Panel Bridges for American use. The Corps of Engineers insisted that American M2s be fully interchangeable with British Baileys, and sent representatives from the companies to visit the British manufacturers. They also borrowed a master set of fabrication gauges from Canadian firms that were building British Baileys. Given the relative simplicity of manufacturing steel girders and trusses—compared with the complex Rolls-Royce Merlin engines that Packard was already mass-producing—it seemed a straightforward matter for the Americans to build fully interchangeable Baileys for Allied use in Europe.

The American Bailey program turned out to be anything but a straightforward matter, and in the words of the Corps of Engineers' official history, it was "almost a complete failure." The army had tasked two tool-and-die companies to manufacture twenty-five sets of fabrication gauges from the borrowed Canadian master set, which only became available in January 1943, well after the first bridges were produced. Although American M2 bridges passed their initial tests, when they arrived in North Africa later in 1943, it was discovered that their components were incompatible with British Baileys. Further inspection showed that the American fabrication gauges were poorly made and inaccurate, and that there were problems with the American design modifications. At that point in time, however, the production lines were too far along to change.[4]

By 1944, all 856 American Bailey panel sets that had arrived in the European theater had to be set aside so as not to be mixed in with the British Baileys—the Royal Engineers even repainted their bridge components brown, so as not to be confused with American parts painted olive drab. While the US Army continued to ship other bridge types into the European theater (10,000 treadway kits, for example), almost all the Baileys used there by the Allies were of British manufacture, including those built in a British-run steel mill captured in Giovinazzo, Italy.

The American Bailey program was actually not a complete failure, because US-made Baileys saw heavy service in the Pacific theater. American army units assigned to the Ledo Road, connecting British India to allied China, used Bailey panels to create a 400-foot-long suspension bridge over the Shweli River in Burma (today Myanmar). As the Allies island-hopped northward through the Pacific, every Marine Corps Engineer Battalion and Navy Construction Battalion (Seabees) was equipped with hundreds of feet of Bailey bridging, which they used for the airfields and bases that sprang up on the newly captured Solomons, New Guinea, and Carolines. The road to Manila was paved with Bailey Bridges, such as the one crossing the Pampanga River on the island of Luzon, as well as the hundreds of smaller streams and rivers across the Philippines. Soon, those islands would host the forces that would land the final blows upon Japan.

THE AMERICAN ISLAND-HOPPING CAMPAIGN across the Pacific theater was paralleled by the advances in the European theater in the summer and fall of 1944. The Normandy breakout and the amphibious invasion in Provence (Operation Dragoon) saw Allied troops overrun crumbling German defenses, take over ports like Antwerp to bring more troops and equipment onto the Continent, and set up forward bases in France, Belgium, and the Netherlands. Over 1,000 Bailey Bridges dotted the landscape, crossing every type of waterway (the "Bailey crap" scene in *A Bridge Too Far* portrays a Bailey being thrown across a wide river, when in fact it was used to cross the narrower Wilhelmina Canal, near Eindhoven, on September 19, 1944).

As the Allies approached the formidable Siegfried Line, famous for its "dragon's teeth" anti-tank barriers, the even more difficult job of crossing the flooded Roer River fell to British, Canadian, and American combat engineers. Churchill, visiting the Siegfried Line at Juelich on March 3, 1945, was so impressed by the Americans' adept use of the British Bailey Bridges that he told the Ninth Army commanding officer, Lieutenant General William Simpson, who offered to drive him across the Roer on one of the Baileys, "After so magnificent a job your troops did here, it is an honor to walk across the bridge." And so he did, side by side with Simpson, accompanied by British generals Montgomery and Alanbrooke (Figure 27).[5]

In late March, Allied troops approached the Rhine River, which marked the unofficial boundary of the German homeland. Most of the bridges had been blown up, but the American First Army seized the still-standing Lundendorff Bridge at Remagen and held it for almost two weeks, pouring troops and supplies across the span until an intense German bombardment collapsed it. By that time, eight floating bridges, including Baileys and treadway pontoons, had been constructed above and below the site.

The biggest push was during the week from March 23 to April 1, when Allied forces made a series of crossings along the length of the Rhine, using landing craft and assault boats. Some of the crossings were defended by DD Shermans, which had successfully navigated the fast-running river and climbed the steep, muddy banks. As troops landed on the opposite shore, engineers began immediately constructing Bailey, treadway, and other bridges at an astonishing rate. Each was given its own nickname, such as Lambeth, Waterloo, and Westminster, echoing the names of the bridges in London. One of the first Baileys to go up was the 1,900-foot-long Sussex Bridge at the Westphalian town of Xanten, built on March 24 by 12th Corps Sappers (who were based in Sussex) in just twenty-six hours. Further south at about the same time, the American 1117th Engineer Combat Group erected a 1,200-foot Bailey Bridge at Wesel, also in a matter of hours. A day later, Churchill and senior Allied generals arrived in the area to cross and recross the Rhine River, secure in the knowledge that those, and the dozens of other bridges now spanning the river, were there to stay for the duration of the war.[6]

"Thanks to Penicillin, He Will Come Home"

The experience of World War One had shown the importance of planning for the medical treatment of soldiers on the battlefront and behind the lines. The state of medical care had advanced dramatically since the mid-nineteenth century, when Florence Nightingale and Clara Barton had tended the wounded in, respectively, the Crimean War and American Civil War. By 1915, most soldiers had field dressings as standard kit, every battalion was assigned a medical officer, and field hospitals and dressing stations were set up close to the fighting. Vaccines against typhoid and other diseases were by then commonplace. Nevertheless, disease and infection (perhaps most horrific being gas gangrene, which causes the tissue to bubble like rising dough) still wreaked havoc at the front lines. To take one example from the Gallipoli Campaign (disastrous in nearly every respect, as we've seen), for every ten Anzac soldiers killed in action, another five died from infections of their wounds or from disease. The development of drugs and medications was still in its infancy, even as other medical research (such as reconstructive surgery) was making leaps and bounds.[7]

Long before World War Two, Roosevelt was an advocate of investing in medical research and improving health care. Paralyzed from the waist down and in a wheelchair at age thirty-nine—from either Guillain–Barré syndrome or polio—he was personally aware of the needs of the infirm and the frail, and put forward Social Security and access to health insurance for workers as major parts of his New Deal program. Roosevelt himself was the driving force behind incorporating military medical research into the new OSRD, which, as noted, subsumed the old NDRC in June 1941. At that time, the army and navy urgently needed scientific assistance for the war they knew was coming, from fighting malaria and tropical diseases to improving combat surgery. The Academy of Sciences was poorly equipped to help, with forty-one disjointed committees and no funding to carry out any investigations. According to Vannevar Bush, Roosevelt "became weary of hearing about medical research, so he sent a message to the Bureau of the Budget, which drew up executive orders, saying that he wanted this medical show put under Bush, and that he did not want to hear a damned thing more about it." Roosevelt's decision caught Bush off guard, as he had no background in medicine; "I told FDR that he had handed me a hot potato," he recounted, for he would have to somehow corral "medicos" (his term) who usually bridled at outside, non-medical authority.[8]

Bush turned to Alfred Newton Richards to lead the Committee for Medical Research (CMR) under OSRD. Richards was the head of pharmacology at the University of Pennsylvania, and his opinions were widely respected. Bush concluded that his own role would be to fund whatever Richards decided upon, but otherwise not to interfere. Richards himself left the day-to-day running of CMR to his executive officer, Chester S. Keefer, previously a physician at Boston University. The CMR was arranged into six research fields, including surgery, medicine, aviation medicine, and malaria, and began letting the first of what would be $25 million in contracts to hundreds of universities and companies.[9]

The committee also established a permanent medical liaison position at the OSRD London Mission from November 1941 onward, in order to keep CMR up to date on the latest British research in military medicine gained from over two years of fighting, at a time when most scientific exchanges were stifled due to security restrictions and wartime postal delays. The medical liaisons—in order of tenure, Kenneth Turner, Joseph Ferrebee, and Hamilton Southworth—made liberal use of diplomatic pouches and their own personal connections across military and medical establishments, to keep up a running exchange between American and British doctors and scientists.

ONE OF THE MOST active areas of transatlantic medical exchange—indeed, the most significant medical achievement of World War Two—was the development of penicillin as an antibiotic. In 1928, microbiologist and former army physician Alexander Fleming, who was researching antibacterial substances to improve on the existing sulfa drugs, found that an airborne mold, *Penicillium*, killed bacterium in a petri dish he had left open for several weeks. After further experimentation he published his results in 1929, though nothing came of them for a decade.[10]

In 1939, a team of Oxford pathologists led by Howard Florey, along with Ernst Chain and Norman Heatley, rediscovered Fleming's paper and a sample of Fleming's mold, and began testing its ability to defeat bacterial infections in mice. Encouraged by the very promising results, in February 1941 they managed to extract enough *Penicillium* mold culture (penicillin) to treat a human patient, an Oxford-area constable, suffering from horribly infected abscesses. His condition greatly improved, but the doctors ran out of penicillin before he was fully cured, and the poor man relapsed and died. Although Florey and his team continued with other human trials, the British medical establishment—now reeling under the Blitz while meeting overwhelming civilian and military demands—was in no position to offer funding or equipment to mass-produce penicillin. Florey now looked across the Atlantic for help. With Lend-Lease just approved, the United States might become not only the arsenal but also the pharmacy of democracy.

Florey had received assistance before from the United States. The American industrialist John D. Rockefeller endowed many institutions that bore his name, including the Rockefeller Institute for Medical Research, which carried out scientific investigations, and the Rockefeller Foundation, which funded many promising researchers. Howard Florey, still a graduate student in 1925, received a Rockefeller Travelling Fellowship to work in the University of Pennsylvania laboratory of Alfred Newton Richards, and had turned several times again to the Rockefeller Foundation to support his research, most recently his penicillin trials.

The head of Rockefeller's Natural Sciences Division, which funded Florey's work, was the mathematician Warren Weaver, who at the same time was head of the NDRC Section D-2 on fire control. Weaver accompanied James Conant and Fred Hovde to London in March 1941 to establish the NDRC (soon OSRD) London Mission, also gathering information on British anti-aircraft fire-control technology and methods. While there, he was injured in an automobile rollover accident and spent several days in a hospital, experiencing at first hand how the British medical establishment coped with the Blitz.[11]

Florey's initial human experiment had just concluded, as noted, both successfully and tragically, when on April 14 he sat at Weaver's bedside and related to him both his excitement at penicillin's potential and his frustration at not getting British companies, or even Britain's Medical Research Council, which had funded Florey's early work, interested in manufacturing penicillin. Weaver immediately grasped the significance of Florey's accomplishments so far, and that he also needed to be linked with

American scientists and industry to see it through. But this was still many months before the CMR was even dreamed of, or before the first medical scientists came aboard the London Mission office; Weaver was now the de facto bridge between British and American researchers. Taking off his NDRC hat and putting on his Rockefeller hat, Weaver told Florey that if he could get permission from the Medical Research Council to leave, the foundation would pay for Florey's trip to the United States to locate "some American mold or yeast raiser who would undertake a large-scale production of this material for a test, say, 10,000 gallons for the first run." Still in his hospital bed amid falling bombs, Weaver wrote a glowing memo back to the Rockefeller Foundation: "This project, if it were indeed successful, would be more revolutionary than the discovery of sulfonamides [sulfa drugs] . . . and must be recognized as a project of the very highest potential importance."[12]

Events moved quickly after that. Weaver was released from the hospital and traveled back to New York on April 21. And Florey received permission from the Medical Research Council to spend three months in the United States. In June, Rockefeller granted Florey and Heatley $6,000 (a half-million dollars today) for the journey, and secretly arranged with the State Department for seats on the Pan Am *Dixie Clipper*, which were at a premium. With vials of freeze-dried penicillin mold in their pockets, they arrived on July 2 in New York, and immediately met with Weaver and others at the Rockefeller Foundation to plan their campaign. Florey spent July 4 with his children at the home of their friend John Fulton in Connecticut, where he and his wife had sent them during the Blitz for safeguarding (as had thousands of other British parents).

THE FOLLOWING WEEK, FLOREY and Heatley went to Washington, DC, first to the National Academy of Sciences and then to the Department of Agriculture, where, after a thirty-minute chat, the head of the Agricultural Research Service sent a telegram to one of his field laboratories in Peoria, Illinois, asking its staff to host the two Oxford scientists in setting up a pilot-scale penicillin production facility. In two days, Florey and Heatley were at the Northern Regional Research Laboratory (NRRL), where with a single letter of agreement and additional funding from the Rockefeller Foundation to support Heatley's stay there, they began production work on July 15.

The NRRL had been established a few years earlier as part of Roosevelt's New Deal, mainly to support midwestern corn farmers by creating new products for their crop. NRRL was beginning to use corn-steep liquor, a by-product of corn milling, which proved to be an excellent growth medium for penicillin. At the time, though, the mold could only be grown in small batches in surface cultures, using nutrient media in shallow petri dishes and small flasks. This was slow, inefficient, and space-consuming; Gladys Hobby, a researcher at Columbia University's Medical School, noted that to grow it for laboratory experiments, "hundreds of two-liter flasks with *Penicillium notatum* ... lined every classroom laboratory bench."[13]

NRRL's head of the Fermentation Division, Robert Coghill, suggested that, in addition to continuing with surface cultures, the team pursue deep culture (also called "deep vat," "deep tank," and "submerged") fermentation, using large tanks, as was done in brewing beer or distilling whiskey, which would be more efficient and capable of industrial-scale production. A third line of research would involve looking for and developing new strains of *Penicillium* mold. While Heatley remained at NRRL to oversee the production experiments, Florey embarked on a series of visits to American pharmaceutical companies in the hopes of gaining their interest for commercial manufacture of penicillin.

Florey visited eight pharmaceutical companies, of which only four—Merck and Company, E. R. Squibb and Sons, Charles Pfizer and Company, and Lederle Laboratories—showed some interest. Several had already experimented with penicillin, but without a well-identified market or outside funding for further work, they were understandably reluctant to undertake such financial risks by themselves. After this disappointing round of talks—Florey later said he felt like "a carpet bag salesman"—on August 7 he stopped in to see his old University of Pennsylvania laboratory supervisor, Alfred Newton Richards. Florey's timing was perfect, for Richards had just been appointed as the head of OSRD's Committee for Medical Research, which only days earlier had had its first meeting, and was even now trying to decide where to spend its considerable funds. Over dinner at the Philadelphia Club, Richards listened intently to Florey's tale and, realizing its vast potential to help the armed services, promised "to see that everything possible was done to expedite the production of penicillin."[14]

Richards was as good as his word. On October 2, 1941, OSRD and the CMR approved placing penicillin in its program of research, and the following week Bush and Richards met with representatives from the Department of Agriculture and the National Academy of Sciences and with the research directors of the four pharmaceutical companies Florey had identified. Only one company, Merck, showed serious interest and was willing to share its results. The CMR convened a second conference with the same participants on December 17, just days after Pearl Harbor, when the urgency of the situation was obvious to everyone. Richards made clear to the companies that they needed to share information with each other as part of the war effort, that doing so would not be considered an antitrust violation by the Department of Justice, and that the information would be shared during monthly meetings with the CMR. No restrictions were placed on any of the companies regarding patents, as long as they did not interfere with the free flow of information.

While Heatley was working with his team at NRRL to improve the yield of surface cultures, another branch was culturing and testing new strains of *Penicillium* mold that could produce more penicillin. Molds came from across the globe: cheese from Connecticut, soil samples collected at various sites by the US Army, shrubs from Norway, wine must from Belgium. The best results came from NRRL's own backyard. In 1942, a moldy cantaloupe from a Peoria market was brought to the laboratory—whether by an NRRL employee or by a local homeowner is still debated—and its surface mold cultured. Designated NRRL 1951, this strain yielded far more penicillin than others, and when irradiated was able to produce 250 times more than Florey's original strain.

Florey himself had returned to Oxford in October 1941, where he and Ernst Chain improved the yields of their own cultures, continuing with clinical trials and bringing the British pharmaceutical industry into the picture. Reports between Britain and the United States were exchanged through the OSRD London Office representatives, where Ken Turner, Joe

Ferrebee, and Hamilton Southworth used their personal connections with Florey and Fleming to keep both sides informed of progress in research and clinical trials.[15]

COMMERCIAL RESEARCH WAS ALSO moving ahead quickly. Soon after the December 1941 CMR meeting, Merck and Squibb signed an agreement to share not just research but also production information. Heatley had by then left NRRL to assist Merck with its pilot plant in Rahway, New Jersey, where in March 1942 they managed to coax enough penicillin to treat one patient. At the request of Florey's friend John Fulton, the CMR allocated it to a dying patient in New Haven, Connecticut, and had it shipped there the next day. Anne Miller was listless and had a temperature of 106 degrees when she began a drip injection. By morning, her temperature had dropped to normal, and within several weeks of continued injections, she became the first patient to be saved by penicillin.

Knowing that this news would unleash a tidal wave of demand, OSRD and CMR, which bought the entire stock of penicillin from the pharmaceuticals, placed Richard's right-hand man, Chester Keefer in charge of allocation. Keefer only allowed for its use by the US armed forces and some clinical trials to determine proper dosage. Heatley, when he returned to Oxford in June 1942, was permitted only a half-gram of American penicillin to bring back to the laboratory where it all began.

By the middle of 1943, American manufacturers had produced 400 million units of penicillin (supplemented by another 200 million units from British companies like Glaxo). This amount, however, was only enough for clinical trials of several hundred wounded troops. Some of those first trials were conducted by Florey and a team of ten surgeons in North Africa, treating the wounded from the fighting there, as well as those from the Sicily campaigns who were flown back to field hospitals. The success of these trials encouraged the CMR to continue supporting research into industrial-scale manufacture of penicillin.

NRRL had been making slow progress on deep culture fermentation, although the strain mentioned above, NRRL 1951, proved to be the most productive for fermentation in tanks, and became the parent for all future penicillin strains. While Merck and Squibb continued pursuing surface cultures, Pfizer's chemical engineers put all their efforts into deep culture fermentation, since it already used that process in its primary business of making feed products for the agricultural and pharmaceutical industries. By August 1943 Pfizer was confident enough to build a pilot 2,000-gallon penicillin production plant, which was so successful that the following month it bought the old Rubel Ice Plant on Marcy Avenue in Brooklyn, installed fourteen 7,500-gallon tanks, and on March 1, 1944, began the first industrial-scale manufacture of penicillin.

BY APRIL 1944, ALL American production of penicillin was taken out of the CMR and placed under the War Production Board, which gave production contracts to twenty-two companies, including Schenley Laboratories, a former bourbon manufacturer that had little difficulty turning its whiskey fermentation process over to penicillin production. Capacity had increased to 100 billion units (enough to treat about 40,000 severely wounded cases) per month, which allowed the US government to permit limited distribution of penicillin to civilian hospitals. Britain's own pharmaceutical industry, even using deep culture fermentation, was only able to produce a small fraction of that, so American penicillin shipped to Britain was distributed among all the Allies prior to the D-Day landings. As the troops hit the beaches and dropped behind the lines on June 6, field hospitals, LST hospital ships, and hospitals back in Britain were stocked with ample quantities of penicillin to treat all the wounded.

As the Allied armies swept across Europe, penicillin supplies followed them at every step, saving 95 percent of all soldiers treated with it and reducing the mortality rate of the dreaded gas gangrene from 15 percent to almost zero. Back in America, pharmaceutical companies ran morale-boosting magazine ads proclaiming, "Thanks to Penicillin, he will come home" (Figure 28). While penicillin certainly saved many tens of thousands of lives during the final year of the European campaign, the Allied armies in general had a higher standard of medical care than the Wehrmacht. When they arrived at the banks of the Rhine River in March 1945, they were in far better shape, both materially and physically, than their German opponents.[16]

Inventions are smarter than their inventors, finding ways of changing and evolving in ways that their original inventors had never imagined. Alexander Fleming always said, "I did not invent penicillin. Nature did that." Howard Florey and his team certainly invented the production of penicillin, but it was inevitable that it would transcend anything they could have dreamed of at the beginning, whether they had brought it to the United States or not. And at exactly the same time as Florey's invention was changing before his eyes, another invention that had been developed by British and German scientists, the splitting of the uranium atom, was being reshaped by American scientists into a form previously unimaginable, not only to its inventors but to all humankind.[17]

CHAPTER 10

THE NEW WORLD STEPS FORTH

World War II was the first war in human history to be affected decisively
by weapons unknown at the outbreak of hostilities.[1]
—Vannevar Bush (1946)

Within weeks of the Allied landings at Normandy, American scientists
from the OSRD London Mission were close behind the advancing troops,
scouring the French countryside for information on German weapons and
defense technologies. The first priority was to gather intelligence about
launch sites of the V-1s that were falling across Britain, the second priority to
get new information on German radars. On D+20 (June 26), a C-47 transport plane carrying a replacement fighter engine and two OSRD London
physicists, Guy Stever and Howard Robertson, landed on a small dirt field
above the cliffs of Omaha Beach. Stever was an expert in radar, Robertson
in explosives (and also fluent in German). The two men were taken by jeep,

passing wrecked gliders and dodging sporadic artillery fire from remaining German troops. They passed Sainte-Mère-Église, which had been the scene of heavy fighting, and went into the heart of the Cotentin Peninsula, where they set up their base camp, sleeping in pup tents with the distant booms of guns echoing over the hedgerows.

Each day, Stever and Robertson went to a new locale to examine what the Germans had left behind. Destroyed V-1 launch sites gave clues to the effectiveness of the Allied bombing campaign, while their examination of Y-Gerät radio guidance stations offered little they did not know already. Near the recently captured port of Cherbourg they investigated one of the most significant sites, a storage and assembly facility for Hitler's newest "vengeance weapon," the V-2 rocket, whose terror was even greater than the V-1 because its supersonic, ballistic trajectory could not be countered. On July 6, while heading to the landing grounds from where they would fly back to Britain, Stever and Robertson were pulled over by military police to let pass a column of tanks. "In the command car stood General George Patton," recalled Stever in his 2002 memoir *In War and Peace*. "He was in full travel costume, with a brass-plated helmet and his famous special pistols on his belt. He stood straight, looking like he was in a victory parade, although the only audience was us." Having just assumed command of the Third Army, Patton was on his way to begin his breakout from Normandy and start upon the long road to Berlin.[2]

The next intelligence mission was to Brittany, no longer a German stronghold but still dangerous, to look for radar installations. This time, OSRD London director Bennett Archambault accompanied Stevers and two army technical officers on the trip. Landing in the Breton capital of Rennes, on August 10 they made their way to the town of Lannion, where they were greeted as liberators. François Tassel, a member of the Maquis, the French Resistance organization, who was one of the eyewitnesses, later recalled that "the four Americans, including the scientist Guy Stevers, made their entry into the town, cheered by the townsfolk. The following day, the main body of American troops arrived, also to great jubilation." Although the town had been liberated, the fighting continued.[3]

After helping liberate Lannion, the OSRD contingent drove to a radar tracking station in the pleasant coastal town of Perros-Guirec, where after summitting a hill, they suddenly saw "many people on both sides of the road wearing German helmets and carrying rifles. German soldiers in the road with rifles ready stopped us. Our senior officer, Colonel [Eric] Bradley, a calm veteran of World War One, told us in a very low voice, Don't say anything." The Germans led them through a minefield to a farmhouse at the Clarté overlook, where hundreds of Germans were camped. A letter from a British secretary at OSRD London Mission, Joyah E. E. Rowland, to David Langmuir, who was on home leave, tells the rest of the story:[4]

> Stever, Arch and Colonel Bradley arrived back on Monday [August 14]. To an admiring crowd Stever told the story of how Arch, Bradley and he went to inspect a site and found that the Maquis had surrounded 450 Nazis and that the Commanding Officer was in the process of surrendering to them, but was diffident about doing so as he thought the French might kill them—so he preferred to surrender to the Americans—thusly, Stever and Arch had the privilege of having 450 so and so's hand in their weapons to them—then Colonel Bradley walked up the road and collared another 1,000. All the local inhabitants were overjoyed and gave them a dinner party in the evening, to which each villager contributed something—drew forth their foie gras, sardines, wines, and most precious of all BREAD. The former delicacies I imagine had been buried for just such rejoicing. Arch and Stever had to kiss French babies, French mothers, aunts, uncles, and everyone. Allied cars and jeeps everywhere were one mass of flowers, flowers thrown at their feet and huge Victory signs in flowers on the roads.

The Germans were eventually handed over to American troops. Stever and Arch both returned from Perros-Guirec with large Nazi flags that they proudly displayed over their desks as war trophies. Stever would be back in France in just two weeks, entering Paris right after it was liberated on August 26. This time he was part of Eisenhower's Combined Intelligence Objectives Sub-Committee, a British-American team gathering technical intelligence on intact German and French laboratories and industries.

As the Allies advanced across Europe, OSRD London Mission established several field offices around Paris to bring science straight to the battlefields. In October 1944, BBRL (radar) and ABL-15 (radar countermeasures) set up laboratories at the Société Française Radioélectrique building in Levallois-Perret, just outside Paris on the banks of the Seine River, and began transferring many of their personnel from Great Malvern to be closer to the action. Working closely with the Army Signal Corps, they sent their scientists to assist the Eighth and Ninth Army Air Forces with solving operational problems as they unfolded. Those combat scientists worked at the front lines, frequently under fire. The head of ABL-15's Paris office, Wallace Caulfield Jr., was on such an operation on December 31, 1944, in Luxembourg when he was wounded in a bombing and strafing attack. He died the following day, and was posthumously awarded a Bronze Star for his actions.[5]

In late November, OSRD London established a field headquarters in the newly opened American embassy near Place de La Concorde, where Archambault moved most of his administrative staff. Vannevar Bush immediately used this office as his base for visiting American ordnance officers along the front lines, to impress upon them the utility of the proximity fuze, which, as already described, would be used to devastating effect against the Germans in the Battle of the Bulge. Another OSRD field office, at 2 Place de l'Opéra, would host an Allied intelligence operation, the Alsos Mission.[6]

Uncovering the German Atomic Program

The Alsos Mission was one of dozens of intelligence operations mounted by Britain and the United States (sometimes jointly, sometimes separately) to identify and recover vital information and matériel from the Nazi regime, as regions were liberated by advancing Allied troops. The most famous of these missions was the Monuments, Fine Arts, and Archives program, popularly known as the Monuments Men, whose members scoured caves, residences, and warehouses for art treasures stolen by the Nazis. The lesser-known

Houghteam (named for its leader, US army major Floyd W. Hough) sought German maps and survey data of strategic value.

Many more missions were aimed at gathering German scientific and technical information, and even the scientists themselves and their equipment. This was in part to aid the continuing conflict; though the German military was being pushed back everywhere, there was still deep Allied anxiety stemming from the "danger of the German scientists, the risk that they would come up with new weapons of devastating destructiveness," as undersecretary of war Robert P. Patterson stated after the war (mentioned previously). This was a well-founded fear, as demonstrated by the recent V-1 and V-2 weapons, as well as the jet-powered Me 262 fighter that had just rolled out.[7]

A larger goal of these missions, however, was to give the Allies a leg up for the competition with the Soviet Union that everyone knew was on the horizon. In addition to the aforementioned Combined Intelligence Objectives Sub-Committee (CIOS), there was the Field Information Agency Technical (FIAT), Joint Intelligence Objectives Agency (JIOA), Target Intelligence Committee (TICOM), T-Force, Naval Technical Mission, and Fedden Mission, each of which had distinct but overlapping interests in basic and applied sciences, intelligence, engineering, and technology. Later missions, such as Operations Epsilon, Surgeon, and Matchbox and the better-known Operation Paperclip, detained German scientists and engineers in order to entice them into applying their skills in postwar Britain, Canada, and the United States. Of these, the Alsos Mission, run jointly by the United States and Britain, was the only one dedicated to uncovering a Nazi atomic program. This was of crucial relevance to the Manhattan Project, which was trying to develop an atomic bomb first.

The British and Americans feared a Nazi atomic program because, just before the war began, German scientists had made great leaps in discovering how to create a chain reaction, the process at the heart of an atomic bomb. British scientists like Patrick Blackett and John Cockcroft had first discovered the process of splitting the atom in the 1920s and early 1930s, but in 1939 the German chemists Otto Hahn and Fritz Strassmann showed how to bombard uranium with slow neutrons to cause fission, a result confirmed by French chemist Frédéric Joliot-Curie, among others. This unleashed a flurry of scientific investigations in Britain, Canada, and the United States, which led to the establishment in September 1942 of the Manhattan Project, led by Brigadier General Leslie Groves.

Groves made security a top priority right from the start, inhibiting the exchange of personnel and information with Britain and Canada. It also stifled any significant gathering of intelligence about German atomic research, since any agent would have to know something about the Manhattan Project to carry out his duties. Apart from information on the transfer in 1940 of high-quality Congolese uranium ore from Belgium to Germany, and the Norwegian intelligence that led to the aforementioned assaults on the Vemork Norsk heavy-water production plant, the Allies were almost blind as to German capabilities.

The Allied invasion of Italy in September 1943 offered an opportunity to get information directly from the source; as troops advanced and liberated European territory, agents could follow in their wake to gather documents and interview scientists connected with the Nazi atomic program. Groves worked with Vannevar Bush and the head of army intelligence, Major General George Strong, to establish a small cadre of military and civilian personnel for this mission. With security at the top of his agenda, Groves would not hand the task to an intelligence service like the OSS, nor could he send anyone with working knowledge of the Manhattan Project in case of capture.

The man picked to lead the mission, Lieutenant Colonel Boris T. Pash, was at first glance not an obvious candidate. Although American-born, he spent much of his youth in Russia and even fought in its army prior to the Russian Revolution. Thereafter a devout anti-communist, Pash's career was in education until he joined the army's counterintelligence unit in 1940. Pash came to Groves's attention when he investigated a security breach at one of the Manhattan Project's laboratories. In November 1943, army intelligence gave the mission the cover name Alsos. It was never made clear who authorized this name, for it is the Greek word for "grove," a reference to the head of the Manhattan Project. Groves was none too pleased but agreed to it anyway, on the grounds that changing it would draw more attention than keeping it.[8]

Arriving in Naples in December 1943, Pash and his army team, leading a small group of scientists from the army, navy, and OSRD, scoured the surrounding Italian countryside for documents and scientific personnel that could reveal atomic secrets. They found nothing and no one of particular interest, though the information they gathered pointed to Rome as a potential source. The American Fifth Army and British Eighth Army, however, remained stymied for months at the Gustav Line south of the city, so the Alsos team had no way of investigating. The team returned to the United States in March 1944, just as advance planning for D-Day was under way.

The Alsos Mission returned in April, with new orders to follow the invading forces and exploit fresh intelligence sources in France, starting with Frédéric Joliot-Curie. Pash formed his military teams, while Vannevar Bush selected Samuel Goudsmit to lead the scientific portions of the mission. Like Pash, Goudsmit was not an obvious choice. He was a Dutch-born physicist who, by his own admission, preferred "the comforts of the civilized world and the quiet of a peaceful laboratory" over "not braving enemy fire or parachuting behind enemy lines." He had previously served in the BBRL performing operations research. Although he was an atomic physicist, he was not then working on the atom bomb. "In other words I was expendable," he admitted, because "the Germans could not hope to get any major bomb secrets out of me." Goudsmit also personally knew many of the European atomic scientist and spoke their languages, as well as the language of atomic physics. Pash and Goudsmit agreed that Pash's teams would carry out the military operations of locating and seizing sites and capturing scientists, while Goudsmit's teams would conduct interrogations and analyze documents.[9]

Goudsmit arrived at the OSRD London Mission on June 9, 1944, to set up his Alsos office, which with forty combat scientists became the largest contingent of the OSRD Office of Field Service. They were joined by another 150 troops, officers, and civilians (including a dozen British personnel). Among Goudsmit's selectees was his countryman Gerard Kuiper, the astronomer who was developing radar countermeasures, and Ed Salant, fresh from the proximity fuze project. Goudsmit conferred with Reginald V. Jones, the British physicist who had deciphered the secrets of Germany's bomber navigation systems, to gain further intelligence on where to locate German scientists of interest.

Pash, meanwhile, took a small military team to just-liberated Rome on June 19 to find and interview Italian physicists at the University of Rome. They claimed that German scientists had never asked them about nuclear fission. They were, however, able to provide locations for persons of interest. In August, Pash received intelligence that the scientist at the top of Alsos's target list, Frédéric Joliot-Curie, had been sighted at his summer home in Arcouest, Brittany. On August 11, while Stever and Archambault were just thirty miles away celebrating their liberation of Lannion, Pash and another military team braved minefields and snipers, only to discover that the house had been unoccupied for some time. They next went to Rennes, where the university yielded documents that pointed to Strasbourg as a potential site of interest.

Within days Pash received word that the Allies were about to enter Paris, where Joliot-Curie's laboratories were located. He and his small Alsos team raced to the Paris suburb of Longjumeau, near Orly airport, where they joined the French 2nd Armored Division for its final push into the city. Just before 9:00 a.m. on August 25 at the Porte d'Orléans, three French M-4 Sherman tanks were the first Allied vehicles to enter the city since 1940. The jeep carrying Pash and his team was the fourth. That afternoon, they raced past snipers to find Joliot-Curie at his laboratory. He told them all he knew about the German atomic program, which was very little other than the fact that it existed. Pash arranged for Goudsmit and his OSRD team to come to Paris as soon as possible, while establishing the Alsos office at the Allied headquarters in the hastily abandoned offices of the German commandant of Paris, at 2 Place de l'Opéra. On August 27, Goudsmit arrived and also interviewed Joliot-Curie, who gave him the names and possible locations of German scientists associated with the atomic program.

AS ALLIED TROOPS ADVANCED, Alsos followed behind in different teams. Its first missions were to Belgium and the Netherlands. Near Antwerp they seized some of the uranium ore that had been mined in Belgian Congo. Further missions located more ore in southern France. These were shipped to the United States. However, the majority of the ore was still somewhere in Germany, as were most of the scientists of interest. When the French 2nd Armored Division liberated Strasbourg in November 1944, it gave the Alsos Mission its first big intelligence break, for documents found in Rennes and Eindhoven had pointed to the Alsatian capital as a center of atomic research. Pash managed to round up several German physicists there who were disguised as medics. Goudsmit followed him there, after receiving Pash's urgent telegram. Interrogations yielded nothing, but a close examination of their papers—read by candlelight while artillery shells were still falling on the city—revealed to Goudsmit's relief that the Germans were nowhere near capable of making an atomic bomb. Further study then confirmed what Reginald Jones had already told Goudsmit—that the most prominent nuclear physicist in Germany, Werner Heisenberg, had moved his laboratories from Berlin to the town of Hechingen in Baden-Württemberg, just seventy miles from Strasbourg. The Allies had learned through several sources, including Heisenberg's own friend the Danish physicist Niels Bohr, that Heisenberg was leading the Nazi atomic program. As soon as the first Bailey Bridges were thrown over the Rhine River in March 1945, Alsos would cross them into the heart of Nazi Germany to locate him.

Heisenberg was not the only target of interest. One Alsos team learned that the Germans had built a uranium processing plant at Oranienburg, near Berlin. Groves requested of General Carl Spaatz that his Eighth Army Air Force destroy the facility, which they did on March 15 in a visual run with high explosives and incendiaries. At the same time, another team arrived at the university town of Heidelberg, where Goudsmit knew his old friend Walther Bothe had his physics laboratory. Any unease that he had about detaining a colleague was put to rest when Bothe embraced him warmly and said, as Goudmit recalled, "I am glad to have someone here to talk physics with." While Bothe did not reveal any atomic secrets—he claimed to be a loyal German if not a Nazi, according to Goudsmit—he did reveal that the entire program consisted of only two dozen scientists plus helpers.[10]

During April 1945, Alsos teams pushed deeper into Germany, in an attempt to reach key sites before the country was divided into Soviet, British, American, and French zones, as had been decided by the national leaders at the Yalta conference back in February. Goudsmit's group captured Otto Hahn and several more scientists, and later learned that the destruction of the heavy-water plant at Vemork Norsk had indeed prevented the German atomic program from advancing. Meanwhile, one of Pash's teams found the remaining uranium ore stockpile in central Germany, and the ore was trucked out over the next two weeks.

Pash next joined with the Sixth Army T-Force to converge on the town of Haigerloch, where on April 23 they found an experimental uranium pile (a primitive nuclear reactor using heavy water to slow the neutrons, which the Nazis believed could become a bomb) in a cave below a castle, with uranium ore and heavy water buried nearby. These were dug up and the pile was dismantled (Figure 29), and all were shipped to the United States.

As the Allies and Soviets were encircling Berlin, Alsos's biggest prize, Werner Heisenberg, continued to elude them. They found his atomic laboratory set up in a corner of an old textile mill in Hechingen, just ten miles from Haigerloch, but Heisenberg himself had left just a few days before they arrived, bicycling almost 200 miles to his winter cabin in Urfeld, high in the Bavarian Alps. Pash immediately set out in pursuit, and his jeep arrived at the base of the mountain, which was still covered with snow, on May 3. The bridge to Urfeld had been blown up and there were SS troops reported in the area, though Hitler was already dead and what was left of the Nazi government was on the verge of surrender. Pash's force of nineteen men clambered up the slopes, arriving at a large hotel, where the innkeeper pointed him to the cabin. Heisenberg was waiting on the veranda. "I have been expecting you," he apparently told Pash. Pash took a deep breath and told him that he and his family would have to be evacuated immediately to Heidelberg. The urgency of the moment was intensified when a small SS contingent came close to the cabin, only to be dispersed with small-arms fire from Pash's troops.[11]

When safely in Allied hands, Heisenberg proudly told his old friend Goudsmit all about his research, which he claimed was for producing energy and not a weapon. As earlier with Bothe, Heisenberg claimed to Goudsmit that he was a nationalist but not a Nazi. He was convinced that his little reactor was the last word in atomic physics, and insisted on staying in Germany to continue his work. Goudsmit came away more depressed than relieved. Heisenberg, in his view, "was the greatest German theoretical physicist," on par with Einstein, but his achievements fell far short of his vision. Goudsmit concluded that "the whole German uranium setup was on a ludicrously small scale. Here was the central group of laboratories, and all it amounted to was a little underground cave and a wing of a small textile factory." He speculated that the US government had "spent more money on our intelligence mission than the Germans had spent on their whole project."[12]

Goudsmit may have been right that the Alsos Mission outspent Heisenberg's program, but he likely would have been astonished to learn that the cost of the Manhattan Project alone (modern estimates put it at about $2 billion, or half a trillion dollars today) was equal to half the entire German annual economy during the war. That one project, though, would prove to be worth the expense.[13]

"As If Somebody Had Turned the Sun On with a Switch"

The term "atomic bomb" was coined in 1914 by H. G. Wells in his novel *The World Set Free,* read both by public figures like Churchill and by nuclear physicists like Leó Szilárd of Hungary. Wells himself had followed the discoveries of Ernest Rutherford and others of the atomic nucleus and nuclear decay, and simply expounded on their military possibilities. But the fact that a novelist was able to develop such ideas from basic research showed the impossibility of keeping military atomic secrets hidden.

All over Europe and the United States, physicists worked to unlock the workings of the atom. Many of them would go on to receive Nobel Prizes for their discoveries. In 1925, Rutherford's pupil Patrick Blackett confirmed with his cloud chamber that atomic nuclei could disintegrate to form two new atoms. In 1932, Cambridge physicist John Cockcroft, at Rutherford's behest, was the first to artificially split the atom (a lithium atom into two helium nuclei), confirming that Albert Einstein's equation $E = mc^2$ meant that the disintegration process could produce vast amounts of energy. That same year, James Chadwick, also at Cambridge, identified the neutron, while Ernest Lawrence at Berkeley developed the cyclotron (atom-smasher).

These events led many other scientists to work toward the invention of artificial nuclear fission. In 1934, Enrico Fermi in Rome discovered the principles of uranium fission by neutron radiation, while in Paris, a team led by Irène Joliot-Curie (daughter of Marie Curie, who discovered radioactivity) and her husband, Frédéric, identified fission in the decay pattern of uranium in 1938. The breakthrough came in Berlin in December 1938, when the team led by Otto Hahn and Fritz Strassmann artificially bombarded uranium with slow neutrons, causing fission into two barium nuclei, releasing energy and additional neutrons in the process. They published the results in the journal *Nature* in February 1939, which immediately electrified the physics world.[14]

Just weeks after the release of these results, experiments by Frédéric Joliot-Curie confirmed that by splitting the uranium atom, the release of neutrons could lead to a cascade of more atoms being split and releasing even more neutrons. This concept of a chain reaction had been thought of back in 1933 by Szilárd, and now here was proof that an atomic bomb of enormous destructive power was possible. When Niels Bohr brought early news of the fission process to the United States, +Szilárd and Fermi— both of whom had arrived in America just weeks earlier—performed experiments that verified the possibility of a fission chain reaction. More money for experimentation was needed, so in August 1939, Szilárd drafted the now-famous letter from Einstein to Roosevelt, explaining the need to develop an atomic research program to beat the Germans to the punch. Authority for the approved program was initially given to the Bureau of Standards but transferred to the Uranium Committee of NDRC when it was created in June 1940; it became the S-1 Section after NDRC was absorbed into OSRD in 1941.

Meanwhile in Britain, Henry Tizard's Committee for the Scientific Survey of Air Warfare, which included Cockcroft, was skeptical that an atomic bomb could be produced, but tasked the University of Birmingham to investigate. Two scientists there, Rudolf Peierls and Otto Frisch, were both refugees from the Nazi regime and therefore not allowed to work on secret projects like radar. In early 1940 Mark Oliphant (who was then supervising Randall and Boot's cavity magnetron) assigned them to the atomic project. Peierls and Frisch soon discovered that the critical mass of uranium isotope U-235 needed for a chain reaction was just a few pounds, far less than had been originally estimated and certainly capable of being made into a bomb that could be carried by an aircraft. U-235 is very rare, only 0.7 percent of raw uranium, so it would need to be separated from the more common U-238 and refined (the fact that the Germans had not recognized how to do this is what led Goudsmit, while at Strasbourg, to realize that they could not produce an atomic bomb).

The two scientists drafted these findings in what became known as the Peierls-Frisch memorandum of March 1940. When Tizard's Air Warfare Committee realized that an atomic bomb might be within their grasp, in June they established a separate committee, called the Maud Committee, to examine the feasibility of producing it. The Maud Committee members included Oliphant, Chadwick, Cockcroft, and Blackett. At the time, many thought that the cover name Maud had to be an acronym. Actually, it came from an April 1940 telegram, sent on behalf of Niels Bohr, to Otto Frisch and other friends in Britain, saying that he was well despite the German invasion of Denmark, and asking them to "inform Cockcroft and Maud Ray Kent." Maud Ray had been governess to Bohr's children and now lived in Kent. Committee members, however, assumed the "u" in Maud referred to a message about "uranium," so they decided the name was both appropriate and innocuous.[15]

The American and British paths to an atomic bomb first crossed when the Tizard Mission met with NDRC from August to November 1940. Cockcroft only held three discussions that touched on atomic matters, mostly concerning separating uranium. He did not reveal the contents of the Peierls-Frisch memorandum or the ongoing Maud Committee investigations, mainly because they were still unconfirmed. Just before returning to Britain in November, Cockcroft met with Fermi, who was still conducting fission experiments, and discovered that the Americans were no further along in nuclear research than was the Maud Committee. Moreover, there was only lackluster support from the NDRC; apparently neither the British nor the Americans believed that their experimentation would result in a practical atomic bomb anytime soon. Both sides were focused on far more promising developments in areas such as airborne radar and anti-aircraft artillery.[16]

The liaison scientists at the OSRD London Mission were certainly not focused on atomic bombs. One of them, Kenneth Bainbridge, was looking at British radar systems when on April 14 he was invited by John Cockcroft to attend a Maud Committee meeting. Bainbridge had been given no notice of the British uranium program prior to coming to London, so the invitation came as a surprise. It appeared that in the five months since Cockcroft had returned to Britain, scientists at four British universities had made enormous strides, to the point where "uranium power prospects appear good," as Bainbridge reported back to Vannevar Bush, and that an atomic bomb might even be feasible in two years. This was enough to make Bush's Uranium Committee look more closely at nuclear fission for creating power, though the committee was not yet convinced of its potential as a weapon.[17]

Charles Lauritsen reported aboard the OSRD London Mission on May 28. Merle Tuve had sent him to coordinate British research on the proximity fuze, but Lauritsen soon found that the testing activities there were lackluster. He was, however, invited to the final Maud Committee meeting on July 2, 1941, which would approve its findings before publication. Lauritsen was given a draft copy of the Maud Report—he never said by whom—and at 11:00 p.m. hurried it to his office on the top floor of 40 Berkeley Square, where Fred Hovde, the head of the mission, was working late. Hovde later related that Lauritsen had told him that the paper, marked "British Top Secret," was so valuable that "we must duplicate it at once and get it back to the States to Bush."

When Hovde asked what it concerned, Lauritsen told him to look for himself. Hovde did and was astonished. He asked Lauritsen where he had gotten it. From "some friends," Lauritsen said evasively. When Hovde reminded Lauritsen that sharing it ran against all their agreements with the British, Lauritsen replied, "They want us to have it, the scientist who gave it to me."[18]

Lauritsen and Hovde stayed until early the next morning duplicating the report, which Hovde sent to Bush in the next day's diplomatic pouch. Lauritsen returned the original document to the Maud Committee member who had given it to him. The main reason for Lauritsen's rush to send off the copy was its opening revelation:[19]

> We have now reached the conclusion that it will be possible to make an effective uranium bomb which, containing some 25 lb. of active material, would be equivalent as regards destructive effect to 1,800 tons of TNT and would also release large quantities of radioactive substances which would make places near to where the bomb exploded dangerous to human life for a long period.

The four universities that contributed to the results had pursued several lines of research. One involved refining the calculations for critical mass and explosive yield. Others investigated different ways to separate the fissionable isotope U-235. The most promising method appeared to be gaseous diffusion, since uranium hexafluoride gas could be pumped through a filter, leaving the heavier U-238 behind and allowing the lighter U-235 to pass through and be collected. Yet another line of research, assisted by the British electrical and electronics firm Metropolitan-Vickers, estimated that an atomic bomb plant could be built in eighteen months for £5 million, with the first bomb ready by the end of 1943. The committee finally raised the question of whether a gas diffusion plant should be built domestically, in Canada, or in the United States. The report was reviewed by various departments until it was briefed to Churchill, who approved the atomic bomb program on August 31, 1941. Under the innocuous cover name Tube Alloys, British science began working on the problem of separating and refining U-235.

After his return to the United States in July, Lauritsen discussed the Maud Committee findings directly with Bush. Bush, however, did not take any concrete action toward a weapons program. Only after Mark Oliphant came to the United States in late August to promote the British atomic program, and after Bush received an official copy of the Maud Committee report on October 3, did he become convinced that an atomic bomb was possible.

He took the results of the report directly to Roosevelt on October 9 and repeated to him, almost word for word, the opening paragraphs and findings of the Maud Committee report. "The British conclusions," Bush told the president, were that the explosive core of an atomic bomb would weigh 25 pounds, with a yield of 1,800 tons of TNT, and require a vast industrial plant to produce it. Roosevelt did not commit that day to making an atomic bomb, but made it clear to Bush that he wanted greatly intensified research, and more importantly that it should involve "complete interchange with Britain on technical matters." Two days later, Roosevelt wrote to Churchill, saying, "We should soon correspond or converse concerning the subject which is under study by your MAUD committee, and by Dr. Bush's organization in this country, in order that any extended efforts may be coordinated or even jointly conducted. . . . I send this message by Mr. Hovde, head of the London office of our scientific organization." Churchill enthusiastically replied in early December, just before Pearl Harbor: "I need not assure you of our readiness to collaborate with the United States administration in this matter. . . . I arranged for Mr. Hovde to have a full discussion."[20]

BY 1942, WITH THE United States in the war, there were two parallel efforts on either side of the Atlantic aimed at making an atomic bomb—Tube Alloys in Britain and the OSRD S-1 Section in the United States. The Tube Alloys directorate was primarily focused on the separation of the two uranium isotopes, and contracted with Metropolitan-Vickers and Imperial Chemical Industries to develop a gaseous diffusion process that would pass uranium hexafluoride through a fine nickel-wire membrane, extracting and refining the U-235. The S-1 Section undertook many research programs at once. One line of research aimed at creating a self-sustaining chain reaction in a small nuclear reactor, which Enrico Fermi's team succeeded in doing in December 1942, under the viewing stands of the University of Chicago football stadium. Another aimed at producing the newly discovered plutonium (theoretically with a greater yield than U-235) by building a much larger nuclear reactor at Hanford, Washington, under the direction of DuPont, which was already busy with shadow gunpowder factories. Several more programs examined different methods of uranium separation.

The largest such project, following on from Tube Alloy's research, was a gaseous diffusion plant built by the engineering construction firm MW Kellogg Company at a massive site in Oak Ridge, Tennessee, which later housed other separation plants using centrifugal and electromagnetic techniques. Connecting the British and American efforts were the OSRD London Mission and the British Central Scientific Office, each of which relayed technical information and arranged for the exchange of scientists. They even forwarded sensitive materials, such as when OSRD London sent to the United States, via diplomatic pouch, ten pounds of powdered nickel from the Mond Nickel Company in Wales, the only producer of the material vital for manufacturing gaseous diffusion membranes, for testing the diffusion concept.[21]

The scale of S-1's program, and the fact that many of the research projects were rapidly becoming production efforts, led Bush and his OSRD team in June 1942 to begin transferring overall control to the US Army Corps of Engineers. The Corps established a new office at 270 Broadway in New York, naming it the Manhattan District, which in turn lent its name to the entire atomic bomb program. In September 1942, General Groves, fresh from supervising the construction of the Pentagon and the Holston Ordnance Works (which made RDX), was given command of the Manhattan Project.

As we have seen, Groves insisted on strict security measures and compartmentalizing information. This, coupled with the fact that the Manhattan Project was already outspending Tube Alloys by roughly 200 to 1, led to an almost complete severing of British-American collaboration in the fall of 1942. Apart from some exchanges with British and Canadian engineers and scientists about gaseous diffusion, Bush made certain that atomic secrets were not divulged to its allies. To the White House he stated that this policy would not delay the project, since America was now doing 90 percent of the work. Roosevelt concurred, though he had promised full cooperation at a meeting with Churchill just months earlier, at a meeting at his home in Hyde Park. Churchill raised the issue with Harry Hopkins at the Casablanca Conference in January 1943, but spring and early summer passed with no sign of an American policy change. The Tube Alloys directorate, determined to build a bomb "if necessary, alone," as Churchill once said, estimated that the project would be feasible if given the highest national priority. But with the Battle of the Atlantic still raging and the planning for Operation Husky—the invasion of Sicily—under way, that probability was infinitesimal.[22]

The matter of atomic cooperation came to a head when Vannevar Bush met with Churchill at 10 Downing Street, toward the end of Bush's tour of British anti-submarine warfare facilities in July 1943. Bush anticipated that the issue would come up and asked the president for direction, but "as usual [Roosevelt gave him] no instructions whatever." Churchill reviewed—heatedly—for Bush the discussions on cooperation he and Roosevelt had had at Hyde Park, while Bush countered that the Americans were not withholding anything. Rather, they were carrying out proper security protocols of compartmentalizing information, so that British scientists only saw information about their work (which was primarily gaseous diffusion). Given that British radar development had operated along the same security principles, this was hard to argue against.[23]

Nonetheless, Churchill and Bush came to an understanding about expanding the scope of cooperation and pooling resources. This became the basis for the Quebec Agreement on atomic research that the prime minister and the president signed on August 19, during the Quadrant Conference, which also laid the groundwork for Operation Overlord. Among other things, the agreement created a top-level Combined Policy Committee, consisting of senior members from the United States, Britain, and Canada, and established the British mission to the Manhattan Project for the liaison scientists who would come to work in the American program. James Chadwick, discoverer of the neutron and a driving force behind Tube Alloys, became the leading member of the British mission and won the respect of Groves for being "punctilious" about security.[24]

By the fall of 1943, the Manhattan Project spanned twenty sites across the United States and Canada, each devoted to a different aspect of developing the two types of atomic bombs: one with a uranium warhead, and the other with a plutonium warhead. Hanford focused on plutonium production, while the Oak Ridge site was devoted to uranium production. Ernest Lawrence's laboratory at Berkeley carried out research on electromagnetic separation of uranium. Finally, a team at the Los Alamos site, led by the physicist Robert Oppenheimer, who also chose the remote location in New Mexico for maximum security, would design and build the atomic bombs themselves.

Chadwick decided that British scientists could contribute more to the war effort by working inside the Manhattan Project than by staying in Britain, even at the expense of the Tube Alloys program. He and two others, Rudolf Peierls and Mark Oliphant, were in the United States before the ink was dry on the Quebec Agreement. Chadwick would end up spending most of his time in Washington, carrying out diplomatic and administrative duties and acting as scientific advisor to the Combined Policy Committee. Oliphant joined Lawrence's laboratory, while Peierls was assigned to gaseous diffusion research before going to Los Alamos.

Following behind those first three came a flood of British scientists in late 1943 and through 1944, thirty-five in all. Many of them had been pulled off various radar projects to work on electromagnetic separation at Berkeley. They included Maurice Wilkins, Joan Curran (who had developed Window radar countermeasures), and Curran's husband, Sam. Another group, fifteen who had worked on the Tube Alloys program, went to Oak Ridge to work on gaseous diffusion. They were able to obtain nickel powder in industrial quantities from the Mond Nickel Company in Britain, through a program known as Reverse Lend-Lease.[25]

Otto Frisch was one of nineteen members of the British delegation at Los Alamos. Even with Groves's security measures, not only were the members of the British mission completely integrated into the Manhattan Project, but some of them also became its leaders. At Berkeley, Mark Oliphant became Lawrence's de facto deputy, and ran the laboratory in Lawrence's absence. At Los Alamos, six teams were led by British scientists, including the Implosion Hydrodynamics group with Peierls at the helm, and former Tube Alloys mathematician William Penney helping to solve the complex fluid dynamics inherent in creating an implosion-type plutonium bomb. Niels Bohr, who had escaped with his family from Denmark, was a frequent visitor to Los Alamos and offered his insights and inspiration to the members.

The members certainly needed inspiration. Life at Los Alamos could be trying, even for Britons who were used to wartime conditions—the housing was ramshackle, the cooking stoves barely functioned, sand got into homes through every crack and crevice, and when it rained the streets turned to mud. Yet the Los Alamos landscape was a wonder of nature—Oppenheimer in his youth spent his summers there, which is partly why he preferred the location—and the camaraderie was palpable, with regular dances, shows, and concerts. Both British and American scientists worked long hours to impossible deadlines. When the news of Roosevelt's death on April 12, 1945, was broadcast over the radio, Otto Frisch still completed one of his critical mass experiments that would lead to the uranium bomb. On May 7, the day Germany surrendered, scientists detonated 100 tons of TNT at the Trinity test site in Alamogordo, New Mexico, to calibrate the instruments that would measure the first atomic blast.

On July 16, 1945, the implosion-type plutonium bomb—"the Gadget"—was detonated at 5:30 a.m. Otto Frisch, who was there along with most of the members of the British mission, reported:[26]

Fearing to be dazzled and burned, I stood with my back to the gadget, and behind the radio truck. I looked at the hills, which were visible in the first faint light of dawn. Suddenly and without any sound, the hills were bathed in brilliant light, as if somebody had turned the sun on with a switch. After that I turned round and tried to look at the light source but found it still too bright to keep my eyes on it. A few short glances gave me the impression of a small very brilliant core, much smaller in appearance than the sun, surrounded by decreasing and reddening brightness. The ball rose slowly, lengthening its stem and getting gradually darker and slightly larger. As the red glow died out it became apparent that the whole structure, in par-ticular the top mushroom, was surrounded by a purplish blue glow. A minute or so later the whole top mushroom appeared to glow feebly in this colour, but this was no longer easy to see, in the increasing light of dawn.

That same day, the cruiser USS *Indianapolis* left San Francisco with the components of the Little Boy uranium bomb, heading for Tinian Island in the Pacific. The second bomb, the plutonium-core Fat Man, was transported by aircraft to Tinian a week later. Both bombs were assembled while their B-29 Silver Plate Superfortresses, *Enola Gay* and *Bockscar*, were prepared for their bombing missions.

The British involvement with the Manhattan Project had not ended at the Trinity test site. It was British engineering that enabled those planes to carry the massive atomic bombs. Conventional bomb release mechanisms were too flimsy for the 10,000-pound atomic bombs, so those were replaced at Wright Field with British Type G single-point attachments and Type F releases, used on modified Lancaster bombers to carry the 12,000-pound Tallboy bombs that had put *Tirpitz* out of action. The B-29s navigated using the Gee, Loran, IFF, and H2X systems, which were developed by British and American scientists working in close collaboration. After President Harry Truman authorized the use of atomic bombs on August 3, *Enola Gay* dropped Little Boy over Hiroshima on August 6, killing 140,000 people. On August 9, *Bockscar* dropped Fat Man over Nagasaki, with 75,000 deaths. Its detonation was witnessed by William Penney, as he flew in the observer plane *Big Stink*. All these aircraft, when they returned to Tinian Island, were guided in by the Ground Control Approach (GCA) system that British and American scientists and engineers had struggled together to make a reality.[27]

Japanese delegates signed the instrument of surrender aboard the battleship USS *Missouri* on September 2, 1945. Anchored in Tokyo Bay, they were surrounded by over 200 ships of several Allied nations, but mainly from the United States and Britain. More than anything else, World War Two demonstrated that their alliance was, in the end, stronger than that between Japan and Germany, each of which had carried out the war largely on its own. Britons and Americans had worked and fought side by side in what Churchill was already referring to as a "special relationship." Their collaboration in creating "weapons unknown at the outbreak of hostilities," as Vannevar Bush had put it, had been crucial to their victory. Archambault ascribed this success (as noted at the beginning of this book) to "Britain's scientific mobilization for war," coupled with "America's engineering capabilities." Edward "Taffy" Bowen told Bush in 1951, "The greatest credit ... goes to our two governments for the fact that we were able to work together during the war, exchanging freely and wholeheartedly."[28]

The success of mobilizing science on national and international scales had been proven in war. It was now time to determine how those efforts would translate to peace.

EPILOGUE

Endless Frontiers

T HE WESTERN UNION overnight cablegram (Figure 30) that arrived at Bennett Archambault's London office the morning of April 24, 1945, delivered happy news:[1]

DIANA WRIGHT LANGMUIR BORN APRIL TWENTY THIRD EIGHT
POUNDS TWO OUNCES EVERYTHING FINE = DAVID LANGMUIR

Even as the war was drawing to an end in mid- to late 1944, after Allied troops had broken out of the Normandy region and were advancing toward Germany, there was a general sense of beginning a new chapter. People began thinking about the future. For David and Nancy Langmuir, it was about starting a family after so many war-torn years apart; that summer, their daughter was conceived almost as soon as David came home on a six-week leave.

That same summer, leaders from forty-four nations met at Bretton Woods, New Hampshire, to hammer out the postwar monetary and financial systems that would reconstruct ravaged economies around the world. And on November 17, Roosevelt, knowing that OSRD would cease to exist after the end of the war (it would be disbanded in 1947), wrote a letter to Vannevar Bush asking him to think about what science would look like beyond that. The president noted that OSRD had been "a unique experiment" that had proven the value of teamwork, cooperation, and coordination "in applying existing scientific knowledge to the solution of the technical problems paramount in war." Now its mission and techniques of bringing together scientists from universities and private industry "should be used in the days of peace ahead for the improvement of the national health, the creation of new enterprises bringing new jobs, and the betterment of the national standard of living." He then went on to ask Bush for a report outlining how these "new frontiers of the mind" could be harnessed by government to the betterment of the nation. Bush assembled committees of scientists to help him answer Roosevelt's questions, not knowing that the president would not live to see those answers.[2]

WHILE BUSH WAS ATTENDING to postwar science, the OSRD London Mission was already beginning to wind down. Langmuir had left London in early February 1945 to be present at the birth of his daughter, with many more scientists departing shortly thereafter. On April 25, Archambault began closing the London and Paris offices, along with the BBRL and ABL-15 offices in Great Malvern. Files had to be packed and shipped backed to the United States, property returned to the American embassy (one Humber sedan, eighteen gas masks, fourteen helmets, one first aid pack . . .), and the office flats in Hereford House restored (new partitions and doors, blackout curtains removed). Letters of thanks and congratulations came pouring in from all quarters: American and British flag and general officers, British ministers, and grateful ambassadors from other nations. On June 18, 1945, OSRD London hosted its farewell party at Claridge's Hotel, where Archambault once again supplied the whiskey. In late June, he led a small OSRD team to visit Germany, to analyze Nazi experimental aircraft and rocket laboratories (Figure 31). Arch himself left the London Mission on July 25, the last man off the ship. The election results the very next day showed that Churchill's party was voted out of office in a land-slide; the public had declared that peace in Britain would look very different from war.[3]

The British were looking away from the war, but they did not forget what the Americans had done for them in the war. In 1948, Vannevar Bush was made an Honorary Knight Commander of the Order of the British Empire, while James Conant and Karl Compton were made Honorary Commanders. Bush remained head of OSRD until its disestablishment, later becoming the president of the Carnegie Corporation. Conant and Compton returned full-time to their presidencies of (respectively) Harvard and MIT. Archambault, along with several other members of the OSRD London Mission, was awarded the King's Medal for Service in the Cause of Freedom.

By that time, Archambault was treasurer (later vice president) of the M. W. Kellogg Company in New York City, the same firm that had built the gaseous diffusion plant at Oak Ridge. Once again, his old friend Carroll Wilson at MIT—who had recruited him for the OSRD position back in 1941—had put Kellogg in contact with him. As Archambault explained to Bush, "This is the fourth position, out of the seven I have had since leaving [MIT], for which Carroll has been responsible." He also met and married his wife, Margaret, that same year. They had three children in the next few years. The OSRD "family" remained close for many years. Carroll Wilson became godfather to Archambault's daughter Michele. Archambault, meanwhile, became godfather to Diana Langmuir (Figure 32), while Langmuir continued working at the Department of Defense. Both Arch and David stayed in touch with Guy Stever (first at MIT, later science advisor to President Gerald Ford), even talking about writing a history of the OSRD London Mission.[4]

The war launched or boosted the careers of many who served at the OSRD London Mission. Several later became Nobel Prize winners for their discoveries in physics: Luis Alvarez (inventor of the GCA system) in 1968 for particle physics (he later co-developed the asteroid/dinosaur extinction hypothesis); Isidor Rabi (who helped develop microwave radar) in 1944 for atomic nuclei research; William Shockley (pioneer in operations research) in 1956 for the transistor. Shockley, along with Fred Terman of RRL, was also credited as being one of the fathers of Silicon Valley in the 1950s.

Others became widely known in scientific circles: Thomas Kuhn at ABL-15 wrote the influential *The Structure of Scientific Revolutions* (1962), which gave us the term "paradigm shift"; James Van Allen, who helped bring the proximity fuze to the Pacific fleet, discovered the eponymous radiation belts that circle the Earth; and Gerard Kuiper, who worked on Window and Alsos, made astronomical discoveries that led the scientists to name the outer-solar-system Kuiper Belt for him. The experience of working with OSRD scientists led Arthur C. Clarke, as we've seen, to write his only non-science-fiction work, *Glide Path*, about the GCA (he later became good friends with Alvarez), and when he was the subject of the BBC's *This Is Your Life* in August 1994, his special guests included colleagues from his GCA days. Two British scientists working under OSRD programs, Howard Florey and Maurice Wilkins, shared Nobel Prizes in Physiology or Medicine: Florey for penicillin in 1945, and Wilkins for the structure of DNA in 1962.[5]

For many, the end of World War Two simply marked the next stage in their careers. The two men responsible for the development of the LST, Rowland Baker and John Niedermair, continued designing warships for many years afterward. Baker was transferred to the Royal Canadian Navy as chief constructor, where he created its iconic postwar frigates and destroyers before returning to Britain to design its first nuclear-powered submarine, HMS *Dreadnought*. Niedermair continued to direct the US Navy's Preliminary Design Branch, where he led the creation of a new Cold War fleet of guided-missile ships, supercarriers, and nuclear submarines. Merle Tuve, after leading the development of the proximity fuze, returned to head the Department of Terrestrial Magnetism, where he pioneered advances in seismology that gave a deeper understanding of Earth's structure. Bernard Lovell and Taffy Bowen both played key roles in the birth of radio astronomy, establishing observatories in (respectively) Britain and Australia. Patrick Blackett and John Cockcroft were both awarded the Nobel Prize (1948 and 1951, respectively) for their prewar work on atomic physics.

Many of the technologies that had been cooperatively developed during the war found new lives in peacetime. At the top of the list is the cavity magnetron, today at the heart of every microwave oven. LORAN, dreamed of by Alfred Loomis based on the British Gee system, became one of the most widely used navigation systems in the world before GPS. Modern radio transponders used to identify aircraft and ships, even thousands of miles out to sea, began with the humble, gear-driven IFF Mark II. GCA, which in the early Cold War proved essential for maintaining the flow of food and supplies during the 1948–1949 Berlin Airlift, was for decades in widespread use at airports around the world before replacement by more automated systems. Today, operations research keeps global supply chains in motion. And Bailey Bridges still carry traffic on American roads (Figure 33).

Finally, the British jet engine, developed by RAF engineer Frank Whittle in the 1930s, was one of the Tizard Mission's true gems, as Americans first realized in the fall of 1940. After further information exchanges, the Army Air Forces contracted with General Electric to build Whittle's engine, while Whittle himself settled in Boston to help with development. Although prototype British and American jet aircraft flew in 1942 and 1943, their production models arrived too late in the war to make any strategic difference (as was the case for Germany's Me 262). The jet engine, of course, revolutionized flight in the twentieth century.[6]

British-American cooperation did not always turn out well. One of the nineteen members of the British delegation at Los Alamos, Karl Fuchs, later confessed to being a Soviet agent during that period, and was responsible for passing information on fission and fusion bombs that may have sped up the Soviet programs. But several other Soviet spies at Los Alamos were American-born, as was the most famous atomic spy, Julius Rosenberg (who actually began his espionage career by passing information on the proximity fuze to the Soviets). On balance, the transatlantic partnership worked very well. As Bush later observed, the two nations "in collaboration went ahead faster than would have been the case if they'd continued to operate independently".[7]

CHURCHILL'S 1946 SPEECH (WHICH opens this book) argued that the "special relationship" between the United States and Britain, which was forged in battle, should continue in the Cold War. Despite their maintaining close political and military ties—America's largest overseas bases were in Britain—the next decade was also marked by divisions. Chief among them was America's initial refusal to share atomic secrets with Britain and Canada, although they were key partners in the Manhattan Project. Britain therefore carried on its atomic programs alone. Its weapons program (headed by William Penney, formerly of the Tube Alloys Program and Manhattan Project) exploded its first atomic bomb in 1952. The following year, after research led by John Cockcroft, work began on Britain's first atomic power station.[8]

When Churchill returned as prime minister in 1951, he brought back Frederick Lindemann as his science advisor, whose portfolio emphasized nuclear R&D. After Churchill visited the United States in 1952, nuclear relations between the two nations began to thaw. Over the next few years, Britain and America agreed to more consultations, until in 1958 they signed the US-UK Mutual Defense Agreement, which allowed extensive cooperation and technology sharing on nuclear energy and weapons. Shortly afterward, Britain embarked on its first nuclear-powered submarine, the aforementioned HMS *Dreadnought*, which saw a close partnership between Rowland Baker and Admiral Hyman Rickover, who by that time was the head of the US Navy's nuclear reactor program.[9]

THE SINEWS OF SCIENCE, like Cicero's "sinews of war" and Churchill's "sinews of peace," consist of money. In the postwar years, America had lots of it, and Britain comparatively little. Prior to the war, the two nations were almost equally prosperous; in 1937, American GDP per capita was just 10 percent above Britain's. After the war, America entered an economic boom period, while British austerity, coupled with a shrinking empire (India became independent in 1947, followed by other nations), stifled its economic growth. By 1950, America's GDP per head was 50 percent higher than Britain's. By the end of the decade, it was double, and the gap continued to increase through the 1960s. With greater wealth, Americans spent more on consumer goods and capital goods, which benefited from the technological advances made during the war. Consequently, the economics of R&D between the two nations also diverged. By 1959, American industry had hired 40 percent more scientists and engineers, and spent three times more on R&D, on a per-capita basis compared with Britain.[10]

British and American science and technology, therefore, took different paths after the war. Although Britain's aviation industry exploited wartime research to develop advanced aircraft—the first passenger jet, the de Havilland Comet, flew in 1949—this was not the case for other industries. To take one example, Britain did not fully capitalize on its wartime electronics advances to create a homegrown computer industry. Those who developed the bombe were sworn to silence by the Official Secrets Act, and the Colossus machines, which, as described, were early versions of an electronic computer, were broken up and discarded. By contrast, Silicon Valley, as mentioned, was begun by scientists such as Fred Terman and William Shockley, who leveraged the technology and expertise they had developed during the war to gain important government contracts that jump-started the American computer industry.[11]

British and American government support for civilian R&D also took different paths. To paraphrase Clausewitz (cited earlier), science is the continuation of politics by other means. Prior to World War Two, both Britain and the United States took generally laissez-faire attitudes toward scientific research, as they did with their economies. In the 1920s, for example, American government support was almost entirely directed toward agricultural research, so industrial R&D facilities such as Bell Labs and General Electric Research Laboratory and private philanthropic organizations like the Rockefeller Foundation and the Carnegie Corporation filled in the rest. The British government, meanwhile, had the Department of Scientific and Industrial Research (DSIR), but its remit was very limited. Apart from defense-related matters, British industry carried out the vast majority of scientific R&D before the war.[12]

During World War Two, the British government had continued to conduct R&D in a fragmented manner, never having developed an equivalent of the American OSRD. Churchill had relied on Lindemann for advice, of course, but Lindemann had had little real authority. Each of the armed services had its own set of R&D laboratories, as did the Ministry of Supply. DSIR played a modest but significant role, hosting the National Physical Laboratory and the Tube Alloys directorate. After the war, DSIR continued until 1965, once the government (prodded on by Patrick Blackett) had created the Ministry of Science and the Ministry of Technology. At the same time, Britain began turning away from large-scale domestic R&D programs in favor of collaboration with other nations. Concorde, Britain's supersonic aircraft, was a joint program with France, while its own space program was subsumed into what became the European Space Agency.

By contrast, World War Two completely changed the American government's relationship with R&D. As described throughout this book, OSRD demonstrated that the government could harness American science at a national level to achieve political and policy goals that were in the public interest. That was the model that Roosevelt had asked Vannevar Bush to develop in his "new frontiers of the mind" letter in August 1944. On July 25, 1945—a week after the first atomic bomb test—Bush released his findings in a report titled *Science: The Endless Frontier*. Based on input from many scientific panels and his own experience leading OSRD, Bush called for centralization and government sponsorship of what he called "basic research . . . general knowledge and an understanding of nature and its laws," which could then be transitioned and applied by private industries and government toward practical results.[13]

Bush's vision was expansive: a single organization to lead the fight against disease, head the drive for national security, and improve public welfare. In 1950, Congress whittled it down to create the National Science Foundation (NSF), which funded basic scientific research but did not include defense, medical, or atomic R&D. The military services, by that point, had established their own research branches, starting with the Office of Naval Research (ONR) in 1946, which included the ONR Branch Office London (later called ONR Global), which, like the former OSRD London Mission, maintains connections between American and international scientists. Combined with the establishment of the Atomic Energy Commission and the expansion of the National Institutes of Health in the 1940s and the creation of NASA in 1959, the United States proved capable of embracing large-scale projects that harnessed American R&D, with outcomes that affected the entire nation.[14]

The SAGE air defense system, developed in the 1950s and 1960s to protect the country against Soviet bombers, led to the creation of the modern interactive computer and the internet. In the 1960s and 1970s, the Apollo moon program, intended to upstage the Soviet Union, created a new generation of scientists and engineers who would go on to revolutionize consumer and industrial technology. Silicon Valley, buoyed by government contracts and attracting talent from around the globe (over half its start-ups have been founded by immigrants), has created some of the largest companies in the world, which continue to dominate markets worldwide.[15]

Ever since the Monroe Doctrine of the 1820s, Americans have assumed that they are an exceptional nation, believing that their national character made them destined for a preeminent role in the world. The country's continued ascendancy has often bolstered the idea that the United States was always meant to be a global leader. Yet this argument misses the point. What makes America exceptional today is what helped it win World War Two: its ability to adopt and adapt the best ideas from its allies across the world, and make them its own.

NOTES

Preface

1. Archambault (ed.), *Report of OSRD Activities*, part 1, p. 9.
2. Coalition warfare: Barr, *Yanks and Limeys*, p. 215.
3. The Foreign Office asked its US ambassador: British Foreign Office to Lord Halifax, August 15, 1941, OSRD London Mission, NARA RG 227 NC-138, Box 54.
4. History from the middle: Kennedy, "History from the Middle"; Kennedy, *Engineers of Victory*, pp. 372–373, 406.
5. "The atom bomb only ended the war": Interview with DuBridge, quoted in Kevles, *The Physicists*, p. 308.
6. For every front-line warfighter, there were five people behind them: This tooth-to-tail ratio is a problematic calculation for which there is no clear method. My assumptions for the year 1944, the height of the war, are: 10.2 million military, of whom 7.5 million are deployed overseas (Dunn [ed.], *Vital Statistics of the United* States, p. vi); of the military deployed overseas, 5 million were in front-line combat (McGrath, *The Other End of the Spear*, pp. 16–23); federal government civilian employees in war agencies, 2.9 million (United States Bureau of the Census, *Government Employment*, p. 1); munitions and essential industries labor force, 18 million (War Manpower Commission, *Manpower Review*, p. 25). Total support personnel, 26 million; front-line combat troops, 5 million; tooth-to-tail ratio, 1 to 5. "Outfought and outproduced": *Budget of the United States Government for the Fiscal Year Ending June 30, 1943*, p. v.
7. Every continent including Antarctica: Operation Tabarin established British military bases in Antarctica in 1943. Impossible to discuss cooperation on every battlefront: Russia, Japan, and most of the Pacific campaign are largely absent from this narrative. During World War Two, Canada and Australia were not the independent nations they are today, instead considered more a part of the larger British Empire. Their stories in the Allied technical cooperation effort still need to be comprehensively told.

A Note on Currency

8. Measuring Worth website, accessed July 2020; OECD PPP website, accessed July 2020. Inflation in Britain and the United States was relatively stable until 1938, after

which it spiked in both nations due to the outbreak of war: See O'Neil, *Interwar U.S. and Japanese National Product and Defense Expenditure*, p. 28.

9. Pound-to-dollar exchange rate: *NYT*, January 1, 1942, p. 46.

Chapter 1: Defend Our Island

1. Roberts, *Churchill*, pp. 891–895; White, *Our Supreme Task*, pp. 57–60.
2. Churchill at Westminster College: Harold B. Hinton, "Briton Speaks Out," *NYT*, March 6, 1945, p. 1; Muller (ed.), *Churchill's Iron Curtain Speech Fifty Years Later*, pp. 1–13, 23.
3. Reynolds, *From World War to Cold War*, p. 64. Catchy turn of phrase: Langworth (ed.), *Churchill by Himself*, p. ix.
4. Allison and Ferreiro (eds.), *The American Revolution*, p. 49; Dimbleby and Reynolds, *An Ocean Apart*, p. 14: Schake, *Safe Passage*, pp. 39–47.
5. The bumpy Anglo-American rapprochement: See Kori Schake's masterful *Safe Passage*.
6. Roberts, *Churchill: Walking with Destiny*, p. 14; "I loved her dearly": Churchill, *A Roving Commission*, p. 5. See Kehoe, *Titled Americans* for an in-depth look at Jennie Churchill's transatlantic ties.
7. "The one indispensable feature": Dimbleby and Reynolds, *An Ocean Apart*, p. 48; "English-speaking peoples": Roberts, *Churchill*, p. 78.
8. One-third of Britain's war costs: Dimbleby and Reynolds, *An Ocean Apart*, p. 59.
9. *CSWW*, vol. 2, p. 15.
10. "Don't let the British pull the wool over your eyes": quoted in Dimbleby and Reynolds, *An Ocean Apart*, p. 67. Exchange of naval constructors: Ferreiro, "Goodall in America." Roosevelt meets Churchill: Lash, *Roosevelt and Churchill*, p. 193.
11. Barr, *Yanks and Limeys*, pp. 58–59; Schake, *Safe Passage*, pp. 224–225. "New international order": Wilson, *Address of the President of the United States*, pp. 4, 7.
12. Dimbleby and Reynolds, *An Ocean Apart*, pp. 73–81; Schake, *Safe Passage*, pp. 226–234. The Senate also did not ratify the Versailles Treaty; a separate peace was signed with each of the Central Powers in 1921.
13. Wiseman and House quotes from Dimbleby and Reynolds, *An Ocean Apart*, p. 83.
14. Kuehn, *Agents of Innovation*, p. 199; Johnsen, *The Origins of the Grand Alliance*, pp. 38–40; Stanley V. Goodall to Eustace Tennyson d'Eyncourt, November 21, 1918, NMM DEY/20.
15. Baer, *One Hundred Years of Sea Power*, pp. 90–103; Kuehn, *Agents of Innovation*, pp. 25–29, 67, 180–187, 198–199.
16. Bell, *The Royal Navy*, pp. 49–57 (Churchill quote p. 49); Knox, *The Eclipse of American Sea Power*, p. vii. Thanks to Andrew Lambert for his observation on the naming of American aircraft carriers.
17. "Merely a form of hostilities": Dimbleby and Reynolds, *An Ocean Apart*, p. 89; "Yankee menace": Bell, *Churchill and Seapower*, p. 125.
18. Grove, *The Royal Navy Since 1815*, pp. 159–163; Baer, *One Hundred Years of Sea Power*, pp. 108–112; Johnsen, *The Origins of the Grand Alliance*, p. 40.

19. A clear explanation of this complex crisis is given in Silber, *When Washington Shut Down Wall Street* ("England has been the exchange place of the world," p. 1; "chief money lender," p. 157).

20. Auld, "The British War Debt," p. 641; Chambers, "Neither a Borrower nor a Lender Be," p. 14; Boyer and Hatton, "New Estimates of British Unemployment," p. 667; US Bureau of the Census, *Historical Statistics of the United States*, vol. 1, pp. 126, 226; Costigliola, "Anglo-American Financial Rivalry in the 1920s" ("vassal state," p. 913; draining Europe of its capital, p. 928). The final World War One loan payment from the Britain to the United States was made in 2015, a century after the war.

21. "Completely smashed": Dimbleby and Reynolds, *An Ocean Apart*, p. 101

22. A classic analysis of the global Great Depression is Kindleberger, *The World in Depression*.

23. Bottelier, "Associated Powers," pp. 124–130; McDonough (ed.), *The Origins of the Second World War*, p. 437.

24. Postan, *British War Production* pp. 9, 14; "Disarmament in my view will not stop war . . . the bomber will always get through": Hansard, *House of Commons Debates*, November 10, 1932, vol. 270, cc631–632.

25. "Bomber will always get through . . . old frontiers are gone": Hansard, *House of Commons Debates*, July 30, 1934, vol. 292, cc2337–2329.

26. Postan, *British War Production*, p. 12.

27. Military spending: Max Roser and Mohamed Nagdy, "Military Spending," OurWorldInData.org, https://ourworldindata.org/military-spending, accessed March 2020. For the period 1933–1938, the United Kingdom's spending on the military grew from 2 percent of GDP to 7 percent of GDP, while for the United States it remained a steady 1 percent of GDP. Britain's military spending was still proportionally less than that of Germany, which averaged 10 percent of GDP in that period. Defense industry employment: Allen, "Mutual Aid Between the U.S. and the British Empire," pp. 247–248. Munitions production: Koistinen, *Arsenal of World War II*, p. 499.

28. "If London was bombed": Reynolds, *The Creation of the Anglo-American Alliance*, p. 50.

29. Johnsen, *The Origins of the Grand Alliance*, pp. 49–63; Bottelier, "Associated Powers," pp. 110–112.

30. "In my thoughts," "It is because you": Lash, *Roosevelt and Churchill*, p. 23.

31. Referred to the navy as "we" but the army as "they": Lash, *Roosevelt and Churchill*, p. 184. Naval intelligence: Florence, *Courting a Reluctant Ally*, pp. 43–56. Additional thanks to Alan G. Kirk (nephew of then-Captain Alan Goodrich Kirk) for personal insights.

32. "Heaven knows," "fight for freedom to the last Briton": Reynolds, *The Creation of the Anglo-American Alliance*, pp. 78–81. Chatfield's "to the last Briton" was echoing the then-famous statement by Joseph Goebbels (and repeated by the German propagandist William Joyce, aka Lord Haw-Haw) that "England will fight Germany down to the last Frenchman." Welles mission: Rofe, *Franklin Roosevelt's Foreign Policy and the Welles Mission*.

33. "Well, boys," "grateful": Reynolds, *The Creation of the Anglo-American Alliance*, pp. 152–153.

34. Hall, *North American Supply*, pp. 105–112 ("absolute minimum," p. 112).

35. Edgerton, *Britain's War Machine*, pp. 11–46 ("allied output," p. 14); Edgerton, *Warfare State*, pp. 42–45; Postan, *British War Production*, pp. 102–114; Postan, Hay, and Scott, *Design and Development of Weapons*, pp. 6, 321, 367–368; Coombs, *British Tank Production and the War Economy*, p. 48; Ruggles and Brodie, "An Empirical Approach to Economic Intelligence in World War II," p. 89; Wark, "British Intelligence on the German Air Force and Aircraft Industry" ("neck and neck," p. 645).

36. Stolfi, "Equipment for Victory in France in 1940."

37. Alexander and Philpott (eds.), *Anglo-French Defence Relations Between the Wars*, pp. 92–120, 209–226 ("we have the closest cooperation," p. 209).

38. Edgerton, *Britain's War Machine*, pp. 44–45.

39. Hansard, *House of Commons Debates*, June 4, 1940, vol. 361, cc787–798.

Chapter 2: Fight with Growing Confidence

1. Churchill's education: Churchill, *A Roving Commission*, pp. 15–60.

2. "Explain to me in lucid, homely terms": *CSWW*, vol. 2, p. 338; "bomb no bigger than an orange": Roberts, *Churchill*, p. 326. For a biography of Lindemann, see Fort, *Prof*. Clementine Churchill and Lindemann at the tennis tournament: Reginald V. Jones, "Churchill as I Knew Him," Enid and R. Crosby Kemper Lecture, 1992, National Churchill Museum, Fulton, MO, https://www.nationalchurchillmuseum.org/kem per-lecture-jones.html.

3. Roberts, *Churchill*, pp. 462–493 ("single sheet of paper," p. 254; "Action this day," p. 469).

4. Fort, *Prof*, pp. 183–228 ("oldest and greatest friends," "Love me, love my dog," p. 242).

5. MD1: Macrae, *Winston Churchill's Toyshop*; Milton, *Churchill's Ministry of Ungentlemanly Warfare*.

6. "Varied from the most brilliant conceptions at one end": Alanbrooke, *War Diaries*, p. 273. "When faced with any problem": MacRae, *Winston Churchill's Toyshop*, p. 142.

7. Death rays: See Fanning, *Death Rays and the Popular Media*. Killing sheep: Rowe, *One Story of Radar*, p. 6.

8. Judkins, "Making Vision into Power," pp. 90–102.

9. Zimmerman, *Britain's Shield*, pp. 11–43.

10. "Radiant energy": Judkins, "Making Vision into Power," p. 102. "Death ray": Watson-Watt, *The Pulse of Radar*, pp. 51–52.

11. "Birth certificate of radar": Watson-Watt, *The Pulse of Radar*, p. 53.

12. Watson-Watt, *Three Steps to Victory*, pp. 108–109. "High respect and partial frustration": Watson-Watt, *The Pulse of Radar*, p. 63.

13. Zimmerman, *Britain's Shield*, pp. 60–131; Judkins, "Making Vision into Power," pp. 104–146.

14. Chain Home: Watson-Watt, *Three Steps to Victory*, pp. 202–246; Rowe, *One Story of Radar*, pp. 20–53; Hanbury Brown, *Boffin*, pp. 4–16; Bowen, *Radar Days*, pp. 1–29; Judkins, "Making Vision into Power," pp. 120–249.

15. "Boffin": Watson-Watt, "The Natural History of the Boffin." "Wizard": *CSWW*, vol. 2, p. 338. Additional thanks to Allen Packwood, director of the Churchill Archives Centre, Churchill College, University of Cambridge. Many scientists used the term "boffin" in their memoirs, e.g., Robert Hanbury Brown's *Boffin*. However, Reginald V. Jones, who helped Churchill write his *Second World War* chapter titled "The Wizard War," broke with other scientists by using that same title for the American version of his memoirs. None of these accounts attribute the word "boffin" to a character in Charles Dickens's novel *Our Mutual Friend* or to any other literary source.

16. Tizard-Lindemann dispute: Zimmerman, *Britain's Shield*, pp. 99–108; Judkins, "Making Vision into Power," pp. 122–123.

17. "Producing atomic bombs": Clark, *The Birth of the Bomb*, p. 58. Autobiography: Watson-Watt, *Three Steps to Victory*. "Synthetic palindrome": Hanbury Brown, *Boffin*, p. 6.

18. German radar: Kroge and Brown (ed., trans.), *GEMA*; Kummritz, "German Radar Development to 1945."

19. Navy radar: Allison, *New Eye for the Navy*. Army radar: Office of the Chief of Military History, *The Signal Corps*, vol. 1, *The Emergency (to December 1941)*. "Physicists' war": Compton, "Physics and the Future."

20. Two excellent books on the Battle of Britain and the Blitz are Holland, *The Battle of Britain*, and Prior, *When Britain Saved the West*.

21. "Observers, with field-glasses": *CSWW*, vol. 2, p. 294. Aerial mines: Edgerton, *Britain's War Machine*, pp. 107–112.

22. A war of factories: Fear, "War of Factories": Overy, *Why the Allies Won*, pp. 180–207. Shadow factories: Barnett, *The Pride and the Fall*, pp. 131–133, 145–146; Edgerton, *Britain's War Machine*, pp. 198–205; Mitchell, *The Shadow Scheme*.

23. Postan, *British War Production*, pp. 116, 164.

24. Losses at Dunkirk: Postan, *British War Production*, pp. 116–117, 185, 192; Skennerton, *Lee-Enfield Story*, p. 286; Hansard, *House of Commons Debates*, July 1, 1942, vol. 381, cc251; Hansard, *House of Lords Debates*, July 1, 1942, vol. 123, cc589; *CSWW*, vol. 2, p. 338. "The Battle of France is over": Hansard, *House of Commons Debates*, June 18, 1940, vol. 362, cc 60.

25. "We have no continental army": Bell, *Churchill and Seapower*, p. 196. Appreciation of Future Strategy: NAUK CAB draft 80/16/60 of August 21, 1940, appreciation CAB 80/17/38 of September 4, 1940. Review of Future Strategy: CAB 80/58/15 of June 22, 1941, CAB 80/59/5 of July 31, 1941. See also Butler, *Grand Strategy*, vol. 2, pp. 343–345, 547–551; Bell, *Churchill and Seapower*, pp. 196–197.

26. "The Navy can lose us the war": *CWP*, vol. 2, pp. 762–764.

27. Skilled labor: Postan, *British War Production*, pp. 95–101. Women's conscription and factory employment: British Information Services, *Women's War Work in Britain*.

28. Munitions supplies: Allen, "Mutual Aid Between the U.S. and the British Empire, 1941–45," p. 268.

29. Cash-and-Carry: Johnsen, *The Origins of the Grand Alliance*, pp. 72–75; Hancock and Gowing, *British War Economy*, pp. 101–135. Anglo-French Purchasing Board: Hall, *North American Supply*, pp. 39–126; Hall and Wrigley, *Studies of Overseas Supply*, pp. 66–80; Bottelier, "Associated Powers," pp. 130–134, 156–186.

30. Machine tools: Cincinnati Milling Machine tools in British factories featured prominently in the 1943 propaganda film *Millions Like Us*. Horse-drawn aircraft: Dimbleby and Reynolds, *An Ocean Apart*, pp. 131–134; Vernon, "Horses on the Payroll."

31. Hall, *North American Supply*, p. 429; Bottelier, "Associated Powers," pp. 122, 134, 162, 181; Holley, *Buying Aircraft*, p. 200. "That's no fire": Cooke, *The American Home Front*, p. 246.

32. Engle, "Half of Everything"; Walton, *Miracle of World War II*, pp. 117–120.

33. Machine tools: Hall, *North American Supply*, pp. 113, 198. Shadow factories: Hall and Wrigley, *Studies of Overseas Supply*, pp. 86–89.

34. Metric to English units: Woodbury, *Battlefronts of Industry*, p. 170. BPC: Foreign Inquiries for Production of Munitions reports, Army Navy Munitions Board memorandum 53, September 10, 1940. "Pursuing an almost entirely American policy": Eden, *The Eden Memoirs*, p. 176. *Foreign Inquiries for Production of Munitions reports.* President Franklin D. Roosevelt's Office Files, 1933–1945 Microfilm reel 35 / 0204. Franklin D. Roosevelt Library and Museum, Hyde Park, NY.

35. Influencing American public opinion: Cull, *Selling War*; Hemming, *Our Man in New York*.

36. Leighton and Coakley, *Global Logistics and Strategy*, pp. 33–34; Johnsen, *The Origins of the Grand Alliance*, p. 95.

37. "Arsenal of Democracy": Monnet, *Memoirs*, pp. 158–169. Gallup poll numbers: See Hemming, *Our Man in New York*.

38. Reynolds, *The Creation of the Anglo-American Alliance*, pp. 121–168; Barr, *Yanks and Limeys*, pp. 114–120; Bailey, *The Arsenal of Democracy*, pp. 14–15, 111–113; Gropman, *Mobilizing U.S. Industry in World War II*, p. 153. "Germany had lost the war": Monnet, *Memoirs*, p. 161.

39. Herman, *Freedom's Forge*, p. 88; United States Civilian Production Administration, *Industrial Mobilization for War*, p. 51. "We did not have enough powder": Carew, *Becoming the Arsenal*, p. 83.

40. Koistinen, *Arsenal of World War II*, pp. 53–64; Wilson, *Destructive Creation*, pp. 62–64.

41. Watson, *The German Genius*, pp. 689–698. "Eliminating German science from the war": Baxter, *Scientists Against Time*, p. 26. Postwar analysis revealed that Japanese science was in many areas equal to that of Germany, though the disdain of the Japanese government for basic science was even deeper than that of the Nazis.

42. Alic, *Trillions for Military Technology*, pp. 35–41.

43. "Complete lack of proper liaison": Bush, *Pieces of the Action*, p. 74.

44. "Answer to a plane is another plane": Zachary, *Endless Frontier*, p. 99.

45. "OK—FDR": Conant, *My Several Lives*, pp. 234–235.

46. The history of NDRC and OSRD is primarily derived from Baxter, *Scientists Against Time* and Stewart, *Organizing Scientific Research for War*. Additional thanks to Dan Else for his expertise and insights. "Spend a few days": "Carroll L. Wilson 1910–1983: Report of the Carroll L. Wilson Awards Committee," MIT Libraries, Institute Archives and Special Collections, T171.M4218.W553.1987, pp. 44–45. "End run": Bush, *Pieces of the Action*, pp. 31–32.

47. Office for Emergency Management: Koistinen, *Arsenal of World War II*, pp. 15–17. Auditorium: correspondence with Potts & Callahan Builders, February 1943, Carnegie Institution for Science, Administration Archives, Box 7, Folder 13. "Van" Bush: Bush, *Pieces of the Action*, p. 277 ("keep abreast of things," p. 94).

48. Conant, *Tuxedo Park*, pp. 105, 129–178.

49. Guerlac, *Radar in World War II*, vol. 1, pp. 247–252; Genuth, "Microwave Radar, the Atomic Bomb" ("decided to write a report," p. 281).

50. Megaw, "The High-Power Pulsed Magnetron."

51. Norden bombsights: See McFarland, *America's Pursuit of Precision Bombing*. "No weapons of special value": Zimmerman, *Top Secret Exchange*, p. 45.

52. Information in this and the following paragraphs is primarily from Zimmerman, *Top Secret Exchange* ("meant a great deal," p. 59); Phelps, *The Tizard Mission* ("closer liaison," p. 69); Clark, *Tizard*, pp. 248–271 ("All offers," p. 253); A. V. Hill, *Memories and Reflections*, pp. 273–278, Papers of Professor A. V. Hill, Churchill Archives Centre, Churchill College, Cambridge, UK ("would have much to gain," p. 275).

53. Tizard's appointment letter: letter from Ministry of Aircraft Production to Henry Tizard, August 3, 1940, NARA RG 227 NC-138 Entry 169, Box 1 (my thanks to Jamie Holmes for identifying it). List of Tizard Mission members: Bowen, "The Tizard Mission to the USA and Canada," p. 296.

54. Cosmos Club: My thanks to Thad Garrett and Spencer Churchill for their assistance with the club archives. Weather for August 28, 1940: Daily Reminder 1940, Wed. Aug. 28, 1940, Papers of James Bryant Conant, Harvard University Archives UAI 15.898, Box 5.

55. "The most valuable cargo": Baxter, *Scientists Against Time*, p. 142.

56. Bought them five years, "a special lab": Daily Reminder 1940, Wed. Oct. 2, 1940, Papers of James Bryant Conant, Harvard University Archives UAI 15.898, Box 5 (thanks to Dan Else for his help with this). Also, Conant, *Man of the Hour*, p. 200.

57. "I am so glad": Buderi, *The Invention That Changed the World*, pp. 44–45.

58. Over fifty projects: Rad Lab, *Five Years at the Radiation Laboratory*, p. 28.

59. Correspondence between Vannevar Bush and the Department of War and Navy, September–November 1940, NARA RG 227 NC-138 Entry 169, Box 1 (my thanks to Jamie Holmes for identifying it).

60. Mk XIV stabilized bombsight: See McFarland, *America's Pursuit of Precision Bombing*. It saw limited combat use after late 1943, most famously to help sink the German battleship *Tirpitz* in November 1944.

61. Combined boards: Koistinen, *Arsenal of World War II*, pp. 268–274.

62. British Central Scientific Office: MacLeod, "All for Each and Each for All"; Hall and Wrigley, *Studies of Overseas Supply*, pp. 379–385; NAUK AVIA 42, British Central Scientific Office Registered Files.

63. Conant mission: Records of the OSRD London Mission, NARA RG 227 NC-138 Entry 176, Box 154 ("your proposal will be welcomed," telephone call from Air Ministry to Bush, February 3, 1941); Wilson, "Trip to Britain with J. B. Conant: CLW Journal, Feb–Apr 1941," Carroll L. Wilson papers, Massachusetts Institute of Technology Libraries, Department of Distinctive Collections, MC-0029, Box 4 F.109 ("A mad place"); Daily Reminder 1941, Papers of James Bryant Conant,

Harvard University Archives UAI 15.898, Box 5 (thanks to Dan Else for his help with both the Wilson and Conant papers); Conant, *My Several Lives*, pp. 248–271 ("up to date," p. 261); Conant, *Man of the Hour*, pp. 206–225; Topping, *The Hovde Years*, pp. 115–135.

64. Archambault (ed.), *Report of OSRD Activities*, part 1, pp. 2–3; "With Winant, Conant [and] Harriman in England": Woollcott, *The Letters of Alexander Woollcott*, p. 283. Pan Am Clippers: Vaz and Hill, *Pan Am at War*.

65. Archambault (ed.), *Report of OSRD Activities*, part 1, pp. 3–4; Topping, *The Hovde Years*, pp. 131–157 ("foolhardy Americans," p. 131).

66. Atlantic Charter: Reynolds, *The Creation of the Anglo-American Alliance*, pp. 212–221 ("believer in bombing," p. 212).

67. "Freezing to death": Topping, *The Hovde Years*, p. 153. "We are all in the same boat now," "Britain would live," "Slept the sleep of the saved and thankful": *CSWW* vol. 3, pp. 538–540. "Well, the war is over": Billotte, *Le temps des armes*, p. 187.

68. "Cram course": Topping, *The Hovde Years*, p. 156. "The British, I think": Oral history interview with Vannevar Bush, 1964, Massachusetts Institute of Technology Libraries, Department of Distinctive Collections, MC-0143, Reel 7, p. 460.

69. "No shadow of a doubt": David Langumir to his wife, Nancy Langmuir, Nov. 20, 1942, personal papers of David Langmuir (my thanks to Jean Langmuir, David's daughter, for providing copies of these documents). Information on Bennett Archambault is from personal papers of Bennett Archambault (my thanks to Michele Archambault, Bennett's daughter, for providing copies of these documents).

70. "American accents": Henrey, *The Incredible City*, p. 40.

71. "It was a beehive": Bush, oral history interview with Vannevar Bush, 1964, Massachusetts Institute of Technology Libraries, Department of Distinctive Collections, MC-0143, Reel 7. Gormless: That would be me, in my role as liaison scientist for the Office of Naval Research Global office in London. "Capable of a greatness": Longmate, *The G.I.'s*, p. 376. Information on the OSRD London Mission is from Archambault (ed.), *Report of OSRD Activities*, and OSRD London Mission files, NARA RG 227 NC-138.

Chapter 3: Fight in the Air

1. "Bombers alone": *CWP*, vol. 2, pp. 762–764.

2. "Masses of men": *CWP*, vol. 2, pp. 947–948.

3. Rowe, TRE, and Sunday Soviets: Rowe, *One Story of Radar*, pp. 83–88; Hartcup, *The Challenge of War*, pp. 24–25; Hartcup, *The Effect of Science on the Second World War*, p. 10; Purbeck Radar Museum Trust, http://www.purbeckradar.org.uk, accessed August 2019.

4. Rowe, *One Story of Radar*, pp. 116–117; Watson-Watt, *The Pulse of Radar*, pp. 382–383; Lovell, *Echoes of War*, pp. 85–92. Additional thanks to Sebastian Cox, head of RAF Air Historical Branch in Ruislip, for his comments on this and other sections.

5. Gee and Oboe: Rowe, *One Story of Radar*, pp. 108–114; Watson-Watt, *The Pulse of Radar*, pp. 335–351; Johnson, *The Secret War*, pp. 84–91; Guerlac, *Radar in World War II*, vol. 2, pp. 766–776.

6. Lovell, "The Cavity Magnetron in World War II," p. 286; Lovell, *Echoes of War*, p. 94.

7. "This is the turning point": Rowe, *One Story of Radar*, p. 117.

8. Megaw, "The High-Power Pulsed Magnetron" ("Colt revolver," p. 982).

9. MIT Rad Lab: Rad Lab, *Five Years at the Radiation Laboratory*; Buderi, *The Invention That Changed the World*, pp. 38–51; Kevles, *The Physicists*, pp. 303–323; Rigden, *Rabi*, pp. 124–145 ("I want to be in on it," p. 132); Guerlac, *Radar in World War II*, vol. 1, pp. 253–303; and Attwood (ed.), *Summary Technical Report of Division 14*. See also the twenty-eight volumes of the *Massachusetts Institute of Technology Radiation Laboratory Series* (Ridenour, ed.)

10. Bowen, *Radar Days*; Robinson, "British Microwave Radar 1939–41"; Denis M. Robinson, interview by Michael Wolff, May 23, 1978, Niels Bohr Library and Archives, www.aip.org/history-programs/niels-bohr-library/oral-histories/4845.

11. "How many Germans will it kill?": Rigden, *Rabi: Scientist and Citizen*, p. 133. Monica Healea: Rossiter, *Women Scientists in America*, p. 6. "How does a whistle work?": Kevles, *The Physicists*, p. 304.

12. Eldridge, "Electronic Eyes for the Allies," pp. 134–138.

13. Bowen, *Radar Days*, pp. 184–186; Lovell, *Echoes of War*, pp. 157–158.

14. Bell Laboratories: Kelly, "Radar and Bell Laboratories"; Lack, "Radar and Western Electric"; Fisk, Hagstrum, and Hartman, "The Magnetron as a Generator of Centimeter Waves"; Gertner, *The Idea*, pp. 67–69.

15. "We're allies now": Denis M. Robinson, interview by Michael Wolff, May 23, 1978, Niels Bohr Library and Archives, www.aip.org/history-programs/niels-bohr-libr ary/oral-histories/4845.

16. Guerlac, *Radar in World War II*, vol. 1, p. 276.

17. Lovell, *Echoes of War*, p. 146; Buderi, *The Invention That Changed the World*, pp. 184–185.

18. Lovell, *Echoes of War*, pp. 96–97; Saward, *The Bomber's Eye*, p. 82; Saward, *Bernard Lovell*, pp. 55–73 ("searing experience," p. 71).

19. "I am deeply disturbed ... any news": *CSWW*, vol. 4, pp. 251–255.

20. "weren't to be outdone by any Britisher," "we no longer have the Americans": Eldridge, "Electronic Eyes for the Allies," pp. 166–177; Bowen, *Radar Days*, p. 188; Papers of Edward G. Bowen, Churchill Archives Centre, Churchill College, Box 1, Folder 14.

21. Eldridge, "Electronic Eyes for the Allies," pp. 177–179.

22. July 5, 1942, Sunday Soviet: I have described these meetings in detail because of Bernard Lovell's claim that the Americans were dead set against radar-guided blind bombing, thus delaying British development of H2S. This narrative has been re-peated ever since by almost every history of radar, yet it is simply not true. Rabi's and Purcell's contemporary diaries and notes of the meetings (Rabi, "Diary of I. I. Rabi"; Purcell, "Official Diary of E. M. Purcell") are in OSRD London Mission, NARA RG 227 NC-138, Box 148. Lovell told his side of the story over fifty years later (starting in 1991), in several places: Lovell, *Echoes of War*, pp. 145–146; Lovell, "The Cavity Magnetron in World War II," pp. 287–288; and interviews conducted in 2007 with Web of Stories (Lovell, "The Americans' Reaction to the Magnetron," https:// www.webofstories.com/play/bernard.lovell/31). I received additional information from his son, Dr. Bryan Lovell, in May 2019. Lovell's half-century-later accounts

differ significantly in several crucial places from Rabi and Purcell's on-the-spot notes: Lovell claimed that the Americans said microwave radar was "unworkable" in Philip Dee's office, but there were no meetings there on that Sunday or any other day during Rabi's visit; the afternoon closed-door meeting was in Herbert Skinner's office, but Lovell was not present; and neither in the Sunday Soviet nor the closed-door meeting was the performance of centimeter radar over land even mentioned. Neither Rowe nor Skinner, in their later writings and correspondence, made any mention of supposed American opposition; and when Lovell wrote to Rabi's biographer John Rigden before publishing *Echoes of War*, Rigden reported to him that neither Rabi, Purcell, nor DuBridge recalled any such opposition. The inescapable conclusion is that Lovell simply misunderstood the Americans' concerns, and in his mind, those concerns morphed into monolithic opposition to the system he was responsible for.

23. Compton Mission: Lee DuBridge, Report on Visit to England, April 28–June 11, 1943, OSRD London Mission, NARA RG 227 NC-138, Box 145 ("most urgent radar problem," p. 1); Archambault (ed.), *Report of OSRD Activities*, part 2, pp. 19–20. Radar research and development: Visit of Compton Mission from U.S.A. to United Kingdom, NAUK AVIA 22/2319; Stever, *In War and Peace*, pp. 34–36; Eldridge, "Electronic Eyes for the Allies," pp. 242–253; Buderi, *The Invention That Changed the World*, pp. 187–189.

24. BBRL: Archambault (ed.), *Report of OSRD Activities*, part 1, pp. 5–7, part 2, pp. 21–23 ("development and effective employment," p. 21); John G. Trump, *A War Diary, 1944–45*, Massachusetts Institute of Technology Libraries, Department of Distinctive Collections, D810S2T78_JGT_1973; Correspondence between Bennett Archambault and Vannevar Bush, February 23–25, 1944, personal papers of Bennett Archambault (my thanks to Michele Archambault, Bennett's daughter, for providing copies of these documents); Guerlac, *Radar in World War II*, vol. 2, pp. 731–756, 817–826; Eldridge, "Electronic Eyes for the Allies," pp. 265–267.

25. Craven and Cate (eds.), *The Army Air Forces in World War II*, vol. 2, p. 691.

26. Lovell, *Echoes of War*, pp. 193–196.

27. Fine, *Blind Bombing*, pp. 178, 196; Philco, *Radar on Wings*; Fisk, Hagstrum, and Hartman, "The Magnetron as a Generator of Centimeter Waves"; Guerlac, *Radar in World War II*, vol. 2, pp. 776–795. A highly fictionalized telling of radar-guided bombing through overcast was the narrative focus of one episode in the 1960s television series *Twelve o'Clock High* (season 2, episode 21, "Back to the Drawing Board," first aired February 7, 1966).

28. Millar, *The Bruneval Raid*; Jones, *Most Secret War*, pp. 223–239; Goodchild, *A Most Enigmatic War*, pp. 260–285.

29. Brown, *Technical and Military Imperatives*; Beyerchen, "From Radio to Radar." "Call me Meier": Shirer, *The Rise and Fall of the Third Reich*, p. 517.

30. *CSWW*, pp. 337–352; Jones, *Most Secret War*, pp. 92–188; Goodchild, *A Most Enigmatic War*, pp. 102–151.

31. Hartcup, *The Challenge of War*, pp. 147–156; Hartcup, *The Effect of Science on the Second World War*, pp. 56–59.

32. "Window": Cockburn, "The Radio War."

33. Gillmor, *Fred Terman at Stanford*, pp. 186–252.

34. "When I arrived back from England": Price, *The History of US Electronic Warfare*, vol. 1, pp. 26–33; Price, *Instruments of Darkness*, pp. 109–116.

35. Chinn (ed.), *Summary Technical Report of Division 15*, pp. 230–248; transcript of interview with Harold F. Elliott, PER 239.72, Tape 8, conducted by Irv Rasmussen, July 1968, Perham Collection of Early Electronics: Sound Recordings, 2003-38, History San Jose Research Library and Archives, http://perhamcollection.history sanjose.org/people-companies/harold-elliott/; Price, *The History of US Electronic Warfare*, vol. 1, pp. 41–42 ("getting financial support"), 273.

36. Price, "A Survey of US Countermeasures During World War II. "I have never seen any American development": Langmuir to Suits, September 29, 1943, OSRD London Mission, NARA RG 227 NC-138, Box 147. "Depends absolutely on American production": Office of the Chief of Military History, *The Signal Corps*, vol. 3, *The Outcome*, p. 311 (the amount of aluminum needed for Window would have cost the RAF 250 Lancaster bombers in lost production, according to Sebastian Cox, head of RAF Air Historical Branch in Ruislip). Chaff did double duty as tinsel foil: Pollard, *Radiation*, p. 131.

37. Thomas Kuhn at ABL-15: OSRD London Mission, NARA RG 227 NC-138, Box 147; Thomas S. Kuhn papers, Massachusetts Institute of Technology Libraries, Department of Distinctive Collections, MC-0240, Box 1.

38. Archambault (ed.), *Report of OSRD Activities*, part 1, pp. 5–6, part 2, pp. 6–7; Suits et al., *Applied Physics*, pp. 55–81; Lovell, *Echoes of War*, pp. 119–125; Malvern Radar and Technology History Society, https://mraths.org.uk/, accessed January 2019.

39. "Effect was stunning": David Langmuir to Nancy Langmuir, November 2, 1942, personal papers of David Langmuir (my thanks to Jean Langmuir, David's daughter, for providing copies of these documents).

40. "Up to our ears": Price, *Instruments of Darkness*, pp. 188–189.

41. "Folding up the entire show": Bennett Archambault to David Langmuir, October 1, 1943, personal papers of David Langmuir. "Improving the relations": Trump, *A War Diary*, p. 6. "I have enormous confidence": Vannevar Bush to Bennett Archambault, February 23, 1944, personal papers of Bennett Archambault. See also Gillmor, *Fred Terman at Stanford*, pp. 246–247.

42. Biddle, *Rhetoric and Reality in Air Warfare*, p. 220.

43. The information on the P-51 Mustang in this and following sections is from Wagner, *Mustang Designer Edgar Schmued and the P-51*; Ethell, *Mustang*; Freeman, *Mustang at War*; Horkey, "The P-51: The Real Story"; Ludwig, *P-51 Mustang*; Bailey, *The Arsenal of Democracy*, pp. 198–237; Anderson, *The Grand Designers*, pp. 156–186.

44. Aviation giants: Koistinen, *Planning War, Pursuing Peace*, p. 189. "The names of RAF fighters": Royal Air Force Museum, London, communication to me, July 2019.

45. The actual participation of Beverly Shenstone in the design of the Mustang continues to be debated. His biographer Lance Cole (*Secrets of the Spitfire*, p. 197) attributes some of the Mustang's aerodynamic design to him. Edgar Schmued (Wagner, *Mustang Designer Edgar Schmued and the P-51*, pp. 61–62) is quoted as giving Shenstone full credit for the air scoop modifications based on aerodynamic theory. Edward Horkey, NAA head of aerodynamics ("The P-51"), took credit for the modifications and does not mention Shenstone at all. However, John Leland "Lee"

Atwood, NAA's chief engineer, took exception to many of Horkey's claims (Atwood, "An Engineer's Perspective on the Mustang"; Anderson, *The Grand Designers*, pp. 180–181). The weight of evidence indicates that Shenstone significantly participated in the Mustang design.

46. P-51s crated and shipped: Turner, *Mustang Pilot*, p. 18. "Definitely the best American fighter": Wagner, *Mustang Designer*, p. 77.

47. "The point which strikes me . . . relatively quick job": Birch, *Rolls-Royce and the Mustang*, pp. 10–11. For Allison engines, see Whitney, *Vee's for Victory!*

48. "If their having the drawings would enable us to win the war": Lloyd, *Rolls-Royce*, pp. 42–44; Pugh, *The Magic of a Name*, pp. 210–211.

49. Draper, *Operation Fish*, pp. 206–234; Switky, *Wealth of an Empire*, pp. 37–52, 85–95; Taber, *Chasing Gold*, pp. 158–171, 284–305.

50. Wilson was "consternated": McDowall, *Quick to the Frontier*, p. 300; Nelson, *Arsenal of Democracy*, pp. 80–81.

51. Morgenthau's office: Kimball, *The Most Unsordid Act*, p. 56.

52. "Bill, we can't make those motors": Beasley, *Knudsen*, p. 264.

53. "Let the American government take over the contract": Beasley, *Knudsen*, p. 264. "You're mixed up. . . . They want war"; Sorensen, *My Forty Years with Ford*, pp. 275–276.

54. "Consider any proposal": Beasley, *Knudsen*, p. 265.

55. Klein, *A Call to Arms*, p. 71. "We can't borrow parts from the British": Melnitsky, *Profiting from Industrial Standardization*, pp. 42–44.

56. The story of the Packard Merlin engine production is from Lloyd, *Rolls-Royce*, pp. 49–56; Walton, *Miracle of World War II*, pp. 84–91; Birch, *Rolls-Royce and the Mustang*; Herman, *Freedom's Forge*, pp. 100–106; Hyde, *Arsenal of Democracy*, pp. 49–52; Wilson, *The Merlin*, pp. 182–190.

57. "Sweet music in the ears": "Packard Begins on Air Engines," *NYT*, August 3, 1941, p. 17. Barrington died in the factory from a heart attack: Michigan Department of Health, Certificate of Death for Thomas B. Barrington, State File No. 309278, July 1, 1943.

58. See Aldrich, *American Hero*.

59. "I am told by an American friend": Ludwig, *P-51 Mustang*, pp. 130–134.

60. Many of them were African Americans: Wilkerson, *The Warmth of Other Suns*, pp. 127–133.

61. This section on the combined bomber offensive is largely from Craven and Cate (eds.), *The Army Air Forces in World War II*, vol. 2, pp. 274–307, 665–706, vol. 3, pp. 30–66; McFarland, *America's Pursuit of Precision Bombing, 1910–1945*, pp. 165–190; Davis, *Carl A. Spaatz and the Air War in Europe*, pp. 287–452; Kennedy, *Engineers of Victory*, pp. 75–143; O'Brien, *How the War Was Won*, pp. 72–82, 266–315.

62. The bombers were "multiplying themselves": Jones, *Most Secret War*, pp. 300–301.

63. "Chaff screening force": Fifteenth Air Force, *Radar Counter Measures*.

64. "Initial spectacular success": Langmuir to Suits, September 29, 1943, OSRD London Mission, NARA RG 227 NC-138, Box 147.

65. Over 90 percent of the bombing raids: Crowther and Whiddington, *Science at War*, p. 69. "Christmas trees": Friedrich, *The Fire*, p. 22. For details on target marking, see Freer, "Circumventing the Law That Humans Cannot See in the Dark."

66. "A few H2X airplanes now": Davis, *Carl A. Spaatz and the Air War in Europe*, pp. 296–297.
67. "Complete destruction . . . mauled . . . The cost of such deep penetrations": Craven and Cate (eds.), *The Army Air Forces in World War II*, vol. 2, pp. 703–704.
68. Davis, *Bombing the European Axis Powers*, pp. 270, 279–290.
69. Kennedy, *Engineers of Victory*, pp. 130–131. See also Holland, *Big Week*.
70. "Long-range fighter escort did appear over Germany at just the saving moment": Arnold, *Global Mission*, p. 376.
71. Strategic bombing histories: Webster and Frankland, *The Strategic Air Offensive Against Germany 1939–1945*; *The United States Strategic Bombing Survey*.
72. Speer interrogation: Miller, *Masters of the Air*, pp. 463–470. Goering interrogation: Johnsen, *Captured Eagles*, pp. 183–185.

Chapter 4: Fight on the Landing Grounds

1. On friendly fire, see Shrader, *Amicicide*.
2. Half of all bomber missions: Conway, *Blind Landings*, p. 164.
3. Watson-Watt, *Three Steps to Victory*, pp. 214–230.
4. "A small device": Watson-Watt, *The Pulse of Radar*, pp. 136–143.
5. "You are in charge": Bowden, "The Story of IFF," p. 436.
6. Trim, "The Development of IFF in the Period up to 1945"; Brown, *Technical and Military Imperatives*, pp. 129–135; Hartcup, *The Challenge of War*, p. 124; Bowen, *Radar Days*, p. ix. "Every unit": Watson-Watt, *The Pulse of Radar*, p. 140. "So many IFF sets were needed": Bowden, "The Story of IFF," p. 436.
7. Allison, *New Eye for the Navy*, pp. 126, 179–180; Office of the Chief of Military History, *The Signal Corps*, vol. 1, *The Emergency*, pp. 264–266.
8. "Vital importance of a common method": Bowen, *Radar Days*, pp. 179–181.
9. Brown, *Technical and Military Imperatives*, pp. 131–132; Office of the Chief of Military History, *The Signal Corps*, vol. 1, *The Emergency*, pp. 264–266; Watson-Watt, *The Pulse of Radar*, p. 140.
10. Philco, *Radar on Wings*, pp. 3–6.
11. Office of the Chief of Military History, *The Signal Corps*, vol. 2, *The Test*, pp. 242–243; *FTP 217*, pp. 95–96. After the war, the IFF Mark IV sets were sold for surplus, almost all of them unused and still in their original sealed packaging.
12. Brown, *Technical and Military Imperatives*, p. 241; Lundstrom, *The First Team*, pp. 73–77, 206, 270.
13. Lundstrom, *The First Team*, pp. 305, 323–324.
14. America accounted for half of the world's 90 million radio sets: Potter, *Wireless Internationalism and Distant Listening*, p. 112.
15. IFF Mark III: oral history interview with Harold Wheeler, 1991, IEEE History Center, https://ethw.org/Oral-History:Harold_Wheeler_(1991); Dettinger and Bachman (eds.), *Harold A. Wheeler's Legacy*; Wheeler, *Hazeltine Corporation in World War II*; Bowden, "The Story of IFF," p. 436; Whitehead, "1973 Pioneer Award," p. 791; *FTP 217*, pp. 95–96; Guerlac, *Radar in World War II*, vol. 1, pp. 367–370; Office of the Chief of Military History, *The Signal Corps*, vol. 2, *The Test*, pp. 242–243.

16. IFF Mark V: Rad Lab, *Five Years at the Radiation Laboratory*, p. 24; Roberts (ed.), *Radar Beacons*, p. 20 ("particularly sacred"); Guerlac, *Radar in World War II*, vol. 1, pp. 370–374; Isidor Rabi, "Diary of I. I. Rabi," and Edward Purcell, "Official Diary of E. M. Purcell," both in OSRD London Mission, NARA RG 227 NC-138, Box 48; Eldridge, "Electronic Eyes for the Allies," pp. 177, 195–208, 268–273; Bowden, "The Story of IFF," pp. 436–437; Whitehead, "1973 Pioneer Award," pp. 791–792; Trim, "The Development of IFF in the Period up to 1945," pp. 450–453; Wheeler, *Hazeltine Corporation in World War II*.
17. "Our friendlies": Eldridge, "Electronic Eyes for the Allies," p. 271.
18. Air-conditioning: Whitehead, "Memoirs of a Boffin."
19. "Sent a signal to the engineers": Bowden, "The Story of IFF," p. 436. Friendly fire study: Shrader, *Amicide*, pp. 65–72. German friendly fire: Holland, *Big Week*, p. 131.
20. Freer, "Circumventing the Law That Humans Cannot See in the Dark," pp. 40, 145. Landing accident rate: Wells, *Courage and Air Warfare*, p. 52. Heavy bomber losses upon landing: David B. Langmuir to Lee DuBridge, January 14, 1943, Central Decimal Correspondence Files, NARA RG 342, Box 404, RD 158, File: Project 102. Thanks to Erik Conway for finding this correspondence.
21. "All bases socked in": Wells, *Courage and Air Warfare*, p. 30. "Vile and unexpected": Otter, *1 Group*, pp. 170–173.
22. Freer, "Circumventing the Law That Humans Cannot See in the Dark," p. 40; Wells, *Courage and Air Warfare*, p. 29; Johnston et al., *Time and Navigation*, pp. 93–94.
23. On early radio navigation systems, see Rankin, "The Geography of Radionavigation"; Blanchard, "Air Navigation Systems."
24. On Gee, see Colin, "Robert J. Dippy"; Watson-Watt, *Three Steps to Victory*, pp. 393–398; Watson-Watt, *The Pulse of Radar*, pp. 335–344. Although rejected by TRE, O'Brien's proposal to Decca was adopted by the Royal Navy in 1942 under the initials QM. It went into commercial production after the war under the name Decca Navigator.
25. "Marshalling in the assembly": Watson-Watt, *Three Steps to Victory*, pp. 394–395.
26. "The final achievement": "Radar Production," p. 295. "Every operational heavy bomber": Connor, "The Lattice of Victory," p. 6. Only 1 percent of Gee-equipped aircraft: Grande et al., *Canadians on Radar*, pp. xvi–7. "Far too numerous": Hall (ed.), *Radar Aids to Navigation*, p. 60.
27. "Epiphany": Conant, *Tuxedo Park*, pp. 199–200.
28. LORAN: Connor, "The Lattice of Victory"; Rad Lab, *Five Years at the Radiation Laboratory*, pp. 176–178; Pierce, McKenzie, and Woodward (eds.), *LORAN, Long-Range Navigation*; Guerlac, *Radar in World War II*, vol. 1, pp. 525–536. Tizard Mission: Zimmerman, *Top Secret Exchange*, pp. 145–146; Phelps, *The Tizard Mission*, pp. 190–194. "Must have been working a 24-hour day": Conant, *Tuxedo Park*, p. 231.
29. Commercial blind landing systems: Conway, *Blind Landings*, pp. 80–122.
30. Development of Ground Control Approach (GCA) at MIT Rad Lab: Alvarez, *Adventures of a Physicist*, pp. 86–110 ("what occurred to me," p. 95); RAND History Project interview of Edward L. Bowles by Martin Collins and Michael Dennis, July 14, 1987, Box 10, Folder 9, National Air and Space Museum Archives, https://sova.si.edu/details/NASM.1999.0037#ref128; Fowler, "Rad Lab, Luie Alvarez, and the

Development of the GCA Radar Landing System"; Getting, *All in a Lifetime*, pp. 104–114, 154–155; Getting, "SCR-584 Radar"; Johnston, "The War Years," pp. 57–62; Guerlac, *Radar in World War II*, vol. 1, pp. 497–506; Mindell, "Automation's Finest Hour"; Conway, *Blind Landings*, pp. 123–136; Pang, "Edward Bowles and Radio Engineering at MIT," pp. 333–335. Additional information from Walter L. Alvarez (Luis Alvarez's son).

31. "Luie envisioned someone": Johnston, "The War Years," p. 58. "The aircraft which are chiefly concerned": David B. Langmuir to Lee DuBridge, January 14, 1943, Central Decimal Correspondence Files, NARA RG 342, Box 404, RD 158, File: Project 102. Thanks to Erik Conway for finding this correspondence.

32. "Disastrous," "I don't want," "happiest times": Alvarez, *Adventures of a Physicist*, pp. 98–99.

33. Homer G. Tasker and Gilfillan Brothers, Inc.: Conway, *Blind Landings*, pp. 128–132; Office of the Chief of Military History, *The Signal Corps*, vol. 1, *The Emergency (to December 1941)*, pp. 223–230; Ward, Fowler, and Lipson, "GCA Radars"; oral history interview with Kathryn and Charles "Bert" Fowler, 1991, IEEE History Center, https://ethw.org/Oral-History:Kathryn_and_Charles_Fowler. Additional information from Andrea Kalas, senior vice president of asset management, Paramount Pictures, Hollywood, CA. The studio system was ended by the Supreme Court case *United States v. Paramount Pictures, Inc.* in May 1948.

34. A flight of three PBYs: oral history interview with Lawrence Johnston, 1991, IEEE History Center, https://ethw.org/Oral-History:Lawrence_Johnston, p. 13; Johnston, "The War Years," pp. 60–66.

35. Jolley, "Invention of Ground Control Approach Radar at the MIT Radiation Laboratories." "Four mysterious youngsters": Hope, *I Never Left Home*, p. 25.

36. Franklin S. Cooper (OSRD) to Bennett Archambault, May 25, 1943, OSRD London Mission, NARA RG 227 NC-138, Box 144; Alvarez, *Adventures of a Physicist*, pp. 104–110 ("grimly aware," pp. 109–110).

37. "Quite another to do so after eight hours": Alvarez, *Adventures of a Physicist*, p. 106.

38. Rad Lab, *Five Years at the Radiation Laboratory*, p. 43; Jolley, "Invention of Ground Control Approach Radar at the MIT Radiation Laboratories."

39. Clarke, *Glide Path* ("absurdly young," p. 19; "Scotch and nylons," p. 60); Clarke, *Ascent to Orbit*, pp. 31–34; McAleer, *Arthur C. Clarke*, pp. 43–57; Clarke, "Extraterrestrial Relays." Clarke was not the only science-fiction author to get his start working as an engineer during World War II: Isaac Asimov, Robert Heinlein, and L. Sprague de Camp were all the Naval Aviation Experimental Station in Philadelphia during the war.

40. "Any fool": Conway, *Blind Landings*, p. 135. GCA deployment: Guerlac, *Radar in World War II*, vol. 1, p. 503; Attwood (ed.), *Summary Technical Report of Division 14*, vol. 1, pp. 73–74.

41. "Combination of blockade, bombing": Watson, *Chief of Staff*, pp. 402–403. "To coordinate all action," "Go and set Europe ablaze!": Roberts, *Churchill*, p. 580.

42. "Invention is the mother of necessity": Kranzberg, "Kranzberg's Laws," p. 545.

43. Development of Rebecca/Eureka: Hanbury Brown, *Boffin*, pp. 68–79 ("to drop agents," p. 71).

44. "Recognition of Beacons": Watson-Watt, *Three Steps to Victory*, p. 387; Watson-Watt, *The Pulse of Radar*, p. 332.

45. SOE operations using Rebecca/Eureka: Bascomb, *The Winter Fortress*, pp. 111–116; Bines, *The Polish Country Section of the Special Operations Executive*, pp. 125, 146; Foot, *SOE in France*, pp. 81–82.

46. Hanbury Brown, *Boffin*, pp. 73–74.

47. United States manufacture of Rebecca/Eureka: Hanbury Brown, *Boffin*, pp. 74–79 ("far too many differences," "seedy hotel," p. 77); Dettinger and Bachman (eds.), *Harold A. Wheeler's Legacy*, p. 7; Wheeler, *Hazeltine Corporation in World War II*, pp. 208–211; Philco, *Radar on Wings*, p. 28; Williams, "The History of Rebecca-Eureka."

48. Burton, "The Eureka-Rebecca Compromises," p. 28; Warren, *Airborne Operations in World War II*, p. 16.

Chapter 5: Fight on the Seas and Oceans

1. "The only thing": *CSWW*, vol. 2, p. 529.

2. Bell, *Churchill and Seapower*, pp. 80–83, 163–167, 219–220.

3. Lambert, "Seapower 1939–1940"; Grove, "The Battle of the Atlantic." "The greatest prize": *CSWW*, vol. 2, p. 445.

4. "Scourge": *CSWW*, vol. 3, p. 99. "The most mischievous naval operations": Arcadia Conference: December 1941–January 1942, Proceeding of the American-British Joint Chiefs of Staff Conference, Washington, DC, https://www.jcs.mil/Portals/36/Documents/History/WWII/Arcadia3.pdf, p. 9.

5. Plumpe, "Ancient Convoying" (additional thanks to historian William M. Murray on ancient convoy operations); Ferreiro, *Brothers at Arms*, pp. 190, 197; Sutton, *Lords of the East*, pp. 48–49.

6. Van der Vat, *The Atlantic Campaign*, pp. 12–42; "Bare and empty": Doenitz, *Memoirs*, p. 4. Appleyard's analyses are detailed in Winton, *Convoy*, pp. 114–122.

7. Murphy, "The British Shipbuilding Industry During the Great War"; Hirshfield, "From Hog Islanders to Liberty Ships"; Thiesen, *Industrializing American Shipbuilding*, pp. 203–208.

8. Murphy, "Labour in the British Shipbuilding and Ship Repairing Industries," pp. 60–61; Varela, Murphy, and van der Linden (eds.), *Shipbuilding and Ship Repair Workers Around the World*, p. 61; Robins, *Standard Ships*, pp. 11–14; Henshaw, *Liberty's Provenance.*

9. Elphick, *Liberty*, pp. 30–41 ("I am not satisfied," pp. 39–40); Johnman and Murphy, "The British Merchant Shipping Mission in the United States," p. 13.

10. Four times greater: Morison, *History of United States Naval Operations in World War II*, vol. 1, *The Battle of the Atlantic: September 1939–May 1943*, p. 294.

11. British Merchant Shipbuilding Mission: Thompson and Hunter, "The British Merchant Shipbuilding Programme in North America"; Johnman and Murphy, "The British Merchant Shipping Mission in the United States" ("helpful as possible," p. 5); Herman, *Freedom's Forge*, pp. 121–122.

12. Of the 200-plus histories of *Liberty* ships and shipbuilding, I have used the following for this and subsequent sections: Lane, *Ships for Victory*; Sawyer and Mitchell, *The Liberty Ship*; Elphick, *Liberty* ("Todd Shipyard Corporation has been practically allocated to us," p. 41; "pure theatre," p. 43); Bourneuf, *Workhorse of the Fleet*. "His telephone calls were legend": Land, *Winning the War with Ships*, p. 171.

13. *Mahan*-class: Heinrich, *Warship Builders*, pp. 59–61. On Gibbs, see Ujifusa, *A Man and His Ship*.

14. Design agents: Ferreiro, *Bridging the Seas*, pp. 223–225.

15. "Oh Hell": Elphick, *Liberty*, p. 47.

16. Final contracts: "Ship Deal Is Signed," *NYT*, December 20, 1940, pp. 1, 6. "I scrambled": Elphick, *Liberty*, p. 50.

17. "When do we pour the keel?": Lane, *Ships for Victory*, p. 248.

18. Plans supplied: Thompson and Hunter, "The British Merchant Shipbuilding Programme in North America," pp. 79–80. Design problems: Brown, "Design Plans, Working Drawings." "Felt very skeptical": Elphick, *Liberty*, p. 56.

19. "Built by the mile": Robins, *Standard Ships*, p. 88. On Canada's shipbuilding program, see Pritchard, *A Bridge of Ships*. Cyril Thompson joined the RAF in 1943, and returned to his shipyard after the war. In total, over 3,000 cargo ships in World War Two were built to Thompson's design, more than any other class of vessel before or since.

20. Pooling resources: See Lindberg and Todd, *Anglo-American Shipbuilding in World War II*. On women in British shipyards, see Murphy, "From the Crinoline to the Boilersuit." "Women were not suitable": Stanley V. Goodall Papers, Diaries, 1932–1946, British Library, Western Manuscripts, ADD MS 52785–52791, entry for October 19, 1940.

21. On women in American shipyards, see Clawson, *Shipyard Diary of a Woman Welder*; Hirshfield, "Rosie Also Welded."

22. Liberty ships made up half: Elphick, *Liberty*, p. 17. Cracking: Ferreiro, *Bridging the Seas*, pp. 159–160.

23. Convoy system: *History of Convoy and Routing*; Hague, *The Allied Convoy System 1939–1945*.

24. Bolero: Ruppenthal, *Logistical Support of the Armies*, vol. 1, pp. 52–113; Leighton and Coakley, *Global Logistics and Strategy, 1940–1943*, pp. 362–376; Barr, *Yanks and Limeys*, pp. 327–330; Reynolds, *Rich Relations*, pp. 90–117.

25. Miller, "Sea Transport." "We've got to have ships!": Dwight D. Eisenhower and Harry D. Butcher, Personal and Official Diary of Lieut. General Dwight D. Eisenhower, Eisenhower Presidential Library, https://www.eisenhowerlibrary.gov/sites/defa ult/files/file/DDE%20Diary%20JanJuly%201942.pdf, pp. 1–2.

26. ASDIC: Franklin, *Britain's Anti-Submarine Capability*, p. 57. Only in 1939, when Churchill publicly acknowledged ASDIC, did the Royal Navy invent the name Allied Submarine Detection Investigation Committee to explain the acronym, even though no such committee ever existed.

27. Jeffrey, "Commodore Edison Joins the Navy"; Hackmann, *Seek and Strike*, p. 257.

28. The information in this section is primarily derived from DeBrosse and Burke, *The Secret in Building 26*; Mundy, *Code Girls*; Budiansky, *Battle of Wits*; Dayton

Codebreakers, https://daytoncodebreakers.org/, accessed December 2020. Additional thanks to David Kohnen for context and clarification.

29. "Full collaboration": Budiansky, *Battle of Wits*, p. 239. The War Department would sign a separate agreement with GC&CS the following year for Army and Air Force decrypts.

30. The former Eastcote satellite facility was later partly occupied by the US Navy's Office of Naval Research Global, where I had an office, completely oblivious at the time to the historical significance of the site. The site is now a residential community.

31. On the Western Approaches Command, see Parkin, *A Game of Birds and Wolves*.

32. The operations research information in this section is primarily derived from Sternhell and Thorndike (eds.), *A Summary of Antisubmarine Warfare Operations in World War II*, pp. 93–176; Budiansky, *Blackett's War*; Hore (ed.), *Patrick Blackett*; Thomas, *Rational Action*, pp. 31–130; Waddington, *O.R. in World War 2*. Additional thanks to Peter Hore and Stephen Budiansky.

33. "Born of radar": Watson-Watt, *Three Steps to Victory*, p. 230. To this day, British sources use the term "operational research," and Americans use "operations research" to describe the same thing.

34. "The proper use of what we have got": Blackett's 1941 essay "Scientists at the Operational Level," republished in Blackett, *Studies of War*, pp. 171–176, quote on p. 176.

35. Morse became dismayed: Morse, *In at the Beginnings*, p. 171. Tate in London: *A Summary of Personnel and the General Assignments*, OSRD London Mission, NARA RG 227 NC-138, Box 134, n.p.; Topping, *The Hovde Years*, pp. 136–138; Budiansky, *Blackett's War*, p. 176. ASDIC and sonar: Hackmann, *Seek and Strike*, p. 263; Weir, *An Ocean in Common*, p. 163.

36. ASWORG: Morse, *In at the Beginnings*, pp. 156–212 ("It didn't take long," p. 173); Shurkin, *Broken Genius*, pp. 63–85; Coleman (ed.), *A Survey of Subsurface Warfare in World War II*, pp. 7–116; "History of the Anti-Submarine Measures Division of the Tenth Fleet," US Army Command and General Staff College, Ike Skelton Combined Arms Research Library Digital Library, https://cgsc.contentdm.oclc.org/digital/collection/p4013coll8/id/1999; Herrick, *Subsurface Warfare*, pp. 45–61; Tidman, *Operations Evaluation Group*, pp. 17–54; Rau, "The Adoption of Operations Research in the United States During World War II"; Meigs, *Slide Rules and Submarines*, pp. 58–63.

37. "Seemed to know everyone": Morse, *In at the Beginnings*, p. 192. Archambault's pocket phone book: personal papers of Bennett Archambault (my thanks to Michele Archambault, Bennett's daughter, for providing copies of these documents). "Analysis of US Aircraft Attacks on U/Boats": OSRD London Mission, NARA RG 227 NC-138, Box 174.

38. Operational effectiveness of microwave radar for bombing: Shockley to Brigadier General Harold McLelland, Feb. 1, 1943, OSRD London Mission, NARA RG 227 NC-138, Box 148. Kenneth Thimann: Hore (ed.), *Patrick Blackett*, p. 158. "Straight face": Morse, *In at the Beginnings*, pp. 185–186.

39. Search theory: Thomas, *Rational Action*, pp. 99–102; Morison, *History of United States Naval Operations in World War II*, vol. 1, *The Battle of the Atlantic*, p. 224.

40. "Prosper to best advantage": Shrader, *History of Operations Research in the United States Army*, p. 16. Tenth Fleet: "History of the Anti-Submarine Measures Division of the Tenth Fleet," US Army Command and General Staff College, Ike Skelton Combined Arms Research Library Digital Library, https://cgsc.contentdm.oclc.org/digital/collection/p4013coll8/id/1999; Tidman, *Operations Evaluation Group*, pp. 54–94.

41. Bush and Archambault tour: OSRD London Mission, NARA RG 227 NC-138, Box 134, "A Summary of Personnel and Their General Assignments"; Bush, *Pieces of the Action*, pp. 84–89; Hackmann, *Seek and Strike*, p. 265. Office of Field Service: Thiesmeyer and Burchhard, *Combat Scientists*.

42. The film scene was closely based on Forester, *The Good Shepherd*, pp. 35–37.

43. "Proud parent," "pet-name": Watson-Watt, *Three Steps to Victory*, p. 359. This section on HF/DF is primarily based on Redgment, "High-Frequency Direction Finding in the Royal Navy," and especially on Kathleen Broome Williams's superbly researched *Secret Weapon*.

44. "Talkative U-boats": Watson-Watt, *Three Steps to Victory*, p. 359.

45. Ghormley: Johnsen, *The Origins of the Grand Alliance*, p. 108. Busignies: Williams, *Secret Weapon*.

46. "Then I propose," "somewhat comparable": Williams, *Secret Weapon*, pp. 135–137.

47. "A convoy is no better than its ears and eyes": Morison, *History of United States Naval Operations in World War II*, vol. 1, *The Battle of the Atlantic*, pp. 226–227.

48. Depth charges: McKee, "An Explosive Story."

49. This section on RDX is primarily from Baxter, *Scientists Against Time*, pp. 256–259, and Baxter, *The Secret History of RDX*. Acknowledgments to Colin Baxter for additional clarifications.

50. "It seems to me": Baxter, *The Secret History of RDX*, p. 117 ("special priority," p. 28).

51. "To interest United States authorities," "it would be best": Baxter, *The Secret History of RDX*, pp. 11–12.

52. Combined boards: Hall, *North American Supply*, pp. 336–393. Additional information thanks to Nick Hewitt, National Museum of the Royal Navy. "Carry an awful wallop," "some risk": Baxter, *The Secret History of RDX*, p. 85.

53. This section on the British development of Hedgehog is from Richardson, "Charles Frederick Goodeve," pp. 329–333; Macrae, *Winston Churchill's Toyshop*, pp. 73–74, 164–165; Pawle, *The Secret War 1939–45*, pp. 113–176; Friedman, *British Destroyers and Frigates*, pp. 138–139.

54. "Time for lunch . . . There is plenty of time to do so": Soames, *A Daughter's Tale*, p. 168.

55. "This anti-submarine gun of yours": Pawle, *The Secret War 1939–45*, p. 113.

56. This section on the American development of Hedgehog is from Burchard, *Rockets, Guns and Targets*, pp. 96–101; Rowland and Boyd, *US Navy Bureau of Ordnance in World War II*, pp. 136–137; OSRD London Mission, NARA RG 227 NC-138, Box 144; Shachtman, *Laboratory Warriors*, pp. 205–206.

57. Thanks to Allen and Ed Galson (sons of Henry Galson) for their oral histories and newsletters recounting the manufacture of Hedgehog at Carrier Corporation.

58. This section on the Battle of the Atlantic is from Central Office of Information, *The Battle of the Atlantic*; Morison, *History of United States Naval Operations in World War II*, vol. 10, *The Atlantic Battle Won*; O'Brien, *How the War Was Won*, pp. 228–265; Milner, *Battle of the Atlantic*. Additional thanks to Randy Papadopoulos.

59. March 1943: Barnett, *Engage the Enemy More Closely*, pp. 600–606; Redford, "The March 1943 Crisis in the Battle of the Atlantic."

60. Convoy SC 154: Rohwer, *Chronology of the War at Sea*, vol. 2, pp. 394–395; Syrett, "Failure at Sea." "Some time elapsed": "U-845 Sunk March 10, 1944: Report on the Interrogation of Survivors, C.B. 04051 (102)," Naval Intelligence Division, Admiralty, May 1944, http://www.uboatarchive.net/Int/U-845INT.htm.

Chapter 6: Fight on the Beaches

1. "London Gets First Bombs for Three Weeks," *Daily Express*, June 5, 1941, p. 1; "German Armies on Stalin's Frontier," *Daily Express*, June 12, 1941, p. 1.

2. *CSWW*, vol. 3, *The Grand Alliance*, pp. 342–346.

3. Billard et al., "Forensic Study of *Bouvet* Capsizing." Modern forensic analyses of *Bouvet*, in which I participated, still cannot determine whether the ship was struck by an Ottoman mine or an artillery shell.

4. Polmar and Mersky, *Amphibious Warfare*, pp. 11–15.

5. *CSWW*, vol. 2, pp. 214–215.

6. *CSWW*, vol. 2, pp. 217–219.

7. "Large armoured irruptions": *CSWW*, vol. 2, p. 572.

8. RCNC: Brown, *A Century of Naval Construction*; Lavery, *Churchill's Navy*, pp. 73–75. Rowland Baker: Brown, "Sir Rowland Baker, RCNC." Additional thanks to David K. Brown, RCNC, and Charles Betts, RCNC, both my former professors, for additional personal information on Baker, for whom they worked. Note that LCTs were originally referred to as TLCs, or Tank Landing Craft, before the British and American navies standardized their notations in July 1942.

9. Bell, *Churchill and Sea Power*, pp. 207–209.

10. Maund, *Assault from the Sea*, p. 73; Fergusson, *The Watery Maze*, pp. 68, 70–71; Marder, *Operation "Menace,"* pp. 171–172, 188–189 ("best engineering brains," p. 189).

11. Brown, *A Century of Naval Construction*, pp. 165–167.

12. Friedman, *U.S. Amphibious Ships and Craft*, pp. 112–113; Stanley V. Goodall Papers, Diaries, 1932–1946, British Library, London: Western Manuscripts, ADD MS 52785–52791, entries for November–December 1940. Thanks to Ian Buxton for additional assistance.

13. Baker, "Ships of the Invasion Fleet"; MacDermott, *Ships Without Names*, pp. 11–13. Information on Sheffer thanks to Barbara Jones of the Lloyd's Register Foundation.

14. Edward Lull Cochrane, "Serial 1448—Great Britain Ship Design, 7 January 1941," NARA RG 19 UD1017 R 470/27/35/01, Box 5, Secret Correspondence

1915–1942. One-third of all Royal Navy ships would be American-built: Herman, *To Rule the Waves*, p. 547.

15. Friedman, *U.S. Amphibious Ships and Craft*, pp. 113–114.

16. James W. S. Dorling, *History of British Admiralty Delegation to USA*, 1945, NAUK ADM 199/1236.

17. "Development of the LST and Other US Navy Ships," June 1944, John C. Niedermair Files, Office of the Curator of Models, Naval Surface Warfare Center Carderock Division, Box 8 (thanks to Dana Wegner for making the documents available); Niedermair, *Reminiscences*, pp. 225–226.

18. Information on John Niedermair is courtesy of the members of the Niedermair family, whom I interviewed from 2017 to 2019. Special thanks to Margaret Moodie and John Niedermair IV for their help with family archives and oral histories. Thanks also to Patricia Long (née Niedermair), Barbara Long, George Edward "Ed" Niedermair, Marion Greer-Knowles, and Philip Niedermair.

19. Baker, "Notes on the Development of Landing Craft"; Brown, "Sir Rowland Baker" ("house on fire," p. 145); Strahan, *Andrew Jackson Higgins*, pp. 95–96. Higgins later claimed that he had developed the LST first, but his small pencil sketch of a similar concept, sent to the British embassy in October 1941, came long after Baker's LSTs were in the water, was never seen by BuShips, and had no impact on the actual program. Thanks to Jerry Strahan for further information on Higgins.

20. Dorling, *History of British Admiralty Delegation to USA*; Thomas A. Hussey, Pontoon causeways testimony, March 12, 1951, Royal Commission on Awards to Inventors, NAUK T 166/126/3 (thanks to Frank Blazich for his help); Fergusson, *The Watery Maze*, pp. 114–115; Friedman, *U.S. Amphibious Ships and Craft*, pp. 118–120. Additional thanks to Andrew Hussey (Thomas Hussey's son).

21. Thomas A. Hussey, Pontoon causeways testimony, March 12, 1951. "Dad's face was ashen": my interview with Patricia Long (née Niedermair), August 20, 2017.

22. Dorling, *History of British Admiralty Delegation to USA*; Maund, *Assault from the Sea*, pp. 82–83. LSTs originally were referred to as ATLCs, Atlantic Tank Landing Craft, before the British and American navies standardized their notations in July 1942. The Lend-Lease contracts for the seven *Boxer*-class ships were diverted to build American Landing Ship Docks (LSDs), based on a design developed by Rowland Baker. LSD-1 *Ashland*-class ships carried smaller landing craft in a well deck and were used extensively in the Pacific theater.

23. "Gave us the benefit": "Development of the LST and Other US Navy Ships," June 1944, John C. Niedermair Files, Office of the Curator of Models, Naval Surface Warfare Center Carderock Division, Box 8. After Baker departed for Britain in February 1942, naval constructor George McCloghrie took his place with a permanent desk in BuShips Design Division.

24. LST priorities: Mowry, *Landing Craft and the War Production Board*, pp. 5, 11. "Under way as quickly as possible": Matloff and Snell, *Strategic Planning for Coalition Warfare*, pp. 192–193.

25. LSTs: Rottman and Bryan, *Landing Ship Tank*; MacDermott, *Ships Without Names*.

26. Pontoons and "Bridging the Gap" trials: Blazich, "Bridging the Gap from Ship to Shore" (thanks to Frank Blazich for also providing me copies of his research).

27. Hussey quotes: Thomas A. Hussey, Pontoon causeways testimony, March 12, 1951. Niedermair quotes: Niedermair, *Reminiscences*, pp. 232–234.

28. *CWC*, vol. 2, pp. 61–83; D'Eyncourt, *A Shipbuilder's Yarn*, pp. 109–128.

29. Edgerton, *Britain's War Machine*, pp. 63–65. Estimates of British tank numbers varied from 217 to 250 to 488 light, medium, and heavy tanks.

30. British first designed a turret and gun for fighting: Chamberlain and Ellis, *British and American Tanks of World War Two*, p. 5. "Most mobile": Barr, *Yanks and Limeys*, p. 99.

31. British Tank Mission: Fletcher, *British Armour in the Second World War*, vol. 1, *The Great Tank Scandal*, pp. 87–105; Hall and Wrigley, *Studies of Overseas Supply*, pp. 96–103; Blue, "The Ram Cruiser Tank," pp. 15–34; Beasley, *Knudsen*, pp. 282–283.

32. "As high as the Tower of Babel": Fletcher, *British Armour in the Second World War*, vol. 1, *The Great Tank Scandal*, p. 90.

33. M3 tanks: Fletcher and Zaloga, *British Battle Tanks*, pp. 36–61.

34. M3 engineering changes: Thomson and Mayo, *The Ordnance Department*, p. 253. M4 Sherman tanks: Fletcher and Zaloga, *British Battle Tanks*, pp. 62–93; Chamberlain and Ellis, *British and American Tanks of World War Two*, pp. 114–137.

35. The sections on Duplex Drive tanks are from Fletcher, *Swimming Shermans*; Zaloga, *US Amphibious Tanks of World War II*; and Stuart Burgess, "The Duplex Drive Tanks of D-Day," http://www.duplexdrivetanks.co.uk, accessed January 2019 to May 2021. I am especially indebted to Stuart Burgess for sharing with me his original research on the design and development of DD tanks.

36. "Unsuccessful": Rowe (ed.), *Summary Technical Report of Division* 12, pp. 165–168; OSRD London Mission, NARA RG 227 NC-138, Box 148.

37. Expedite production: Zaloga, *US Amphibious Tanks of World War II*, p. 15.

Chapter 7: Fight in France

1. Operation Ironclad: Grehan, *Churchill's Secret Invasion*, pp. 48–57.

2. Operation Jubilee: Symonds, *Neptune*, pp. 75–76.

3. LSTs in Operation Torch: MacDermott, *Ships Without Names*, p. 19.

4. My thanks to Douglas Nash, historian at the Marine Corps University Quantico, for guiding me through the operational experience of WWII amphibious assaults using the LST.

5. "Looked like a rehearsal": Symonds, *Neptune*, p. 115. "The first real test": Truscott's memoir is quoted in Tomblin, *With Utmost Spirit*, pp. 163–164.

6. *LST-386*: MacDermott, *Ships Without Names*, p. 112; Stillwell (ed.), *Assault on Normandy*, pp. 165–169.

7. Appreciation of Future Strategy: Butler, *Grand Strategy*, vol. 2, pp. 343–345, 547–551; Bell, *Churchill and Seapower*, pp. 196–197.

8. American troop buildup: Reynolds, *Rich Relations*, pp. 99–103.

9. Eisenhower delays the date of D-Day: Symonds, *Neptune*, p. 181.

10. "All turned upon LSTs": *CSWW*, vol. 5, p. 428. "Destinies of two great empires": Harrison, *The European Theater of Operations*, p. 54. Churchill later

bowdlerized his "destinies" telegram in *Closing the Ring* (*CSWW*, vol. 5, p. 454), but the original has more immediacy.

11. Slapton Sands exercises: Symonds, *Neptune*, pp. 195–221.

12. Out of more than 3,000 English-language books on the D-Day landings, I have found Symonds's *Neptune*, Ambrose's *D-Day*, Keegan's *Six Armies in Normandy*, and Caddick-Adams's *Sand and Steel* to be the most comprehensive and useful works.

13. Taxable, Glimmer, and Moonshine: Twinn, "The Use of Window (Chaff) to Simulate the Approach of a Convoy of Ships"; Latham and Stobbs (eds.), *Pioneers of Radar*, pp. 188–193. Operation Taxable was flown by the celebrated No. 617 RAF "Dambusters" squadron.

14. Warren, *Airborne Operations in World War II*, pp. 32–80; Moran, *American Airborne Pathfinders in World War II*; Preisler, *First to Jump*.

15. Pathfinder success rate: Office of the Chief of Military History, *The Signal Corps*, vol. 3, *The Outcome*, pp. 96–98; Warren, *Airborne Operations in World War II*, pp. 58–60. Frank Lillyman survived the battle and the war, but Robert de LaTour was mortally wounded in battle three weeks after D-Day.

16. DD tanks at Normandy: Fletcher, *Swimming Shermans*, pp. 20–24; Zaloga, *US Amphibious Tanks of World War II*, pp. 21–28 ("saved the day," p. 25).

17. M29 Weasels and DUKWs: Rowe (ed.), *Summary Technical Report of Division 12*, pp. 11–150.

18. Bangalore torpedoes: Coll, Keith, and Rosenthal, *The Corps of Engineers*, pp. 468–470.

19. "Had the misfortune": Stillwell (ed.), *Assault on Normandy*, p. 167.

Chapter 8: Fight in the Hills

1. "I'd hate to have to prove to anyone," "Everyone is talking about them": David Langmuir to Carroll Wilson, July 4, 1944, personal papers of David Langmuuir.

2. Tip-and-run raids: Chamberlin, *Life in Wartime Britain*, pp. 72–74. "The show was Casablanca": David Langmuir to Nancy Langmuir, January 31, 1943, personal papers of David Langmuir.

3. "That is a security violation": Stever, *In War and Peace*, p. 33. "There is a risk": David Langmuir to Nancy Langmuir, November 12, 1943, and "Arch has come to the conclusion," David Langmuir to Charles Langmuir, April 19, 1944, personal papers of David Langmuir.

4. AA guns: Werrell, *Archie, Flak, AAA, and SAM*, pp. 1–69.

5. Radar gun-laying: Getting, *All in a Lifetime*, pp. 101–153 ("draw first blood," p. 133); Getting, "SCR-584 Radar"; Mindell, "Automation's Finest Hour."

6. The complete saga of how the Oerlikon 20 mm gun came to be a major Allied anti-aircraft weapon has never been coherently told; its "biography" is yet to be written. I have pieced together a summary from primary and secondary sources, as follows.

   George Ross, Steuart Mitchell, and smuggling the Oerlikon gun out of Switzerland: Ross, "How the Oerlikon Gun Came to Britain" ("her blonde hair," p. 19); Wylie, "British Smuggling

Operations from Switzerland"; Pawle, *The Secret War*, pp. 62–65; McGeoh, *The Princely Sailor*, pp. 31–32. Mitchell's exploits are fictionalized in A. P. Martin's novel *Spy Trap*.

British manufacture of the Oerlikon gun: Richardson, "Charles Frederick Goodeve," pp. 325–329; Pawle, *The Secret War*, pp. 66–73.

American interest in the Oerlikon gun, Antoine Gazda, and the British Purchasing Commission: Diary of John J. McCloy, 1942, John J. McCloy Papers, Box DY1, Folders 4–7, Archives and Special Collections, Amherst College Library; *Altman v. Gazda*, Appellate Division of the Supreme Court of New York, First Department, 269 App. Div. 654 (February 9, 1945); *Oerlikon Machine Tool Works Buehrle Co. v. United States*, 121 Ct. Cl. 616, 102 F. Supp. 417, 418 (1952); Litigation on Licence to Admiralty for Manufacture of the Oerlikon Anti-Aircraft Cannon and Ammunition, NAUK TS 32/462 to TS 32/467; United States 82nd Congress, House Committee on the Judiciary, Special Subcommittee to Investigate the Department of Justice, House Resolution 95, serial 20, part 2 (1952), pp. 1122–1126; Chinn, *The Machine Gun*, vol. 3, parts 8 and 9, pp. 547–551; Friedman, *Naval Anti-Aircraft Guns*, pp. 175–176, 214–215; Brodie, "Our Ships Strike Back"; Rowland and Boyd, *US Navy Bureau of Ordnance in World War II*, pp. 234–240.

American manufacture of the Oerlikon gun: Rowland and Boyd, *US Navy Bureau of Ordnance in World War II*, pp. 234–247; Borth, *Masters of Mass Production*, pp. 197–199; Nelson, *Arsenal of Democracy*, pp. 260–268; Hyde, *Arsenal of Democracy*, pp. 182–186; McBurney, *World War II Rhode Island*, p. 74.

7. When I was working at the US Navy Office of Naval Research Global in London, I lived in Ruislip and daily passed the train depot sheds, completely unaware of their importance to the history of the Oerlikon gun.

8. "We'll buy that!": Pawle, *The Secret War*, p. 72.

9. Two of many court cases are *Altman v. Gazda*, Appellate Division of the Supreme Court of New York, First Department, 269 App. Div. 654 (February 9, 1945), and *Oerlikon Machine Tool Works Buehrle Co. v. United States*, 121 Ct. Cl. 616, 102 F. Supp. 417, 418 (1952)..

10. McLoy: Diary of John J. McCloy, 1942. Biltmore Hotel: United States 82nd Congress, House Committee on the Judiciary, pp. 1122–1126. The Providence Biltmore Hotel is today the Graduate Providence and still has a Suite 1009, though a 1970s reconstruction reconfigured all the room arrangements.

11. Unlike the Oerlikon gun, the biography of the Bofors 40 mm gun was written in 2013: Gander, *The Bofors Gun*. Other sources for this section: Rowland and Boyd, *US Navy Bureau of Ordnance in World War II*, pp. 221–234; Thomson and Mayo, *The Ordnance Department*, pp. 77–78; Chinn, *The Machine Gun*, vol. 3, parts 8 and 9, pp. 575–580; Borth, *Masters of Mass Production*, pp. 199–203; Friedman, *Naval Anti-Aircraft Guns*, pp. 174–175, 263–266. Kerrison Predictor: Singer, *Singer in World War II*, pp. 7–22; Phelps, *The Tizard Mission*, p. 297; Boyce (ed.), *New Weapons for Air Warfare*, pp. 15, 27, 68.

12. Henry Howard and Axel Wenner-Green, yachtsmen: John, "Southward Ho!"

13. "The demonstration was about as international an affair as it could be": Rowland and Boyd, *US Navy Bureau of Ordnance in World War II*, p. 223.

14. "Jump in the Lake": Gander, *The Bofors Gun*, p. 83. As with the Oerlikon gun, lawsuits between AB Bofors and the US government continued long after the war was over.

15. Kerrison Predictor: Hartcup, *The Challenge of War*, pp. 160–163; Phelps, *The Tizard Mission*, p. 297; Gander, *The Bofors Gun*, pp. 48–50; Singer, *Singer in World War II*, pp. 7–22 ("overwhelming," p. 7); Boyce (ed.), *New Weapons for Air Warfare*, pp. 15, 27, 68.

16. Friedman, *Naval Anti-Aircraft Guns*, pp. 263–266.

17. The proximity fuze has several biographies, which I have drawn extensively from. Jamie Holmes's *12 Seconds of Silence* gives the fullest context for the story, and I also thank him for sharing with me his original research. Ralph Baldwin, who worked on the proximity fuze project, includes in his two books *The Deadly Fuze* and *They Never Knew What Hit Them* many firsthand technical and programmatic details of the fuze. Other sources are Boyce (ed.), *New Weapons for Air Warfare*, pp. 102–163: Burns, "Factors Affecting the Development of the Radio Proximity Fuse"; Brennen, "The Proximity Fuze: Whose Brainchild?" Primary-source documents: Carnegie Institution for Science, Department of Terrestrial Magnetism Archives, "Section T Proximity Fuze Records, 1940–[1999], Bulk 1941–1943" (thanks to Shaun Hardy for his assistance); Johns Hopkins University Applied Physics Labs Archives, "Section T and British Cooperative Work" and "Task A (VT Fuze Development)—British Correspondence July 1943—October 1944" (thanks to Stephen Phillips and Dan Wilt for helping me locate pertinent documents); OSRD London Mission, NARA RG 227 NC-138, Box 137, Section T History of Proximity Fuzes, November 20, 1945.

18. "Please go out and get it for us": Baldwin, *The Deadly Fuze*, p. 18.

19. "Anxious to serve": Holmes, *12 Seconds of Silence*, p. 40. The farm was originally owned by Gardiner Means and Caroline Ware, who were Roosevelt's friends and advisors for his New Deal. It is today Meadowlark Gardens in Vienna, VA.

20. "Became the prime mode of operation": Carnegie Institution for Science, Department of Terrestrial Magnetism Archives, "Section T Proximity Fuze Records," Tuve's Reports Part 2, p. 382.

21. Tuve's running orders: Baldwin, *They Never Knew What Hit Them*, pp. 16–17.

22. British and American exchange reports, correspondence, and bills of lading of samples: Carnegie Institution for Science, Department of Terrestrial Magnetism Archives, "Section T Proximity Fuze Records," Box 9, Folder 1. University of Toronto research: Avery, *The Science of War*, pp. 102–104. "Time is shorter than we think": Holmes, *12 Seconds of Silence*, p. 101.

23. "It is most urgent": Holmes, *12 Seconds of Silence*, p. 114.

24. "Three runs, three hits, and no errors": Holmes, *12 Seconds of Silence*, p. 146.

25. "Continually struggled": Cockcroft, "Memories of Radar Research," p. 337.

26. Pile's "urgent request": OSRD London Mission, NARA RG 227 NC-138, Box 137, Section T History of Proximity Fuzes, November 20, 1945, p. 22.

27. "Bob Hopes": Chamberlin, *Life in Wartime Britain*, p. 73.

28. There are over 100 books (many of which are firsthand accounts) on the V-1 campaign. I have chosen to rely on the excellent summaries in Werrell, *Archie, Flak, AAA, and SAM*; Holmes, *12 Seconds of Silence*; and Baldwin's *The Deadly Fuze* and *They Never Knew What Hit Them*.

29. "Impersonal as a plague": Waugh, *Unconditional Surrender*, p. 184. "Robot bombs": William M. Breazeale (MIT Rad Lab) to Bennett Archambault, July 13, 1944, OSRD London Mission, NARA RG 227 NC-138, Box 143.

30. "With my compliments to OSRD": OSRD London Mission, NARA RG 227 NC-138, Box 137, Section T History of Proximity Fuzes, November 20, 1945, p. 26.
31. "Funny fuze": Baldwin, *The Deadly Fuze*, pp. xxxi, 279. Patton's December 29, 1944, letter is displayed at an exhibit on the proximity fuze at the Johns Hopkins University Applied Physics Laboratory in Laurel, MD.

Chapter 9: Fight in the Fields and in the Streets

1. This section on the Bailey Bridge is primarily based on the biography of its inventor, Donald C. Bailey (Harpur, *A Bridge to Victory*). Further technical explanations are from Bailey, "The Bailey Bridge and Its Developments." Additional sources: Joiner, *One More River to Cross*; Roberts, "The Bailey"; Coll, Keith, and Rosenthal, *The Corps of Engineers*. I extend thanks to the Royal Engineers Historical Society (Séan Scullion, secretary) and especially to Peter Mallett, who shared with me his extensive research for his forthcoming biography of the Bailey Bridge.
2. Jostled in the staff car: Harpur, *A Bridge to Victory*, p. 3. Niedermair's salary: John C. Niedermair Files, Office of the Curator of Models, Naval Surface Warfare Center Carderock Division, Box 4.
3. "Modification of the British Bailey Panel Bridge": Roberts, "The Bailey," p. 185.
4. "Almost a complete failure": Coll, Keith, and Rosenthal, *The Corps of Engineers*, p. 549.
5. "After so magnificent a job": Sydney Gruson, "Churchill Visits Rhine Front Areas," *NYT*, March 7, 1945, pp. 1, 4.
6. Joiner, *One More River to Cross*, p. 678; *CSWW*, vol. 6, pp. 364–365; Alanbrooke, *War Diaries*, p. 678. Thanks to Peter Mallett for his help.
7. Gallipoli: *Statistics of the Military Effort of the British Empire During the Great War*, p. 284.
8. "Became weary . . . hot potato . . . medicos": Bush, *Pieces of the Action*, pp. 44–45.
9. CMR: Baxter, *Scientists Against Time*, pp. 299–393; Stewart, *Organizing Scientific Research for War*, pp. 98–119; Andrus et al. (eds.), *Advances in Military Medicine*, vol. 1, pp. xli–liv.
10. This section on penicillin is based on Wilson, *In Search of Penicillin*; Hobby, *Penicillin*; Lax, *The Mold in Dr. Florey's Coat*; Bud, *Penicillin*; Andrus et al. (eds.), *Advances in Military Medicine*, vol. 2, pp. 717–745; Richards, "Production of Penicillin in the United States." The story of penicillin is fictionalized in Lauren Belfer's 2010 novel, *A Fierce Radiance*. Primary sources for OSRD London Mission's role in developing penicillin: Archambault (ed.), *Report of OSRD Activities*, Part 13, "Military Medicine"; OSRD London Mission, NARA RG 227 NC-138, Box 154, Penicillin Exchange.
11. Warren Weaver in London: Archambault (ed.), *Report of OSRD Activities*, part 2, p. 5; Boyce (ed.), *New Weapons for Air Warfare*, p. 20; Topping, *The Hovde Years*, pp. 136–137; Jonas, *The Circuit Riders*, pp. 301–303.
12. "Some American mold or yeast raiser": Bud, *Penicillin*, p. 33. "More revolutionary than the discovery of sulfonamides": Lax, *The Mold in Dr. Florey's Coat*, p. 159.

13. "Hundreds of two-liter flasks": Hobby, *Penicillin*, p. 75.
14. "A carpet bag salesman": Lax, *The Mold in Dr. Florey's Coat*, p. 186 ("To see that everything possible," p. 197).
15. Reports between Britain and the United States were exchanged: Archambault (ed.), *Report of OSRD Activities*, Part 13, "Military Medicine," p. 6; OSRD London Mission, NARA RG 227 NC-138, Box 154, Penicillin Exchange.
16. Saving 95 percent of all soldiers . . . gas gangrene: Jonas, *The Circuit Riders*, p. 308. Allies had a much higher standard of medical care: Bud, *Penicillin*, p. 57.
17. "I did not invent penicillin": Macfarlane, *Alexander Fleming*, p. 260.

Chapter 10: The New World Steps Forth

1. "First war in human history": Vannevar Bush's foreword to Irvin Stewart's history of OSRD, *Organizing Scientific Research for War*, p. ix.
2. Stever, *In War and Peace*, pp. 42–48 ("In the command car," p. 48).
3. "The four Americans": "Le commandant raconte la libération de la ville."
4. "Don't say anything": Stever, *In War and Peace*, p. 49. "Stever, Arch, and Colonel Bradley arrived": Joyah E. E. Rowland to David Langmuir, August 17, 1944, personal papers of David Langmuir.
5. Wallace Caulfield Jr.: OSRD London Mission, NARA RG 227 NC-138, Box 134, "A Summary of Personnel and Their General Assignments."
6. OSRD Paris offices: Archambault (ed.), *Report of OSRD Activities*, Part 2, pp. 34–39; Stever, *In War and Peace*, pp. 51–53; Bush, *Pieces of the Action*, pp. 111–113.
7. "Danger of the German scientists": Baxter, *Scientists Against Time*, p. 26.
8. I have used the following biographies of the Alsos Mission for this section: Pash, *The Alsos Mission*; Goudsmit, *Alsos*; Kean, *The Bastard Brigade*. Other information from Groves, *Now It Can Be Told*, pp. 185–249; Thiesmeyer and Burchhard, *Combat Scientists*, pp. 160–181; Jones, *Most Secret War*, pp. 478–483; Archambault (ed.), *Report of OSRD Activities*, part 1, pp. 6–7.
9. "Comforts of the civilized world": Pash, *The Alsos Mission*, p. 36. "I was expendable": Goudsmit, *Alsos*, p. 15.
10. "I am glad to have": Goudsmit, *Alsos*, p. 78.
11. "I have been expecting you": quoted by Groves in *Now It Can Be Told*, p. 243.
12. "Greatest German theoretical physicist": Goudsmit, *Alsos*, p. 113 ("The whole German uranium setup," pp. 107–108).
13. Manhattan Project cost: Rhodes, *The Making of the Atomic Bomb*, p. 605. Was worth half the entire German annual economy: Harrison (ed.), *The Economics of World War II*, p. 10.
14. See Rhodes, *The Making of the Atomic Bomb* for the full history of the atomic bomb, which is highly abbreviated here.
15. The Maud Committee, Tube Alloys program, and subsequent British/Canadian participation in the Manhattan Project are extensively covered in many works dedicated to these subjects, some of which I have used for this section: Gowing, *Britain and Atomic Energy* ("Inform Cockcroft," p. 45); Ruane, *Churchill and the Bomb in War*

and Cold War; Farmelo, *Churchill's Bomb*; Szasz, *British Scientists and the Manhattan Project*. Additional sources: Rhodes, *The Making of the Atomic Bomb*; Groves, *Now It Can Be Told*; Jones, *Manhattan*; Avery, *The Science of War*.

16. Tizard Mission and the atomic bomb: Zimmerman, *Top Secret Exchange*, pp. 149–153.
17. "Uranium power prospects": Goldberg, "Inventing a Climate of Opinion," p. 436.
18. "We must duplicate it at once": Topping, *The Hovde Years*, p. 163.
19. "We have now reached the conclusion": Gowing, *Britain and Atomic Energy*, pp. 76–77.
20. "The British conclusions . . . complete interchange": Rhodes, *The Making of the Atomic Bomb*, pp. 377–378. "We should soon correspond": *CRCC*, vol. 1, p. 249. "I need not assure you": *CRCC*, vol. 1, p. 279.
21. OSRD London Mission, NARA RG 227 NC-138, Box 140, Bennett Archambault, "Nickel Powder to Be Sent to Dr. P[aul] D[yer] Merica of International Nickel Company," August 14, 1942.
22. 90 percent of the work: Gowing, *Britain and Atomic Energy*, p. 149 ("if necessary, alone," p. 157).
23. "No instructions whatever": Bush, *Pieces of the Action*, p. 282.
24. "Punctilious": Groves, *Now It Can Be Told*, p. 144.
25. Reverse Lend-Lease was the provision by Britain and other Allies of in-kind services, matériel, and equipment (e.g., housing, transportation, aircraft parts, combat bridges, food and petroleum) to American forces at home and overseas.
26. "I stood with my back to the gadget": Gowing, *Britain and Atomic Energy*, pp. 441–442.
27. See Campbell, *The Silverplate Bombers* for the British equipment carried by the B-29s configured to carry atomic bombs.
28. "Britain's scientific mobilization for war": Archambault (ed.), *Report of OSRD Activities*, Part 1, p. 9. "The greatest credit": Edward Bowles to Vannevar Bush, June 22, 1951, Vannevar Bush papers, Collection MSS14498, Box 13, Library of Congress, Washington, DC. Thanks to Jamie Holmes for locating this.

Epilogue: Endless Frontiers

1. David Langmuir to Bennett Archambault, April 24, 1945, OSRD London Mission, NARA RG 227 NC-138, Box 147.
2. "A unique experiment": Zachary, *Endless Frontier*, p. 224. England, "Dr. Bush Writes a Report," makes it clear that Roosevelt himself, not Bush, wrote the "new frontiers of the mind" letter.
3. Files pertaining to the closing of OSRD London Mission, BBRL, and ABL-15, as well as the visit to Germany, are in OSRD London Mission, NARA RG 227 NC-138, Boxes 130, 132, 133, and 181.
4. "This is the fourth": Bennett Archambault to Vannevar Bush, September 28, 1945, personal papers of Bennett Archambault. Writing a history of OSRD London Mission was mentioned in numerous papers and letters in personal papers of David Langmuir.
5. BBC's *This Is Your Life*: personal communication from Arthur C. Clarke to me, September 3, 1994.

6. On the development of jet engines, see Giffard, *Making Jet Engines in World War II*.
7. "In collaboration went ahead faster": Oral history interview with Vannevar Bush, 1964, Massachusetts Institute of Technology Libraries, Department of Distinctive Collections, MC-0143, reel 11-A, p. 701-A.
8. Edgerton, *Warfare State*, pp. 231–237.
9. Ball, "Military Nuclear Relations Between the United States and Great Britain." The word "nuclear" began replacing "atomic" after the first hydrogen (thermonuclear) bomb was exploded in 1951.
10. R&D economic numbers based on Edgerton, *Science, Technology and the British Industrial "Decline,"* pp. 49, 59, 60.
11. On the role of government in American technology industries, see Weiss, *America Inc.?*
12. Edgerton, *Science, Technology and the British Industrial "Decline,"* pp. 38, 43.
13. Bush, *Science* ("basic research," p. 17).
14. History of ONR: Sapolsky, *Science and the Navy*; Buderi, *Naval Innovation for the 21st Century*. History of NSF: Bush, *Science*, pp. iii–x.
15. On large-scale projects, see Hughes, *Rescuing Prometheus*.

BIBLIOGRAPHY

Commonly Used Abbreviations

CRCC: Winston Churchill and Franklin D. Roosevelt. *Churchill and Roosevelt: The Complete Correspondence*. 3 vols. Edited by Warren F. Kimball. Princeton: Princeton University Press, 1984.

CSWW: Winston Churchill, *The Second World War*. 6 vols. London: Cassell & Co., 1948–1954.

CWC: Winston Churchill, *The World Crisis*. 5 vols. London: Thornton Butterworth Ltd., 1923–1931.

CWP: Winston Churchill, *The Churchill War Papers*. 3 vols. Edited by Martin Gilbert. New York: W. W. Norton, 1993–2001.

GPO: United States Government Printing Office, Washington, DC.

HMSO: Her/His Majesty's Stationery Office, London.

IWM: Imperial War Museums, London.

NARA: National Archives and Records Administration, College Park, MD.

NAUK: National Archives of the United Kingdom, Richmond.

NHHC: Naval History and Heritage Command, Washington, DC.

NMM: National Maritime Museum, Caird Library and Archive, Greenwich, UK

NDRC: National Defense Research Committee, Washington, DC.

NYT: *New York Times*.

OSRD: Office of Scientific Research and Development, Washington, DC.

Rad Lab: MIT Radiation Laboratory, Cambridge, MA.

Archival Sources

Altman v. Gazda, Apellate Division of the Supreme Court of New York, First Department, 269 App. Div. 654 (February 9, 1945).

Arcadia Conference: December 1941–January 1942, Proceeding of the American-British Joint Chiefs of Staff Conference, Washington, DC., https://www.jcs.mil/Portals/36/Documents/History/WWII/Arcadia3.pdf.

Archambault, Bennett (ed.). *Report of OSRD Activities in the European Theater During the Period March 1941 Through July 1945* (April 15, 1946). NARA RG 227 NC-138 Entry 176, Box 128A.

Archambault, Michele (daughter of Bennett Archambault). Personal papers of Bennett Archambault.

Bowles, Edward L. Rand History Project Interview of Edward L. Bowles by Martin Collins and Michael Dennis, July 14, 1987. Box 10, Folder 9, National Air and Space Museum Archives, Chantilly, VA. https://sova.si.edu/details/NASM.1999.0037#ref128.

Bowen, Edward G. Papers of Edward G. Bowen, Churchill Archives Centre, Churchill College, Cambridge, UK.

British War Cabinet and Cabinet: Chiefs of Staff Committee: Memoranda, NAUK CAB 80.

British Central Scientific Office Its Successor the British Commonwealth Scientific Office: Registered Files, NAUK AVIA 42.

Burgess, Stuart. *Duplex Drive Tanks of D-Day*, http://www.duplexdrivetanks.co.uk/.

Bush, Vannevar. Oral history interview with Vannevar Bush, 1964. Massachusetts Institute of Technology Libraries, Department of Distinctive Collections, MC-0143, Cambridge, MA.

Bush, Vannevar. Vannevar Bush papers, Collection MSS14498. Library of Congress, Washington, DC.

Carnegie Institution for Science. Administration Archives. Washington, DC.

Carnegie Institution for Science. Department of Terrestrial Magnetism Archives. Washington, DC.

"Carroll L. Wilson 1910–1983: Report of the Carroll L. Wilson Awards Committee." MIT Libraries, Institute Archives and Special Collections, T171.M4218.W553.1987, Cambridge, MA.

Central Decimal Correspondence Files, Engineering Division, Material Command, Wright-Patterson Air Force Base (The Sarah Clark Files). NARA RG 342.

Cochrane, Edward Lull. "Serial 1448—Great Britain Ship Design, 7 January 1941." NARA RG 19 UD1017 R 470/27/35/01, Box 5 Secret Correspondence 1915–1942.

Conant, James B. Papers of James Bryant Conant, 1862–1987. Cambridge, MA: Harvard University Archives UAI 15.898.

Dayton Codebreakers, https://daytoncodebreakers.org/.

D'Eyncourt, Eustace Henry William Tennyson. Papers and correspondence, 1898–1939. NMM DEY.

Dorling, James W. S. *History of British Admiralty Delegation to USA*, NAUK ADM 199/1236 (uneven pagination), 1945.

Eisenhower, Dwight D. and Harry D. Butcher. *Personal and Official Diary of Lieut. General Dwight D. Eisenhower*. Abilene, KS: Eisenhower Presidential Library, Museum & Boyhood Home, https://www.eisenhowerlibrary.gov/sites/default/files/file/DDE%20Diary%20JanJuly%201942.pdf.

Elliott, Harold F. Transcript of Interview with Harold F. Elliott (PER 239.72, Tape 8, conducted by Irv Rasmussen, July 1968). Perham Collection of Early Electronics: Sound Recordings, 2003-38. Santa Fe, NM: History San Jose Research Library & Archives, http://perhamcollection.historysanjose.org/people-companies/harold-elliott/.

Foreign Inquiries for Production of Munitions reports. President Franklin D. Roosevelt's Office Files, 1933–1945 Microfilm reel 35 / 0204. Franklin D. Roosevelt Library and Museum, Hyde Park, NY.

Fowler, Charles A., and Kathryn Fowler. Oral history interview with Kathryn and Charles "Bert" Fowler, 1991. Institute of Electrical and Electronics Engineers (IEEE) History Center, Hoboken NJ, https://ethw.org/Oral-History:Kathryn_and_Charles_Fowler.

Goodall, Stanley V. Goodall Papers: Diaries; 1932–1946, British Library, London: Western Manuscripts, ADD MS 52785–52791.

Hansard, *House of Commons Debates / House of Lords Debates*, https://hansard.parliam ent.uk/.

Hill, Archibald Vivian. *Memories and Reflections*. Papers of Professor A. V. Hill, Churchill Archives Centre, Churchill College, Cambridge, UK.

History of the Anti-submarine Measures Division of the Tenth Fleet. Manuscript, United States Navy. Fort Leavenworth, KS: US Army Command and General Staff College, Ike Skelton Combined Arms Research Library Digital Library, https://cgsc.conten tdm.oclc.org/digital/collection/p4013coll8/id/1999.

Hussey Thomas A. Pontoon causeways, Hussey testimony given Monday, 12th March 1951. NAUK T 166/126/3 Royal Commission on Awards to Inventors.

Johns Hopkins University Applied Physics Labs. Archives. Laurel, MD.

Johnston, Lawrence. Oral history interview with Lawrence Johnston, 1991. Institute of Electrical and Electronics Engineers (IEEE) History Center, Hoboken, NJ, https://ethw.org/Oral-History:Lawrence_Johnston.

Jones, Reginald V. "Churchill as I Knew Him." Enid and R. Crosby Kemper Lecture, 1992. National Churchill Museum, Fulton, MO, https://www.nationalchurchillmus eum.org/kemper-lecture-jones.html.

Kuhn, Thomas S. Thomas S. Kuhn papers. Massachusetts Institute of Technology Libraries, Department of Distinctive Collections, MC-0240, Cambridge, MA.

Langmuir, Jean (daughter of David Langmuir). Personal papers of David Langmuir.

Litigation on Licence to Admiralty for Manufacture of the Oerlikon Anti-Aircraft Cannon and Ammunition, NAUK TS 32/462 to TS 32/467.

Lovell, Bernard. "The Americans' Reaction to the Magnetron." *Web of Stories* 2007, https://www.webofstories.com/play/bernard.lovell/31.

Malvern Radar and Technology History Society, https://mraths.org.uk/.

McLoy, John J. *Diary of John J. McCloy, 1942* in John J. McCloy Papers (Box DY1, folders 4- 7). Amherst, MA: Archives and Special Collections, Amherst College Library.

Measuring Worth, https://www.measuringworth.com/.

Niedermair, John C. Niedermair Files, 17 boxes, Bethesda, MD: Office of the Curator of Models, Naval Surface Warfare Center Carderock Division (NSWC-CD).

Purbeck Radar Museum Trust, http://www.purbeckradar.org.uk.

Robinson Denis M. Interview by Michael Wolff on 1978 May 23, Niels Bohr Library & Archives. College Park, MD: American Institute of Physics, www.aip.org/history-programs/niels-bohr-library/oral-histories/4845.

Roser, Max and Mohamed Nagdy. "Military Spending." OurWorldInData.org, https://ourworldindata.org/military-spending.

Trump, John G. *A War Diary, 1944–45.* Massachusetts Institute of Technology Libraries, Department of Distinctive Collections, D810S2T78_JGT_1973, Cambridge, MA.

"U-845 Sunk March 10, 1944: Report on the Interrogation of Survivors," C.B. 04051 (102), Naval Intelligence Division, Admiralty, May 1944, http://www.uboatarchive. net/Int/U-845INT.htm.

United States 82nd Congress. House Committee on the Judiciary, Special Subcommittee to Investigate the Department of Justice, House Resolution 95, serial 20 part 2. Washington, DC: GPO, 1952.

Wheeler, Harold. Oral history interview with Harold Wheeler, 1991. Institute of Electrical and Electronics Engineers (IEEE) History Center, Hoboken NJ, https:// ethw.org/Oral-History:Harold_Wheeler_(1991).

Wilson, Carroll Louis. Carroll L. Wilson papers, 1926–1983. Massachusetts Institute of Technology Libraries, Department of Distinctive Collections, MC-0029, Cambridge, MA.

Primary Sources

Alanbrooke, Alan Brooke. *War Diaries, 1939–1945.* Edited by Alex Danchev and Daniel Todman. London: Phoenix Press, 2002.

Alvarez, Luis W. *Alvarez: Adventures of a Physicist.* New York: Basic Books, 1987.

Arnold, Henry Harley. *Global Mission.* New York: Harper, 1949.

Atwood, John Leland. "An Engineer's Perspective on the Mustang." *Flight Journal,* June 1999, pp. 113–114.

Attwood, Stephen S (ed.). *Summary Technical Report of Division 14 [Radar], National Defense Research Committee (NDRC).* 3 vols. Washington, DC: NDRC, 1946.

Bailey, Donald C., Robert A. Foulds, and Rodman Digby-Smith. "The Bailey Bridge and Its Developments." In *The Civil Engineer in War: A Symposium of Papers on Wartime Engineering Problems,* pp. 373–410. London: Institution of Civil Engineers, 1948.

Baker, Rowland. "Ships of the Invasion Fleet." *Transactions of the Institution of Naval Architects* 88 (1947), pp. 50–72.

Baker, Rowland. "Notes on the Development of Landing Craft." *Transactions of the Institution of Naval Architects* 88 (1947), pp. 218–258.

Billard, Jean-Yves, François Grinnaert, Isabelle Delumeau, Pierre Vonier, Paul Creismeas, Jean-François Leguen, and Larrie D. Ferreiro. "Forensic Study of *Bouvet* Capsizing." In *Proceedings of the 14th International Ship Stability Workshop,* Kuala Lumpur, 2014.

Billotte, Pierre. *Le temps des armes.* Paris: Plon, 1972.

Blackett, Patrick M. S. *Studies of War: Nuclear and Conventional.* New York: Hill and Wang, 1962.

Bowden, Bertram Vivian. "The Story of IFF (Identification Friend or Foe)." *IEE Proceedings,* 132/A/6 (October 1985), pp. 435–437.

Bowen, Edward G. *Radar Days.* Bristol: Adam Hilger, 1987.

Bowen, Edward G. "The Tizard Mission to the USA and Canada." In Russell W. Burns (ed.), *Radar Development to 1945,* pp. 296–307. London: Peter Peregrinus, 1988.

British Information Services. *Women's War Work in Britain*. New York: British Information Services, Information Division, 1943.

Budget of the United States Government for the Fiscal Year Ending June 30, 1943. Washington, DC: GPO, 1942.

Bush, Vannevar. *Pieces of the Action*. New York: William Morrow and Co., 1970.

Bush, Vannevar. *Science: The Endless Frontier: 75th Anniversary Edition*. Washington, DC: National Science Foundation, 2020.

Chinn, Howard A. (ed.). *Summary Technical Report of Division 15 [Radar Countermeasures], National Defense Research Committee (NDRC)*. Washington, DC: NDRC, 1946.

Churchill, Winston. *A Roving Commission: My Early Life*. New York: Charles Scribner's Sons. 1930.

Clarke, Arthur C. *Ascent to Orbit: A Scientific Autobiography*. New York: John Wiley & Sons, 1984.

Clarke, Arthur C. "Extra-Terrestrial Relays: Can Rocket Stations Give World-Wide Radio Coverage?" *Wireless World Radio and Electronics* 51/10 (October 1945), pp. 305–308.

Clarke, Arthur C. *Glide Path*. New York: Harcourt, Brace & World, 1963.

Clawson, Augusta Homes. *Shipyard Diary of a Woman Welder*. New York: Penguin Books, 1944.

Cockburn, Robert. "The Radio War." *IEEE Proceedings*, 132/A/6 (October 1985), pp. 423–434.

Cockcroft, John D. "Memories of Radar Research." *IEEE Proceedings*, 132/A/6 (October 1985), pp. 327–339.

Coleman, John S. (ed.). *A Survey of Subsurface Warfare in World War II*. Washington, D.C.: Office of Scientific Research and Development, National Defense Research Committee, Division 6, 1946.

Compton, Arthur Holly. "Physics and the Future." *Nature* 148 (August 30, 1941), pp. 236–237.

Conant, James B. *My Several Lives: Memoirs of a Social Inventor*. New York: Harper & Row, 1970.

Dettinger, David, and Henry L. Bachman (eds.). *Harold A. Wheeler's Legacy: Recollections of Wheeler Laboratories During the Heyday of Radar*. New York: Marconi Advanced Systems Division, 1999.

D'Eyncourt, Eustace Henry William Tennyson. *A Shipbuilder's Yarn: The Record of a Naval Constructor*. London: Hutchinson & Co., 1948.

Doenitz, Karl. *Memoirs: Ten Years and Twenty Days*. Annapolis, MD: Naval Institute Press, 2012.

Dunn, Halbert L. (ed.). *Vital Statistics of the United States 1944, Part 1*. Washington, DC: GPO, 1946.

Eden, Anthony. *The Eden Memoirs, Volume 2: The Reckoning*. London: Cassell, 1965.

Fifteenth Air Force. *Radar Counter Measures: Bombing with Chaff*. Maxwell Air Force Base, AL: Air Force Historical Research Agency, Air Force History Index, Roll A5771 (frames 1914–1924), 1945.

Fisk, James B., Homer D. Hagstrum, and Paul L. Hartman. "The Magnetron as a Generator of Centimeter Waves." *The Bell System Technical Journal* 25/2 (April 1946), pp. 167–349.

Forester, C. S. *The Good Shepherd*. Boston: Little, Brown and Co., 1955.

Fowler, Charles A. "Rad Lab, Luie Alvarez, and the Development of the GCA Radar Landing System: A Memoir." *IEEE Aerospace and Electronic Systems Magazine* 23/5 (May 2008), pp. A1–A16.

FTP 217: U.S. Radar: Operational Characteristics of Radar Classified by Tactical Application. Washington, DC: Joint Chiefs of Staff, 1943.

Getting, Ivan A. *All in a Lifetime: Science in the Defense of Democracy*. New York: Vantage Press, 1989.

Getting, Ivan A. "SCR-584 Radar and the Mark 56 Naval Gun Fire Control System." *IEEE Transactions on Aerospace and Electronic Systems* 11 (September 1975), pp. 922–936.

Goudsmit, Samuel A. *Alsos*. Los Angeles: Tomash, 1983.

Groves, Leslie R. *Now It Can Be Told: The Story of the Manhattan Project*. New York: Harper & Row, 1962.

Hanbury Brown, Robert. *Boffin: A Personal Story of the Early Days of Radar, Radio Astronomy and Quantum Optics*. Bristol, UK: Adam Hilger, 1991.

Henrey, Mrs. Robert (Madeleine Mathilde). *The Incredible City*. London: J. M. Dent & Sons Ltd., 1944.

Herrick, John. *Subsurface Warfare: The History of Division 6, NDRC*. Washington, DC: Department of Defense, Research and Development Board, 1951.

History of Convoy and Routing. United States Naval Administration in World War II, vol. 11. Washington, DC: Navy Department, 1945.

Hope, Bob. *I Never Left Home*. New York: Simon and Schuster, 1944.

Horkey, Edward. "The P-51: The Real Story." *American Aviation Historical Society Journal* 41/3 (Fall 1996), pp. 178–189.

Johnston, Lawrence. "The War Years." In Luis W. Alvarez, *Discovering Alvarez: Selected Works of Luis W. Alvarez with Commentary by His Students and Colleagues*, pp. 55–76. Edited by William Peter Trower. Chicago: University of Chicago Press, 1987.

Jolley, Neal A. "Invention of Ground Control Approach Radar at the MIT Radiation Laboratories." *IEEE Aerospace and Electronic Systems Magazine* 8/5 (May 1993), p. 57.

John, Solly. "Southward Ho!" *Motor Boating* (January 1944), p. 89.

Jones, Reginald V. *Most Secret War: British Scientific Intelligence, 1939–1945*. London: Hamilton, 1978. (Published in the United States under the title *The Wizard War*.)

Kelly, Mervin J. "Radar and Bell Laboratories." *Bell Telephone Magazine*, Winter 1945/1946, pp. 221–255.

Knox, Dudley Wright. *The Eclipse of American Sea Power*. New York: American Army & Navy Journal, 1922.

Kranzberg, Melvin. "Kranzberg's Laws." *Technology and Culture* 27/3 (July 1986), pp. 544–560.

Lack, Frederick R. "Radar and Western Electric." *Bell Telephone Magazine*, Winter 1945/1946, pp. 283–294.

Land, Emory Scott. *Winning the War with Ships: Land, Sea and Air—Mostly Land*. New York: Robert M. McBride Co., 1958.

Latham, Colin, and Anne Stobbs (eds.). *Pioneers of Radar*. Thrupp, Stroud, Gloucestershire: Alan Sutton Publishing Ltd., 1996.

"Le commandant raconte la libération de la ville: François Tassel, alias, le commandant Gilbert, a vécu de l'intérieur la libération de Lannion, le 11 août 1944." *Ouest-France, Info Lannion-Perros*, March 11, 2009, p. 1.

Lovell, Bernard. "The Cavity Magnetron in World War II: Was the Secrecy Justified?" *Notes and Records of the Royal Society of London* 58/3 (September 2004), pp. 283–294.

Lovell, Bernard. *Echoes of War: The Story of H2S Radar*. Bristol, UK: Adam Hilger, 1991.

Macrae, Stuart. *Winston Churchill's Toyshop: The Inside Story of Military Intelligence (Research)*. Stroud, UK: Amberley, 2010.

Martin, A. P. *Spy Trap: Spymaster Pym Book 2*. Amazon CreateSpace, 2017.

Maund, Loben E. H. *Assault from the Sea*. London: Methuen, 1949.

Megaw, Eric C. S. "The High-Power Pulsed Magnetron: A Review of Early Developments." *Journal of the Institution of Electrical Engineers—Part IIIA: Radiolocation* 93/5 (1946), pp. 977–984.

Monnet, Jean. *Memoirs*. Translated by Richard Mayne. Garden City, NY: Doubleday and Co., 1978.

Morse, Philip M. *In at the Beginnings: A Physicist's Life*. Cambridge, MA: MIT Press, 1977.

Mowry, George E. *Landing Craft and the War Production Board, April 1942 to May 1944*. Washington, DC: US Civilian Production Administration, Bureau of Demobilization, 1946.

Niedermair, John C. *Reminiscences of John C. Niedermair (Naval Architect—Bureau of Ships)*. Interviewed by John T. Mason Jr. Annapolis, MD: Naval Institute Press, 1978.

Pash, Boris T. *The Alsos Mission*. New York: Award House, 1969.

Philco. *Radar on Wings*. Philadelphia: Philco Corporation, 1945.

Pollard, Ernest C. *Radiation: One Story of the MIT Radiation Laboratory*. Durham, NC: Woodburn Press, 1982.

Rad Lab. *Five Years at the Radiation Laboratory*. Cambridge, MA: MIT, 1947.

"Radar Production: Wartime Triumph of the Industry." *Wireless World Radio and Electronics* 51/10 (October 1945), pp. 290–295.

Richards, Alfred Newton. "Production of Penicillin in the United States (1941–1946)." *Nature* 201/4918 (February 1, 1964), pp. 441–445.

Ridenour, Louis N. (ed.). Massachusetts Institute of Technology Radiation Laboratory Series. 28 vols. New York: McGraw-Hill, 1947–1953.

Roberts, Arthur (ed.). *Radar Beacons*. Massachusetts Institute of Technology Radiation Laboratory Series, vol. 3. New York: McGraw-Hill, 1947.

Robinson, Denis M. "British Microwave Radar 1939–41." *Proceedings of the American Philosophical Society*, 127/1 (February 1983), pp. 26–31.

Ross, George. "How the Oerlikon Gun Came to Britain." *Naval Review* 69/1 (1954), pp. 19–22.

Rowe, A. P. *One Story of Radar*. Cambridge, UK: Cambridge University Press, 1948.

Rowe, Hartley (ed.). *Summary Technical Report of Division 12 [Transportation Equipment], National Defense Research Committee (NDRC)*. Washington, DC: NDRC, 1946.

Singer Manufacturing Company. *Singer in World War II, 1939–1945*. New York: Singer, 1946.

Soames, Mary. *A Daughter's Tale: The Memoir of Winston Churchill's Youngest Child.* New York: Random House, 2013.

Sorensen, Charles E. *My Forty Years with Ford.* New York: Collier Books, 1962.

Statistics of the Military Effort of the British Empire During the Great War, 1914–1920. London: HMSO, 1922.

Sternhell, Charles M., and Alan M. Thorndike (eds.). *A Summary of Antisubmarine Warfare Operations in World War II.* Washington, DC: NDRC, 1946.

Stever, Horton Guyford. *In War and Peace: My Life in Science and Technology.* Washington, DC: Joseph Henry Press, 2002.

Stillwell, Paul (ed.). *Assault on Normandy: First-Person Accounts from the Sea Services.* Annapolis, MD: Naval Institute Press, 1994.

Suits, Chauncey G., George R. Harrison, and Louis Jordan. *Applied Physics: Electronics, Optics, Metallurgy.* Science in World War II—Office of Scientific Research and Development. Boston: Atlantic Monthly/Little, Brown and Co., 1948.

Thompson, Robert Cyril, and Harry Hunter. "The British Merchant Shipbuilding Programme in North America, 1940–42." *Transactions of the North-East Coast Institution of Engineers and Shipbuilders* 59 (1943), pp. 61–92, D47–D64.

Turner, Richard E. *Mustang Pilot.* London: William Kimber, 1970.

The United States Strategic Bombing Survey: Summary Report (European War). Washington, DC: GPO, 1945.

United States Bureau of the Census. *Government Employment,* vol. 5, no. 5, for third quarter 1944 (March 1945).

United States Bureau of the Census. *Historical Statistics of the United States, Colonial Times to 1970.* 2 vols. Washington, DC: GPO, 1975.

United States Civilian Production Administration. *Industrial Mobilization for War; History of the War Production Board and Predecessor Agencies, 1940–1945.* New York: Greenwood Press, 1969.

War Manpower Commission, *Manpower Review* 10/3 (March 1943).

Watson-Watt, Robert. "The Natural History of the Boffin." *Proceedings of the Institute of Radio Engineers* 41/12 (December 1953), p. 1699.

Watson-Watt, Robert. *Three Steps to Victory: A Personal Account by Radar's Greatest Pioneer.* London: Odhams Press, 1957.

Watson-Watt, Robert. *The Pulse of Radar: The Autobiography of Sir Robert Watson-Watt.* New York: Dial Press, 1959.

Waugh, Evelyn. *Unconditional Surrender.* London: Chapman & Hall, 1961.

Webster, Charles, and Noble Frankland. *The Strategic Air Offensive Against Germany 1939–1945.* 4 vols. London: HMSO, 1961.

Wheeler, Harold Alden. *Hazeltine Corporation in World War II.* Ventura, CA: Pathfinder Publishing of California, 1993.

Whitehead, James Rennie. "1973 Pioneer Award." *IEEE Transactions on Aerospace and Electronic Systems* 9/5 (September 1973), pp. 788–797.

Whitehead, James Rennie. "Memoirs of a Boffin." In Colin Latham and Anne Stobbs (eds.), *Pioneers of Radar,* pp. 54–62. Thrupp, Stroud, Gloucestershire: Alan Sutton Publishing Ltd., 1996.

Wilson, Woodrow. *Address of the President of the United States, Delivered at a Joint Session of the Two Houses of Congress, February 11, 1918*. Washington, DC: GPO, 1918.

Woollcott, Alexander. *The Letters of Alexander Woollcott*. Edited by Beatrice Bakrow and Joseph Hennessey. New York: Viking Press, 1944.

Secondary Sources

Alexander, Martin S., and William J. Philpott (eds.). *Anglo-French Defence Relations Between the Wars*. Basingstoke, UK: Palgrave Macmillan, 2002.

Alic, John A. *Trillions for Military Technology: How the Pentagon Innovates and Why It Costs So Much*. New York: Palgrave Macmillan, 2007.

Aldrich, Nelson W. *American Hero: The True Story of Tommy Hitchcock: Sports Star, War Hero, and Champion of the War-Winning P-51 Mustang*. Guildford, CT: Lyons Press, 2016.

Allen, Roy George Douglas. "Mutual Aid Between the U.S. and the British Empire, 1941–45." *Journal of the Royal Statistical Society* 109/3 (1946), pp. 243–277.

Allison, David K. *New Eye for the Navy: The Origin of Radar at the Naval Research Laboratory*. Washington, DC: Naval Research Laboratory, 1981.

Allison, David K., and Larrie D. Ferreiro (eds.). *The American Revolution: A World War*. Washington, DC: Smithsonian Books, 2019.

Ambrose, Stephen E. *D-Day, June 6, 1944: The Climactic Battle of World War II*. New York: Simon & Schuster, 1994.

Anderson, Jr., John D. *The Grand Designers: The Evolution of the Airplane in the 20th Century*. Cambridge, UK: Cambridge University Press, 2018.

Andrus, Edwin Cowles, et al. (eds.). *Advances in Military Medicine*. 2 vols. Boston: Little, Brown and Co., 1948.

Auld, George P. "The British War Debt: Retrospect and Prospect." *Foreign Affairs* 16/4 (July 1938), pp. 640–650.

Avery, Donald H. *The Science of War: Canadian Scientists and Allied Military Technology during the Second World War*. Toronto: University of Toronto Press, 1998.

Baer, George W. *One Hundred Years of Sea Power: The U.S. Navy, 1890–1990*. Stanford, CA: Stanford University Press, 1998.

Bailey, Gavin J. *The Arsenal of Democracy: Aircraft Supply and the Anglo-American Alliance, 1938–1942*. Edinburgh: Edinburgh University Press, 2013.

Baldwin, Ralph B. *The Deadly Fuze: The Secret Weapon of World War II*. London: Jane's Publishing Co., 1980.

Baldwin, Ralph B. *They Never Knew What Hit Them: The Story of the Best Kept Secret of World War II*. Naples, FL: Reynier Press, 1999.

Ball, Simon J. "Military Nuclear Relations Between the United States and Great Britain Under the Terms of the McMahon Act, 1946–1958." *The Historical Journal* 38/2 (June 1995), pp. 439–454.

Barnett, Correlli. *The Pride and the Fall: The Dream and Illusion of Britain as a Great Nation*. New York: Free Press, 1986.

Barnett, Correlli. *Engage the Enemy More Closely: The Royal Navy in the Second World War.* New York: W. W. Norton, 1991.

Barr, Niall. *Yanks and Limeys: Alliance Warfare in the Second World War.* London: Jonathan Cape, 2019. (Originally published as *Eisenhower's Armies: The American-British Alliance During World War II.* New York: Pegasus Books, 2015.)

Baxter, Colin F. *The Secret History of RDX: The Super-Explosive That Helped Win World War II.* Lexington: University Press of Kentucky, 2018.

Baxter, James Phinney. *Scientists Against Time.* Boston: Little, Brown and Co., 1946.

Beasley, Norman. *Knudsen: A Biography.* New York, McGraw-Hill, 1947.

Bell, Christopher. *The Royal Navy, Seapower and Strategy Between the Wars.* London: Palgrave Macmillan, 2000.

Bell, Christopher. *Churchill and Seapower.* Oxford: Oxford University Press, 2013.

Beyerchen, Alan. "From Radio to Radar: Interwar Military Adaptation to Technological Change in Germany, the United Kingdom, and the United States." In Williamson Murray and Allan R. Millett (eds.), *Military Innovation in the Interwar Period*, pp. 265–299. Cambridge, UK: Cambridge University Press, 1996.

Birch, David. *Rolls-Royce and the Mustang.* Derby, UK: Rolls-Royce Heritage Trust, 1987.

Blazich, Frank A. Jr. "Bridging the Gap from Ship to Shore." *Naval History* 35/4 (August 2021), pp. 34–41.

Blue, Bruce Alexander. "The Ram Cruiser Tank: An Ambitious Failure." MA thesis, Concordia University, Montreal, 2010.

Borth, Christy. *Masters of Mass Production.* Indianapolis: Bobbs-Merrill Co., 1945.

Bottelier, Thomas. "Associated Powers: Britain, France, the United States and the Defence of World Order, 1931–1943." PhD dissertation, King's College London, 2018.

Bourneuf, Gus Jr. *Workhorse of the Fleet: A History of the Design and Experiences of the Liberty Ships Built by American Shipbuilders During WWII.* Houston: American Bureau of Shipping, 2008.

Boyce, Joseph (ed). *New Weapons for Air Warfare: Fire-Control Equipment, Proximity Fuzes, and Guided Missiles.* Boston: Little, Brown and Co., 1947.

Boyer, George R. and Timothy J. Hatton, "New Estimates of British Unemployment, 1870–1913." *Journal of Economic History* 62/3 (2002), pp. 643–675.

Brennen, James W. "The Proximity Fuze: Whose Brainchild?" *United States Naval Institute Proceedings* 94/9 (1968), pp. 73–78.

Brodie, Bernard. "Our Ships Strike Back." *The Virginia Quarterly Review* 21/2 (Spring 1945), pp. 186–206.

Brown, David K. *A Century of Naval Construction: The History of the Royal Corps of Naval Constructors.* London: Conway Maritime Press, 1983.

Brown, David K. "Sir Rowland Baker, RCNC." In John Roberts (ed.), *Warship 1995*, pp. 141–154. London: Conway Maritime Press, 1995.

Brown, John K. "Design Plans, Working Drawings, National Styles: Engineering Practice in Great Britain and the United States, 1775–1945." *Technology and Culture* 41/2 (April 2000), pp. 195–238.

Brown, Louis. *Technical and Military Imperatives: A Radar History of World War II.* Philadelphia: Institute of Physics Publishing, 1999.

Bud, Robert. *Penicillin: Triumph and Tragedy.* Oxford: Oxford University Press, 2007.

Buderi, Robert. *The Invention That Changed the World: How a Small Group of Radar Pioneers Won the Second World War and Launched a Technological Revolution.* New York: Simon & Schuster, 1996.

Buderi, Robert. *Naval Innovation for the 21st Century: The Office of Naval Research Since the End of the Cold War.* Annapolis, MD: Naval Institute Press, 2013.

Budiansky, Stephen. *Battle of Wits: The Complete Story of Codebreaking in World War II.* New York: The Free Press, 2000.

Budiansky, Stephen. *Blackett's War: The Men Who Defeated the Nazi U-boats and Brought Science to the Art of Warfare.* New York: Alfred A. Knopf, 2013.

Burchard, John E. *Rockets, Guns and Targets.* Boston: Little, Brown and Co., 1948.

Burns, Russell W. (ed.). *Radar Development to 1945.* London: Peter Peregrinus, 1988.

Burns, Russell W. "Factors Affecting the Development of the Radio Proximity Fuse 1940–1944." *IEEE Proceedings—Science, Measurement and Technology* 143/1 (January 1996), pp. 1–9.

Burton, Chris. "The Eureka-Rebecca Compromises: Another Look at Special Operations Security During World War II." *Air Power History* 52/4 (Winter 2005), pp. 25–37.

Butler, James Ramsay Montagu. *Grand Strategy,* vol. 2, *September 1939–June 1941.* London: HMSO, 1957.

Caddick-Adams, Peter. *Sand and Steel: The D-Day Invasion and the Liberation of France.* Oxford: Oxford University Press, 2019.

Campbell, Richard H. *The Silverplate Bombers: A History and Registry of the Enola Gay and Other B-29s Configured to Carry Atomic Bombs.* Jefferson, NC: McFarland & Co., Inc., 2005.

Carew, Michael G. *Becoming the Arsenal: The American Industrial Mobilization for World War II, 1938–1942.* Lanham, MD: University Press of America, 2010.

Central Office of Information. *The Battle of the Atlantic: The Official Account of the Fight Against the U-Boats, 1939–1945.* London: HMSO, 1946.

Chamberlain, Peter, and Chris Ellis. *British and American Tanks of World War Two: The Complete Illustrated History of British, American and Commonwealth Tanks, 1939–45.* London: Cassell, 2000.

Chamberlin, Eric Russell. *Life in Wartime Britain.* London: B. T. Batsford Ltd., 1972.

Chambers, James. "Neither a Borrower nor a Lender Be: America Attempts to Collect Its War Debts 1922–1934." MA thesis, East Tennessee State University, 2011.

Chinn, George M. *The Machine Gun.* 5 vols. Washington, DC: GPO, 1951–1987.

Clark, Ronald W. *The Birth of the Bomb: The Untold Story of Britain's Part in the Weapon That Changed the World.* London: Phoenix House, 1961.

Clark, Ronald W. *Tizard.* Cambridge, MA: MIT Press, 1965.

Cole, Lance. *Secrets of the Spitfire: The Story of Beverly Shenstone, the Man Who Perfected the Elliptical Wing.* Barnsley UK: Pen & Sword Aviation, 2012.

Colin, Robert I. "Robert J. Dippy: The Hyperbolic Radio Navigation System." *IEEE Transactions on Aerospace and Electronic Systems* 2/4 (July 1966), pp. 476–481.

Coll, Blanche D., Jean E. Keith, and Herbert H. Rosenthal. *The Corps of Engineers: Troops and Equipment.* Washington, DC: GPO, 1958.

Conant, Jennet. *Man of the Hour: James B. Conant, Warrior Scientist.* New York: Simon & Schuster, 2017.

Conant, Jennet. *Tuxedo Park: A Wall Street Tycoon and the Secret Palace of Science That Changed the Course of World War II*. New York: Simon & Schuster, 2003.

Connor, Roger. "The Lattice of Victory: American, Canadian, and British Cooperation in Hyperbolic Navigation, 1940–1945." Paper presented at the 75th anniversary of the Tizard Mission symposium held at the Embassy of Canada, hosted jointly with the US Office of Naval Research and the British Embassy, November 17, 2015.

Conway, Erik M. *Blind Landings: Low-Visibility Operations in American Aviation, 1918–1958*. Baltimore: Johns Hopkins University Press, 2006.

Cooke, Alistair. *The American Home Front, 1941–1942*. New York: Grove Press, 2006.

Coombs, Benjamin. *British Tank Production and the War Economy, 1934–1945*. London: Bloomsbury Publishing, 2013.

Costigliola, Frank C. "Anglo-American Financial Rivalry in the 1920s." *The Journal of Economic History* 37/4 (Dec. 1977), pp. 911–934.

Craven, Wesley Frank, and James Lea Cate (eds.), *The Army Air Forces in World War II*. 7 vols. Chicago: University of Chicago Press, 1948–1958.

Crowther, James Gerald, and Richard Whiddington. *Science at War*. London: HMSO, 1947.

Cull, Nicholas John. *Selling War: The British Propaganda Campaign Against American "Neutrality" in World War II*. New York: Oxford University Press, 1995.

Davis, Richard G. *Bombing the European Axis Powers: A Historical Digest of the Combined Bomber Offensive 1939–1945*. Maxwell Air Force Base, AL: Air University Press, 2006.

Davis, Richard G. *Carl A. Spaatz and the Air War in Europe*. Washington, DC: GPO, 1993.

DeBrosse, Jim, and Colin B. Burke. *The Secret in Building 26: The Untold Story of America's Ultra War Against the U-boat Enigma Codes*. New York: Random House, 2004.

Dimbleby, David, and David Reynolds. *An Ocean Apart: The Relationship Between Britain and America in the Twentieth Century*. New York: Random House, 1988.

Draper, Alfred. *Operation Fish: The Race to Save Europe's Wealth 1939–1945*. London: Cassell, 1979.

Edgerton, David. *Science, Technology and the British Industrial "Decline," 1870–1970*. Cambridge, UK: Cambridge University Press, 1996.

Edgerton, David. *Warfare State: Britain, 1920–1970*. Cambridge, UK: Cambridge University Press, 2006.

Edgerton, David. *Britain's War Machine: Weapons, Resources, and Experts in the Second World War*. Oxford: Oxford University Press, 2011.

Eldridge, Christopher A. "Electronic Eyes for the Allies: Anglo-American Cooperation on Radar Development During World War II." PhD dissertation, Lehigh University, 2001.

Elphick, Peter. *Liberty: The Ships That Won the War*. Annapolis, MD: Naval Institute Press, 2001.

England, James Merton. "Dr. Bush Writes a Report: Science—The Endless Frontier." *Science*, n.s., 191/4222 (January 9, 1976), pp. 41–47.

Engle, Leonard. "Half of Everything: An American's Survey of Orders Placed in the United States." *Flight and the Aircraft Engineer* 38/1667 (December 5, 1940), pp. 472–474.

Ethell, Jeffrey L. *Mustang: A Documentary History of the P-51*. London: Jane's, 1981.

Fanning, Jr., William J. *Death Rays and the Popular Media, 1876–1939: A Study of Directed Energy Weapons in Fact, Fiction and Film*. Jefferson, NC: McFarland & Co., Inc., 2015.

Farmelo, Graham. *Churchill's Bomb: How the United States Overtook Britain in the First Nuclear Arms Race*. New York: Basic Books, 2013.

Faulkner, Marcus, and Christopher M. Bell. *Decision in the Atlantic: The Allies and the Longest Campaign of the Second World War*. Lexington: The University Press of Kentucky, 2019.

Fear, Jeffrey. "War of the Factories." In Michael Geyer and Adam Tooze (eds.), *The Cambridge History of the Second World War*, vol. 3, pp. 94–121. Cambridge, UK: Cambridge University Press, 2015.

Fergusson, Bernard. *The Watery Maze: The Story of Combined Operations*. New York: Holt, Rinehart and Winston, 1961.

Ferreiro, Larrie D. *Bridging the Seas: The Rise of Naval Architecture in the Industrial Age, 1800–2000*. Cambridge, MA: MIT Press, 2020.

Ferreiro, Larrie D. *Brothers at Arms: American Independence and the Men of France and Spain Who Saved It*. New York: Alfred A. Knopf, 2016.

Ferreiro, Larrie D. "Goodall in America: The Exchange Engineer as Vector in International Technology Transfer." *Comparative Technology Transfer and Society* 4/2 (August 2006), pp. 172–193.

Fine, Norman. *Blind Bombing: How Microwave Radar Brought the Allies to D-Day and Victory in World War II*. Lincoln, NE: Potomac Books, 2019.

Fletcher, David. *British Armour in the Second World War*. 2 vols. London: HMSO, 1989–1993.

Fletcher, David. *Swimming Shermans: Sherman DD Amphibious Tank of World War II*. Oxford: Osprey Publishing, 2006.

Fletcher, David, and Steven J. Zaloga. *British Battle Tanks: American-Made World War II Tanks*. Oxford: Osprey Publishing, 2018.

Florence, Gregory J. *Courting a Reluctant Ally: An Evaluation of U.S./UK Naval Intelligence Cooperation, 1935–1941*. Washington, DC: Center for Strategic Intelligence Research, Joint Military Intelligence College, 2004.

Foot, Michael R. D. *SOE in France: An Account of the Work of the British Special Operations Executive in France 1940–1944*. London: HMSO, 1966.

Fort, Adrian. *Prof: The Life of Frederick Lindemann*. London: Pimlico, 2003.

Franklin, George. *Britain's Anti-Submarine Capability, 1919–1939*. Abingdon, UK: Routledge, 2004.

Freeman, Roger A. *Mustang at War*. New York: Doubleday & Co., 1974.

Freer, Paul George. "Circumventing the Law That Humans Cannot See in the Dark: An Assessment of the Development of Target Marking Techniques to the Prosecution of the Bombing Offensive During the Second World War." PhD dissertation, University of Exeter, 2017.

Friedrich, Jörg. *The Fire: The Bombing of Germany, 1940–1945*. Translated by Allison Brown. New York: Columbia University Press, 2006.

Friedman, Norman. *British Destroyers and Frigates: The Second World War and After*. Barnsley, UK: Seaforth Publishing, 2008.

Friedman, Norman. *Naval Anti-Aircraft Guns and Gunnery*. Annapolis: Naval Institute Press, 2013.

Friedman, Norman. *U.S. Amphibious Ships and Craft: An Illustrated Design History*. Annapolis: Naval Institute Press, 2002.

Gander, Terry. *The Bofors Gun*. Barnsley UK: Pen & Sword Military, 2013.

Genuth, Joel. "Microwave Radar, the Atomic Bomb, and the Background to U. S. Research Priorities in World War II." *Science, Technology, & Human Values*, 13/3–4 (Summer–Autumn 1988), pp. 276–289.

Gertner, Jon. *The Idea Factory: Bell Labs and the Great Age of American Innovation*. New York: Penguin Press, 2012.

Geyer, Michael, and Adam Tooze (eds.). *The Cambridge History of the Second World War*. 3 vols. Cambridge, UK: Cambridge University Press, 2015.

Giffard, Hermione. *Making Jet Engines in World War II: Britain, Germany, and the United States*. Chicago: University of Chicago Press, 2016.

Gillmor, Charles Stewart. *Fred Terman at Stanford: Building a Discipline, a University, and Silicon Valley*. Stanford, CA: Stanford University Press, 2004.

Goodchild, James. *A Most Enigmatic War: R. V. Jones and the Genesis of British Scientific Intelligence, 1939–1945*. Solihull, UK: Helion and Co., 2017.

Goldberg, Stanley. "Inventing a Climate of Opinion: Vannevar Bush and the Decision to Build the Bomb." *Isis* 83/3 (September 1992), pp. 429–452.

Gowing, Margaret M. *Britain and Atomic Energy, 1939–1945*. London: Macmillan & Co Ltd., 1964.

Grande, George K., Sheila M. Linden, and Horace R. Macaulay. *Canadians on Radar: Royal Canadian Air Force, 1940–1945*. Ottawa: The Canadian Radar History Project, 2000.

Grehan, John. *Churchill's Secret Invasion: Britain's First Large-Scale Combined Operations Offensive 1942*. Barnsley, UK: Pen and Sword, 2013.

Gropman, Alan L. *Mobilizing U.S. Industry in World War II: Myth and Reality*. Washington, DC: GPO, 2004.

Grove, Eric. *The Royal Navy Since 1815: A New Short History*. New York: Palgrave Macmillan, 2005.

Grove, Eric. "The Battle of the Atlantic: A Legend Deconstructed." *Mariner's Mirror* 105/3 (2019), pp. 336–339.

Guerlac, Henry E. *Radar in World War II*. 2 vols. Los Angeles: Tomash Publishers, 1987.

Hague, Arnold. *The Allied Convoy System 1939–1945: Its Organization, Defence and Operation*. Annapolis, MD: Naval Institute Press, 2000.

Hackmann, Willem. *Seek and Strike: Sonar, Anti-Submarine Warfare and the Royal Navy 1914–54*. London: HMSO, 1984.

Hall, Hessel Duncan. *North American Supply*. London: HMSO, 1955.

Hall, Hessel Duncan, and Christopher C. Wrigley. *Studies of Overseas Supply*. London: HMSO, 1956.

Hall, John S. (ed.). *Radar Aids to Navigation*. Massachusetts Institute of Technology Radiation Laboratory Series, vol 2. New York: McGraw-Hill, 1947.

Hancock, William Keith, and Margaret M. Gowing. *British War Economy*. London: HMSO, 1949.

Harrison, Gordon A. *The European Theater of Operations: Cross-Channel Attack.* Washington, DC: GPO, 1951.

Harrison, Mark (ed.). *The Economics of World War II: Six Great Powers in International Comparison.* Cambridge, UK: Cambridge University Press, 2000.

Harpur, Brian. *A Bridge to Victory: The Untold Story of the Bailey Bridge.* London: HMSO, 1991.

Hartcup, Guy. *The Challenge of War: Britain's Scientific and Engineering Contributions to World War Two.* New York: Taplinger Publishing Co., 1970.

Hartcup, Guy. *The Effect of Science on the Second World War.* London: Macmillan Press, 2000.

Heinrich, Thomas. *Warship Builders: An Industrial History of US Naval Shipbuilding, 1922–1945.* Annapolis, MD: Naval Institute Press, 2020.

Hemming, Henry. *Our Man in New York: The British Plot to Bring America into the Second World War.* London: Quercus, 2019.

Henshaw, John. *Liberty's Provenance: The Evolution of the Liberty Ship from its Sunderland Origins.* Barnsley, UK: Seaforth Publishing, 2019.

Herman, Arthur. *To Rule the Waves: How the British Navy Shaped the Modern World.* New York: HarperCollins Publishers, 2004.

Herman, Arthur. *Freedom's Forge: How American Business Produced Victory in World War II.* New York: Random House, 2012.

Hirshfield, Deborah A. "From Hog Islanders to Liberty Ships: The American Government and Merchant Ship Construction in Two World Wars." *The American Neptune* 54/2 (Spring 1994), pp. 85–98.

Hirshfield, Deborah A. "Rosie Also Welded: Women and Technology in Shipbuilding During World War II." PhD dissertation. University of California, Irvine, 1987.

Hobby, Gladys L. *Penicillin: Meeting the Challenge.* New Haven: Yale University Press, 1985.

Holland, James. *Big Week: The Biggest Air Battle of World War II.* New York: Atlantic Monthly Press, 2018.

Holland, James. *The Battle of Britain: Five Months That Changed History, May–October 1940.* New York: St. Martin's Press, 2010.

Holley, Irving Brinton Jr. *Buying Aircraft: Matériel Procurement for the Army Air Forces.* Washington, DC.: GPO, 1964.

Holmes, Jamie. *12 Seconds of Silence: How a Team of Inventors, Tinkerers, and Spies Took Down a Nazi Superweapon.* Boston: Houghton Mifflin Harcourt, 2020.

Hore, Peter G. (ed.). *Patrick Blackett: Sailor, Scientist and Socialist.* London: Frank Cass & Co. Ltd., 2003.

Hughes, Thomas P. *Rescuing Prometheus: Four Monumental Projects That Changed the Modern World.* New York: Pantheon Books, 1998.

Hyde, Charles K. *Arsenal of Democracy: The American Automobile Industry in World War II.* Detroit: Wayne State University Press, 2013.

Jeffrey, Thomas E. "Commodore Edison Joins the Navy: Thomas Alva Edison and the Naval Consulting Board." *Journal of Military History* 80/2 (April 2016), pp. 411–445.

Johnman, Lewis, and Hugh Murphy. "The British Merchant Shipping Mission in the United States and British Merchant Shipbuilding in the Second World War." *The Northern Mariner/Le marin du nord* 12/3 (July 2002), pp. 1–15.

Johnsen, Frederick A. *Captured Eagles: Secrets of the Luftwaffe*. London: Bloomsbury Publishing, 2014.

Johnsen, William T. *The Origins of the Grand Alliance: Anglo-American Military Collaboration from the Panay Incident to Pearl Harbor*. Lexington: University Press of Kentucky, 2016.

Johnson, Brian. *The Secret War*. Barnsley UK: Pen & Sword Military, 1978.

Johnston, Andrew K., Roger Connor, Carlene E. Stephens, and Paul E Ceruzzi. *Time and Navigation: The Untold Story of Getting from Here to There*. Washington, DC: Smithsonian Books, 2015.

Joiner, John H. *One More River to Cross: The Story of British Military Bridging*. Barnsley, UK: Leo Cooper, 2001.

Jonas, Gerald. *The Circuit Riders: Rockefeller Money and the Rise of Modern Science*. New York: W. W. Norton, 1989.

Jones, Vincent C. *Manhattan: The Army and the Atomic Bomb*. Washington, DC: GPO, 1985.

Judkins, Phillip Edward. "Making Vision into Power: Britain's Acquisition of the World's First Radar-Based Integrated Air Defence System, 1935–1941." PhD dissertation, Cranfield University, Shrivenham, UK, 2007.

Kean, Sam. *The Bastard Brigade: The True Story of the Renegade Scientists and Spies Who Sabotaged the Nazi Atomic Bomb*. New York: Little, Brown and Co., 2019.

Keegan, John. *Six Armies in Normandy: From D-Day to the Liberation of Paris; June 6–Aug. 5, 1944*. New York: The Viking Press, 1982.

Kehoe, Elisabeth. *Titled Americans: Three American Sisters and the British Aristocratic World into Which They Married*. New York: Atlantic Monthly Press, 2004.

Kennedy, Paul. *Engineers of Victory: The Problem Solvers Who Turned the Tide in the Second World War*. New York: Random House, 2013.

Kennedy, Paul. "History from the Middle: The Case of the Second World War." *The Journal of Military History* 74/1 (January 2010), pp. 35–51.

Kevles, Daniel J. *The Physicists: The History of a Scientific Community in Modern America*. New York: Vintage Books, 1971.

Kimball, Warren F. *The Most Unsordid Act: Lend-Lease, 1939–1941*. Baltimore: Johns Hopkins University Press, 1969.

Kindleberger, Charles. *The World in Depression, 1929–1939*. 40th anniversary edition. Berkeley, CA: University of California Press, 2013.

Klein, Maury. *A Call to Arms: Mobilizing America for World War II*. New York: Bloomsbury Press, 2013.

Koistinen, Paul A. C. *Arsenal of World War II: The Political Economy of American Warfare, 1940–1945*. Lawrence: University Press of Kansas, 2004.

Koistinen, Paul A. C. *Planning War, Pursuing Peace: The Political Economy of American Warfare, 1940–1945*. Lawrence: University Press of Kansas, 1998.

Kroge, Harry von. *GEMA: Birthplace of German Radar and Sonar*. Edited and translated by Louis Brown. Bristol, UK: Institute of Physics Publishing, 1998/2000.

Kuehn, John. *Agents of Innovation: The General Board and the Design of the Fleet that Defeated the Japanese Navy*. Annapolis, MD: Naval Institute Press, 2013.

Kummritz, Herbert. "German Radar Development to 1945." In Russell W. Burns (ed.), *Radar Development to 1945*, pp. 209–226. London: Peter Peregrinus, 1988.

Lambert, Andrew. "Seapower 1939–1940: Churchill and the Strategic Origins of the Battle of the Atlantic." *The Journal of Strategic Studies* 17/1 (1994), pp. 86–108.

Lane, Frederic C. *Ships for Victory: A History of Shipbuilding Under the U. S. Maritime Commission in World War II*. Baltimore: Johns Hopkins University Press, 1951.

Langworth, Richard M. (ed.). *Churchill by Himself: The Definitive Collection of Quotations*. London: Ebury Press, 2008.

Lash, Joseph P. *Roosevelt and Churchill, 1939–1941: The Partnership That Saved the West*. New York: W. W. Norton, 1976.

Lavery, Brian. *Churchill's Navy: The Ships, Men and Organisation, 1939–1945*. London: Conway Maritime Press, 2006.

Lax, Eric. *The Mold in Dr. Florey's Coat: The Story of the Penicillin Miracle*. New York: Henry Holt and Co., 2004.

Leighton, Richard M., and Robert W. Coakley. *Global Logistics and Strategy, 1940–1943*. Washington, DC: GPO, 1955.

Leighton, Richard M., and Robert W. Coakley. *Global Logistics and Strategy, 1943–1945*. Washington, DC: GPO, 1968.

Lindberg, Michael, and Daniel Todd, *Anglo-American Shipbuilding in World War II: A Geographical Perspective*. Westport, CT: Praeger, 2004.

Lloyd, Ian. *Rolls-Royce: The Merlin at War*. London: Macmillan Press, 1978.

Longmate, Norman. *The G.I.'s: The Americans in Britain 1942–1945*. London: Hutchinson, 1975.

Ludwig, Paul A. *P-51 Mustang: Development of the Long-Range Escort Fighter*. Hersham, UK: Classic Publications, 2003.

Lundstrom, John B. *The First Team: Pacific Naval Air Combat from Pearl Harbor to Midway*. Annapolis, MD: Naval Institute Press, 2005.

MacDermott, Brian. *Ships Without Names: The Story of the Royal Navy's Tank Landing Ships of World War Two*. London: Arms and Armor Press, 1992.

Macfarlane, Gwyn. *Alexander Fleming: The Man and the Myth*. London: Chatto & Windus, 1984.

MacLeod, Roy. "All for Each and Each for All: Reflections on Anglo-American and Commonwealth Scientific Cooperation, 1940–1945." *Albion: A Quarterly Journal Concerned with British Studies*, 26/1 (Spring, 1994), pp. 79–112.

Marder, Arthur. *Operation "Menace": The Dakar Expedition and the Dudley North Affair*. London: Oxford University Press, 1976.

Matloff, Maurice, and Edwin M. Snell. *Strategic Planning for Coalition Warfare 1941–1942*. Washington, DC: GPO, 1953.

McAleer, Neil. *Arthur C. Clarke: The Authorized Biography*. Chicago: Contemporary Books, 1992.

McBurney, Christian, et al. *World War II Rhode Island*. Mount Pleasant, SC: Arcadia Publishing, 2017.

McDonough, Frank (ed.). *The Origins of the Second World War: An International Perspective*. London: Bloomsbury Publishing, 2011.

McDowall, Duncan. *Quick to the Frontier: Canada's Royal Bank*. Toronto: McClelland &. Stewart Inc., 1993.

McFarland, Stephen L. *America's Pursuit of Precision Bombing, 1910–1945*. Tuscaloosa: University of Alabama Press, 1995.

McGeoh, Ian. *The Princely Sailor: Mountbatten of Burma*. London: Brassey's, 1996.

McGrath, John J. *The Other End of the Spear: The Tooth-to-Tail Ratio (T3R) in Modern Military Operations*. Fort Leavenworth, KS: Combat Studies Institute Press, 2007.

McKee, Fraser M. "An Explosive Story: The Rise and Fall of the Common Depth Charge." *The Northern Mariner/Le Marin du nord*, 3/1 (January 1993), pp. 45–58.

Meigs, Montgomery C. *Slide Rules and Submarines: American Scientists and Subsurface Warfare in World War II*. Washington, DC: National Defense University Press, 1989.

Melnitsky, Benjamin. *Profiting from Industrial Standardization*. New York: Conover-Mast Publications, 1953.

Millar, George R. *The Bruneval Raid: Flashpoint of the Radar War*. Garden City NY: Doubleday, 1975.

Miller, Donald L. *Masters of the Air: America's Bomber Boys Who Fought the Air War Against Nazi Germany*. New York: Simon & Schuster, 2006.

Miller, Michael. "Sea Transport." In Michael Geyer and Adam Tooze (eds.), *The Cambridge History of the Second World War*, vol. 3, pp. 174–195. Cambridge, UK: Cambridge University Press, 2015.

Milner, Marc. *Battle of the Atlantic*. Stroud, UK: Tempus Publishing Ltd., 2001.

Milton, Giles. *Churchill's Ministry of Ungentlemanly Warfare: The Mavericks Who Plotted Hitler's Defeat*. New York: Picador, 2016.

Mindell, David A. "Automation's Finest Hour: Radar and System Integration in World War II." In Agatha C. Hughes and Thomas P. Hughes (eds.), *Systems, Experts, and Computers: The Systems Approach in Management and Engineering, World War II and After*, pp. 27–56. Cambridge, MA: MIT Press, 2000.

Mitchell, David. *The Shadow Scheme*. Documentary film. Coventry, UK: Dave Mitchell Films and Coventry Transport Museum, 2013.

Moran, Jeff. *American Airborne Pathfinders in World War II*. Atglen, PA: Schiffer Military History, 2003.

Morison, Samuel Eliot. *History of United States Naval Operations in World War II*. 15 vols. Boston: Little, Brown and Co., 1947–1962.

Muller, James W. (ed.). *Churchill's Iron Curtain Speech Fifty Years Later*. Columbia, MO: University of Missouri Press, 1999.

Mundy, Liza. *Code Girls: The Untold Story of the American Women Code Breakers Who Helped Win World War II*. New York: Hachette Books, 2017.

Murphy, Hugh. "The British Shipbuilding Industry During the Great War: A Contextual Overview Incorporating Standardization and the National Shipyards, 1916–1920." *International Journal of Maritime History* 24/2 (2012), pp. 19–68.

Murphy, Hugh. "From the Crinoline to the Boilersuit: Women Workers in British Shipbuilding During the Second World War." *Contemporary British History* 13/4 (1999), pp. 82–104.

Murphy, Hugh. "Labour in the British Shipbuilding and Ship Repairing Industries in the Twentieth Century." In Raquel Varela, Hugh Murphy, and Marcel van der Linden (eds.), *Shipbuilding and Ship Repair Workers Around the World: Case Studies 1950–2010*, pp. 47–116. Amsterdam: Amsterdam University Press, 2017.

Nelson, Donald M. *Arsenal of Democracy: The Story of American War Production*. New York: Harcourt, Brace and Co., 1946.

O'Brien, Phillips Payson. *How the War Was Won: Air-Sea Power and Allied Victory in World War II*. Cambridge, UK: Cambridge University Press, 2015.

Office of the Chief of Military History. *The Signal Corps*. 3 vols. Washington, DC: GPO, 1956–1966. (Reprint by the US Army Center of Military History, 1994–2008.)

O'Neil, William D. *Interwar U.S. and Japanese National Product and Defense Expenditure*. Alexandria, VA: CNA Corporation, 2003.

Otter, Patrick. *1 Group: Swift to Attack: Bomber Command's Unsung Heroes*. Barnsley, UK: Pen & Sword Aviation, 2012.

Overy, Richard. *Why the Allies Won*. New York: W.W. Norton & Company, 1995.

Pang, Alex Soojung-Kim. "Edward Bowles and Radio Engineering at MIT, 1920–1940." *Historical Studies in the Physical and Biological Sciences* 20/2 (1990), pp. 313–337.

Parkin, Simon. *A Game of Birds and Wolves: The Ingenious Young Women Whose Secret Board Game Helped Win World War II*. New York: Little, Brown and Co., 2020.

Pawle, Gerald. *The Secret War 1939–45*. London: Harrap, 1956. (Reprinted as *The Wheezers and Dodgers*, Barnsley: Seaforth Publishing, 2009).

Phelps, Stephen. *The Tizard Mission: The Top-Secret Operation That Changed the Course of World War II*. Yardley, PA: Westholme Publishing, 2010.

Pierce, John A., A. A. McKenzie, and Richard H. Woodward (eds.). *LORAN, Long-Range Navigation*. Massachusetts Institute of Technology Radiation Laboratory series, vol 4. New York: McGraw-Hill, 1948.

Plumpe, Joseph C. "Ancient Convoying." *The Classical Weekly* 36/4 (October 26, 1942), pp. 39–45.

Polmar, Norman, and Peter B. Mersky. *Amphibious Warfare: An Illustrated History*. London: Blanford Press, 1988.

Postan, Michael M. *British War Production*. London: HMSO, 1952.

Postan, Michael M., Dennis Hay, and John D. Scott. *Design and Development of Weapons: Studies in Government and Industrial Organisation*. London: HMSO, 1964.

Potter, Simon J. *Wireless Internationalism and Distant Listening: Britain, Propaganda, and the Invention of Global Radio, 1920–1939*. Oxford: Oxford University Press, 2020.

Preisler, Jerome. *First to Jump: How the Band of Brothers was Aided by the Brave Paratroopers of Pathfinders Company*. New York: Berkley Caliber, 2014.

Price, Alfred A. *The History of US Electronic Warfare*. 3 vols. Arlington, VA: Association of Old Crows, 1984–2000.

Price, Alfred A. *Instruments of Darkness: The History of Electronic Warfare*. Barnsley, UK: Greenhill Books, 2005.

Price, Alfred A. "A Survey of US Countermeasures During World War II." In Russell W. Burns (ed.), *Radar Development to 1945*, pp. 357–364. London: Peter Peregrinus, 1988.

Prior, Robin. *When Britain Saved the West: The Story of 1940*. New Haven, CT: Yale University Press, 2015.

Pritchard, James S. *A Bridge of Ships: Canadian Shipbuilding During the Second World War*. Montreal: McGill-Queen's University Press, 2011.

Pugh, Peter. *The Magic of a Name: The Rolls-Royce Story, The First 40 Years*. Duxford, UK: Icon Books, 2000.

Rankin, William. "The Geography of Radionavigation and the Politics of Intangible Artifacts." *Technology and Culture* 55/3 (July 2014), pp. 622–674.

Rau, Erik P. "The Adoption of Operations Research in the United States During World War II." In Agatha C. Hughes and Thomas P. Hughes (eds.), *Systems, Experts, and Computers: The Systems Approach in Management and Engineering, World War II and After*, pp. 57–92. Cambridge, MA: MIT Press, 2000.

Redford, Duncan. "The March 1943 Crisis in the Battle of the Atlantic: Myth and Reality." *History* 92/1 (305, January 2007), pp. 64–83.

Redgment, Peter G. "High-Frequency Direction Finding in the Royal Navy: Development of Anti-U-Boat Equipment, 1941–5." In Fred A. Kingsley (ed.), *The Applications of Radar and other Electronic Systems in the Royal Navy in World War 2*, pp. 229–265. London: Macmillan Press Ltd., 1995.

Reynolds, David. *The Creation of the Anglo-American Alliance, 1937–1941: A Study in Competitive Co-operation*. Chapel Hill: University of North Carolina Press, 1982.

Reynolds, David. *From World War to Cold War: Churchill, Roosevelt, and the International History of the 1940s*. Oxford: Oxford University Press, 2006.

Reynolds, David. *Rich Relations: The American Occupation of Britain 1942–1945*. New York: Random House, 1995.

Rhodes, Richard. *The Making of the Atomic Bomb*. New York: Simon & Schuster, 1986.

Richardson, Frederick Denys. "Charles Frederick Goodeve, 21 February 1904–7 April 1980." *Biographical Memoirs of Fellows of the Royal Society* 27 (November 1981), pp. 306–353.

Rigden, John S. *Rabi: Scientist and Citizen*. Cambridge, MA: Harvard University Press, 1997.

Roberts, Andrew. *Churchill: Walking with Destiny*. New York: Viking, 2018.

Roberts, Larry D. "The Bailey: The Amazing, All-Purpose Bridge." In Barry W. Fowle (ed.), *Builders and Fighters, U.S. Army Engineers in World War II*, pp. 181–193. Fort Belvoir, VA: US Army Corps of Engineers, 1992.

Robins, Nick. *Standard Ships*. Barnsley, UK: Seaforth Publishing, 2017.

Rofe, J. Simon. *Franklin Roosevelt's Foreign Policy and the Welles Mission*. Basingstoke, UK: Palgrave Macmillan, 2007.

Rohwer, Jurgen. *Chronology of the War at Sea, 1939–1945*. 2 vols. New York: Arco Publishing Co., 1972.

Rossiter, Margaret W. *Women Scientists in America: Before Affirmative Action, 1940–1972*. Baltimore: Johns Hopkins University Press, 1995.

Rottman, Gordon L. *Landing Ship Tank (LST) 1942–2002*. Illustrated by Tony Bryan. Oxford: Osprey Publishing, 2005.

Rowland, Buford, and William B. Boyd. *US Navy Bureau of Ordnance in World War II*. Washington, DC: GPO, 1953.

Ruane, Kevin. *Churchill and the Bomb in War and Cold War*. London: Bloomsbury Academic, 2016.

Ruggles, Richard, and Henry Brodie. "An Empirical Approach to Economic Intelligence in World War II." *Journal of the American Statistical Association* 42/237 (March 1947), pp. 72–91.

Ruppenthal, Roland G. *Logistical Support of the Armies*. 2 vols. Washington, DC: GPO, 1953–1959. (Reprint by the US Army Center of Military History, 1995.)

Sapolsky, Harvey M. *Science and the Navy: The History of the Office of Naval Research*. Princeton: Princeton University Press, 1990.

Saward, Dudley. *Bernard Lovell; A Biography*. London: Robert Hale, 1984.

Saward, Dudley. *The Bomber's Eye*. London: Cassell, 1959.

Sawyer, Leonard A., and William H. Mitchell. *The Liberty Ship: The History of the "Emergency" Type Cargo Ships Constructed in the United States During the Second World War*. New York: Lloyd's of London Press Inc., 1985.

Schake, Kori. *Safe Passage: The Transition from British to American Hegemony*. Cambridge, MA: Harvard University Press, 2017.

Shachtman, Tom. *Laboratory Warriors: How Allied Science and Technology Tipped the Balance in World War II*. New York: Perennial, 2003.

Shirer, William L. *The Rise and Fall of the Third Reich: A History of Nazi Germany*. New York: Simon & Schuster, 1960.

Shrader, Charles R. *Amicicide: The Problem of Friendly Fire in Modern War*. Honolulu: University Press of the Pacific, 2005.

Shrader, Charles R. *History of Operations Research in the United States Army*. 3 vols. Washington, DC: GPO, 2006.

Shurkin, Joel N. *Broken Genius: The Rise and Fall of William Shockley, Creator of the Electronic Age*. London: Macmillan, 2006.

Silber, William L. *When Washington Shut Down Wall Street: The Great Financial Crisis of 1914 and the Origins of America's Monetary Supremacy*. Princeton, NJ: Princeton University Press, 2007.

Skennerton, Ian. *Lee-Enfield Story*. London: Greenhill Books, 1993.

Stewart, Irvin. *Organizing Scientific Research for War: The Administrative History of the Office of Scientific Research and Development*. Boston: Little, Brown and Co., 1948.

Stolfi, Russel H. S. "Equipment for Victory in France in 1940." *History* 55/183 (1970), pp. 1–20.

Strahan, Jerry E. *Andrew Jackson Higgins and the Boats That Won World War II*. Baton Rouge: Louisiana State University Press, 1994.

Sutton, Jean: *Lords of the East: The East India Company and Its Ships*. London: Conway Maritime Press, 1981.

Sweeting, George Vincent. "Building the Arsenal of Democracy: The Government's Role in Expansion of Industrial Capacity, 1940 to 1945." PhD dissertation, Columbia University, 1994.

Switky, Robert. *Wealth of an Empire: The Treasure Shipments That Saved Britain and the World*. Washington, DC: Potomac Books, 2013.

Symonds, Craig L. *Neptune: The Allied Invasion of Europe and the D-Day Landings*. Oxford: Oxford University Press, 2014.

Syrett, David. "Failure at Sea: Wolf Pack Operations in the North Atlantic, 10 February–22 March 1944." *The Northern Mariner/Le Marin du nord* 5/1 (January 1995), pp. 33–43.

Szasz, Ferenc Morton. *British Scientists and the Manhattan Project: The Los Alamos Years*. New York: St. Martin's Press, 1992.

Taber, George M. *Chasing Gold: The Incredible Story of How the Nazis Stole Europe's Bullion*. New York: Pegasus Books, 2014.

Thiesmeyer, Lincoln R., and John E. Burchhard. *Combat Scientists*. Boston: Little, Brown and Co., 1947.

Thiesen, William H. *Industrializing American Shipbuilding: The Transformation of Ship Design and Construction, 1820–1920*. Gainesville: University of Florida Press, 2006.

Thomas, William. *Rational Action: The Sciences of Policy in Britain and America, 1940–1960*. Cambridge, MA: MIT Press, 2015.

Thomson, Harry C., and Lida Mayo. *The Ordnance Department: Procurement and Supply*. Washington, DC: GPO, 1960.

Tidman, Keith R. *Operations Evaluation Group: A History of Naval Operations Analysis*. Annapolis, MD: Naval Institute Press, 1984.

Tomblin, Barbara Brooks. *With Utmost Spirit: Allied Naval Operations in the Mediterranean, 1942–1945*. Lexington: University Press of Kentucky, 2004.

Topping, Robert W. *The Hovde Years: A Biography of Frederick L. Hovde*. West Lafayette, IN: Purdue University, 1980.

Trim, Richard M. "The Development of IFF in the Period up to 1945." In Russell W. Burns (ed.), *Radar Development to 1945*, pp. 436–457. London: Peter Peregrinus, 1988.

Twinn, John E. "The Use of Window (Chaff) to Simulate the Approach of a Convoy of Ships Towards a Coastline." In Russell W. Burns (ed.), *Radar Development to 1945*, pp. 416–422. London: Peter Peregrinus, 1988.

Ujifusa, Steven. *A Man and His Ship: America's Greatest Naval Architect and His Quest to Build the S.S. United States*. New York: Simon and Schuster, 2012.

Van der Vat, Dan. *The Atlantic Campaign: World War II's Greatest Struggle*. New York: Harper & Row, 1988.

Varela, Raquel, Hugh Murphy, and Marcel van der Linden (eds.). *Shipbuilding and Ship Repair Workers Around the World: Case Studies 1950–2010*. Amsterdam: Amsterdam University Press B.V., 2017.

Vaz, Mark Cotta, and John H. Hill. *Pan Am at War: How the Airline Secretly Helped America Fight World War II*. New York: Skyhorse Publishing, 2019.

Vernon, Jerry E. "Horses on the Payroll." *Royal Canadian Air Force Journal* 5/2 (Spring 2016), pp. 80–95.

Waddington, Conrad Hall. *O.R. in World War 2: Operational Research Against the U-Boat*. London: Elek Science, 1973.

Wagner, Ray. *Mustang Designer Edgar Schmued and the P-51*. Washington, DC: Smithsonian Institution Press, 1990.

Walton, Francis. *Miracle of World War II: How American Industry Made Victory Possible*. New York: Macmillan Co., 1956.

Ward, Harold, Charles A. Fowler, and Herbert I. Lipson. "GCA Radars: Their History and State of Development." *Proceedings of the IEEE* 62/6 (June 1974), pp. 705–716.

Wark, Wesley K. "British Intelligence on the German Air Force and Aircraft Industry, 1933–1939." *The Historical Journal* 25/3 (September 1982), pp. 627–648.

Warren, John C. *Airborne Operations in World War II*. Maxwell Air Force Base, AL: Air University, 1956.

Watson, Mark Skinner. *Chief of Staff: Prewar Plans and Preparations. United States Army in World War II: The War Department.* Washington, DC: GPO, 1950.

Watson, Peter. *The German Genius: Europe's Third Renaissance, the Second Scientific Revolution, and the Twentieth Century.* New York: Harper, 2010.

Weir, Gary E. *An Ocean in Common: American Naval Officers, Scientists, and the Ocean Environment.* College Station, TX: Texas A&M University Press, 2001.

Weiss, Linda. *America Inc.?: Innovation and Enterprise in the National Security State.* Ithaca, NY: Cornell University Press, 2014.

Wells, Mark K. *Courage and Air Warfare: The Allied Aircrew Experience in the Second World War.* Abingdon, UK: Routledge, 2013.

Werrell, Kenneth P. *Archie, Flak, AAA, and SAM: A Short Operational History of Ground-Based Air Defense.* Maxwell Air Force Base, AL: Air University Press, 1988.

White, Philip. *Our Supreme Task: How Winston Churchill's Iron Curtain Speech Defined the Cold War Alliance.* New York: Public Affairs, 2012.

Whitney, Daniel D. *Vee's for Victory! The Story of the Allison V-1710 Aircraft Engine, 1929–1948.* Atglen, PA: Schiffer Military History, 1998.

Wilkerson, Isabel. *The Warmth of Other Suns: The Epic Story of America's Great Migration.* New York: Random House, 2010.

Williams, Eric K. "The History of Rebecca-Eureka." In Russell W. Burns (ed.), *Radar Development to 1945*, pp. 308–318. London: Peter Peregrinus, 1988.

Williams, Kathleen Broome. *Secret Weapon: U.S. High-Frequency Direction Finding in the Battle of the Atlantic.* Annapolis, MD: Naval Institute Press, 1996.

Wilson, David. *In Search of Penicillin.* New York: Alfred A. Knopf, 1976.

Wilson, Gordon A. A. *The Merlin: The Engine That Won the Second World War.* Stroud, UK: Amberley Publishing, 2018.

Wilson, Mark R. *Destructive Creation: American Business and the Winning of World War II.* Philadelphia: University of Pennsylvania Press, 2016.

Winton, John. *Convoy: The Defence of Sea Trade, 1890–1990.* London: Michael Joseph Ltd., 1983.

Woodbury, David Oakes. *Battlefronts of Industry: Westinghouse in World War II.* New York: J. Wiley, 1948.

Wylie, Neville. "British Smuggling Operations from Switzerland, 1940–1944." *The Historical Journal* 48/4 (December 2005), pp. 1077–1102.

Zachary, Gregg Pascal. *Endless Frontier: Vannevar Bush, Engineer of the American Century.* New York: Free Press, 1997.

Zaloga, Steven J. *US Amphibious Tanks of World War II.* Oxford: Osprey Publishing, 2012.

Zimmerman, David. *Britain's Shield: Radar and the Defeat of the Luftwaffe.* Stroud, UK: Sutton, 2001.

Zimmerman, David. *Top Secret Exchange: The Tizard Mission and the Scientific War.* Montreal: McGill-Queen's University Press, 1996.

INDEX